PAUL: A NOVEL

Theologian, literary scholar
and performance storyteller, Walter
Wangerin, Jr, has written a great many
books including fiction, children's books,
poetry, short stories and theology.

His first novel, *The Book of the Dun Cow*
won the National Book Award in America
and was the *New York Times'* Book of the
Year. *The Book of God*, published in 1996,
has been a worldwide bestseller with
editions in more than a dozen languages.

He has won many other awards for his books,
which include *Ragman and Other Cries of
Faith* and *The Book of Sorrows*. He is writer-
in-residence at Valparaiso University. He and
his wife live in Valparaiso, Indiana, USA.

For my brother, Felipe Wangerin,
Pescador on the west coast of Mexico
near Caborca, Sonora

PAUL

A NOVEL

WALTER
WANGERIN

LION

A Lion Book
an imprint of
Lion Hudson plc
Mayfield House, 256 Banbury Road,
Oxford OX2 7DH, England
www.lionhudson.com
ISBN 0 7459 5055 8

First hardback edition 2000
First paperback edition 2001
This edition 2005
10 9 8 7 6 5 4 3 2 1 0

Published in the USA by Zondervan Publishing House,
Grand Rapids, Michigan 49530

Published in association with the literary agency of Alive
Communications, 1465 Kelly Johnson Blvd, Suite 320,
Colorado Springs, Colorado 80920

A catalogue record for this book is available
from the British Library

Printed and bound in Great Britain by
Cox and Wyman Ltd, Reading

Walter Wangerin's website address is:
www.walterwangerinjr.org

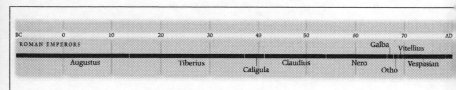

First-century Roman emperors

Contents

Prologue

CORINTH

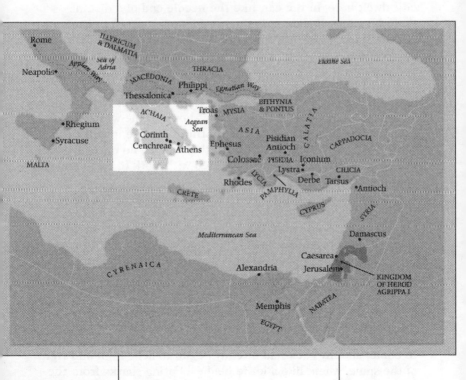

Prisca

1

There was a Voice in the morning. There came a Voice through the wet air, like a long flag lifted on the wind: *eucharistoumen*, it was saying, and, *to theo pantote peri panton humon...*

There was this single Voice which, though it came up from the city, dwelt here, in the ear, like the needle end of a distant thread, saying: *mneian poioumenoi epi ton proseuchon hemon...*

That Voice – the bare sound of it even before the words made sense to me – pricked my hearing and drew me out of the house and down to the city.

Truly, I had no intention of going to the market that day. Aquila was already there, delivering three pieces of finished goods – awnings, they were – to one of the shops on the western side, the side that was blinded by the morning sun. He meant to return early with supplies. Besides that we had no other business in the marketplace. I sat at my bench with work to hand and the dear hope of receiving a client or two.

Cutting with the round-edged knife, I was, bent over the leather, my hair bound back and none to talk to since none but me was there. Four Sabbaths before, on the first boat to arrive since the winter storms had stilled, had come a letter to me bearing the news that my mother had died. 'Of a broken heart,' my father wrote, 'not ten days after you left her alone in Rome.' No, none but me was there. The news was six months late a-coming. But the sorrow was only four weeks old.

Cutting along the grain of the leather with my round-edged knife in order to make a strong edge for the hem and the holes to come, and my back had already begun to ache high and right of the spine, when, like a knife blade shooting sparks from the spin of the whetstone – that Voice!

I hadn't noticed it straightaway. It was like the mosquito that whines below your knowing which, when suddenly it changes pitch, makes you aware of it.

So the sound of the Voice rose a degree – not as if it were loud, you understand, but insistent – and I noticed it.

Now, the market in the morning is a boil of human noise, empty carts clattering the stones of the roads that lead away, oxen dropping a heavy foot, the mason's hammer shaping rock, and folks will shout the nature of their wares, and I don't know the soldier that does not laugh and clamour when he's free of duties, and children shriek, and with what wondrous lungs the beggars bemoan their poor conditions, and some of these are philosophers who decry the rich for riches, and others of a philosophical commitment will rise up and deliver lectures unbidden in singsong conviction, and the ladies who come to purchase surround themselves with slaves to bear their purchases away, and the men will gather under porches to gossip of governments and games, and the dogs that we hate are barking, and yet – and yet, arising like an obelisk above the human boil, that Voice! Not loud. Never loud, but single, solo, separate.

Well, if it had *harmonized*, you know, I'd have lost it in the morning noise.

Or if it weren't so high in the nose, so biggety-sounding, I could have ignored it.

Or if it had quit!

So I was walking before I was done cutting my round of leather, and before I thought to cover my head, I was descending steps to the marketplace. Following sound, I was. Obeying my hungry ears.

We hadn't been in Corinth more than six months, the winter months from autumn to spring, and this was the spring of that year.

We had travelled east by the sea, suddenly, lightly, the two of us alone in the dangerous days before the winter storms shut the sea doors altogether. We had no choice. We grabbed what we could and flew, driven from Rome by the command of the emperor.

My husband and I: 'We.' Hum. Does that make us seem important? – I mean, that Titus Claudius Caesar Augustus

Germanicus should look down from the Palatine and pluck up two Jews to send them grandly away from the foremost city on earth?

If you could see me now, you would know that I am laughing. No, we were of no importance. We are Jews; isn't that enough to say? Jews, in an empire whose emperors grow sick with suspicion, get vomited out. Or dipped in pitch and raised as flaming torches for the night-time parties of the powerful.

But forgive me: that's the bitterness speaking, and it is not enough to say.

In those days Claudius wanted to renew the old religions of Rome. The man had witnessed signs and wonders. Four legions of his armies had finally invaded that white northern island which even Julius Caesar could not conquer – his legions invaded, said the emperor, *with* his gods, who deserved the worship, therefore, of every Roman.

So Claudius ordered and presided over a solemn celebration of the eight-hundredth anniversary of the founding of Rome. Festivals we had on a splendid scale, games and contests and glory and crowns: the *ludi saeculares*. It should not have affected us, but the next thing the emperor did was to expand the *pomerium*. This is the most ancient boundary of old Rome. Actually, it's an imaginary circle around the 'pure' part of the city where none but Roman gods can be honoured and acknowledged. But Aquila and I belonged to a synagogue on the Aventine, the only hill that had stood outside the *pomerium*. All at once the hill and the synagogue were inside, and our congregation had to disband or else move. It was a little like kicking over an anthill. What had been hidden now rushed and tumbled into the sunlight, and the private tensions of our community became very public, and the emperor reacted.

These private tensions ran deep. Some of us believed that the Messiah had come to earth, that he had died on a cross and had been buried but then on the third day was raised to life again. It was here that my father and I parted opinions. He was among the others – the great majority of others – who could not believe that the Anointed One of God would come to die. My mother was caught between. Her heart was with us. Her life was with her husband.

Truth to tell, though, this difference alone didn't sever my father and me, or else divide the congregation. Over the years many of our people, devout and honest, had believed in a variety of messiahs without tearing the community apart. No, but lately some Greek-speaking Jews had come to Rome teaching that salvation through *this* Messiah was worldwide. For his death had made Gentiles, just as they are, equal to Jews.

The Gentiles in the synagogue, God-fearing folk among us, were glad to hear that teaching.

But the leaders were insulted.

'Who are we?' they argued. 'We're the chosen people of God. No matter where we live, we are the holy nation, separate from every other nation – and the mark of that separation is circumcision! No true Messiah of the God of Abraham would cancel the mark of the covenant!'

The travelling Jews argued back with eloquence. But the leaders of the synagogue stopped debating and started commanding. They called it blasphemy to teach that God could forsake his covenant with the Jews. 'Apostasy!' they cried. 'Obey the Law or leave!'

But that happened just when we had all been driven out of our synagogue on the Aventine. When we lost the building we lost the privacy of our dissensions. Worse, we lost restraint upon ourselves. Soon Jews were fighting in public on the Sabbath. Jews beating Jews! How could the authorities *not* take notice of us?

And as if that weren't enough, the travelling Jews were ignorant of conditions in Rome. Their talk excited the suspicions of the emperor himself.

They prophesied famine.

We begged them to be still.

But they rose up in spite of us and uttered dire oracles of a worldwide shortage of grain!

Foolish, foolish men, however true their words might be. For Claudius feared two things terribly. He hated magics, divinations, astrologies, *prophecies*, and *prophets*! He hated, you see, any hidden means by which his enemies might seek to destroy his government or to assassinate him.

This was no secret. We knew. Everybody knew. For example, in the year of the *ludi saeculares*, a citizen named Petra told of a dream he had dreamed in which silver coins crumbled into dust. Petra was not a slave or a foreigner or a magician. He was a plain Roman. Yet the people thought his dream was a prediction of the failure of the money of the empire, and when poor Petra would not deny that he had ever dreamed such a dream, the emperor chopped off his head.

'Shut up and sit down!' we said to the foolish prophets among us. 'Don't you see how nervous the Romans are?'

In those days Romans were noticing how birds of ill omen had begun to perch on high places, glowering down on the capitol. They told of houses being overturned by the continual shocks of earthquake.

Well, and the second fear of the emperor was almost worse than the first: he believed that the basic systems of the empire could collapse, turning all Rome against him. Famine, you see, was an unthinkable disaster. It could kill an emperor. And already in those days there *were* shortages of grain in the city.

One morning, in fact, while Claudius was sitting on his judgment seat in the Forum, a crowd surrounded him demanding food. I was swept helplessly along. So sudden and so bold was the mob that it drove Claudius back into a far corner before his guards could break in to save him. Poor Claudius! He cut a miserable figure. His legs were thin, his body huge, his arms and legs for ever trembling. His head doddered and his fingers twiddled. The man's tongue was too big for its mouth, thickening all his speech. He had no dignity, you see. He couldn't command a bunch of roughnecks. They scared him in the open forum; in private he must have despised them.

So, then: what else should we have expected in our own Jewish situation? Our religion was already scorned by Roman teachers and Roman writers – like Seneca, that famous philosopher, who called it *superstitio*; and the brawls of our congregation had awakened the city authorities; and the famine-talk curdled the blood of the emperor. No, I wasn't surprised. Just sad that we would have to leave.

In the eighth year of his reign, Claudius published an edict expelling from Rome the most obstreperous Jews, whom he identified as those that followed 'Chrestus'. He meant, of course, the followers of *Christ*. He meant the Messiah, the crucified one, Jesus of Nazareth – that one.

Aquila and I followed that one.

You see, then, that we were not important. We were not loud or antagonistic or belligerent or, so far as we knew, obstreperous. But something in believing made us stubborn, and we prepared to leave.

My father told us to stay with him.

'In hiding?' I said.

'In blood and kinship,' he said.

'We cannot deny our Lord Messiah,' I said. 'We have no choice.'

He said, 'What Messiah divides families? What Messiah sets a daughter against her father?'

'Not the Messiah, Father,' I said. 'The Roman emperor is doing this thing.'

He did not kiss me. He did not so much as speak. He turned and walked away, leaving even my mother unattended. My father went one way and we went another, for ever.

My mother stood helpless, alone in the space between us, weeping.

'Mother,' I begged. I took her hands in mine. 'Mother, come with us.'

At my touch, the woman shivered. She sank to her knees. She crumpled down to the floor, weeping. She never answered my supplication.

Aquila and I left Rome alone. We rushed east along the Appian Way and boarded one of the last ships to sail from Brindisi before the winter storms destroyed the sea-lanes. We arrived at Corinth in chill weather. We found two rooms to rent in a house on the first risings of the southern hills. We paid taxes to the Manager of the Public Markets in order to practise our trade there. And though we did in fact – did deeply – miss Rome and our dear ones living in peril there, we settled.

Ou thelomen de humas agnoein, adelphoi, peri ton koimomenon...

It was the word *koimomenon* that triggered understanding. I was listening now. I hurried down the stone steps. I wanted to catch the sense, to comprehend what the Voice was saying.

The wind freshened as I descended. The sky was at war between sunstreams and billowing cloud. Dust blew up in the marketplace. The robes below me swelled and snapped around their human bodies. Folks began to scatter. Labourers held their hammers and peered upward.

Koimomenon. It means 'those fallen asleep'. But the tone of the Voice had made it mean more: 'those sleeping the sleep of death'.

13

The Voice said: 'But I don't want you to be unknowing about those who sleep the sleep of death.'

I stood in the middle of the busy marketplace turning my head left and right, trying to find the source, the location, of the Voice.

There: the line of northern shops. And there: under the colonnade at the western reach of those shops. Okay, so I bent my head against the weather and walked that way.

Great drops of water were potting the dust. Then here came a high wind spitting rain, raging with rain, a rain that stung the skin. People dashed for cover. My tunic was suddenly so soaked that it clung to my legs. Children shrieked with fear and glee. Yet, like the cricket that sits in your ear, the Voice continued in my hearing: '... so that you will not grieve as others do who have no hope'.

So that you will not grieve.

The colonnade was crowded. Scarcely a cranny for a small woman among the bodies.

An angry cry made me step backward. 'Stinking, filthy beggar!' There came the muffed sound of wood on human bone, an immediate *Yipe*, and my own particular Voice fell silent, but the crowd was howling outrage: 'What's wrong with you, Apelles?'

'He's blocking my doorway!'

'It's raining! No one's doing business now.'

'Bloody beggar! Miserable Jew!'

There came a second smack-sound, and the crowd roared: 'Get out! Apelles, get out! Throw that *echidna* out of here!'

The bodies parted just in front of me and a man flew out face forward, landing in a long smear across the wet ground. He rose cursing and ran off to the southeast.

In that same instant I slipped through the opening into the crowd – and now when the Voice began again to speak, it was a physical thing before me.

A man said, 'As others do who have no hope. Did you get that?'

Another man said, 'Yes.'

The first man said: '*Ei gar pisteuomen hoti Iesous apethanen...* For since we believe that Jesus died and rose again, even so through Jesus will God bring with him those who have fallen asleep...'

Oh, my! Oh, my heart! Here was no one of any bodily advantage. Here was a small man sitting cross-legged on the

14

stone floor of the colonnade, leatherwork spread around him, his tools and materials close to hand, his head, a monument for hugeness, now bowed over his fingers as if too heavy for his stalk of a neck, and patches of blood marking two parts on the crown of it. His fingers were flying. He was saying, 'For this we declare to you by the word of the Lord,' and his amazing fingers were sewing a felling stitch between two pieces of leather, making a tight seam, a waterproof seam.

He was saying, '... by the word of the Lord, that we who are alive, who are left until the coming of the Lord, shall not precede those who have fallen asleep'.

And I saw that the other man – much younger, with a ringlet fall of honey hair, sitting cross-legged like his elder and facing him – was writing furiously a kind of shorthand on papyrus. The words were not being lost. I didn't have to memorize them. They could be found again, Oh, my heart!

For it was the words that took my breath away – not the skinny man, but the Voice, the Voice itself.

The rainy day and the wet Corinthians around us and the work I should have been doing and lack of Aquila – all these things vanished from my knowing. Only the little man. Only the words that arose from him like birds in a bright, ascending flight. Only this: 'For the Lord himself will descend from heaven with a cry of command,' the man was saying, 'with the archangel's call and the sound of the trumpet of God.' Even so did he speak while his fingers were stitching, and I was caught between laughing and sobbing at the vision, between believing and fearing it, for the name *Jesus* was so dear to me, so familiar, and the thought of his coming swelled in me like the breath of well-being, a tingling in my heart, a thump of delight at all things soon to be made right – but where was my mother, then, and would my mother hear that cry, and how would she feel before the sound of the trumpet of God? 'And the dead in Christ will rise first,' the man of the monstrous head was saying, and I found myself sinking to my knees, for he was saying, 'then we who are alive, who are left – we will be caught up together with them in clouds to meet the Lord in the air; and so we will always be with the Lord. Therefore, comfort one another – '

'Noxious little Jew-roach! Why will you keep sitting when confronted by your superiors?'

Suddenly the rain and the day returned. I jumped to my feet.

So did the young scribe jump to his feet, spilling an ink pot – while his elder merely raised his face to gaze upon this newly approaching speaker.

Everyone had moved back, in fact, to make room for him. He was an official person with a fat, official presence. Behind him Apelles the shoemaker was dripping and glowering and repeating, 'Jump, Jew! Jump for Erastus!' And behind Apelles were four soldiers bearing weapons, the force that gave this official a real and present authority.

Erastus – pink, magnificent, the Manager of the Public Markets in Corinth, to whom Aquila and I had paid our taxes six months ago – Erastus said, 'Apparently you don't know my position. Or else you don't know the position you're in right now.'

'Well,' the little man grinned, 'I should have thought that my position is obvious.' He gestured to the tuck of his legs. It was a joke.

The grin did not improve his face: eyebrows thick and dark and joined in the middle; his nose both narrow and hooked; his eyes red-rimmed in that tremendous skull; a swift mouth, moist red lips. Patchy blood on the top of his head, an orange worm of a scar at the hairline – a smile on him looked thievish.

Nor did the joke improve the mood of the Manager of Markets.

'Sir,' said Erastus, 'Apelles the shoemaker has lodged a complaint against you. I can shut you out of commerce here altogether, especially since you haven't so much as registered with my office.'

'Registered for what?'

'For the right to do business here,' said Erastus.

'Well, to tell you the truth,' said the skinny man, his voice growing more nasal and irritating, 'I'm not doing business here.'

With surprising quickness, the fat Erastus reached down, snatched the leather and tore the stitching apart. 'This isn't business?' he said.

The little man stood up. 'No, it's a gift. I'm making a tent for my friend here, for his travels.'

Erastus turned his corpulence toward the young 'friend'.

'What's your name?'

'Timothy.'

'Timothy the Scribe,' he said, 'do you write the words that this man dictates?'

'Yes.'

'And what, with your craft, are you making of his words?'

'A letter.'

'Ah. And who will carry this letter to those unto whom it is addressed?'

'I will.'

'*You* will? Yes, yes, of course you will. You are a good and reliable labourer. Unto whom, then, will you go, Timothy? How many days will it take? How many nights must you sleep?'

'To Thessalonica. Fourteen nights.'

'Fourteen nights under the open stars?'

'No.'

'Under *what*, Timothy? Under what sort of shelter, Timothy the Scribe?'

'Under a tent.'

'Well! And who made the tent?'

'He did. Paul.'

'And who *gave* you the tent, Timothy?'

'Paul.'

'Now listen to me,' Erastus lifted his voice to the people standing nearby. 'A scribe gives a leatherworker two things: a piece of writing and four weeks' time in order to read the letter aloud in Thessalonica. In return a leatherworker gives the scribe a tent. What do you call that?'

'An exchange,' screamed Apelles.

'And what's an exchange?' called Erastus, his face as red as a pomegranate.

'BUSINESS! BUSINESS!'

The weight of opinion was not with these two, this Paul and this Timothy.

Erastus turned to the little man and stretched out a fat hand, palm upward. 'Remit the market tax now, freely,' he growled, 'or my soldiers will cut it from the leather of your buttocks.'

Everything went still. Rain fell in runnels from the eaves of the colonnade, stitching the puddles beneath them. The man named Paul stood wordlessly, grinning, bouncing lightly on his skinny legs, his bow-legs. Clearly, he wasn't about to do a thing, neither pay nor argue on his own behalf.

Apelles the shoemaker hissed, 'Slash him, slash him.'

The Manager of Markets shrugged. He withdrew his empty hand and began to raise it to signal the soldiers behind him.

But then I acted. Me, Prisca – I did something. Or else it was the Lord, since I had no idea *what* to do.

I leaped and grabbed that fat official's hand and hung on, crying, 'But his taxes *are* paid! I paid them myself!'

Erastus took my wrist in his thumb and forefinger and pinched hard between the bones. I had to let go.

'Who are you?' He spoke with high disdain.

'Prisca,' I said, 'the wife of Aquila. We're leatherworkers from Rome. Surely you remember, sir.'

'I remember,' he said, 'that you paid taxes for one concern, not two.'

'Yes! Indeed! And this man has just come to Corinth for the very purpose of working for us. One concern, you see. Our taxes *are* his taxes, because he is ours.'

... kai houtos pantote syn kurio esometha...

And so we shall always be with the Lord. Therefore, comfort one another with these words.

Here begins the story of Paul,
the apostle that was

Part One

*D*AMASCUS

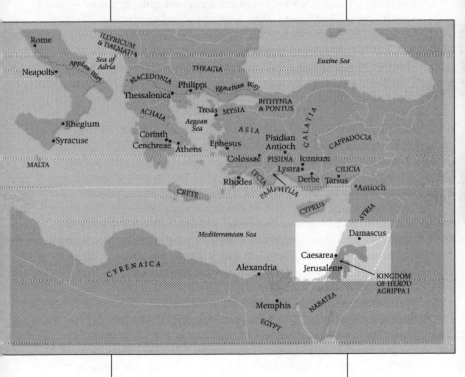

James

2

I begin with an admission: I did not like Stephen. Others did. Others accorded him unqualified honour. I could not.

Cephas and the twelve, in fact, contrived a means whereby that band of Greekish Jews – Stephen foremost among them – could speak and act with authority among us. I disapproved. Not because they had not seen the Lord alive, though they had not. Not because they'd only lately arrived in Jerusalem, heedless of Hebrew, their mouths full of Greek. And certainly not because I *dis*liked them in any way. I disapproved because these men were constrained neither by Moses nor by Aaron. The Law and the Temple were empty before them. Worse, they made themselves open enemies of Torah and the Holy Place. The only thing these men seemed to know of Jesus was the shame he had heaped on hollow ritual. It is true that Jesus despised a self-serving priesthood. So did Jeremiah. But let's be precise in matters as elemental as these: Jesus and Jeremiah hated the *abuses* of the Temple and the sinfulness of them that served there. Stephen, on the other hand, and the fellows who associated themselves with him, changed the focus of our Lord's accusations, heaping them on the Temple itself, on the ancient restraints, on the very wisdom of God. They gave no thought to *consequence*!

But those were the early days, when all the church lived in a sort of feral excitement, glad and breathless, perpetually amazed. Scarcely mindful. No one was considering consequence. For the Holy Spirit blazed in daylight in the touch of an apostle, and people leaped up who had never walked in their lives before. For the Holy Spirit could utter sudden thunder in the voice of Cephas, and liars fell dead at his feet. The end of the world was as near as the storm clouds that sweep in from the sea – so we said, and so we felt, for there were stories of the dead already emerging from their tombs. Hymns spouted from the mouths of the untutored. In those days decisions were made by enthusiasms, not by a quiet rabbinic wisdom. And the Greekish Stephen did indeed work wonders, and, yes, the Hebrew believers were glad of it, for this was a sign that Jerusalem, ever the centre of things, was drawing Jews home, now, drawing the children home from every nation under heaven to meet the Lord at his return in glory.

So the twelve laid their hands on seven. I disapproved, but to no avail. When we took Stephen plus six unto our bosom, it seemed to me that we had taken an adder there, rash, outrageous, and dangerous.

3

The Jew who rejects Judaism in the privacy of his own soul, although he is an apostate, is nevertheless a trouble unto himself alone. His silence makes him tolerable, even in the Holy City, because his sin is hidden.

But the Jew who chooses to *preach* such rejection, and thereby to urge it upon others – he has become a public trouble and an abomination. And the finer, more forceful his mind and his speaking, why, the greater the danger he! Anyone who strives to divide the People of God 'does evil in the sight of the Lord your God, transgressing his covenant'.

Allow me to quote Torah, the fifth book, since it was Torah that the authorities sought faithfully to obey when they executed Stephen.

Listen: *If there is found among you... a man or woman who does what is evil in the sight of the Lord your God, in transgressing his covenant, and has gone and served other gods and worshipped them, or the sun or the moon or any of the host of heaven, which I have forbidden, and it is told unto you and you hear of it, then you shall inquire diligently, and if it is true and certain that such an abominable thing has been done in Israel...*

Stop for a moment. Grant me an interruption to analyse the conditions established here for the action that must follow.

Those who love God love his Law. Those who love the Law are bound to do the Law. Living itself consists in obeying, death in disobedience. And the Law, which is the love of the invisible God for all the earth, is itself given place and shape and visibility in the behaviours of an obedient people.

Here, in the portion of Torah which I have quoted for you, the Law presents five distinct conditions upon which dreadful action must be taken by those who would be an obedient people.

First: The evil, the 'abominable thing', occurs in this, that the Lord God (who is defined on earth by his covenant with Israel, the very name of whose mercy is *Torah*), the Lord God, I say, is superseded in human worship by any other thing, by any other covenant whatsoever.

Second: The evil is 'found' among you. That is, it becomes known to someone in the community, whether a close relative or a watchful neighbour. And the evil is found 'among you'. That is, the evildoer is one of you, a member of the covenant people of God.

Third: The evil is 'told unto you and you hear it'. At this point, when people of authority have been made aware of the evil, there is no alternative. Knowledge constrains the faithful. The first discovery of evil by a member of the community may be accidental; this second communication is intentional. It must be the unifying of all intents: the people's, the Lord's, and the leaders'. The sequence which follows now *must* follow for the sake of the life and the health of the nation.

Fourth (being the first intentional step toward the purification of the people again): Leaders must 'inquire diligently' after the facts in order to assess what sin has been sinned, whether the apostasy of false worship, or else the communal distress of false witness. The inquiry will therefore depend upon, as Torah says, *the evidence of two witnesses or of three witnesses. A person shall not be put to death on the evidence of one witness.*

Fifth (being its own single and distinct action): The leaders shall come to an agreement internally, and then shall publicly announce that 'it is true and certain that such an abominable thing has been done in Israel'.

What then? What action must follow these five conditions?

Return to Torah: *Then you shall bring forth to your gates that man or woman who has done this evil thing, and you shall stone that man or woman to death with stones. The hand of the witnesses shall be first against him to put him to death, and afterward the hand of all the people. So you shall purge the evil from the midst of you.*

And have you the stomach to view the event? I shall describe it to you as my teachers described it to me, for it is not Torah but tradition that preserves the picture:

The accused is bound and led outside the city wall to a hill and a sheer drop which must be twice as deep as the sinner is tall.

The witness whose testimony convicted the evil one (whether it be a close relative or a watchful neighbour) now steps forward and bodily casts the accused down from the brow of the hill. He must land on his back.

If he dies from the fall, the execution is complete.

But if he continues to live, a second witness now heaves high a heavy stone, steps to the edge of the hill, and drops the stone on the chest of the accused, directly over his heart. It is meant to crush ribs and explode the heart, and so to kill the man or the woman. If it succeeds, the execution is complete.

But if the evil one survives this boulder too, then all the people shall pick up stones and throw them down upon the accused until he is dead indeed.

That is our tradition. That is the Law, both terrible and holy.

4

What could he have been thinking? Perhaps if the man had not gone *into* the courts of the Temple in order to denounce it – yes, in his Greekish dress, with Greek in his mouth – he might have had more time to contemplate consequences. Ah, but he *meant* to be public. He was bold; he trusted his eloquence; and he *meant* to lodge his accusations in the very ears of those whom he accused.

In a twinkling he had his desire. Opponents rushed to argue with him, Jews like himself from the Diaspora, from Alexandria and Cyrene and Asia – and one notable young fellow from Cilicia.

Stephen, standing by one of the columns of Solomon's Portico, had asked, 'Where does God dwell?'

Several men gestured toward the Temple, gleaming in the sunlight of a summer's noon. 'There,' they said. 'In terrible darkness,' they said, 'and in the midst of his people. There.'

Supercilious Stephen nodded. 'How do you know that?' he said.

'We have the scriptures,' they answered. 'Scriptures declare that wherever the tabernacle was erected – even in the days of their wandering – there was God in the midst of the people.'

'The Tabernacle is not the Temple.'

'Both are under the covenant of God, a covenant God renewed with David and again with Solomon, the builder of the Temple.'

'How do you know?'

'Scripture is our witness.'

'Yes, yes,' Stephen said, touching his knuckles to the smooth stone of a column. 'If there is a truth, it must have the witness of scripture. But scripture can be twisted.'

Now that young Cilician spoke, though he had not arisen. He sat on his heels like a nomad, his knee beneath his chin. 'There can be no twisting,' he said, 'when the witness *and* the truth have been joined and taught for generations as a single thing. We, sir, speak with the weight and the age of Abraham and all his generations, beginning with circumcision and even down to the lambs of the Passover here. There. On that altar. Would you gainsay a whole history?'

Stephen glanced down and grinned. 'Oh, no: not me, sir. But the God who utters histories says through the prophet, *Forget the former things! Dismiss the things of old. Behold, I am doing a new thing; even now it springs forth. Don't you perceive it?*'

The Cilician shrugged. 'Your "new thing" as well as your prophet were both of them already old when Ezra was born to enforce the Law four hundred years ago. The old will always confound you and your kind, while it must confirm us and ours. Listen to scripture,' said the Cilician – and I confess, I leaned forward to hear him. His manner was entirely confident.

'Listen,' he said: 'A thousand years ago at the dedication of Solomon's Temple its rooms were filled with a smoke so thick that the priests came out choking. That cloud was the glory of the Lord, sir! Yes, and Solomon himself said, *The Lord has set the sun in the heavens, but he said that he would dwell in thick darkness.* And Solomon said, *I have built thee an exalted house, a place for thee to dwell in for ever.*'

It was a good answer, perfectly quoted. I appreciated the man who carried the books so lightly in his mind.

Stephen rubbed his bare chin, grinning still. 'What, then? Would you bind God to one place?' he said. 'And if so, why choose *this* place? Why not the land between the rivers, where Abraham first met God? Why not Egypt, where God raised Joseph up? Too far away? So what about Sinai, where God spoke to Moses face-to-face?'

Stephen was filled with delight. His eye glittered for the stroke to come. He said: 'As for Solomon's house, didn't the Most High God himself say, *Heaven is my throne and earth my footstool. What house will you build for me? Or what is the place of my rest? Did not my hand make all these things?*'

The Cilician didn't move, but the other debaters grew angry. 'Fool! You fool!' they cried at Stephen. 'This is the twisting of scripture! The God of heaven and earth can *choose* to dwell wherever he pleases – and he has chosen this house!'

'Chose once, and now un-chooses,' Stephen replied. '*Do justice and righteousness*, the Lord God said,' said Stephen. '*Do no wrong or violence, nor shed innocent blood in this place, or I swear by myself that this house shall become a desolation.*'

'What? What?' they cried. 'You declare the Temple *empty*?'

Glancing at me, Stephen said, 'Even my dear friend James will testify that you've shed innocent blood.'

His eye and his word caught me by surprise and shamed me. I resented the gesture. I detested the association. Almost I stalked away – but no one was noticing me.

They were fixed on Stephen, shouting, 'How *dare* you call the Temple of the Lord *empty*?'

'I said "desolate". Abandoned. Forsaken. There's a difference. Unless – ' Stephen's lip curled into a smile. 'Unless it is a den,' he said, 'and then it's very full. Of thieves.'

'Ahhh!' they choked on their emotion. 'First he insults the house of God, then he insults the priests of God!'

'No, no, you don't understand,' Stephen cried, lifting up his hands: 'I intend to insult no one but *you*!'

'Us? *Us*?'

'You and all who hide behind this hollow creed, *The Temple of the Lord, the Temple of the Lord, the Temple of the Lord*.'

'Break his teeth!' they shouted. 'Cut his tongue out!'

'But these are not my words,' Stephen cried. 'They're Jeremiah's.'

Men spat and made fists.

This fury is precisely the danger I dreaded. It could swell, grow careless, and destroy the whole community of believers, not just Stephen and his kind.

But a high, nasal voice cut through the clamour: 'For a man who believes that all is new', the voice sang out, 'you rely on very old authority. Ancient, I'd say. Un-chosen. Overturned.'

The angrier debaters backed away, revealing the young Cilician, still sitting on his heels, hugging his knees, uttering a sound like the sharp snarl of a trumpet.

'Why should we listen to you?' the Cilician said, fixing Stephen with his eyes. 'By whose authority do you undo *our* authorities, sir, our covenants and sacrifices and all our history? We are a people chosen by God. We are Jews. It is in these things that we remain Jews. By what right do you strive to tear down the wall that has saved us alive for centuries among the nations?'

Stephen drew breath, swelled his chest, and announced: 'In the name and by the power of Jesus of Nazareth, the Messiah of God and my own Lord. *He* has now become the wall that saves all people alive.'

There ran a fierce blustering through the other men, but the Cilician smiled and said, 'So it is this Jesus of Nazareth that makes thieves of our priests and a desolation of our holy places?'

'No, sir! He only saw it so. And then they proved it so by crucifying him. His is the innocent blood that was shed. But that horror is followed by this hope: he is also the new thing springing forth.'

The growlings increased.

The Cilician said, 'Hush, hush, let's consider the conclusions such an assertion must lead us to. If, as you say, this Jesus of Nazareth has now become the wall that saves the people – saves *all* the people, I think you said – alive, then the Jewishness of the Jews must now be nothing, right?'

Stephen said it. He did not shrink from saying it. He said, 'Right.'

'But how can such a wonderful something suddenly become a nothing?' the Cilician asked. 'Only the Creator can uncreate. And to do that, God would have to deny himself, which is impossible.'

Oh, I liked this Cilician! With confident fluency he had softened the debate and sharpened it, both at once. No one was shouting any more. Everyone was listening. Anger had turned to reason – and what excellent reasoning it was! I confess that I felt a greater kinship with the Cilician than with Stephen: for though I did, as Stephen did, believe that Jesus was God's Messiah come to the earth, I did *not*, with Stephen, reject the Jewishness of Jesus. Messiah was as Jewish as King David. Messiah was promised to Jews. Messiah was sent first to the Jews and then, *through* the Jews, to the whole world. The Cilician was right: Jewishness must absolutely be preserved, even for the sake of the world!

'And how do you know', the young Cilician was saying to Stephen, 'that there is power in your Jesus?'

'By the words and the prophecy of Torah,' Stephen responded. 'By the authority *you* obey. For the Lord God himself said to Moses, *I will raise up for them a prophet like you, and I will put my words in his mouth, and he shall speak to them all that I commanded him*. Jesus is that prophet. His power comes straight from God. His words bespeak the new Law that replaces the old Law of Moses. Moreover, sir,' said Stephen, 'the God who keeps his promises, even as he has kept this promise, does not deny himself thereby. He exalts himself in glory!'

The Cilician closed his eyes and quoted the rest of the passage that Stephen had quoted: '*But the prophet*,' he said, '*who presumes to speak a word in my name which I have not commanded him to speak, that same prophet shall die.*'

The Cilician opened flaming eyes. Suddenly he flew to his feet and thrust his face into Stephen's face, crying: 'Which is exactly how your prophet fulfilled *that* prophecy. He died! He died a cursed death – proof, proof that he had never spoken the words commanded by God. And that, sir, is the only promise God kept regarding Jesus of Nazareth. He cursed him and he died!'

Stephen, physically bigger than the Cilician, roared in return: 'Yes, he died. You killed him. But then the Lord God raised him to life again!'

'No!' cried the Cilician, clapping his hands as if to drive wild dogs away. 'No, sir, God did not raise him to life again. Bring witnesses. Bring ten thousand witnesses to support your blasphemous claim, and I will vanquish them every one with *my* sole, irrefutable witness: Holy Torah. For the death your Jesus died was nothing less than the death of cursing. It was the death of holy hatred, for it is written: *Cursed be everyone who hangs on a tree*! God despised your Jesus. God so loathed the man that with cursing he took his life away so that any one who idolizes him shall perish apart from the kingdom. Behold, no house is more desolate or more forsaken than your own!'

I personally believe that it was the Cilician who fulfilled the third step of the Stoning Law. I think he went to the council and accused Stephen of worshipping another besides the Lord God – worshipping, in fact, a dead man.

The fourth step occurred with dizzy speed – and all this no more than two years after the crucifixion of our Lord!

The fourth step: Stephen was brought before the council and questioned. Believers prayed for him. Yes, I prayed for him. I did not like him. I feared the ruin he was bringing down upon us all. But he was my brother. I went to the Temple and knelt on stone steps through three watches, praying for him.

But while I prayed, Stephen was racing from drama to drama: In the midst of his trial he sank to his knees. His eyes rolled upward, his face grew bright, and he sang aloud, 'Look! Oh, look! I see the heavens opened and the Son of Man standing at the right hand of God!'

Such a public rage was loosed by this proud blasphemy that even I could hear the shouts of those who were tying Stephen's arms with ropes. I rose up and followed the sound of their roaring as they dragged him outside the city. The day had deepened into evening. I saw all things in silhouette. Oh, my Lord – I watched that dark party climb to the edge of a steep hill. Some men removed their robes and bound their tunics tight in their belts. One of them lifted Stephen in two strong arms, carried him to the lip of the hill, and hurled him down to the rocks. He hit with a heavy sound, then made a motion as if to rise and kneel. Another man heaved up a heavy boulder and dropped it mightily on the chest of my brother. But Stephen made the motion again, as if to kneel. Immediately, a black hail of stones rained down on him. He struggled. He would not cease struggling. *Lie down*, I whispered. *Lie down and die*. But he continue to struggle until by slow force he achieved his knees, and I heard him say, 'Lord, receive my spirit,' and then, astoundingly, he shouted: 'Ahhh, God, don't blame them for this!'

Suddenly he slumped. And though stones continued to trouble the ground around him, the struggle was done. Stephen was dead.

5

I've never shrunk from speaking the truth aloud. I shall not shrink from it now.

There was for us an immediate benefit in Stephen's death. The Greekish Jews who had shared sympathy with him now fled Jerusalem. They travelled to Samaria, Tyre, Antioch, Damascus, taking with them the antagonisms they had engendered.

We were unhindered, then, and unquestioned in our celebrations of the Holy Festivals, our sacrifices of burnt offering and whole burnt offering, our faithful love of Torah. We were Jews among Jews again and well received, and I went daily to the Temple to pray.

In those days I possessed very little authority among my own people, those who believed in the name of Jesus. Nevertheless, I grew strong in prayer. I prayed so devoutly and long that over the years my knees developed patches of callus which, so went the joke, were as tough as the knees of a camel. Among Jews in general, though, my devotion drew an honour which brought favour to the whole church and which, years later, granted me a certain credit when I had to negotiate with them for our lives.

In those days, too, my love of Torah caused people to give me a sobriquet I myself have never used: *Just*. James the Just.

6

The young Cilician who had debated Stephen with such a swift and scribal knowledge of the scripture was also present at his execution. He sat to one side, his great head balanced, unmoving. If he participated, it was as an officer of the council whose report of the stoning would seal the matter. That, at least, was my assumption.

I did not know his name then. I do now, of course. Perhaps the whole world knows his name by now.

Let me conclude this particular account with a second admission: because of the affliction he has visited upon Jerusalem and the churches down to this day – requiring of me more negotiation than the energies of one man can sustain – I could dearly wish I had never heard the name. I would have lived in plain piety without the knowledge. Yet, though he has strained the goodness in me, he has sometimes caused in me the heat that proves me living.

He was 'Saul', of the tribe of Benjamin.

In Greek (the language of his life and all his letters) he is 'Paul'.

$\mathcal{L}$. Annaeus Seneca

7

Seneca, lately arrived in Rome,
  To Novatus, my brother in Cordoba,
  This seventeenth year of the reign of Tiberius:

Greetings!
You know that I pray ceaselessly for your health and for nothing
more than the healing of this grim *suspirium* which we have shared,
you and I, all the days of our lives. But with this letter, *mi Novati*,
I am able to send more than desires and devotion. I have a fact at
hand, a thing you can do to salubrious effect: go to Egypt. Live in
Egypt. Breathe Egypt for the space of half a year, and your lungs
will know the benefit. My own breathing improved remarkably
while I was visiting our aunt and our uncle Galerius in Alexandria,
and though I have only just now returned to Rome, I believe the
improvement is real and will last.

In Alexandria they call our condition by its Greek name:
asthma. A 'panting'. A 'shortness of breath' – indeed! The Latin
suspirium is less effete and more functional. But you and I both
know that the best, most descriptive term of all is *hoc animum
egerere*. It is a continual 'breathing one's last', isn't it? Oh, *mi
Novati*, how close to dying we have come! While we suffer, it is
again and again *almost* to 'give up the ghost'. No matter how
brief the attack, it comes like a squall at sea – and I, by violent
efforts producing a mere squeaking sound, wonder in the silence
of my mind whether the breath that just fled me will ever return.
Will it have been my last breath after all? Novatus, do you, in that
last blackening moment, do the same as I? Do you make it a
meditation on death, a practising to die, as it were?

Well, abide a while in Egypt, my brother. Drink the dry air.
Astonish yourself with the freedom of deep breathing, when

your lungs shall be like leaves of the pine trees, causing soft sighs.

Go to Egypt – but not immediately. Don't go now. The emperor has roused himself to clean house. The emperor is furiously sacking officials in every province under his direct control. The emperor is suddenly as predictable as a babbling Jewish magician. Wait till he withdraws again into his usual reclusion, and then go.

It's this business with Sejanus that has drawn the great beast from his lavish lair on Capri. I don't mean that Tiberius has actually *come* to Rome, but that he is suddenly exerting a bloody influence here, executing Sejanus through the actions of the Senate and striving thereby to resurrect his own power. I doubt it was the horrors that the Praetorian Prefect imposed on Rome that troubled Tiberius (capable of horrors of his own). Rather, it was the golden statues of Sejanus. It was the impolitic pride with which Sejanus allowed his birthday to be declared a holiday. It was Sejanus's power – more than the substance, the *form* thereof. Tiberius squashed power. Yet in his poor bedevilled brains, the execution of Sejanus has not been enough. The emperor, now a perfect hive of suspicions, is changing policy. Once he trusted his provincial governors as he would his own right hand. Once he let them hold office for decades, creating a blessed consistency abroad. Now he makes a dogma of *dis*trust and recalls them for no reason at all.

And that's the command that ended my sojourn in Egypt. Wasn't it sixteen years ago that Tiberius appointed Uncle Galerius to govern it? Almost half my life. And, though the rest of that province is a miserable backwater, I had come to love the learning in Alexandria and would have stayed a decade in philosophic meditations. Who could have anticipated the violent changes to come?

Not only that we had to hasten from Egypt.

But also that we had truly to face and outface death on the way.

Mi Novati, here is the principal news of this letter. I have been avoiding the words. Heavily now, I lift my reed to write them: Uncle Galerius is dead.

His wife, on the other hand – his widow, I should say, our aunt – has emerged from the event as a she-eagle of noble and stubborn strength.

When we meet again I will give you a fuller account of the experience. Here and now, in the immediate grieving of my heart, I can but sketch the story of his dying, thus:

The emperor's recall was both sudden and impatient. Within a fortnight, then, we took passage on a grain ship out of the port of Alexandria. We promised both captain and crew a handsome payment at the end of the voyage. A generous tent, therefore, was erected on the deck of the vessel for our privacy and comfort. Interior couches and tables were fixed to the floor; closets and boxes and games and carpets furnished the small apartment; and to console my troubled uncle there were, besides his wife, an Egyptian cook, a musician who blew a soft pipe, and his affectionate nephew: I spent a good deal of time reading aloud to our aunt and uncle, especially from the writings of Papirius Fabianus.

But then, five days into the voyage, a squall struck down on us so suddenly that the rigging snapped and we wallowed broadside to the wind. The tent gulped and bellied inward, straining its ropes. I heard the shouts of the sailors outside. I told my uncle to bind his wife and himself to one of the couches, then I went out into the weather. The deck was awash. The water foamed and tore at my ankles. Two men were fighting with the tangled rigging amidships. Three others strove to cut the sail they could not lower. The captain cried me back into the tent – and I would have obeyed him, but at that moment the whole ship heaved and listed to a violent angle. I lost footing. Equipment slid down the deck and into the sea. Sailors grabbed the tackle to save themselves. A spar swung wildly over my head. It slashed the wall of the tent. A shrieking arose on the wind, familiar anguish. Even as the captain started yelling, '*Mittite scapham*! Lower the boat!' I crawled back to the collapsing tent. I drew myself through its fallen door and found our dear aunt lying across her husband on his couch. The side of his head was split open, bleeding. Her face was a ghastly map of his blood. But his eyes were open and fixed.

The ship pitched. The spar wandered drunkenly over my uncle's skull. Everywhere the tent shivered and snapped. All things shifted. Nothing was stable. Nothing but those staring eyes and the wife that kept kissing his hands.

I said, 'Let him go. Let him go. *Matertera*, come: Galerius is dead.'

She did not answer me.

I said, 'They're lowering a boat. We have to escape in the boat. Come with me.' I put my hands on her shoulders, but she shook me off.

The Egyptian was cowering under the table, shrieking. Hers was the anguish I had heard. In that instant she put a human face on the terrors we had entered.

'*Matertera*!' I shouted. 'There's no help for it. Leave him behind! Leave the body behind and save yourself!'

A strong knife ripped through the tent wall. The weather exploded around us. In the midst of that violence the captain appeared and cried, 'We're abandoning ship!' He reached and took my aunt's arm. 'Woman,' he shouted, 'you first.'

And suddenly the woman had a voice.

'No,' she said, taking her arm back. 'My husband goes first.'

The captain glanced at the stark eyes. 'Madam! The man is dead.'

'Why should that matter to you?' she said.

'It's a small boat! There isn't space for a dead man!'

'Then two shall die! Will that give you space enough?'

'Madam, please! Why would you save a dead man?'

'For the dignity, sir!' my aunt cried out, turning her full face toward the captain. The wind made whips of her hair. Her forehead streamed rain and blood together. She cried: 'A good man lost position. A good man lost his life. He shall not lose his soul to the sea! He shall be rightly buried!'

The captain searched my eyes with a panicked appeal. 'Sir, *you* tell her the need.'

Novatus, my brother, the bravado of our aunt caused me to astonish myself, for I raised my voice and bellowed above the wind: 'If this ship survives with the body and the wife of Galerius, we'll double the reward to all hands equally! If not, then not. Nothing! Nothing!' I roared to all hands. 'You might as well die now!'

The Egyptian cook passed out.

But the sailors went straight to work. They jettisoned the weaponry, boxes, furniture, the tent, and every heavy object on deck. They threw overboard not only the grain, but the clay containers as well. They released a sheet anchor from the bow of the ship in order to turn our nose into the wind – and they succeeded.

Galerius rests in a marble tomb. The nine days of mourning are past. The days of obligation have begun. The grandeur of his funeral equalled indeed the accomplishments of his life, as well as the nobility of his wife.

And now that wife, our aunt, has turned her strength of purpose unto the two of us, dear brother. We have become her present project. She begs me to beg you, Novatus, to travel hither to Rome. This newly garrulous woman wants to introduce us to her most influential friends. She says that we have languished too long outside the magistries of government. She is currying favour, sir, in order that we may finally be elected to the quaestorship and so embark upon the public careers that shall raise us to the senatorial ranks her husband never enjoyed.

And why not? I may as well climb poorly, panting and practising death, since I cannot swim at all.

Jude the Damascene

8

'Meet me,' the Pharisee wrote, 'at the foot of Hermon, where the holy Jordan begins.'

He meant the city that the Romans call Caesarea Philippi. We call it Paneas. He himself – Saul himself – liked religious names better. I figured that out pretty quickly. And he meant an exact spot, too: a well-known cave with a spring of water that runs south to become the Jordan River. He wanted someone to lead him back to Damascus and then to give him food and a room while he was doing his work here, restoring order to our synagogues.

It takes two days to travel from here to Paneas on the back of my donkey. It takes me three when I walk beside it. Stiff legs. Slow bones. And the days grow shorter and shorter for me. But I decided this time to walk. I've got nothing else to do. And I love Mount Hermon. I love the look of that grand old man lying down in the distance. And I thought maybe to sell some cushions at Paneas.

So the day after Shabbat I filled two leather pouches with bread and cheese and flasks of wine, enough for three days to and three days back; I bound seven cushions together and heaped them all on the back of my little donkey.

'Godspeed! Godspeed!' my neighbour Zephaniah said to me.

'I'll be back in six days with the Pharisee,' I said to him. 'Perhaps you'll have a dinner ready?'

So I walked east on Straight Street, waving with my left hand and leading my donkey with the right. I turned south at the theatre, then went out of the city by the little gate, the one that the Romans have started to call the Gate of Mars. So much newness around us. Too much newness. Caesarea Philippi, for example, is filled with fresh, white buildings younger than me. In the sunlight I have to blink to see them – so bright they hurt my eyes. Stone-dust still fills their rooms so that they even smell new. And that's a new name, too: Caesarea Philippi. Philip the Tetrarch put a name on the city that forces us to praise him and Caesar both, all in one breath.

My donkey is old. I am old. I became suddenly very old when Hodesh died and left me alone. We used to run our little business together, Hodesh and I. I got the materials, feathers and wool and silk, different fabrics for different qualities. She sewed the ticking and stuffed it and beautified some of our cushions with her needlework – so beautiful! So beautiful, in fact, that royal blood bought them and sat on them. We two sold our goods side by side in our shop. And I would travel some, me and my donkey – like this trip to Paneas.

'God speed you on your way,' my neighbour Zephaniah said to me. He's old too, and scared. He and I and most of the Jews here are scared of the changes, not so much in our city as in our synagogues. It's tearing the people apart! My neighbour Zephaniah said, 'God give you good speed,' and he meant that God should make this trip successful, that the Pharisee's work among us should also be successful, so that these new teachings should die right now, should die a fast, cold death. Too much newness! Roman newness is one thing. You can live with it because they figured out about heat and water and building high, and they have made even my little travels safer. But some newness is a plain and hateful enemy. You kill it before it kills you. You kill it like crushing the head of a snake!

The old things, O Lord! O Lord my God, the old things are the good things. This is one of the reasons why, as I led my donkey west toward Hermon, I looked and looked with love at that high old mountain. He fills the whole horizon, left and right as far as I could see: white-haired, mighty, grizzled, ancient. Look at him. He remembers the word that God used for making the creatures that creep on him. Even before Abraham, the people who lived here knew that the mountain was sacred. Oh, look at him: three peaks, the highest one in the south where Panea is. All year round snow covers the three peaks, and in winter the ridges between wear white as well, turbans and shawls and fringes. And on that day the morning sun behind my back made the snow to blush a golden pink. Like the blush of Hodesh, ah.

The face of old Hermon is wrinkled with gorges and chasms.

He weeps waterfalls. He wears green forests like a robe of a thousand folds. He gathers the dewfall waters for the streams that give drink to the beasts of the fields. King David said that the Lord God makes Mount Hermon skip like a wild young ox. I don't understand that. But I understand this, that when I look at him, Hermon makes my *heart* skip like a wild young ox.

Almond trees grow on the western slopes.

For a good long portion of the first day, I walked west over the dry flatland toward the mountain. Then I turned and followed the lie of its foothills to the southwest. Sheep and goats are there, wool and milk and cheese.

I remember the day our troubles began. It was the Shabbat before Passover. During prayers four strange men walked into the synagogue – Jews, to be sure, but when we asked them who they were, they said they were followers of 'The Way'.

Oh, but they were so tattered and hungry that we took them straight to our houses and washed them and fed them and gave them fresh clothes. Then we heard their story. They told us that they were forced to flee from Jerusalem with nothing but their lives, that they had suffered persecution there, and that one of their leaders, a man named Stephen, had just been murdered.

They spoke Greek the same as us. They weren't citizens of Jerusalem. They came from other cities in the empire. And we know how hard Jerusalem can be, grim and suspicious, especially for foreigners. So we received these 'Way' folks with real sympathy. But already in the first days they looked a little wild to me, trembling all the time with passions and excitements I couldn't rightly understand. Like they were drunk. And to my way of thinking, they were just *too* happy. It didn't bother them that people wanted to beat them or kill them. Well, and then when they got up in our synagogues and started to talk, the sympathy got divided. They lost mine.

To tell the truth, we have never been as fanatical as Jerusalem about the purities of being born children of Abraham. We invite Gentiles to worship with us – and if they come to fear God as the One True God, and if they keep the Law and are circumcised, well, then we say that the salvation of Israel is theirs too, same as ours.

But listen to this: the 'Way' that these new Jews talked about? It turned out to be a shortcut! It skipped the Law. It skipped circumcision. It skipped the whole of Israel and went straight to salvation! O Lord, how could *anyone* have sympathy with such blasphemy? Oh, yes, it was blasphemy. I'm no scholar. All my life I've been a merchant of cushions. Yet even I could see that their teachings blasphemed the Lord, the One True and Holy God of Israel, because they said that their 'Way' was not a *path*-way, a way of life. They said it was a *person*! A man, a fellow named Jesus, born in Nazareth, executed in Jerusalem. All that a Gentile had to do, they said, was get washed in the name of this Jesus, and suddenly that same Gentile was as close to God as any Jew. And directly they were washing Gentiles in the Amana River north of Damascus.

Did I say sympathy got divided? Sympathy split down the middle like a tree hit by lightning. And if it didn't completely split our synagogues too, it surely did distress them. Most of the Gentiles rejoiced to learn of such freedoms. We lost them. God lost their voices and their praise. On Shabbat our congregations looked as if a sickness had taken men away from us. But it wasn't only Gentiles. There were Jews now, too, who declared that Jesus of Nazareth was the Anointed One of God.

My old friend Ananias could hardly raise his face to me, and I said, 'Ananias, why can't you look at your old friend any more?'

He said, 'I do. I look at you, Jude.'

'Well, if you do,' I said, 'it's quick and nervous, Ananias. Why do you glance away when I come?'

'I don't know about quick and nervous,' Ananias said. 'Maybe it's worry you see in me. I am worried about you, my old friend.'

'Who should be worried about whom?'

'You are frightened,' he said. 'You cannot see that things are better, not worse.'

'Better? Better?' I said. 'Everything is upside down!'

And Ananias said to me, 'Messiah has come, Jude. How can the world be the same? The world cannot be the same. Messiah has come, and soon he will come again.'

Oh, my poor legs started to shake. I could not stop them from shaking.

'Ananias, Ananias,' I whispered, 'this is what I feared. This is why you cannot look at me.'

My eyes were stinging. I felt the same great sorrow that I felt when Hodesh closed her eyes and died. My heart was crying.

Then Ananias moved close to me. I could tell that he wanted to embrace me. There was a pity in his face that caused a sudden anger to rush through me. I lifted my chin and said, 'So now what, Ananias? Will you now invite yourself into a Romish house and sit down to a bite of pork?'

'No, Jude,' he said. 'My old friend, you know better than that. I love Torah. I will always love Torah – '

But me, I could not listen to him. I had already turned away from him.

I went to the synagogue, where people were screaming at each other. Brothers were cursing brothers even while Torah was unrolled and open in the room. I sat down in a corner and pulled my shawl over my head and wept. My shoulders heaved and shook. I sobbed from the very roots inside of me.

O Lord God, look down and see what newness has done to us! It is an enemy. It is killing us.

So therefore I was present when the leaders of the synagogues gathered to write a letter to the High Priest in Jerusalem, begging for some kind of help to restore peace and order in Damascus.

And I was there again when two letters from Jerusalem were read aloud in the congregation, one right after the other. The first letter was from the High Priest, recommending a Pharisee named Saul as the best warrior to fight on our side.

The other letter came from this man Saul himself. Here are some sentences which he wrote in his letter:

'I refute the teachings of these!' Saul wrote. '*Anathema esto!*' he wrote. 'For if any man should preach – even but once! – that the washing of some baptism is a substitute for circumcision, that man despises the entire Law of God. And why? Because the Law is one. It is the word of the God Who is One! Therefore, to revoke a single statute like circumcision is to dismiss the whole covenant and the entire Law. Now, salvation comes only through the Law, for the Law is the good and perfect will of God, the saviour of Israel; and obedience unto that Law makes the will of God a manifest, visible thing on earth. If circumcision can be superseded; if the name of a *dead* man can take the place of living Torah, making Jews and Gentiles equal before God, then salvation is lost, because *the walls are coming down!* And that is the greatest horror. Behold how the holiness of the people of God – their necessary separation from the rest of the world – is being destroyed. The walls of Abraham, his covenant with God, and the walls of Moses, *our* covenant with God, are cracking and collapsing! Oh, and I have fallen into a mighty zeal to destroy these destroyers of Israel. Therefore, I shall come to you. Have someone meet me at the foot of Hermon, where the holy Jordan begins. Tell him to seek a man newly bald. For love of you and for the work to be done in Damascus, I have made a vow. I shall let no razor touch my hair, neither shall I drink strong drink for twenty-nine days. On the thirtieth day I'll go to the Temple that my hair be cut and offered with offerings to the Lord. Early the thirty-first day, I shall rise and fly to you.'

9

Look for a man newly bald. I was more interested in trying to figure out what 'newly bald' meant than in selling cushions. I walked down the middle of a shining marble street in Panea with a cushion held high in my left hand and the bridle of my little donkey in the right. I moved past counters and shops toward the temple that Herod the Great built fifty years ago – built it right at the foot of the mountain. Maybe somebody wanted to buy my cushion. I didn't notice. There was a dark cloud coming from the west, getting ready to collide with the side of the mountain. The rainy season was about to start any day now. They had finished sowing their wheat fields west of Mount Hermon. Maybe it was going to rain. My little donkey needed oats before the day was done.

Newly bald: What would that look like? When you come to Herod's temple from the city, you come first to its back, as if the building were busy about other things. Its porch faces the mountain. Actually, the porch faces a cave in the base of the mountain, a very, very old cave so holy that all people, even the Greeks, know of its holiness. Many gods have been worshipped there. For example, the god the Greeks call Pan, which is how the city got its old name, Panea. But only one God made the world. And only the Lord is One. Between the temple porch and the mouth of the cave, there is a space of green garden and low stone walls and ancient trees and pools of bright water. That is the particular spot that the Pharisee named Saul had chosen, where I should meet him. So I tethered my little donkey on the city side of the marble temple and walked around the building, and there he was. In the end I had no trouble finding 'newly bald'.

The fellow had a huge head, and perhaps that would have been enough to notice, but there was a more perfect sign: his head was sunburnt from ear to ear and nape to brow. Sunburnt and blistered. The whole scalp looked like a bubbling gruel. I guess he hadn't worn a turban all the way from Jerusalem.

He was huffing and puffing, as if he was running a race – but the man was only talking. It turned out that that's the way Saul always talked, headlong and lickety-split. He was talking to two young fellows – but as soon as his little eye caught sight of me, he stopped and grinned and said, 'If you're for me, then I'm for you.'

I thought it was amazing, how he could pick me out of all the people passing by. I nodded and said, 'Jude'.

He came straight up to me and took the cushion that I had forgot was in my hand.

'I knew it was you, Jude,' he said, holding my cushion up high. 'I knew it was you in the midst of a trip,' he cried, bursting into laughter and embracing me: 'Here's an old Jew like my father the Jew, who comforts his backside travelling!'

I liked him right away. My heart went straight out to Saul the Pharisee, and I felt glad that it was me come to meet him. I grinned and grinned at his silly joke.

He was short and bright and very quick, small eyes in his head, long fingers, I noticed, and a run of words that, once it got going, couldn't get stopped.

He pointed to one of the young fellows with him, saying, 'Mattithias', and to the other, saying, 'Pedaiah'. They were lads with downy cheeks, but they had the sense to wear turbans.

Then Saul the Pharisee was serious. 'I was telling my companions', he said, 'that this is the northern corner of the land. Did you know that, Jude? Do you remember? Come here. Stand in the mouth of the cave.'

We four moved toward darkness and the echoing stone.

Suddenly Saul threw back his head and cried a line of scripture: *'So Joshua took all that land, as far as Baal-gad in the valley of Lebanon below Mount Hermon.'* Birds flew up from the bushes. People moved away from us.

Saul kneeled down and placed the palms of his two hands on the ground. 'Here it is,' he whispered: 'Baal-gad, the northern corner of the Promised Land, sacred for ages to the nations, but given to us by the Lord our God twelve hundred years ago. And from under the caverns of this cave,' he said, 'arise the springs of the Jordan River, where even a pagan king can wash his body clean again.'

It rained. There were some thunderclaps in the clouds on the mountain, then water poured down for about an hour, and then the

47

sky was clear again – but we had already started walking eastward when the rain began, and we kept right on walking through it. Saul, that little man, had a springing step as if his bandy legs were soldier's bows. He bounded along at a good clip. But my old bones are stiff. I gave thought to riding the donkey.

He was talking: 'Mattithias and Pedaiah and I will spend three days in silence, observing, listening. We'll catch these ravening beasts with the lies in their throats. On the morning of the fourth day, the first day of the week, I'll dictate a letter to the Council in Jerusalem. Pedaiah will carry it south, and then Mattithias and I and you, Jude, and the leaders of the synagogues will in the righteousness of God punish those who would destroy the people of God.'

'Excuse me, excuse me,' I called behind him. 'How will we do this? How will we punish them?'

Saul stopped and turned around to answer me. My legs and my lungs were grateful for the rest, but there was another sort of panting inside of me. With all my heart I wanted to return our congregations to peace again. Oh, how I hated the people who had come to tear us apart. But I was also thinking of Ananias. So I said, 'How will we punish them?'

'With words, sir,' he said, searching my face with his little eyes. 'And with rods and with imprisonment,' he said, 'and with death, if that becomes necessary again.'

'With death?' I said. 'Does it have to be death?'

As if my donkey were his donkey, Saul went to the little beast and untied one of the pouches and brought out two loaves of barley bread and a leather flask of wine. From among his own pack he took a large piece of leather and spread it on the ground.

'Sit,' he said.

We did, all four – though he himself squatted on his heels.

Saul broke the bread and we shared the wine, and while we drank he spoke to me, teaching me as if we sat in a synagogue together.

'Do you remember the story of Phinehas?' he asked. 'Jude, I will tell you the story of Phinehas, since it bears heavily upon this present age.'

Saul's brow is like a ridge on my dear Mount Hermon, a strong outcropping. It makes his eyes look small and fierce and deep as wells. But on that day he tilted his head with tenderness and

I saw love in him and it was love that talked to me, for this thin young man loved the things he had to say.

He said, 'The story tells of a terrible deed and a yet more terrible thing, the anger of God; terrible too – but good as well – was the means that turned his wrath away and saved the people alive.'

Saul's long fingers began to trace pictures in the dust. He said: 'The children of Israel were encamped in Shittim on the plains of Moab east of the Jordan River. The time was nigh for them to cross into the Promised Land. They were at the very end of their long journey through the wilderness, Jude – forty *years* in the wilderness, during which time the Lord God, who had brought them out of captivity, had also led them and fed them and kept them safe, never leaving them alone.

'Then it was that the people began to play the harlot with the daughters of Moab. Moreover, they ate with Moab; they bowed down to their gods; they yoked themselves to the Ba'al of Pe'or.

'And the wrath of the Lord God was kindled against Israel.

'The Lord God commanded that all the chiefs of the people should be hung in the sun before him, and that all who had yoked themselves to the Ba'al of Pe'or should be slain, in order to turn his fierce anger away.

'A plague began to spread through Israel, so the entire people gathered at the door of the tent of meeting and began to weep and beg for the forgiveness of the Lord.

'And then – even then, while the people were weeping – a man of Israel named Zimri took into his tent a woman of Midian named Cozbi. They went into his innermost room together.

'Now, Phinehas the son of Eleazar saw what was happening. He rose up and left the congregation and took a spear in his hand and went after Zimri and, finding the man and the woman in the very act, he pierced them through, body to body, both bodies at once, with a single thrust of the spear.

'Jude?'

It took me a moment to realize that Saul had spoken my name. Again, staring at me, he said, 'Jude?'

'Yes?'

'What did Phinehas do to Zimri?'

'He killed him.'

'Yes, he killed him,' said Saul. 'Now hear what the Lord said. The Lord God said, *Phinehas the son of Eleazar has turned back my wrath from the people of Israel, in that he was jealous with my jealousy among them, so that I did not consume the people of Israel in my jealousy. Behold, I give to him my covenant of peace; and it shall be to him, and to his descendants after him, the covenant of a perpetual priesthood, because he was jealous for his God, and made atonement for the people of Israel.*

'Sometimes, Jude,' Saul said rising, ready to walk again, 'sometimes it takes the death of one or two to atone for the sin of the whole people.'

That evening I paid a Syrian farmer the price of two silk cushions to let us sleep on the roof of his house. Kindly he offered us goats' milk and some dried prunes. He fed my little donkey good oats.

Saul put his great head down on one of my pillows, too.

Oh, how sore and weary were my old bones! Yet there was a true heat in my heart now. Something was coming. Something good was coming to our dear community.

I lay a long time unmoving, thinking. This is the way it is with me, now: I can't find sleep as easily as I used to when Hodesh put her pallet down by mine. Nor have I slept in the presence of any other person – certainly not in the presence of strangers – since the night she closed her eyes and went away from me.

But Saul, Saul, this Pharisee named Saul, hardly seemed a stranger any more. So wiry tough. So intense. I don't know; he was already as familiar as a fixed thing, like the moon or the mountain, or like someone's son. My son.

Suddenly he spoke. As if he just opened his mouth on a conversation that was going on in his head, he said, 'It must be the zeal of a few that protects the lives of all. It must be. And death may be the only act that finally makes the difference. But death is not always a punishment. Sometimes it's a sacrifice. I promise you, Judas of Damascus,' Saul said in the starry darkness, 'if it ever comes to this, I will deliver even my body to be burned.'

Right away he sighed and started to snore. That fast the man was sleeping. And I thought about his poor wretched head, because the blisters must have been breaking, and the tender flesh beneath the torn skin must have felt like fire.

Sometime in the night I woke up and found that tears were running from my eyes. Perhaps it was closer to morning. Yes, it had to be morning, in the dark before the dawning. It seemed to me that my father had been sitting near me, rocking with his head bent forward, rocking with his shoulders hunched, singing softly and granting me once more the great comfort of love, and nothing was changed, and every good thing was still the same, except that I was a child and my father had come to sing the morning prayers for me.

My tears were the tears of thanksgiving. I had never thought to feel so beloved again.

In a soft voice, a sweet bird-whistling voice, very pretty and very clear, the Hebrew words were being sung by someone in my ear: *Hear, O Israel: the Lord, our God, the Lord, is one!*

The first words of my baby life, they were – the words of my lying down and my rising up, both evening and morning. I woke supposing that I was home again and that nothing was wrong, and that all was well. I woke weeping and singing: *And you shall love the Lord your God with all your heart, and with all your soul, and with all your might...*

In my bosom it was a man's voice; it was the voice of a very old man.

But beside me on the roof of the Syrian's house, another voice was singing sweetly, the voice of the young Pharisee. And still the warm tears flowed from my eyes, because Saul had roused me into the world of God and the love of God, and if all was not well, yet it would be.

Together, in Hebrew, we sang softly: *Blessed art thou, O Lord our God, King of the Universe, who forms light and creates darkness, who makes peace and creates all things...*

And then I must have slipped back to sleep again, because I had the strange sense that the singing floated higher and higher until all the stars made a rain of the song, saying, *Blessed art thou, O Lord, who hast chosen thy people Israel in love...*

10

The sun came up at our right shoulders. We made long, traipsing shadows that stretched over rocky ground halfway to Mount Hermon – odd, knee-popping shadows as tall as cedar trees. My face was glad for the warmth. The morning air was growing colder, and my joints were tightening against the winter.

By sunrise we had already been travelling for several hours. The little Pharisee had struck out at such a busy pace that I reckoned we'd be home before the night. Two days! On my own two skinny legs! I don't know the last time I had such speed in me. Saul made folks breathe faster, rush harder, laugh gladder. Die sooner.

'Jude!' he cried out ahead of me. He didn't turn around. He didn't pause or slow down. He just kept right on kicking dust with that springing bow-legged sprint of his, and he hollered to the air in front of him, 'Jude!'

I gathered my own breath to holler back: 'What?'

And he shouted, 'You're a good man, Jude! You're a decent, upright man, and I'm proud to be called your friend!'

He kept on walking – giggling, I think, if I could hear it right – but he knocked me off my stride a little. Even just to smile can make an old man forget he's walking.

'You should have a talk with Mattithias,' Saul called, 'the pretty one, the dark-haired one beside you there. One day he will be a good man too.'

The lad named Mattithias blushed and frowned. He did, though: he had the bloom of beauty, the sharp cheekbone, a dark and even brow. Cedar of Lebanon, he was growing into the grace and strength of a handsome man.

Saul called back, 'What do you think, Jude? Mattithias has an eye for my sister. What do you think? Should I give him reason to smile?'

Mattithias wasn't smiling. His beautiful cheeks were oven red, his mouth a straight white line, his eyes fiercely forward. The other lad walking beside him kept glancing nervously into his companion's eyes as if seeking his own right response.

Suddenly Saul turned round and saw the effect of his talk on the callow lads. He burst into a high squealing laugh.

'Jude!' he shouted. 'The day sweet Mattithias takes my sister into his own home, into his own bed – that's the day he'll be a good man too, and a good man indeed!'

By noon we had turned to the east. We walked strung out in a line, none of us talking – almost as if pieces of us had gone to sleep in the heat. Our shadows were small pools at our left feet, and the sun had stripped me of all but a thin tunic. My little donkey carried everything uncomplaining.

Suddenly, in the noonday silence, I felt a blow at the back of my skull. I started to turn around, but was struck a second time, snapping my jaw shut. The third hit came down so hard it felt like rock against my neck. It drove me to the ground. But I swear there was no *thing*, and no *one* was hitting me. It was *light*, a brighter light beating us down, blocks of a blinding light from the sky, and both of the lads were laid as low as me.

In silence! There was no sound, just us grunting when we went down, like we were children pretending, but we weren't!

But then, as if the firmament had torn apart, there came a roaring from above, a steady thunder like waterfalls, and I tried to cry out, but there was no voice in me, there was no breath left in me. The ground was trembling. I shut my eyes and covered my head – and this next thing is impossible, but true: In the midst of the roaring I heard three perfect words, *Tis ei, Kyrie?* So I opened my eyes, and in a blood-red seeing I recognized Saul, flat on his back, his own eyes gaping straight to the light. He said, *Who are you, Lord?* And the thunder doubled itself, and I should not have been able to hear anything in such a sound, but I did. I heard Saul say, *Ti poieso, Kyrie? O Lord, what shall I do?* All at once he jammed his fists into his eye sockets and rolled over on his side as if he was suffering a fire in his face, and under the weight of the light I started to stand up while Saul kept rolling, rolled onto his knees and crouched forward and ground his poor bloody skull down on the stony earth.

And that's how it ended.

The roaring stopped. It was gone so suddenly and so completely that I almost couldn't remember it. The light was bright and hot, but normal. I felt let loose, as if I would suddenly start floating. But Saul was all rolled into himself like a porcupine.

From between his knees he whispered, 'Jude?'

I heard him call my name, *Jude, Jude*, but I couldn't move to answer him. My joints were locked. I had stopped breathing.

Saul said, 'Jude? Are you there?'

Slowly he unfolded his arms to their length and pushed himself up so that he was wallowing on his hands and his knees. He raised his face. He swung it to the right and then to the left, and I saw that the rims of his eyes were as red as fire, but that the pupils were gone. The living centres of his eyes had vanished.

'Jude,' he said. 'Jude, my friend, I need you. Please come and help me. I can't see. I can't see...'

He said, *I need you*, and that gave me motion again, and I went to him.

11

It was dusk when we entered the little gate in the south wall of Damascus. The sky was the colour of polished amethyst; you could look deep into it, deep and still and purple.

I had settled Saul on my donkey, which I led by the bridle. It was no good leading the man himself, because he didn't know how to be blind. He kept going first and stumbling, and mostly I was catching him more than leading him.

The two lads that had come with him from Jerusalem were walking some little way behind us – in shadows, whispering with each other. They were afraid. I didn't blame them.

When at noon he had finally risen to his feet again, they rained questions on him: 'Are you all right? What's the matter? What happened? What should we do now?'

Poor fellows. Saul wasn't talking to anyone. He was struggling to walk and leaning on me. He was driving himself forward. I'd say he was lunging forward, but he kept tripping on the rocky soil, then clinging to me not to fall.

'Sir, please,' Mattithias had said, 'Saul, what's the matter with you?'

'What the matter is,' I said, 'he's blind.'

'I know that!' Mattithias snapped. 'But how?'

Pedaiah said, 'Why? Why is he blind? Saul, why are you blind?'

Young Pedaiah broke into tears. 'What are we going to do now?' he wailed.

Ah, the poor lads! Their bodies were coming to manhood, but their moods were still caught in youth, and they were so afraid. Yet how should anyone act when a holy thing has just happened?

Saul stopped struggling. He held my arm in his left hand and reached his right into the air before him. 'Mattithias,' he said.

Mattithias came and said, 'Here I am.'

Saul said, 'Take my hand.'

The beautiful boy took his hand.

Saul said, 'Easy, easy, *adelphe*. You want to know what to do? Go home. You and Pedaiah, go back to Jerusalem. Go home.'

Mattithias glanced back and forth between me and Saul: at me as if I could explain what his master had said, at Saul as if trying to find his master behind the blank eyes. I held still. I had nothing to say.

The lad said, 'We can't do that! Why should we do that? What about you? We'll go back when you do.'

Saul's wounded eyes were pouring forth water, though he wasn't blinking. He drew the lad's hand to himself and kissed it and said, 'I'm not going home. I don't have a home.'

Mattithias opened his mouth wide, as if Saul's kiss were burning him. In a tiny voice he said, 'Why not?'

Saul said, 'I've been commanded to go to Damascus and wait for orders there.'

'We know that!' Mattithias fairly screamed. He took his hand back. 'We're *all* supposed to go to Damascus. It's the reason we came. Why don't you want us with you any more? Why are you sending us away?'

Saul shrugged and shook his head. He stood still a while, water flowing from his eyes. Finally he murmured, 'Everything is changed, Mattithias. Go home,' and he started walking again, but much more slowly, leaning the more on me.

The lads fluttered around the two of us like sparrows. 'You're blind!' they whimpered. 'Why can't you see? What happened? What devil struck us down in the road? What do you know? What won't you tell us?'

But Saul didn't answer. Saul said nothing at all.

We toiled along. His bodily weight in the crook of my right arm raised in me a great tenderness, as a father must feel when his son returns home weak and in need. The little man would slip, and I would catch him and hold him a moment and set him on his feet again. I was his tree. He was lighter than Hodesh. I was his strength. And I must have felt free to make decisions for us all, now.

'Saul,' I said, 'let me make our journey easier.' Then I lifted him and put him between two pillows on the back of my little donkey, and so we came to the city at dusk.

As we moved into the old streets south of the theatre the night became suddenly dark. No one lights a torch here, and all the doors are shut. My own street, though, is neither narrow nor crooked. It is as straight as its name. And it's wide, with colonnades on either side. Easy for a walker to find his way, even in the dark. The lads were in a strange country and frightened, but I was home and glad of that. Here I could be of more help.

As we passed by the house of my neighbour Zephaniah, he stuck his head out of his door and called: 'Jude! I'm surprised to see you. I didn't expect you till tomorrow.'

'Well, but we made good time,' I said.

'Did the Lord God grant you success then, Jude?' my old neighbour asked. 'Is that the Pharisee there? Did you bring the Pharisee with you?'

'Yes,' I said. 'Here he is, riding on my donkey.'

'Welcome!' Zephaniah cried. He bustled over to us and bowed a greeting. He straightened, then bowed again, but Saul didn't respond. Of course not. He was blind. But I felt embarrassed to say so in front of him.

So I said, 'Saul, meet my neighbour Zephaniah.'

It is possible that Saul nodded, then, and that the nod was meant for a greeting.

Mattithias announced, 'He's not talking any more. Something's wrong with him.'

Zephaniah looked at me and said, 'Let me keep my promise, Jude. Let me go and cook a meal for you.'

'Thank you, Zephaniah,' I said.

Yes, truly: I had succeeded. I'd brought the Pharisee that would help us bring order to our synagogues again. But he had said, *Jude, I need you*, and that had gone straight to my heart, and now there was so much more to do.

In the atrium of my house I tend a tiny garden where a fountain trickles into a small, shallow pool. After supper and after I had shown the young lads to a room upstairs, I led Saul to my garden. He sat down on the stone bench where Hodesh and I would sit of an evening. I knelt before him with clean towels. I began to wash him. He did not refuse me.

There was no help for it but that I must remove his tunic. I laid sponges of warm water upon his chest and felt with my hands how narrow his ribs were, how thin the man was. And his skin almost shone in the dark for paleness.

'Saul, Saul,' I said.

The man said nothing. He permitted me to lift his arms for the washing. His lips pursed, as if thoughts were going unspoken through his mind.

His sight was gone. What else was gone? Voice? Words?
Saul, can you hear me now?

I dried his body with linen cloths and wrapped him in a robe. Then I straddled the bench beside him. 'Medicines,' I whispered, 'for your poor head.'

The sunburn blisters were torn and running. I cut away the loose skin. On the sores themselves I poured a lotion of myrrh. His nostrils flared.

'Myrrh will keep the flesh from corruption,' I murmured. 'Can you bow? Saul, can you bow your head a little?'

He did. My heart gave a sweet start: he had heard me.

I anointed his whole scalp with a mixture of olive oil, verdigris and a powder of lead. The oil would keep my bandage from sticking to the wounds. So now I wound a long linen cloth round and round his great head, whispering, 'This is the turban you should have worn from Jerusalem, my friend.'

But when it came to comforting his eyes, I failed. Oil of aloe could not cool the flaming eyelids. Nor could it soften the crust that knit them together. I feared I might tear the tender lids and make them bleed. Searching closely the ruin of his sight, I brought my face near his. I heard breathing at his nostrils. I felt his warm breath on my cheek. The touch of my fingertip made him flinch.

Jude, my friend, I need you.

But I could not help his eyes.

I stood up. 'Come, my son,' I said. I blushed. I raised him gently to his feet.

'Hear, O Israel,' I chanted softly as I led Saul to a pallet, his weight borne in the crook of my arm: 'The Lord, our God, the Lord, one. And you shall love the Lord your God with all your heart, and with all your soul, and with all your might.'

In the black hours of the morning Saul's two young companions came into my room and stood there, waiting for me to wake. They carried an oil lamp. In the flickering light I saw how grim and frowning they were. It seemed to me that they came carrying convictions like weapons. They no longer were afraid.

The one named Mattithias said, 'Old man, we have something to say.'

I said, 'What is it?'

He stiffened his neck and announced: 'Either we've seen the work of a demon, or else we've witnessed the punishment of heaven. One way or the other, there's evil in this blindness.'

Pedaiah didn't wait for me to respond. Right away he started making a speech, and soon I recognized that it had been planned between them.

Pedaiah said, 'In the Book of Tobit it is written that while he slept in the courtyard some sparrow droppings fell into Tobit's eyes and blinded him. We understand that a demon or a fallen angel did that thing, because no doctor could heal him. For four years Tobit prayed, but no one at all could heal him until the angel Raphael came to help. It was Raphael who showed them that they should put the gall of a fish on Tobit's eyes. That's how he was healed. An angel healed him. So we know that a demon has blinded him. Demons can blind a man.'

Mattithias, his neck still stiff, nearly shouted: 'Or remember what the angel of the Lord did to the wicked men of Sodom. He blinded them! He blinded them to stop their sinning and to punish them. Blindings and blindings – and in the middle of the day Saul is suddenly struck blind by no hand we could see. One way or the other, old man, this blindness is a curse, and you should renounce him the same as we do. He will be no help to you.'

And then they left.

I mean that they turned and went out of my room and out of my house and out of the city, disappointed.

12

The leaders of the synagogues in Damascus are good and faithful men, some of them my oldest friends. They danced when Hodesh and I were married. They invited us to the circumcisions of their sons. They wept when I laid Hodesh in her grave. We are all of the same mind. We love God. We love Torah. And we yearn to preserve these things for our children and our children's children.

At noon the leaders of the synagogues came to my house and knocked on the door.

'Jude,' they said, 'is Saul the Pharisee here?'

'Yes,' I said, 'he is here.'

I stood in the doorway, nodding, *Yes, yes*, but I didn't move.

'That's what we have heard,' they said. 'Zephaniah told us that he met the Pharisee when you came home last night.'

'Zephaniah is a good man,' I said, nodding. 'It was very late when we arrived, yet he cooked a supper for us.'

I still didn't move. I looked down at my feet.

'We have come to welcome your guest,' they said, 'and to hear what he might have to say to us.'

I scratched my chin whiskers. 'You will be very impressed,' I said. 'Saul is a righteous man, full of learning and strength and vigour,' I said. 'When he walks he makes me tired, ha, ha. But when he talks he makes me wise. Yes, the Lord has sent us a teacher. Yes, indeed.'

'Jude,' they said, 'why don't you invite us in? Then we can see this good man for ourselves.'

'Well, but I have some bad news,' I said, now lifting my face and looking at them with a kind of pleading. 'While we were travelling yesterday, he fell down sick.'

'Sick?' Their expressions showed a true sympathy. 'What is the matter?'

'It's his eyes,' I said. 'He is having trouble with his eyes.'

'Ah, that explains why Zephaniah thought he was acting strange last night.'

'So you see that this is not a good time to visit.'

The leaders of the synagogues looked at one another and, by their looking alone, came to a decision.

'Jude, you are a kind and generous host,' they said. 'Please greet Saul for us, and when he is ready, call us. We will wait upon your word.'

Such gratitude flooded my soul that I could hardly speak. It surprised me how moved I was. 'Oh, my friends, my dear old friends,' I said, embracing them. 'Saul will be well. And when he is well, I promise you, he will *do* well, too.'

I watched them go with gladness in my heart and with worry, too.

Only slightly had I changed the truth before the leaders of the synagogues. But it was necessary to change the truth a little. I was a man in ignorance. Also, I had great tenderness for Saul, to protect him, both his body and his reputation, until he was strong again. Yet how to make him strong again? – I did not know this. Ignorance made me helpless.

Not once that day did he speak or eat or drink. I laid the food beside him, but he didn't touch it. I laid a cup of water against his lips and tipped it, but the water only dribbled down his chin. Saul didn't so much as wave the flies away from his eyes. They landed where moisture leaked through the crust. They ate and drank, while Saul sat cross-legged on his pallet and rocked. All day long he rocked and sighed and groaned softly to himself.

Only when I knelt beside him and began to chant the evening prayer did he cease groaning. It seemed he was listening. I took comfort in that.

But neither of us slept that night. It is hard for me to sleep at any time. But when there is a guest in my house whose groans are so deep that there are no words for them, sleep is impossible.

Jude, I need you. Well, and that seemed impossible too. God gave me the guest; but God hadn't told me what to do for him.

The next day was Shabbat.

I finished my usual preparations before going to the synagogue. I stepped into Saul's room to tell him that I would be gone for a while. Whether he could hear me or not, it seemed good to warn him that he would be in the house alone.

'Saul,' I said, 'after the readings, when the men are praying, I will offer up prayers for you.'

Then my guest, the man who seemed like my son, opened his mouth and astonished me.

Still cross-legged on his pallet, Saul said, 'Jude, don't go.'

I cried, 'Saul! Saul!' I shouted, 'You're talking! Are you hungry? Do you want to drink something?'

He raised his hand, and I stopped. In spite of his words, the man stayed hidden behind his blindness. The raising of a hand, then, seemed to me a grave and weighty gesture, and I held my peace.

He said, 'Stay in the house to answer your door. A man is coming to see me.'

Because his hand did not go down again, because it stayed up as if he were a priest concentrating on the act of blessing, I waited. I did not talk again. The day was different. Saul was different, if only because he had spoken. I *felt* different, on account of, I finally had three good things to do: first, wait for a knock at the door; second, answer the door; third, usher a man into my house to see Saul. And all this caused a tingling in me, as if my bones had been numb and now the blood was rushing back and waking them. I tingled because, how did he know a man was coming to see him? Saul must have had a vision behind his eyes. The hand of God had reached down. The hand of God was doing this thing!

So I looked and found some wine. And there was good wheat bread already baked. I could not cook a stew, because it was Shabbat; but I could lay out food that took no preparation, fresh olives and prunes and other dried fruits and some smoked fish, very expensive, and pistachio nuts.

Tingling and panting and feeling such a warmth under my heart, that when I heard three raps at the door I dropped the dish that I was holding.

I knelt down to pick up the pieces in my trembling hands. That's how foolish I was. Not till I heard three more raps did I remember that I'd left the man still standing outside, so I laid the shards back on the floor and walked through the little hallway to the street door and opened it, and then it took two or three looks to realize that I knew this man. I knew him very well. And he could not have chosen a worse time to come and visit me.

'Ananias,' I said, 'what are you doing here?'

'Good Shabbat, friend,' Ananias said. 'There is a man from Tarsus staying with you. I've come to see that man.'

'Tarsus?' I said. 'There's no one here from Tarsus. Ananias, go away. I have other business. Come back next week.'

I started to close the door. This was an outrageous interruption.

'Jude,' he said. 'Jude, have you noticed that I am looking straight into your eyes? There is no fear in me, my old friend. There is only the Holy Spirit and a command from my Lord.'

It is true that the eyes of Ananias were bright and his brow was confident. His voice was very strong. But I was going to close the door anyway, until he took my wrist and said: 'The man's name is Saul, a Pharisee sent from Jerusalem, where he caused much grief for those who follow the Lord Jesus. You have no choice, Jude. You must let me in.'

He knew the name of my guest! Everyone knew the name of my guest, but Ananias knew even the city where he was born. A coldness started to clutch my heart: this was *Ananias* here – the heartbreak of our synagogue, because he believed the teachings of those renegade Jews – and what if...?

I stood still. I did not shut the door. I did not widen the door. I could not think or speak or do.

And then there came behind me the voice of Saul himself, killing my morning's glad anticipations.

He said, 'Is your name Ananias?'

Ananias looked past me and said, 'Yes. And you are Saul of Tarsus.'

And Saul said: 'Jude, this is the man.'

I turned. My little guest was feeling his way along the wall of the hallway, approaching us. He said, 'This is the man, Jude. Let him in.'

I am very old. When I was young I could control my emotions so well that no one had to suffer them except myself. When Hodesh wept, I did not weep. I comforted her. But now in these latter days my emotions control me. And they are terribly strong. It is embarrassing, how loud a show they make in me. I am no longer my own man.

So it was with a sob that I said to Saul, 'What is happening? What happened to you? Why is Ananias here?'

Saul kept feeling his way toward us. I did not move to help him. Instead, Ananias entered my house and passed me by and went to him and placed his hands on Saul's shoulders.

'Brother Saul,' he said, 'the Lord Jesus who appeared to you on the road by which you came has sent me that you may regain your sight and be filled with the Holy Spirit.'

I started weeping. Sadness was like a storm in me. I couldn't contain it. Out of my mouth came a childish noise: *Waaa*! Yet I watched the two men touching each other, and I saw the crust on Saul's eyes crumble and flutter down his white cheeks like fish scales, and then he was blinking, and then he was seeing.

The Lord Jesus who appeared to you... What should I think of such words? What was happening among us?

I myself – I never had the boldness to call him *brother* Saul. *Waaa.*

My eyes wide open, I watched Saul bow his head, shining, shining with a strange white fire! Ananias began to unwind the bandage I had given him.

Ananias was saying: 'You, Saul, are a chosen instrument of the Lord's, to carry his name before the Gentiles and kings and the children of Israel. And the Lord will show you how much you must suffer for the sake of his name.'

Sight and light and a giggling joy in Saul! And he was beaming on Ananias, and something good was gone from me.

Waaa! But perhaps I wasn't crying aloud any more. Perhaps it was the sound of my soul and loneliness.

The two men walked back into my house, Saul on his own feet leading the way.

They went into the atrium where my little fountain trickled into a shallow pool. I did not follow. I didn't move, still standing by the open door. But I heard water splashing, and I heard the voice of Ananias say: 'I baptize you in the name of our Lord Jesus Christ' – and then that high voice of Saul, hooting, 'Jesus Christ is my Lord!' – and then laughter. Saul made *hee-hee* giggles, a silly-sounding laughter. I stopped crying. I went out my door and closed it and walked to the synagogue.

13

The name of my wife is a beautiful name. In Hebrew it means
new. Like the new moon of a new month. And so she was, in all
her ways and all her days, ever new to me and ever young, but
never the newness that destroys the old. Hodesh was youth to
me. Don't you see? She kept my old self young. I had already
entered the forty-fifth year of my age when we married, and she
but seventeen! There was in me no deserving of such a gift of
God. And then, exactly twenty-one days before the Feast of
Tabernacles, she became sick. But this was the year we had
planned to make a pilgrimage to Jerusalem for the Feast. It
would have been her first pilgrimage to the Holy City. But she fell
sick, and she lay down on her pallet, and I nursed her. I did not
cry. I comforted her. Ah, but my Hodesh could not keep food in
her stomach, and soon she loathed the taste of it. And if she
drank anything at all, she threw it up with terrible convulsions.
And then on the evening of the eighteenth day before the Feast,
she smiled at me. All her pain was gone. She smiled a pale smile,
as thin and white as the crescent moon, and then she closed her
eyes and released a long, long sigh, and then she died.

It was the day after the Feast of Tabernacles that I and others
met with the leaders of our synagogues and together wrote
letters to the High Priest in Jerusalem, begging help because a
different sort of newness had come to Damascus to kill us. And
the help they sent us was Saul, the Pharisee, a zealous man.

When I returned to my house after going to the synagogue that
Shabbat, it was already the night. I had lingered there till the day
itself was done.

I saw lamplight in one window of my house. I entered and
walked to the room of that window, which was the room I had
given Saul. He was in it, sitting cross-legged on the pallet I had
also offered him in good faith.

He could see now. He raised his large head and watched me as

I stepped into the room. We both cast monstrous shadows from the single flame.

I said, 'The pallet on which you are sitting – it belongs to my wife.'

He fixed his eyes on me and said, 'Jude, there is only one thing you need to know. That Jesus of Nazareth, he who was crucified eighteen months ago – he is alive.'

I bent down and began to stuff his possessions into his leather bag.

I said, 'For my wife's sake, I need this room and this pallet back again. Please be sure you leave nothing of yours in my house when you go.'

'Jude,' he said, 'it was Jesus himself who met me on the road. God raised him from the dead. This makes all the difference.'

I said, 'Go, Saul. Go.'

He rose to his feet. Now he was the one looking down on me, because I continued to squat.

He said, 'Jude of Damascus, you have been like a father to me.'

This is a moment of which I am the most proud and for which I give thanks to God: I did not cry. I did not wince. I controlled my emotions. I stood up and faced him, my eyes to his eyes. I handed him his bag, and I said, 'Go.'

$\mathcal{L}$. Annaeus Seneca

14

Seneca, in exile on Corsica,
   To Helvia, my mother in Cordoba,
   This first year of the reign of Claudius:

Greetings!
I will not call it 'exile', *mater optima*, and neither should you.
We will call it 'an involuntary change of residence', realizing that
the man required to make such a change need not himself be
changed. He is who he was and what he may always be.

O Mother, often since the Senate tore us asunder and drove
me alone to this rock I've wanted to write you a letter of
consolations; but I mistrusted myself. My own grieving choked
every good word in me, unspoken, unspeakable, unwritten.

But six months have passed. Perhaps your sorrow has eased
enough to receive my remedies. Surely I have banished mine.

So I write.

Please don't think me cruel if I begin with a list of your past
misfortunes. The pampered, luxuriant mind shrinks from the
slightest injury; but the woman who has survived a succession of
calamities can bear the heaviest blow with resolution. You are
that woman, Mother – even from the beginning.

On the day you were born, your own mother died.

Ten years ago you endured the horrors of shipwreck, believing
that your sister and her husband and I myself, all three, had gone
down to the seabed, drowned. It was Galerius in fact that had
died. We were able to meet and kiss and embrace, you and I,
while he lay down on his marble bed for ever.

But then your husband, my father and my namesake, died.

This man once saved my life. Did you know? Before my sojourn
in Egypt, my sickness, my grim *suspirium*, used to cause such

anguish, keeping me ever thin and coughing and cold, that I thought to cut the problem out by cutting my life out altogether. It was care for my dear old father that prevented me. I didn't so much worry whether I had the strength to die as whether he had the strength to endure my dying.

But then it was his death we had to endure, you and I, but separately since a sea divided us. Next, so soon upon the loss of your husband, came the losses of three of your grandchildren. And one of these was mine, my own, my youngest son, who died against your bosom, mother, and under the rain of your gentle kisses.

Finally, I, your second-born, have been torn from you and sent alive to this forsaken crag, this stony grave. It is a new sort of mourning, isn't it? – to mourn the living.

There: Not a single misfortune have I overlooked, because I intend not to cover them, but to conquer them.

And I start with the last: Do you grieve because you think I grieve? Don't. Because I don't! I have schooled myself in contentment, Mother. In my forty-third year, when other men are attaining the height of their powers, I've *lost* power, as well as freedom and the use of my whole estate. But this is my contentment, that I've lost what I never needed, and what I need I can never lose: these two things, universal nature and one's personal virtue.

For this is the intention of the creator of the world, whatever he may be – whether an all-powerful Deity, or some incorporeal Reason contriving vast works, or a divine Spirit pervading all things from the least to the largest with a uniform energy, or Fate, or an inalterable sequence of Causes clinging one to another – whatever the Intender, I say, this is his intention: that nothing of ours can fall under the control of others except that which is finally and truly worthless to us.

The best of any man lies beyond the powers of other men, either to give it or to take it away.

Listen to me. This firmament, arching over you as it does over me; this firmament, more ordered and proportioned, more mobile and lovely than anything else that Nature has fashioned; this brave firmament, Mother, and the most glorious part of it – that is, the human mind capable of surveying and delighting in it – is ours for ever! As long as we are, and are looking, it shall be. And as long as I can behold the realms of God, the sun and moon, the wandering planets rising and setting and swift and slow, the myriad stars in circular courses or fixed or shooting; as long as I can commune with celestial beings, raising my sight to my cousins on high, why should I care what ground is underneath my feet?

And what if an exile is reduced to bread in a hut? Why, the lowliest hovel can be furnished with virtues. Justice and temperance make room for grand companies of friends. Wisdom and righteousness are the chairs and tables. A sweet and proper division of duties produces a hundred serving hands. And the knowledge of God is food and drink indeed. Lo, how a hut is a palace after all.

I have never loved Fortune, even when she seemed most to love me. I never considered her treasures mine, neither her money, nor her office nor her influence. Her theft of these things, therefore, has taken away nothing of my own. Mother, my roof is the stars. My house is human goodness. My body is clothed. My stomach is full. And the thirstier part of me, my soul, drinks gladly from the pool of my books.

So much for me. I am just fine.

As for you, I know your heart. I know what saddens you and what does not. Neither jewels nor pearls have ever moved you. Riches don't glitter in your eyes. You were never embarrassed by the number of your children, as if it proved you old, nor did you hide a pregnancy for the sake of silly beauty. You've never defiled your face with paints nor exposed your body through gauzy garments. Your greatest ornament has ever been your modesty. For you the loss of external things is no loss at all. But that which is internal, *that* is the wound in you: spirit and love and taking thought and the absolute walls of mortality.

What then, Mother? Why, then study philosophy!

I wish my father had been less bound to the customs of his forefathers. I wish he had relented and let you receive a genuine education. A knowledge of the teachings of philosophy would be your ward and protector now, even as it is for me. Ah, he was old-fashioned while he lived.

But now it is your life and altogether your deciding. And you know how to read. And the foundations of philosophy are already established in your alert, enquiring mind. So go back to the books. They will comfort you and cheer you. If earnestly you work with them, neither sorrow nor anxiety nor distress nor suffering need trouble your mind any more, no, not evermore.

But until you've achieved the dear detachment of wisdom,
O Mother, lean on my brothers! Delight in their achievements.

Novatus has done wonderfully well since he was adopted by the senator, L. Junius Gallio. We call my luminous brother by his new name, Gallio. We praise his easy charm and rejoice in his public honours. And while your oldest son shines bright in the Roman sky, he shines on you!

And if Mela, your youngest son, has chosen to live in contemplations, scorning the honours of the public arena in order to take his leisure near you, then his leisure is *for* you!

Gallio helps you. Mela pleases you. Gallio protects you. Mela consoles you. Surely, together they fill the space that has been left by me, and you lack for nothing now, except the bare number, three.

Oh, and I know that you have already turned to your grandson Marcus, sweet and winsome in all his ways. How can sorrow live in the light of the face of that child? What heart so hurt, it could not heal in his innocent huggings? What tears so great, they could not dry in his lively chatter? And whose joy would not rise and laugh out loud in the rhymes he makes, the verses he shouts from hall to hall, the epics in a baby's brain? Mark my words, Marcus will be a poet one day.

And I pray the gods that we all may die before he does.

Oh, let the ravagings of Fate stop here with me! Whatever aches you are doomed to suffer, Mother and Grandmother – let them all fall on me! May the rest of my family know no change hereafter. I shall not lament my present state, neither the exile nor the death of my son, if only I may be the scapegoat for the rest of those whom I love, and if all their sorrows end with me.

James

15

I possess one particular memory of Saul so pure, so luminous that it is, as it were, a pearl within me. According to the admonitions of our Lord, I carry nearly nothing in my worldly scrip; yet that pearl is there. That pearl remains. And in spite of all that has gone between, the memory ennobles our common past.

It occurs at our second encounter, three years after I had watched the young man, the Pharisee, defend Torah before Stephen, three years after he had departed Jerusalem.

Saul is reclining on a rude cushion in Simon Peter's house, his left elbow planted on the table, his jaw in the palm of that hand, his head in a maiden's tilt. The fingers of his left hand are slender and very long. They cradle his face from cheek to temple, the tip of the little one caught in the corner of his eye. Saul is gazing at me.

Simon's table is shaped like a horseshoe. Simon himself, as host for the two of us, reclines at the central section. Saul and I occupy the extremities, opposite one another. Neither one of us has spoken since we exchanged greetings at my entering in. Even as I was following Simon into the dining room, Saul rose and spoke. He said, 'James', and then he said with explicit care: 'The peace of our Lord Jesus Christ be with you, James.'

I replied, I'm afraid, as something of a bumpkin, muttering, 'Peace', in return.

He grinned in wordless delight, then sank down again, and so did I, and Simon has not yet ceased his chatter, but Saul, his head in a light, inquiring tilt, gazes at me in silence.

This is our first actual meeting.

He seems, by the look of him, to know something about me.

I, for my part, have heard of his conversion. Believers in

Jerusalem are highly doubtful of the truth of it, but this is precisely what Simon Peter is protesting before me with boisterous joy: 'It's true! James, it's all true. He saw the Lord. The Lord cut him down like a broom tree, then built him like planks of a good wood into a whole new temple!'

Simon's joy overwhelms all.

And I believe him. I look at Saul and I see, truly, a servant of Christ and a brother to me.

Oh, how I wish I could say some perfect thing to welcome him into our company. The man loves Torah as much as I do. And with his eyes alone he is awaiting my word – *my* word, clearly – and I am moved, for this is his personal choice; not even Simon recognizes the supplication in the tilt of the good man's head. Saul is, by this reverent, expectant silence, honouring me.

Ah, what a grace! What a memory!

And to round the moment into a pearl of radiant light, the Holy Spirit grants me now, in this very hour, the formal, appropriate word.

It is Simon Peter's wife who interrupts his talk. She enters the dining room carrying a flagon of wine and a single cup. She places these on the table in front of her husband, then turns and leaves.

I open my mouth, and even before I know the word, I speak it. 'And finally to you,' I say.

Simon says, 'What? What? What did you say?'

But Saul lifts his head and folds his hands, preparing to hear more. Curiously, it is his very preparing that floods me with the rest of my welcome.

'Saul,' I say, tasting the pleasure of my own participation in this sacred exchange: 'This we have known, and this we have spoken so often in the last four years that the language has become fixed. We've said it ever the same – until now. Now we must unfix the ending and change it, Saul, for you. We say, *Christ died for our sins in accordance with the scriptures. He was buried. He was raised on the third day in accordance with the scriptures. He appeared to Peter, then to the twelve. Then he appeared to more than five hundred believers at one time. Then he appeared to James* – to me, we mean,' I say softly, '*then to all the apostles –* '

I pause. Simon Peter is quiet, aware. So is Saul. Water is rising in his eyes. He neither blinks nor wipes them.

Softly, with ceremony, I say: *'Then to all the apostles.* That's what the ending was. But now the ending must say, *And finally Christ appeared on the road to Damascus also to Saul.* Also to you. Welcome, Saul of Tarsus.'

Again, Simon's wife is in the room, this time with a loaf of flat bread on a round clay dish. She approaches the central table, kneels down across from her husband and places the dish before him.

And these, too, are elements of my blessed memory:

Simon Peter is praying, his great arms swept wide open.

Saul, in an unpretty voice, is singing 'Amen', over and over again: 'Amen! Hallelujah.'

Simon is holding the bread in two hands, saying, 'This is what Jesus did among us before he died. He took bread and blessed it and broke it and gave it to each of us, saying, *This is my body which is for you; do this in remembrance of me.*' And Simon is tearing pieces from the loaf, giving them to Saul on his right, his wife before him, and then to me on his left.

Simon is pouring wine into the cup, saying, 'After we had eaten supper, Jesus took a cup, and when he had given thanks he gave the cup to us all, and we drank, and he said, *This cup is the new covenant in my blood; do this, as often as you drink it, in remembrance of me.*' And Simon Peter is drinking, and his wife is drinking, and he hands the cup to Saul, who is drinking, but then Saul is rising up and walking from his table to mine, and now Saul is kneeling down beside me and handing me the cup, and I am drinking, I am drinking slowly and tastingly and deeply, and as I lower the cup from my lips, Saul is whispering, 'But I am the least, James. And in me it can be nothing but grace, because I persecuted the people of God.'

And that is the close and the purity of my pearl.

In spite of all that has happened between Saul and me in the decades following that perfect moment, I have preserved this pearl as a sacred thing, my private consolation.

Simon Peter says, *'Marana tha'.*

I say, 'Amen'.

Saul takes the cup from my hand and says, 'Amen'.

$\mathcal{L}$. Annaeus Seneca

16

Wild and barbarous Corsica! Imprisoning me completely by its cliffs, wastes and desolations! The autumn is fruitless, the winter grey, the spring a flood that drowns all tender shoots.

I have tried to write. I've tried to maintain a personal discipline, to read, to think, to observe, to *write*! – but have only driven myself to despair. My brains are rusted in disuse. How can I fashion one graceful sentence when the only language I hear is so coarse that it wounds the ear of the savage who speaks it?

How do I do? You want a description? Foodless, drinkless, lifeless, and not so much as a spark to light my funeral fire! Two words alone can define my life and me: an 'exile' *in* an 'exile'!

I hate this island. I hate this shrubby, burning, dirtless rock. The summer comes beastly early, and then what? Why, then the beast grows mad and rabid when the Dog-star shows his tooth.

Gods! – I am banished to a tomb, and the only mercy I beg is that the earth lie lightly on the ashes of the living dead.

Part Two

ANTIOCH

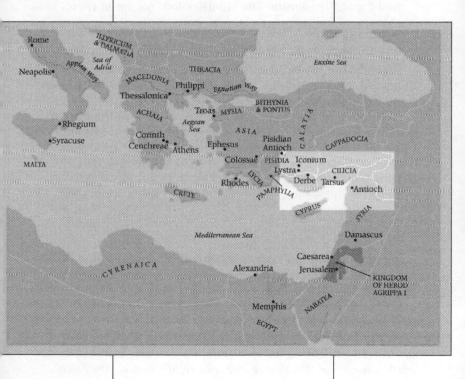

$\mathscr{B}$arnabas

17

Saul said: 'In Damascus once I ate a thrush served on a nest of asparagus. It's a nibble dish. You eat the meat in slivers.'

'Garum,' I said.

'What?' he said.

And I said, 'Try garum. The Gentiles love garum in their cooking.'

'What is it?'

'Ha, ha! Do you see how much we have to look forward to?'

Actually, I'm the one who loves to eat. I have absolutely delighted in our freedoms. For Saul, food's a necessity he often forgets. Or else he uses it for formal declarations.

'Garum: it's a fish sauce,' I said. 'You make it by steeping the guts of a mackerel in salt. Or a tunny. They make it and ship it in huge clay jars. The best stuff comes from Cades.'

Saul said, 'Down in Daphne once I ate a dormouse, little carcass on a little spit.'

I burst into laughter. In my mind's eye I saw a big-headed, grimacing Saul tweaking mouse-bones in his fingers. 'Another nibble dish!' I roared.

Saul smiled a wintry smile.

We were sitting in a corner of Simeon's house, passing the time while people gathered for the weekly meal and worship. Simeon's servants had been preparing dishes all day long. Guests came bearing food of their own. It had triggered our topic, Saul's and mine. Neither one of us cooked.

At the top of my lungs, I quoted Leviticus: '*And these are unclean to you among the swarming things that swarm upon the earth: the weasel, the mouse, the mouse, the mouse, the great lizard, the gecko, the land crocodile, and the mouse*! The bright-eyed, busy dormouse!' Half my laughter was knowing that Saul had a purpose in dining on the tiny rodent. I thought I'd drive that purpose to its extremes.

'Here,' I said, poking him in the ribs. 'Let me give you a recipe with more substance. It's called 'The Garden Piglet'. First you gut a sweet young pig through its mouth, like a goatskin bottle. Then you cram it with chickens and sausages and stoned dates and smoked onions and snails and herbs – oh, and thrushes too, my friend! Sew it up. Roast it. When it's done to a turn, make a thin cut in the piglet's back and saturate the flesh with a sauce of rue, sweet wine, honey, oil – and garum! What do you think of that?'

Saul said, 'Give me porridge.' The man can make a smile as thin as his leg bone.

'Wait! Wait!' I cried, clapping my hands. 'What about a sow's udder shaped to look like a fish? Is it pig if it doesn't *look* like pig?'

About five years ago, shortly after I had invited Saul to Antioch, we were crossing Herod Street when suddenly he turned aside to one of those cook-shops that sell roasted meats by the slice. We had been discussing freedoms. I was telling him of the two times in my life when I'd felt such a glad rush of freedom that I thought I would explode. The first was when I sold my land and all my possessions, and laid the proceeds at the feet of the apostles. I panted as I did that, experiencing a physical lightness, as if I could float like thistledown.

My second discovery of freedom came more gradually, here in Antioch, where the apostles had sent me to exhort the Antiochene believers in faithfulness. The great majority of believers were Gentiles. Already when I came, distinctions were disappearing. No longer were there 'God-fearers' and 'proselytes' among the Gentiles; no longer Jew and non-Jew, higher and lower, freeman and slave. Everyone who followed Christ as Lord was the same as every one else, equal – a family! Even the Romans noticed our amazing unity. They classed us and named us 'Christians'. Pretty soon all the laws that had separated Jews from Gentiles *also* became as nothing to me, and that was my second experience of the lightness of freedom.

I told Saul that it caused in me such a giddiness – such a physically tickling joy – that laughter was always bubbling just below my throat. *Always, always!* is what I was saying to Saul – when suddenly he turned aside to a cook-shop, raised one long finger, and pointed at a piglet revolving on a spit, its fat flaring in the coals below.

'One small portion, please,' he said.

A woman with huge arms cut him the smallest of portions and laid it on a green leaf and accepted his penny for her food.

I fell silent. I had never seen this before. And though I delighted in our new freedoms, what Saul was doing seemed as risky as stepping off a cliff.

He pinched the pork in its folded leaf and with two delicate fingers pulled off a greasy piece. He carried the meat to his mouth, crossing his eyes as it came. He put out his tongue and touched the bit of pig to the tip of it, where it stuck. Then, scarcely breathing, Saul drew the meat into his mouth and chewed and chewed and swallowed it. He blinked rapidly – checking, it seemed, his vitals inside. Then he grinned and plucked at my sleeve and began to laugh. A gasping sort of laughter, like a man who jumped but did not drown.

The little Pharisee had eaten pork. He had climbed the mount to Moses and said, 'No more! We don't need Torah any more.' And then he descended to us and began to use food as a formal declaration and the evidence of a new life. Here in Antioch, when Saul ate among Gentiles he ate *like* a Gentile, and to all the believers he announced, 'For freedom Christ has set us free!'

Well, yes, and so he said. But Saul's freedoms weren't entirely free. He had to pay for them. New foods gave him diarrhoea. My grim, my sober brother! While I chuckled always in the freedoms of the Lord, he glowered – which tickled me no end.

'Wait! Wait!' I shouted. People were crowding in on us now. Friends and believers, the whole congregation. They turned inquisitive faces in my direction, and I couldn't help laughing with the joy of my own joke: 'What about a sow's udder shaped to look like a fish?' I shouted. 'If it doesn't *look* like diarrhoea, how can it *give* you diarrhoea?'

Rufus, one of Simeon's sons, came down upon us like a red bush burning. He grinned and squatted and punched my shoulder.

'Barnabas, will you sing tonight?' he said.

'Nope,' I said. 'I have been invited to hold my peace – and my tongue, and my voice. Time for old Barnabas to be quiet.'

Rufus turned to my companion and said, 'Brother, will you preach tonight?' He meant that *brother* more affectionately than most people do, since Saul lived here in the same house with him, very much like an older brother.

Saul shook his head. 'Your father wants to speak tonight,' he said.

'I'll bet he tells his story again,' said Rufus.

'It's a good story,' Saul said. 'It's the only story. There is no other story in all the world except that sole story alone.'

Noisier and noisier the house was growing. People were carrying food, eating in the dining rooms, moving through the walkway surrounding Simeon's atrium, sitting on the marble pavement inside of the atrium itself. It was a good and gracious space, that atrium: six pillars upholding an open roof, a cistern and a fountain below, and polished marble slabs both black and white. People sat, too, on the low stone wall that bound pillar to pillar. When we gather, we're like a hive of bees in a low, splendid humming. I am washed in the sound.

Saul grabbed my beard and turned my face directly to his own. He looked at me a moment with fierce, tiny eyes. 'That was a joke, wasn't it?'

'What joke?'

'Did someone truly tell you to hold your peace?'

'Ah, well, yes.'

'Who? Who has the gall?'

'James.'

'Which James?'

'Not the brother of John. James, the brother of our Lord. He wrote me a letter.'

Saul let go my beard. He kept looking at me, but his eyes became preoccupied.

When he's troubled, Saul's gestures become quick and cramped, like that of the thrushes he eats, or the mice. He plucks at the hem of his robe. He pulls out bits of thread without noticing.

'James wrote you a letter?'

'A letter for me particularly,' I said, 'but it's directed at others too. At you, maybe. I brought it with me, in case I should read it to the whole congregation. Here.' I pulled the stiff paper from my pouch and handed it to Saul. He began to read it aloud, but slowly, gravely. James wrote in Aramaic, Saul's more difficult tongue.

'The times require a watchful sobriety everywhere among us. King Agrippa is back from Rome. He has chosen to act in a

messianic manner. He's making friends with the Zealots. He curries the favour and the power of the Sadducees, and is growing ever more dangerous. At the very least he will restrict our lives. More likely, he will imprison us. Beat us. And I believe he may go so far as to kill us. Barnabas, we must not give him cause! Barnabas, we must cease those activities that make us loathsome to our Jewish elders. Barnabas, you will agree that I have good reason to fear and to resent the free association some have established with uncircumcised pagans. And the more that Torah is flouted by libertines, the likelier is Agrippa to give ALL believers a political scourging. As for you, why must you make a spectacle of yourself?'

Saul's face was pink. He muttered, '*Kuno-tharses*! Bitch-impudence!' He turned to me and with a low intensity said, 'Joy is not a spectacle, Barnabas. It is a gift of the Holy Spirit. You have no choice but to sing. And so what if Herod Agrippa has come to Jerusalem? The Lord Jesus Christ is coming too, with a glory to explode all Herods, all powers, and every authority together.'

In those days Saul was more than a partner to me; he was the soberer, smarter, bolder side of my own self. James should have been glad that there was someone to balance my compulsions, the roaring and singing and laughing me. In fact, it was at his, James's, suggestion that I brought Saul to Antioch in the first place. He said that Saul knew Torah. So it was James who led me to the man who completed me. Then blessed be God for James, his minister! Because Saul and I were halves of a whole.

I can get by in Greek, but my native tongue is Aramaic. Saul, whose Aramaic is bookish, spoke Greek like a sailor or a rhetor, take your pick. In his mouth the Greek language could be a blizzard to dumbfound you, or the golden thread that snared your heart. In Greek he called himself Paul; in Aramaic, Saul. So I used to joke that *Saul* waddled like a verbal duck, but *Paul* could soar like the eagle.

He laboured for a living. So did I. He sewed leather and canvas, while I worked metals and precious stones.

He was short, constructed of spit and twigs. I am taller and broader in the shoulder than your average ox.

He had studied the Law, both the written and the spoken traditions. I had studied Levitical ritual. Together we were Moses and Aaron – but neither of us, in those heady days, felt bounden to either model any more. We were free. And the Lord was coming soon. And there seemed to be no better place for spending the meantime than in Antioch on the Orontes.

Saul leaned over to me – that hooked nose of his filling my view – and kissed me.

'Sing, Barnabas,' he said. 'When you sing, I weep. Sing.'

Simeon Niger carried a stool into the atrium and set it down in the centre. Those nearest moved backward to grant him a circle of space. He sat. He would rotate slowly as he spoke since he sat in a sea of people, men and women, young and old, Jews and Gentiles – but mostly Gentiles, for whom this story was their closest vision of Jesus. Everywhere we covered cushions and couches and benches and all the floors on rugs and pallets. Some in the farther rooms stood up in order to see him. Others bowed their heads, rather to listen than to look.

Simeon said: 'Brother Saul asks about the tree. *And what of the tree?* Saul says to me, and I say, *What tree do you mean?* and our brother says, *The tree on which they hanged the Lord. The tree of cursing. What do you know of the tree?'*

Simeon paused, looking in our direction.

The man has midnight eyes. Rufus his son is reddish, but Simeon Niger is African, as black as the name we call him by. It's a wonderful puzzle, isn't it? Well, and here's the answer: the mother of Rufus and Alexander – the wife of her husband Simeon – is a pale Jew from Bethany. The milk of her face milked the faces of her children, and a drop of the blood of the ruddy King David must have dribbled through her into baby Rufus.

Simeon was gazing at Saul, who nodded acknowledgment: yes, he had asked about the tree – some years ago, in fact, but this is how Simeon always began the story when Saul was present. He thought of Saul as a son.

'Someone must have told our brother,' Simeon said, 'that I am the one who carried that tree, who carried a limb of it out of the city to Golgotha.

'I wish it had been my wisdom, my will, my choice,' Simeon said. 'I wish I had known enough and loved enough to beg to suffer the weight of that tree. But I knew nothing, and I did not choose.

'Let me show you the depth of my ignorance: When I was chosen, I thought it was a Roman that had chosen me.

'My sons and I were in Jerusalem to celebrate the Passover. We had purchased the lamb. We were taking it to the Temple for slaughter and the butchering. We had just entered the city southward, through the Garden Gate. We were pushing through crowds of people when a Roman soldier grabbed my shoulder and said, *Here! Take the beam. Carry the criminal's beam!*

'*Patibulum* is what he called it in Latin. The crosspiece of a cross, the beam from which to hang a man. The greatest limb of the tree.

'I looked and saw the criminal lying on the ground. The crowd had backed away from him. He lay in an island of emptiness. His back and shoulders had been ripped to ribbons, a thickish, glistening blood congealing. Of course he couldn't carry the rough wood there. It lay beside him.

'But I lifted the lamb in my arms and said, *I'm sorry, sir. My sons and I are going to the Temple –*

'The soldier snatched the lamb and tossed it into the crowd. We lost it. The lamb was gone. He yanked me forward and growled, *Barbarian! You got no pity for the dying?* He put his hands under the arms of the criminal and raised him to his feet.

'I had no choice.

'I bent beneath the wood. Rufus and Alexander, terrified, dashed out of Jerusalem, home to Bethany. I followed the soldiers and bleeding man. Then I noticed that there were women all around me moving in the same direction. They were sobbing and wailing and groaning and crying. Why, it was a funeral procession!

'Soon the dead man stopped and turned. Everyone stopped. He said to me, *Don't weep for me. Weep for yourselves and your children* – for Rufus? For Alexander? They were just boys! The dying man said, *The days are coming when people will say, Blessed are the barren, the wombs that never bore, the breasts that never gave suck! And everyone will cry to the mountains, Fall on us! And to the hills, Cover us!*

'The dead man looked at me and sighed. As he turned away again he said, *For if they do this when the wood is green, what will they do when the wood is dry?*

'At Golgotha the soldier commanded me to drop the beam.

'*You can go*, he said. But I didn't go.

'I watched them lay the poor man down on the wood and stretch his arms from end to end. I watched them drive the spikes through his flesh and bone into the wood. He didn't cry out. He didn't complain. He was not unconscious. His eyes were open. He knew everything, everything that was happening to him, everything, but he didn't scream, he didn't curse, and they put ropes around the *patibulum* that I had carried, then pulled it up the front of a tall, strong post in the ground. They dropped it on a firm peg at the top. Nailed to that crosspiece his body went swinging up from me, hanging from the arms, and his whole body snapped when the beam was dropped into place, and all the skin shivered with the pain, the teeth began to chatter with the pain, and that was the tree, brother Saul. I watched a man hang wide awake and aware on the Tree of Cursing, but even then he didn't cry out, and then they were driving a new spike through his feet, and while they were doing that I heard the man say, *Father, forgive them*. He said, *Forgive them, for they know not what they do*, and now I was shivering too, and next I learned the name of the man, because a soldier set a ladder at the back of the cross and climbed up to the top of it, and there he nailed a shingle with words on it, and I read the words in Aramaic, and they said, *JESUS OF NAZARETH, KING OF THE JEWS*, so then his name was JESUS OF NAZARETH, yes, yes: JESUS was his name, and some of the women that had been crying in his funeral procession were still there, standing near me, watching, too, and JESUS looked down to one of them, and I heard him say, *Woman, behold your son*, so then that's what she was doing, looking up at the man on the cross and crying, and that must have been her son, but her knees began to buckle and another man caught her and held her tenderly, and JESUS said to that man, *Behold your mother*, and they were both crying, and now so was I, I was crying too, so now I could not leave, how could I leave? – I stayed even when a storm bore down on the earth and darkened it, I stayed when everyone else had left except the women and the soldier in charge, I stayed until he died, I was there when he died, and this is the astounding nature of his dying, that finally he did cry out, he threw back his head and forced his body forward, he drove his chest away from the cross like Winged Victory, and the veins in his neck stood out, and when he uttered his voice under the black firmament, it was a *phone megale* that he made, a soldier's cry of triumph!

'He died in triumph.

'And the first one to teach me the meaning of these things was that Roman soldier himself, for he gazed at the dead man, at that poor broken figure on the tree, and whispered, *This man really was the Son of God.*

'But my second teacher was Simon Peter, because from him I heard the impossible thing that happened next and I knew why I had been walking around for weeks after that death without a heart in my breast, and I learned where my heart had gone: it was with JESUS OF NAZARETH, KING OF THE JEWS.

'On Pentecost Simon Peter talked straight to me and in my language while I stood in the middle of another crowd. He said, *This Jesus whom you crucified,* and that was me, because I had carried the wood that cursed him. Simon Peter said, *This Jesus whom you crucified by the hands of outlaws, God raised up!*

'That's the thing that happened next, and I hadn't known about it: Jesus was raised from the dead! The curse was overcome. The tree was nothing any more. Simon Peter said to me, *Repent, and for the forgiveness of your sins be baptized in the name of Jesus, whom God has made both Lord and Christ.*

'And when I was baptized, and when I came up out of the water, and when the Holy Spirit moved inside of me, I, Simeon, a man from Cyrene, realized for the first time who had chosen me. Brother Saul, I did not chose. I had been chosen. But it was no Roman who chose me to carry the tree. It was Jesus! Jesus had chosen me. Jesus picked me. Jesus raised me and made me his own, and when I came up out of the water, I shouted my own cry of triumph in the voice of the shout of Jesus: I shouted, *Jesus!* At the top of my lungs, I cried, *Jesus! Jesus! Lord of my life, I belong to you!*'

At the end of his story, Simeon's clothes were dark with sweat. This happened whenever he told it; Simeon was always transported, almost bodily, back to the time he first met Jesus. But here's a more amazing thing: Whenever he told it, we too met the Lord Jesus again, dying and rising and raised from the dead.

Therefore, as soon as Simeon Niger was done, even before he left his stool, and through no choice of my own either, I was singing.

My chest expands to song. When I am singing, song is the life inside of me, huge and urgent, yearning to stroke the invisible air as an eagle strokes the wind with flight.

My eyes were closed, my great mouth open. A chant came out: '*The Lord to my Lord says,*' I chanted, and I heard the people answer, '*Down, down, my Son, sit down.*'

Again, more fully, I chanted: '*The Lord to my Lord says,*' and they answered, '*Down and down, sit down,*' and so, on the wind of their voices, I flew. I rocked my body and sang:

Sit down, down at my right hand,
  till I bow them low,
  till I lay them low!

My Son, sit down and take command
  till I make thy foes
    thy footstool!

My eyelids were fluttering. Lamplight and shadow and the people around me formed a burning space, orange and black – and now I was on my feet and spinning slowly around. The Holy Spirit was in me. I could feel the Spirit like a fire of song, and I sang a thing I'd never sung before, though I knew immediately that it was the answering utterance for Simeon's story: 'A mystery! A mystery!' I sang: 'The mystery we believe!'

Then I was seized by a new voice and new words. I sang:

Thou! – who in flesh wast manifest –
Art in the Spirit righteousness:
  And angels bow before thee.

Thou! – thy strong name we'll preach abroad,
Till all the world can know, 'twas God
  That snatched thee up in glory.

There was laughter around me. And people were crying.

And a maiden sang out: 'In the name of Jesus!' As soon as they heard that, the whole congregation rose up in order to kneel down.

'In the name of Jesus!' the maiden cried again, and spontaneously, all of us knelt.

'Amen! Amen!' Voices erupted everywhere: 'Amen!'

A young lad, a Gentile named Titus, began to speak rapidly, wildly: 'Bah-bah-bah! Bah-bah-bah!' He got up and danced two steps left, two steps right, and the people clapped, and so he spoke more forcefully: 'Bah-bah-bah!' Titus always did this when the name of Jesus was cried out in the midst of the congregation. The Spirit in me was song. The Spirit in him was a tongue no one could understand. Oh, heavenly days and glorious nights! – the Spirit was here! And we who faced that lad could feel the heat.

Then the voice of an older woman, a prophet, ascended over all. With sense and clarity she declared: 'The Spirit of Jesus has told me to talk! The Spirit has something to say!'

Young Titus fell silent. Everyone held still.

This was Simeon's wife, the mother of Rufus. She did not speak in repetitions, nor were her prophecies triggered by some regular gesture in our worship. Only when the Spirit required it did she speak; and then she said the thing but once and it was said. She was a woman of reverence and respect. The whole congregation sat down.

'The Spirit of Jesus has something to say,' she said, 'regarding these two.'

She was moving toward Saul and me. My stomach started to twist at her approach. Saul watched her steadfastly. She walked to a spot behind us. I bowed my head and instantly felt her hand on the back of my neck.

She whispered then: 'The Spirit says: *Set two people apart for the work to which I have called them. This one, Barnabas. And this one, Saul. Send them out to preach the mighty name of Jesus Christ our Lord.*'

I heard her word, and I knew the truth of it. The twist in my stomach snapped, and I began to giggle.

The apostles had sent me to Antioch to exhort the people here. But this was the Spirit of Jesus himself, sending us out into the world!

Suddenly, Saul sang out, '*Marana tha!*'

I lifted my voice too and roaring with laughter, bellowed: '*Marana tha!*'

Then all the people shouted, '*Marana tha!*'

And I heard the prophet, Simeon's wife, breathe in the air behind me, 'Amen.'

'Bring bread,' I cried. 'Bring wine! Come, let us eat the supper of our Lord Jesus Christ.'

Amen, amen, and it was so.

James

18

I knew the assault was coming. I had lived in continual dread of
it. For more than a decade I'd prayed both privately and publicly
that the Lord preserve us from persecutions in Jerusalem; yet
I could not shake the dread and the expectation. It was coming.
Unless behaviour changed, it was most certainly coming.

Some of those who professed Jesus to be the Christ also
preached religious apostasy. Our leaders did not disapprove. Our
leaders took no stand at all. I begged them to put a palpable
distance between the libertines and ourselves, but these leaders
did nothing. Therefore, I cannot blame the authorities for seeing
all the followers of Jesus as a single, undifferentiated sect. Truth
be told, the majority of believers in Jerusalem were horrified by
the cavalier dismissal of circumcision and the disdain some
brothers expressed for Torah. This had never been the teaching of
Jesus. Jesus had not come to destroy the Law! He came to fulfill
it. Not a jot of the words of Moses would he change or erase. So
I said. So I argued. No one listened.

And the assault came as I had feared it would.

Ah, God, it gives me no pleasure to record the accuracy of my
anticipations. I am no prophet. There was no mystery here. I'm a
plain man who reads what is plainly in view, the feelings and
deeds of people, both powerful and weak.

So King Herod Agrippa, already beloved of his citizens, gave
greater joy to the Zealots and the Sadducees and the priests: he
arrested James, the brother of John and the son of Zebedee. It
may have been a religious matter only. No matter. The king
wanted to display his political potency in the empire at large.
Therefore he did not stone James, which Torah would require;
rather, he killed him according to methods more Roman.

James, my namesake, was beheaded.

A sword and a single stroke cut clean through the neck of that apostle, one of the twelve, the first of that company to die.

Nothing was the same thereafter.

Jerusalem rejoiced.

King Herod, thinking to double the delight, next arrested Simon Peter. While the sacred days of the Passover forestalled his execution, Simon escaped prison under the guidance of an angel. Quickly – and rightly – he departed Jerusalem.

So did most of the twelve.

In their absence, by a terrible default, leadership fell to me.

I did not seek this! I did not *want* to be right. But once it was mine to choose for the church of Jesus the Christ, my brother, I put my own advice into practice. My pieties were seen by faithful Jews as faithfulness. Obedience became the rock of the church, the fastness to protect it against rain and flood and the beatings of wind: it would not fall. I was no threat in Jerusalem. I was honoured. I ate no meat. I laid no razor to my head. I never anointed myself with the oils of Roman decadence. I never went to the baths. I never wore wool, but linen only. And I alone, among believers, was permitted to go so near the Temple of God, almost to go *into* it, where I knelt and prayed continually for the sake of my people.

It was I who sent messages to the believers abroad, news of the death of James and exhortations to live within the house of Israel. I was most anxious that Antioch receive my messages. And it did. But Barnabas and Saul did not. They had been absent for more than half a year, and no one knew where to find them.

Timothy

19

Once when we were travelling home from some work my father
had done in the west, he stopped the carriage by a wide marsh
and raised his hand and pointed over the green water, over the
rotting tree trunks, toward a little hill in the distance.

'Look there,' he said.

I looked and saw two living trees, very old, surrounded by a
stone wall. There were wreaths hanging from the branches, some
new and colourful, some dead brown.

'An oak and a linden,' Papa said, 'the only trees alive in all this
region. Emptiness, emptiness,' Papa whispered, spreading his
arms around. 'Where are the towns? Where are the farms and the
houses and the people?'

He shook his head and started to heave a big sigh, but the sigh
broke into a cough. My father bent forward with the coughing.
His face swelled up a little. He spat a pinkish thing into the
green water and wiped his mouth, and then he said to me, 'But
I know where the people went.'

He smiled and winked and slapped the donkey, and so we were
moving again, homeward to Lystra. I was just a little boy. I was
very glad to leave the marsh and the withering wreaths.

'Papa,' I said, 'where did the people go?'

'Ah,' he sighed, then he sang to the donkey, 'what a good
student I have for a son! He knows the perfect question to ask.
And don't I have the perfect answer?'

Papa climbed into the cart and sat beside me and said, 'Once
upon a time, Zeus and his son Hermes...'

He told me the story of the two trees. All the way home he told
me this story. Often we paused to give other travellers rides in
our cart, but Papa just kept on telling the story, collecting his
audience as he went. He was a good storyteller.

He made it end exactly when we arrived home. I ran into the house, shouting, 'Mama! Mama! I know where all the people went! They drowned!'

Once upon a time, Zeus and his son Hermes came down to earth and travelled through the hills of Phrygia disguised as mortal men. Zeus carried no bolt of lightning. Hermes wore no wings on his heels. Both were tired. They were looking for somewhere to stay.

But nobody took them in.

The farmers and villagers said, 'No.' Merchants and landowners all turned the gods away. They went to a thousand houses and a thousand doors were shut against them.

Finally they came to the humblest cottage of all. Its roof was thatch and reeds. They knocked. An old woman opened the door.

They said, 'May we speak with your master or mistress?'

The old woman laughed and laughed. 'Speak to me, good sirs,' she said, 'since I am maid and mistress both, and my husband is slave and master too, and we are the whole of the household. There's none but me, named Baucis, and old Philemon over there. Come in. Come in and be well.'

So the gods bent down their great heads and entered the lowly doorway. Philemon smiled and brought them chairs. Baucis covered the chairs in old cloths.

'Sit down,' she said, and she began to stir yesterday's ashes to find the spark to light some leaves and small wood chips. She blew and blew and raised a flame. Then she reached for some twigs from the edge of the roof and dropped these in the fire and hung her little pot above it.

Philemon brought vegetables from the garden. Baucis stripped them of leaves for the pot, while her husband took a two-pronged fork and lifted down from the blackened rafters a side of bacon, smoked and good. He cut a large piece and put it also in the pot to boil.

They chatted brightly, the man and the woman, keeping their guests amused. Philemon poured warm water into a beechwood bowl, so that Zeus and Hermes could wash themselves. Baucis spread threadbare covers over a couch whose legs were willow-wood, whose mattress was stuffed with dry sedge grass.

'Sirs, take your places,' she said, bowing, then she tucked up

her thin robe and with shaky hands placed a table before them. She wiped the top with fresh mint, then set the table with clay dishes and the first foods of the dinner: cherries picked in autumn and saved in lees of wine; endives and radishes and pieces of cheese; eggs lightly roasted in ashes not too hot.

Next she brought wine in a flagon and beechwood cups lined on the inside with yellow wax.

After that she brought the stew that had been bubbling on the hearth. And finally the lighter fare: nuts and figs and wrinkled dates, plums and apples in shallow baskets, black grapes, a shining honeycomb, and cheerful company.

But then the old man and the old woman saw a miracle, and they became afraid. For the flagon, after it was poured, filled itself up again. And their own wine was thin and young, but this wine was rich and old.

They fell down on their knees. 'Forgive us!' they cried. 'Forgive our meagre meal, our poor preparations!'

Straightway they jumped up and started to chase their goose, their only goose, the guardian of the cottage. 'Give over!' Philemon cried. 'You're food for our visitors!' But the goose flew through the room to the guests, who covered it under their arms.

'Don't kill the creature,' they said. 'There is no need. We are gods, you see.'

Baucis and Philemon gaped in terror.

'No, don't be afraid,' Zeus said to them. 'As mortal men, we were refused by everyone except you. As gods, now, we are about to punish everyone except you. Old man, old woman, come. Leave your home and climb the mountainside with us.'

They did. Baucis and Philemon, leaning on sticks, struggled up the long slope westward. Near the top, they turned and saw that all the region had begun to drown in a thick green water. Only their house was left standing. At first they wept for the fate of their neighbours, but then they saw that their little cottage was changing: It became a temple with marble columns, a roof bright yellow, thatched with gold, doors adorned with carvings, mosaics inlaid on the floors.

Zeus, watching the faces of the old couple, said, 'Ask me a gift, and I will give it to you.'

In an instant they knew their hearts' desire.

'Let us be your priests,' they said, 'to serve your shrine till we die. And when we do die, O mighty Zeus, let us die together, so *neither one need see the other laid down on the funeral bier.'*

And so it was that they kept this temple all the rest of their lives.

Then one evening as they stood on the sacred steps, bowed down by the winters of their years, Baucis saw leaves in her husband's hair, and Philemon saw that his wife's skin was turning barky. Twigs and branches emerged from the brown spots on their flesh, and just before the grizzled bark enclosed their faces, husband and wife cried out in unison: 'Good-bye! Good-bye, my dear one!'

So then, one became the oak, and the other the linden, and people hang wreaths on the sacred trees, even down to this day.

I was eight or nine years old when my father first told me the story of Baucis and Philemon. I was sixteen when he died. He was born a Greek, my father. He gave me a Greek name: *Timotheos*, 'one who honours God.' But he accommodated himself to the Roman modes of living because it was Rome that he served. The administration of our city was based completely on the Roman way. Caesar Augustus himself had made Lystra a Roman colony, and though most of its citizens were native to the region, neither Greek nor Roman, its governance was Romish and imperious. My father's life's work was to keep records for the city magistrates. His life depended upon their goodwill. He said he 'accommodated' himself, as if it were the likeliest thing in all the world to do, and so I believed that he loved Rome. After he died, my mother declared that it had all been a pose, a necessary imposture, because Rome did not love *him* and, she said with rather more gravity than he, 'His life depended on it.'

He raised me Roman.

On the ninth day of my life, my naming day, he offered a ceremonial sacrifice for his son's purification. Then he hung around my neck a *bulla*, a small golden case with a tiny amulet to protect me against witchcraft and the *fascinatio*, the evil eye. I wore that *bulla* always, all the years of my growing.

My father taught me reading and writing in Greek and Latin. He told me stories of the gods and the heroes. 'It was up the road in Iconium,' he said, 'where Perseus cut off the head of Medusa, writhing with snakes – and Homer calls Perseus the most renowned of men.' Papa quoted long passages of the anger of

Achilles and the melancholy glory of Hector. Whatever he quoted I repeated, shouting the words at the top of my lungs until I'd memorized them. Then he would kiss me and tell me how he hoped to grow as old as Priam, but more gladly than Priam since *his* son would not die in bloody slaughter.

'Honour the gods,' he said.

By words and encouragement and an astonishing knowledge of the human body, my father also taught me the things he could not do any more: wrestling, handling the short sword and the shield, throwing the javelin. Most intently, he trained me to run. In this he was completely Greek. He thought I should enter one of the Hellenic Games and honour the gods by racing. 'At Isthmia, near Corinth,' he said, I would by my triumph 'worship the child-god Melikertes, who was borne on the back of a Dolphin from the place where his mother leaped into the sea – the Molourian Rocks – even to the shores of Isthmia. They burn the black bull there,' he said. 'They sacrifice the whole black bull, uncut! And I will go with you, my son,' he said. 'I will die with joy to see you crowned.'

All this set my mother's teeth on edge. 'Peaceable life,' she sniffed. She loved neither the athletic contests of the Greeks nor the bloody combats of the Romans. She feared for my father, who could not do what he wanted me to do, and she hated his references to death: Papa coughed. Papa had no breath for his own physical endeavour.

It was planned that I would depart childhood and enter my majority on the seventeenth day of March, in the sixteenth year of my age. My father chose that date, the Roman celebration of the Feast of Liber – the *Liberalia* – so that the leaders of the city might recognize me and perceive in me excellent preparation for some governmental post, whether or not they saw fit to attend the ceremonies themselves.

Early on that chosen morning I was to approach the altar of our household gods, kneel down and, for the first time since my ninth day of life, remove the *bulla* from my neck and place it on the altar. Next I would remove the crimson-bordered *toga praetexta* of boyhood, lay it too on the altar, offer with my father a little sacrifice of dedication, then put on the *tunica recta*, woven all of one piece to hang straight down to my ankles without a belt, the garment of personal freedom. Finally, my father expressed the wish that my mother should drape over me the pure white toga of a man, the *toga virilis*. She never truly agreed to do that, but neither did she disagree, so my father had hope.

In fact, it was his final wish.

He died on the first day of March. He wasn't there to make me a man on the seventeenth. No matter. Death made me a man. And it was my mother who, on the night of the day he died, seized the *bulla* at my chest and snapped it off. She opened the door and threw it into the middle of the road, where the filth of the city flowed.

'A man!' my mother cried. 'A man! Let the man come help me wipe the blood of his father, the blood that broke and drowned him in his throat!'

My father's body lay white and clean in our largest room. Neighbours had seen to that. Tomorrow we would bear him on a wooden bier and walk him to a Roman tomb. But the private thing was in his bedroom. Blood had spouted down his couch to the floor. My mother and I kneeled side by side, with clean rags washing wood and stone – with water and lye, my father's blood away.

'Accommodation!' she growled, crouching on her hands and knees, striking the floor with the bloody rags. 'Meekness made him their man. Kindness, obedience – and that dreamy nature! First they took his freedom, then they stole his soul, and now they have his life. Well, well – they shall not have his son!'

That same night my mother led me to an eastern window in our house and told me to kneel down. From her personal possessions she brought out a square woollen cloth with white tassels at the corners, each tassel shot through with a single blue thread. This cloth she draped over my head. She fell prostrate on the floor beside me and began to cry.

'Too long! Too long! Too long,' she wept.

Then softly, with extreme speed, she hissed, 'There is none holy like the Lord, none besides thee; there is no rock like our God, no, none but thee. Here is my son. Here is the son of my womb for thee.'

My mother's voice whistled with such anguish that I became afraid. I was crying with her. I said, 'Mama?'

Suddenly she grabbed my wrist and hissed, 'Timothy, say the words that I say. Say them!'

And then she uttered words in a language I did not know, but I copied her sound for sound:

'Hear, O Israel: the Lord, our God, the Lord, one! And you shall love the Lord your God with all your heart, and with all your soul, and with all your might.

'Hebrew, child,' she whispered after a long silence. 'It's time I found someone to teach you Hebrew. Hush,' she murmured. 'Hush. You needn't cry any more. You're a man, now, remember?'

I lay down on the floor beside my mother and put my arm around her. In a little while I felt sobbings in her body, and then she whispered something to the God of her childhood, the God of her people and of my people, too: the God of the Jews.

'Ah, but break my heart,' she whispered, 'how I loved the man, and I am almost dead without him.'

There were no synagogues in Lystra and very few Jews. From that day forward, from the first of March my sixteenth year, my mother sought a Jew to teach me Hebrew as well as I knew Greek and Latin.

Shortly before the Passover of my seventeenth year she came into the house in a fever of excitement.

'I found him!' she cried. 'I found the scholar to teach you Hebrew.' My mother's eyes danced with the joy of her discovery. 'Timothy, come to the market with me. He says he's got the Greek scriptures by heart in the Greek – but he can read the Hebrew. He calls himself Paul. He has a friend who calls him Saul – though this little man looks nothing like our first king.'

Luke

20

So, being sent out by the Holy Spirit, Barnabas and Saul – and John Mark with them – travelled afoot from Antioch on the Orontes to the seaport at Seleucia. From there they sailed to the island of Cyprus.

When they arrived at Salamis, they proclaimed the word of God in the synagogues of the Jews, then they went through the whole island west by southwest, even to Paphos, the city from which the Roman proconsul governed the entire province of Cyprus.

In Paphos a certain magician practised his arts, a Jewish false prophet named Bar-Jesus. He was a part of the entourage of the proconsul Sergius Paulus, who was himself a man of intelligence. Sergius Paulus summoned Barnabas and Saul in order to hear from them directly the word of God.

But when they came into his presence, the magician, that *Elymas*, that dreamer, interpreter of dreams, loudly denounced them, striving to keep his keeper from the believing.

Saul, who is also called Paul, was suddenly filled with the Holy Spirit. He glared at Bar-Jesus and said: 'You son of the Devil! You assassin of righteousness, fat with lies and villainies! When will you stop twisting the straight ways of the Lord? Well, sir – now! Right now, for the hand of the Lord is on you, striking your eyes as blind as your mind. You will spend a season seeing nothing, not even the sun.'

Immediately mists and darkness fell on Bar-Jesus, and he went about seeking someone to lead him by the hand.

Swiftly, too, when he saw what had occurred, the proconsul believed. He was astonished at the teaching of the Lord.

Now Paul and his company set sail from Paphos around the western horn of the island, north to the city of Perga in Pamphylia. John Mark left them there and returned to Jerusalem. But Paul and Barnabas crossed the Taurus mountains together and came to Antioch in Pisidia.

On the Sabbath day they entered the synagogue and sat down. After the reading of the Law and the Prophets, the rulers of the synagogue sent word to them, asking: 'Brethren, do you have a word of exhortation for the people?'

Paul did.

He rose to his feet and raised his hands yet higher for silence. When everyone was paying attention, he said: 'Men of Israel, God-fearers too, I speak equally to you all.

'The God of Israel chose our fathers. He multiplied our people in Egypt, then with a mighty arm he led them out of the country, out of slavery. For forty years he bore with Israel in the wilderness. And when he had destroyed seven nations in the land of Canaan, he gave them that land as an inheritance. For four hundred and fifty years God took care of Israel, and then he gave them judges, two hundred years of judges, until Samuel the prophet. Then they begged for a king, and God gave them forty years of Saul the son of Kish, of the tribe of Benjamin. And when he had removed their first king, God raised up David as king – of whom he testified: *I have found in David a man after my heart, who will do all my will*. Now, listen: From the posterity of faithful King David, God has in these latter days brought to Israel a Saviour, Jesus, even as he promised!

'Before the appearing of Jesus, John preached a baptism of repentance to all the people of Israel. But as John was finishing his own course, he said, *What do you suppose I am? I am not he! No, but after me comes one the sandals of whose feet I am not worthy to untie!*

'Brethren! Children of Abraham, and you Gentiles who fear God – to us all the message of this salvation has been sent!

'But the rulers in Jerusalem didn't recognize Jesus. They didn't understand the prophets whom they themselves read Sabbath after Sabbath. By condemning Jesus, then, they fulfilled those same prophecies! And though they could find no charge against Jesus deserving death, yet they asked Pilate to execute him anyway. And when they had fulfilled all that was written of him, they took him down from the tree and laid him in a tomb.

'But God raised Jesus from the dead! And for many days he appeared to those that had travelled with him from Galilee, people who are now his witnesses. And we bring you this good news: The promises of God to our fathers – these he has fulfilled for us, the children, by raising Jesus. *Thou art my Son,* God said in the Psalms; *today have I begotten thee.* And to support the fact that he raised him from the dead no more to suffer corruption, he said: *I will give you the holy and sure blessing of David.* And, in another psalm: *Thou wilt not let thy Holy One see corruption.* But David, when he was done serving God, fell asleep; and then he did see corruption; but the one whom God raised up, that one saw no corruption, so that through him the forgiveness of sins is proclaimed to you, and by him those who believe are set free as the Law of Moses could never set you free.

'Beware! Beware and do not scorn this news! Oh, beware lest this word of the prophets fall down upon you: *You scoffers, behold and wonder – and then perish! For I am doing a deed in your days, but you do not believe it, even if one declares it to you!*'

With that passage from Habakkuk, Paul ended his exhortation.

But many people, even before they left the synagogue, went to him and to the rulers, begging that he might preach again on the following Sabbath. Moreover, both Jews and God-fearing Gentiles followed Paul and Barnabas out of the synagogue, clamouring for more.

'Continue,' Paul said to the people. 'Continue in the grace of God.'

By the next Sabbath, news of the preaching had raised such excitement that almost the whole of Antioch gathered to hear the word of God.

But the size of the multitudes caused envy in the leaders of the synagogues; so when Paul rose to speak this time, they too rose up and contradicted him. Fiercely, loudly, they reviled him.

Paul and Barnabas entered the dispute with vigour: 'It was necessary,' they shouted, 'that first the word of God be preached to you. But you thrust it aside. You thrust eternal life aside! So now we turn from you to the Gentiles! For the Lord himself commands us, saying, *I have set you to be a light for the Gentiles, that you may bring salvation to the uttermost parts of the earth.*'

When the Gentiles heard this declaration, they broke into an applause that went on and on. They glorified the word of God.

And as many as were ordained to eternal life believed. And the word of the Lord spread throughout all the region.

But those same Jewish leaders approached certain devout Gentiles, women of high standing, men of civil authority; and using the public enthusiasms as evidence of things to come, caused them to fear, persuaded them to persecute Paul and Barnabas, and so drove them from the district of Pisidia altogether.

When they left, they shook off the dust from their feet as a sign against their enemies and travelled on to Iconium. But the disciples whom they left behind were filled with joy and with the Holy Spirit.

Now, at Iconium they entered the Jewish synagogue and spoke with such success that a great company believed, both of Jews and of Gentiles.

But the unbelieving Jews stirred up certain Gentiles and poisoned their minds against the brethren.

Paul and Barnabas remained a good long while, speaking boldly for the Lord, who bore witness to the word of his grace with signs and wonders done by their hands. But the people of the city were divided, some siding with unbelieving Jews, some siding with the apostles.

Then the Gentiles and the Jews who rejected them, together with their rulers, prepared to molest Paul and Barnabas – to stone them. But they learned of the plan and immediately fled the city.

They walked about twenty-five miles on the Roman road from Iconium to Lystra, a city of Lycaonia, and there they preached the gospel.

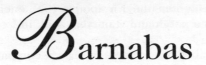

Barnabas

21

They wanted to kill us in Iconium. We had stayed there long enough to make disciples and enemies, both – and both with feelings in the extreme. Saul had that knack: an absolutely fearless little fighter, a headful of words and a voice like a whip. The farther we travelled, the more I let him do the preaching. Me – I just stood back in amazement. Saul would start in a reasonable tone, as if to say, 'Nobody wants to be stupid, do you? Of course not. Nor do we *want* you to be ignorant...' And he meant it! He meant it! He wasn't sarcastic. He had such a thing to tell them, and such a need to say it soon, to say it fast, that the reasonable tone of his voice would change to urgency. So then his sentences got longer, and the words burst from his mouth like flocks of birds, and the faith of the man was a high wind at the hearts of the people, and some of them gasped in delight, and these are the ones who rose up and flew; but others were insulted, and others afraid of the sacred passions, and these are the ones who came to hate him, and that's what happened in Iconium. Those who believed in his preaching caused those who did not to become suspicious and scared of the changes in their city. 'The man's a menace,' our enemies said, 'ruinous to the very order of things. Why, he turns the whole world upside down!' So they planned to kill us in Iconium. Even the rulers were going to stone us.

But our disciples warned us in advance, and we fled to Lystra, twenty-five miles south on a good Roman road.

There's a temple to Zeus in front of the city gates of Lystra, a functional sort of building without gardens or fountains. It's a small forest of columns under a wooden roof, enclosing a statue of Zeus. There's a porch and stair-steps and, in front of them, an altar.

As we approached that temple, we saw a company of people at the altar. Someone shouted: 'Let there be silence!' Not all the travellers around us stopped, but some did – old women with sad ankles, old men leaning on sticks, young mothers with children.

'The pious,' Saul muttered beside me, 'the devout at their dangerous devotions.'

'Dangerous?' I said.

A fire burned on the altar. A priest was washing his hands in a silver bowl held by one of his attendants. He dried his hands in the towel of another attendant, then pulled the hood of his robe up and over his head.

Suddenly someone blew a piercing note on a flute. He blew and blew and did not quit.

Saul stopped walking and shook his head. 'That noise isn't meant for music,' he said. 'It's for drowning out unlucky sounds. It makes me want to shout.'

A boy led a white lamb to the priest, its little horns all gilded, a heavy garland of flowers around its neck. I know the sacrifice of lambs, but I didn't like the pagan gold or the pagan garland. The priest dribbled wine on the lamb's head, and meal and salt, then cut off some of the wool from between its horns and cast that on the altar fire. He raised his hands and called out foreign words, and I could hear Saul clucking beside me. 'Futile prayers. Vain words. Dangerous!'

Now another attendant stepped forward with a heavy mallet, hefted it high and struck the lamb a single blow on the forehead. It dropped dead. It was a good job, a good hit. I'd seen worse ones in the Temple in Jerusalem. This fellow knew what he was doing. Immediately he was on his knees. With a knife he cut one side of the neck and caught the blood in a basin. This he handed to the priest, who poured it, with more wine and a little cake, on the altar fire. At the same time the attendant was cutting open the belly of the lamb, and then everyone looked at the guts inside, murmuring, murmuring pagan things. The flute was still shrilling and Saul muttering and I too was loathing the thing we were seeing, because they were searching the guts for signs from their gods. Then the priest reached in and pulled out the gall and the intestines and the liver. Wine and meal were sprinkled on these, and the whole mass was put on the altar fire, where it hissed and crackled and made a savoury white smoke.

When the flute ceased, and the populations around us returned to their morning, Saul was talking. He had not stopped talking. He was saying, 'Dangerous for whole nations of pagans!

'Look! Look in there!' he said, raising his arm in a gesture so dramatic that people turned and looked. He was pointing past the altar, past the porch, into the temple at the statue of Zeus, broad-chested, fierce-bearded, a contemptuous lip, stone.

'They've exchanged the glory of the immortal God for images resembling a mortal man,' Saul said.

'You know,' I chuckled, taking his elbow and walking again, 'when I was just a simple Levite, a Jew among Jews, I never worried my head about pagans. Life,' I grinned, giving his arm a squeeze, 'is getting complicated.'

But my partner refused my jokes. 'The wrath of God,' he snapped, 'is revealed from heaven against ungodliness, against the wickedness that hides the truth!' He took his arm back and strode ahead.

I had supposed he was talking to me. As far as I was concerned, we were still approaching a new city, preparing to find a forum for preaching. Foolish me! Saul was already launched. The words were already gathering to burst like birds from his mouth.

And even as he entered the gates of the city, my fellow apostle had launched into a sermon for the population: 'That which can be known of the true and living God is plain to all people. All people!' he cried, while citizens and merchants and farmers began to watch him, to listen.

'Ever since the creation of the world,' Saul announced, 'the invisible nature of the one true God – his eternal power, his deity – has been visible in the things that he made. So no one has an excuse. All people have known God. *You* people have known God. Therefore, this is your error: that you do not honour him *as* God or give *him* the thanks. You have exchanged the truth for a lie. You bow down to stone images carved by human hands. You worship the creature instead of the Creator, who is blessed for ever! Amen!'

I tried to stay close to Saul. The size of the crowd was swelling with surprising speed. These people! It didn't seem to matter how harsh my brother's words were. They were smiling, grinning, showing their teeth. Someone seized my hand and tried to kiss it.

When Saul said, *Amen*, I heard twenty or thirty 'amens' to mimic him. No, but they were exact mimics! They took *effort*, and then I realized what the problem was, and I burst out laughing.

'Saul,' I cried.

But he was caught up in the stream of his sentences, saying, 'And since you haven't acknowledged God, God has given you over to wickedness, evil, covetousness, malice – '

'Saul!' I bellowed. 'Saul, listen to them! They're speaking a foreign tongue. They don't understand a word you're saying!'

Ah, my dear friend! In that moment I was pretty sure I understood things better than he. He fell silent, and I expected him to laugh with me at the silliness of our situation.

Instead of laughter, however, I heard Saul whisper, 'Thanks be to God, here is one before me!'

I looked and saw that he'd fixed his eyes on a cripple, a beggar sitting by the wall inside the gate – and the beggar was gazing straight back at him.

Softly, softly my partner murmured, 'Sir, I perceive that you have the faith to be made well.'

The intensity of these two men – Saul and the bent beggar – had a hushing effect on the crowd. Everyone fell silent. No one was speaking. The whole city seemed to crouch in anticipation.

All at once Saul clapped his hands and cried, '*Anastethi*! Stand up! Stand up on your feet!'

And that's exactly what the beggar did. As if he were a spring released, he leaped straight into the air. He walked. He jumped. He cavorted, and the people gasped. The people began to babble and shout and holler, and some of them ran out of the city, and some ran down the streets of the city. Some came to me with greetings more furious than ever, caressing my beard, tugging my long hair. *Zeus*, they said. Among the clamour I thought I heard the word *Zeus*.

Saul was swept away from me. For all my strength, I could not follow. Soon I couldn't even see him.

Someone behind me threw a truly luxurious toga over my shoulders. People in front of me ran their hands over my chest. They touched the muscles of my forearms, my fingers, my toes. 'What?' I shouted. That's all I could think to say in the pressure of so many people: 'What's happening?'

Now new droves of people were pouring up the streets, out of the buildings, out of the shops. It seemed as if the whole city were coming. The crippled man was raised high on the shoulders of strong men, while others pointed and explained loudly things I could not understand. People were dancing and singing and celebrating. I wondered if this was the Holy Spirit blowing again as it did on Pentecost seventeen years ago.

'What?' I blustered. 'What's happening?'

Amazingly, a voice answered me in perfect Greek. 'Every woman is Baucis now, and every man Philemon.' I turned and saw a matron of darker skin. 'But I,' she said, 'am a Jew like you.'

Suddenly I heard that sacrificial flute screaming in the air. The crowds choked their noises. Songs and shoutings ceased. People restrained themselves and faced the gates of the city.

Tambourines and rattles and that flute: and there in the gate was the priest from the temple of Zeus. He had donned sleeves and a long white linen. He carried an axe. His attendants led two great oxen on either side of him, beasts adorned with woollen garlands, colourful ribbons, prepared for sacrifice.

In front of these, another attendant raised high a white rod, and the music ceased.

'To Zeus!' that attendant cried. 'And to Hermes.'

Then, as if an invisible blade had cut the field flat, the entire city fell down to the ground in worship, and only three were left standing: Saul, across the forum from me, I myself, and a woman beside me.

She said, 'They think you are gods come down in mortal form.'

And more's the horror: the citizens of Lystra had prostrated themselves toward us! In our direction, I mean. To Saul and to me!

I threw off the rich toga and began to tear my tunic in anguish. Saul, on the other hand – my blazing partner – took to his heels. He yanked his robe up to his waist and raced on naked bandy legs to the stone rostrum at the east of the forum. He fairly flew to its top, then dropped to his knees and released a long and grievous wailing sound.

'Why do you do this? Why do you do this?' he wailed. He peeled his robe away. He grabbed his tunic in two hands at the throat and ripped it open revealing a thin, pale chest.

'We are people no different from you!' he wailed. 'We live in a flesh like yours, breathing and bleeding and weeping tears. We are not gods. We are creatures *of* God, created *by* God. How could we be gods ourselves?'

Saul stood up. 'But we *know* God!' he cried. 'We know the one, true, living God! We know him so well that we call him Father.

'Yes,' Saul yelled, moving to the left of the rostrum, 'and this is the God who made the heavens and drenched them in light, who made the earth and dressed it green, who scooped the deep places and filled them with seas, who filled the world with birds and fish and beasts. This is the God whom we call Father!'

Saul bounded to the right side of the rostrum. 'In the past,' he declared, 'God allowed the nations to walk in your own ways, to worship vain things, the wood and stone of human hands. But never, never did he leave himself without a witness! Nature has always shown forth his glory! And he is the God who sent from heaven rains upon you. He is the God who has given you goodness and fruitful seasons, satisfying your hearts with food and gladness.

'And now, in these latter times, this God has sent a Son into the world, by whom we all – all of us, all the people of every nation – can call God *Father*.

'We are his messengers! Not gods, not angels, but preachers, the both of us, Barnabas over there, and me, Paul, an apostle of Jesus.'

Back and forth my brother prowled the rostrum. Did he know whether these people were able to understand him? I didn't. Perhaps there were those who spoke Greek, like the woman beside me; but as Saul's words lost the terrible urgency of his grieving, people had begun to lean back on their heels. They sagged into various sitting positions.

The priest of Zeus and his attendants were withdrawing from the gates in obvious disgust, pulling the garlands from their oxen. To them Saul must have seemed crazy, a babbler.

Suddenly he stopped dead centre on the rostrum and cried at the top of his lungs, '*Anastethi*! People of Lystra, stand up! Stand up on your feet. Bow down to no one! Worship nothing except the true God. Come to his Son, the living Lord Jesus. Come to his Son before the judgment of God falls down upon the world. Come, and you will not perish, but you will live, and you like little children will stand before God on that final day and say, "Father, Father, you are my Father."'

All at once it was over.

Saul took the stone steps down from the rostrum. The people got up and went away, though there were five or six who moved in his direction.

But I! – I stood wordless, humming softly to myself, amazed at the thing that Saul had just done. He had preached to pagans nothing of Israel, nothing of the God of Israel, nothing of our scripture, nothing of covenant, Abraham, Moses, the prophets! For the first time ever Saul had cut himself free of the whole religion, of all the history of the Jews. To pagans his sermon shot straight from creation to Jesus.

But I am a Levite still. And a Jew like Saul.

I stood very still, wondering whether I should feel abandoned. Well, and at the same time I wondered whether I would have to follow where Saul had gone and leave this last thing too – my Jewishness, I mean – behind. I'd left my possessions at the feet of the apostles. In Antioch I'd left the synagogue to worship in the homes of the faithful. But this – the scripture and all my heritage: Would that, too, be required of me?

For freedom, Christ had set us free.

Someone was tugging my tunic. It was the Jewish woman. She looked earnestly into my eyes and asked, 'Can you read Hebrew?'

It was exactly seven days later, under the cover of night, that a gang of toughs attacked my brother Saul.

We don't know who set them on. Maybe the priest of Zeus. Maybe our enemies had taken a day-trip down from Iconium to finish the business they'd planned back there. Clearly, the attack wasn't an accident, since they chose Saul specifically, to kill him. I believe they meant to kill him.

We had accepted an invitation from the Jewish woman to stay with her as long as we were in Lystra. Eunice. Saul had agreed to teach Hebrew to her son, Timothy. The house belonged to her mother Lois. All three were hungry for the news of the Jews, and then of Jesus – and I myself delighted now more than ever to hear the scriptures in the mouth of my brother.

One night as we were returning to the house through a narrow street, five men blocked our passage, two before us and three behind. Silently, without a shout, the back three tripped me and pinned me to the ground, while the other two approached Saul. I roared and bellowed and struggled, but I couldn't shake the men from my body or help him. Saul said nothing. He faced his attackers, and I realized that he was waiting! Concentrating!

Run, Saul! Run!

He didn't run. He took a terrible blow to his chest. He bent forward and took another blow in the small of his back. He fell. Strangely, his attackers jumped backward. Then I thought I heard the patter of rainfall, but I felt no water. No, but there was no water. Soon I saw what storm was striking: Dark men on the roofs above us were dropping stones, throwing stones straight down. They were stoning Saul! I heard the crack of stones on the street. I heard the punch of the stones on his body. *Saul! Saul!* I watched him stiffen under the storm. I saw him fold into himself. Then he sighed and went slack. One great rock bounced off his head, but he didn't move, neither twitched nor shivered. He had become a broken doll on the dark street. Men grabbed his arms and dragged him away.

Those who restrained me kept me down a while longer. Then they said, 'You'll find his body at the third mile-marker, in a ditch.' And they left.

For an instant I lay still, utterly dumb. Then my whole body began to shake. I stood up and sank to one knee. I stood up again and began to run to Eunice's house. I banged on the door. 'Timothy! Timothy, I need you!' I shouted, and as soon as he stepped out in the street, I started to run for the city gates.

'They've stoned Saul,' I yelled. 'They've killed him, Timothy! I think they've killed him!'

No one was abroad that night. The guards at the gates had left them open. We dashed through and struck down the road, and in my soul I was calling, *Saul! My brother, Saul!*

The lamb, struck once with a mallet in the centre of its skull, dropped and was instantly dead. Plainly dead. There was no recovery, then. *Saul, Saul, what have they done to you?*

In a ditch! He must have been thrown into the ditch. Just beyond the third mile-marker we found him halfway down the near side of a wadi, his legs doubled beneath him, his arms flopped up over his face and his bloody head. I jumped down into a muddy water deeper than he, and with the hem of my robe began to wipe the thickening blood. Timothy stood frozen above us. *Saul, Saul.*

'We'll carry him home,' I whispered – and just that, the uttering of words and the sound of my sorrowful voice broke me down, and I started to cry.

Then with scorn and with humour together, my brother, my partner apostle said, 'Oh, Barnabas, that's silly.'

Saul's eyes were open! Glints of light reflected from his eyeballs! He was looking at me. He moved. He shifted his weight. He reached up and touched the side of my nose.

'No need for tears,' he said, then turning onto his hands and knees, he climbed from the ditch and stood up and said, 'Come on,' and began to walk back to the city.

Timothy was quicker than I. He rushed to the man, to this miracle of the Lord Jesus Christ, and gave him a strong young shoulder for leaning on.

Yes, yes, yes, O Jesus, yes: even my Jewishness! I could give over the whole of my heritage to follow where that little, bold and bandy-legged man was going.

Luke

22

On the next day Paul went on with Barnabas to Derbe.

When they had preached the gospel to that city and had made many disciples, they returned to Lystra and to Iconium and to Antioch, strengthening the souls of the disciples, exhorting them to continue in the faith, and declaring that we must through many tribulations enter the kingdom of God.

And when with prayer and fasting they had appointed elders for them in every church, they committed them to the Lord in whom they believed.

Then they passed through Pisidia and came to Pamphylia. And when they had spoken the word to Perga, they went down to Attalia. From there they sailed home again to Antioch, where they had first been commended to the grace of God for the work which they now had accomplished.

In Antioch Paul and Barnabas gathered the church together and declared all that God had done with them, how he had opened a door of faith to the Gentiles. And they remained no little time with the disciples.

$\mathcal{L}$. Annaeus Seneca

23

Seneca, in the final month of exile on Corsica,
  To Gallio, my brother in Rome,
  This ninth year of the reign of Claudius:

Greetings!

Look for me, *mi Galli*: I'm coming home. In a fortnight, cast
your eyes toward the streets of Rome and seek a long, bald figure
clothed in a toga of grey wool, a man made gaunt by nine years'
enforced austerities, a man of a yellowish complexion and a
face displaying the hectic flush of our common affliction, our
suspirium. Approach that man. Embrace him. Observe the tears
that spill from his eyes, then gently ask if he be Seneca.

He will be Seneca. And he will kiss thee and sigh to see thee
again.

Ah, *mi Galli*, in my fifty-third year I am rising from the dead
and ascending to a position of some little influence in the city –
though how much influence, and how safely I may exert it,
remain to be seen. Agrippina – the sudden wife of our most
massive Emperor Claudius – has obtained from her husband
my release and is conferring upon me two offices: first, the
praetorship (and wouldn't our aunt be delighted to see
me act the magistrate, since she worked so hard for our
advancements). And second, the tutelage of her young son,
Lucius Domitius. This latter gift has the lesser repute; but it
puts me in the household of the emperor, where a private
influence can be powerful – or perilous. I will not turn
Agrippina down, of course; but I *do* turn the tutelage over in
my mind, seeking the claws the kitten may grow when he grows
to be a lion.

You know as well as I do that people in the household of

Caesar are likelier than garbage dogs to die of what they eat. The closer to power we go, the closer we come to avarice and malice and smiling murders. How did the previous wife of Claudius die? What's the rumour, Gallio? Surely *not* of age or a wasting disease. And how did Agrippina turn the old man's head toward marriage again? And how, in the name of Goodness, did she persuade the Senate to overthrow the sturdiest laws of human morality, the unbreakable codes of Rome? She's his niece! He's her uncle! This is incest! And yet I've heard that a great crowd of Romans marched to the Palatine, *clamouring* for Agrippina's incestuous alliance, and straightway the Senate voted an exemption, and the old glutton, our emperor, now lies entwined in the long white limbs of a lioness.

In offering me the tutelage of her son, Agrippina tells me that Claudius will doubtless adopt the boy in less than a year. She indicates what a treasure, therefore, she is placing in my safekeeping. Blithely she writes that this son of an emperor will himself be emperor one day – this, despite the presence of Claudius's blood-born son, Britannicus. But she ratified her prediction by telling me a story, which I repeat here in my own hand so that you, brother, might take the measure of this inestimable woman.

It seems that when she was six months pregnant with the boy, Agrippina sought his horoscope from a Persian astrologer. 'You will give birth to a son,' the astrologer said, 'who shall be emperor, and who as emperor shall assassinate his mother.'

Immediately the grim Agrippina replied: '*Necet me dum regnet.* Let him kill me – so long as he rule!'

This is the woman I go to work for.

As for her son, at his adoption he will receive a name that means 'strong' and 'valiant': She will call him *Nero*, and then we'll see what such a name can accomplish. I understand that the lad at twelve is skinny-legged; that his mouth droops at the corners; that his pale blue and protuberant eyes are nearsighted; that his hair is auburn, coppery; that he loves dances and music and poetry more than martial pursuits or the structures of law and governmental administration. And this is my clay. This is the thing I am commanded to mould into a *Nero*: 'valiant'. An emperor. Hum.

Mi Galli, I am a philosopher. Even on a barren island I can be free in my contemplations. Tell me, then, and tell me truly: Can

I be as free in the imperial palace where lions switch their tails in casual power?

Well, perhaps the philosopher can tame the kit in spite of its dam and mould a good king after all.

James

24

James, in Jerusalem,
To Simon Peter in Caesarea:

Please: throw off your cloak of hiding a while and come
with deliberate speed to Jerusalem. Saul of Tarsus and Joseph
Barnabas are presently travelling hither from Antioch, by what
route I do not know; whether by land or by sea, I do not know. It
is possible that they shall put in at the port of Caesarea and even
be near you by the time you read this letter; but I desire that you
come here ahead of them. We must discuss the things that are
happening in Antioch before we confront its leaders.

Feelings in Jerusalem are running high. They always do, of
course (and we do well to live in discipline, and so to maintain
stability despite the ferocities of this city). But I'm referring to
the feelings of our own communities.

Last month Judas Barsabbas returned from Antioch in a
fury, filled with condemnations. He had gone there on his own
recognizance (I didn't send him) 'to greet Saul and Barnabas',
so he said, at the conclusion of their yearlong journey to Cyprus
and provinces north. He, like Saul, is a Pharisee. He protests that
he wanted to open a dialogue with the man who had studied
under *Raban* Gamaliel. Barsabbas himself was refused by that
great teacher.

Now Barsabbas is back, pulling on his beard and telling me
how astounded he was to discover that the believers in Antioch
are despised by the synagogues and rejected as apostates and
blasphemers. Jews, Barsabbas says, have divided into two bodies
having nothing to do with each other. The believers, who are now
called 'Christians', swell their numbers with Greeks and pagans
straight from the streets, while the synagogues shrink because

God-fearing Gentiles and proselytes are deserting them ('*And* the Lord God!' Barsabbas thunders) for the house-churches sick with laxity.

'Deserting the Lord God,' Judas Barsabbas thunders, 'because in Antioch these "Christians" teach that Gentiles don't have to be circumcised! Baptism is enough and Jesus is all!' Barsabbas paces in my little room in great agitation. 'They can ignore the Law!' he says. 'Why, inside their house-worshipping churches I've seen the clean and the unclean sitting side by side, eating flesh that was killed with the blood in it, eating meats that were slaughtered and butchered in pagan ritual!

'And the loudest leader of all,' Barsabbas says, pulling his beard and shaking his head, 'is Saul of Tarsus. Oh, I had hoped to admire him! But I found him preaching directly to the pagans, teaching nothing of Israel, nothing of Moses, nothing at all of Abraham; nor does he require anything of these pagans for their salvation, except that they believe in Jesus, dead and risen and coming soon.'

Simon, you and I both know Judas Barsabbas, how passionate and unrestrained he can be. But I tell you, his heart is good. He truly yearns for the salvation of every people. And he fears that Saul is perverting the word so wretchedly that the pagans who trust him will not receive salvation. So he, Barsabbas, stayed in Antioch half the year, arguing publicly against Saul and Barnabas, and teaching people directly that 'unless you are circumcised according to the customs of Moses, you cannot be saved!' He tells me that God has granted him some success. He has caused many people to question the leadership in Antioch, and some have openly withdrawn from Saul and Barnabas. But he believes that this is not enough.

So Judas Barsabbas has delivered his angry speeches everywhere among believers here in Jerusalem. During this last month he has stirred up the passions especially of the Pharisees among us. He wants to 'purify the church,' he says, 'and wash the name of Jesus clean of these treacherous lies'. He argues that even the Greek-speaking Stephen never broke from the synagogues, nor have Stephen's people – Philip, Timon, Prochorus – ever gone anywhere except to those who would know and worship the God of Abraham and Isaac and Jacob.

I must tell you, Simon, that Barsabbas is not alone in his fears. He's only the most emotional.

And now I hear that Antioch is sending a delegation to Jerusalem to argue its own cause. Saul and Barnabas are on their way, accompanied by some young Gentile. Word of their coming and of their intensity precedes them here.

Oh, may the Spirit of the Lord Jesus Christ give us the words and wisdom in the clash to come!

Do you know where Thomas is? I haven't heard from Thomas in eighteen months.

Bring Philip.

Let your wife remain behind. Don't endanger her. Travel light.

Please, Simon: hurry.

itus

25

I'm out of breath. I can hardly keep up. Barnabas said we should
ship south. Paul said, 'No, we're going to walk.' Barnabas said,
'Why?' Paul said, 'So's to talk to everyone on the way.' And that's
what we've been doing. Hardly a day's break. No rest. It's the
rainy season, but Paul wakes up before dawn and takes off
running rain or shine. Or it seems to me it's running. We follow
lickety-split. At noon he comes to a village where some believers
live (how does he know where all the believers live?) and we go to
their house. We eat a little lunch and Paul tells his story. I mean
the story of meeting Jesus on the road to Damascus. The farther
south we go, the more people who've never seen Paul face-to-face,
so for them it's a wonderful tale. I hear it over and over. Paul
says, 'I persecuted the church of God. I tried to destroy it.' He
says, 'I was so zealous for the traditions of the Jews that I
advanced in religion past everyone my own age.' Then he slaps
the table or something, and he says, 'But God set me apart
before I was born! And when I was travelling on the road to
Damascus, he revealed his Son to me. Jesus of Nazareth appeared
to me and said, *Saul, Saul*! and called me to be an apostle to the
Gentiles!'

That's it. That's what Paul says wherever we stop. And
sometimes the people cry right there, mumbling tears of happiness
at the change in him. Always and everywhere they say, 'Praise God!
Glory to God the Father,' things like that. Then Paul goes on to tell
them what happened when he and Barnabas preached to the
pagans, how the Holy Spirit came to the pagans the same as the
Jews – and then our hosts really go wild. Everybody starts to sing
hymns, and if somebody yells, *In the name of Jesus*, well, then I do
my thing, which is this funny little dance and I speak in tongues.
The Holy Spirit makes me speak in tongues.

I say to Paul: 'Why am I invited? What do I do when we get to Jerusalem?' He says to me, 'Nothing. Do nothing.' Well, that's a poser; so I say, 'I don't get it.' He looks me dead in the eye then, and says, 'Titus,' says my name solemn and serious and scared, even; it seems to *me*, it's scared. 'Titus,' he says, 'the gospel I preach to the Gentiles must not be preached in vain. I cannot be running in vain. Some false brothers have been spying on our freedom which we have in Christ Jesus. They want to bring us back to bondage. They want to make my preaching into nothing. But you, little brother – you are my proof. Who you are, what you do, what has not been done to you: It's proof of the power of Jesus.'

Well, and when he says that, the only thing going through my mind is, *At your speed, the running's not in vain: It's doing a bang-up job of killing me*. So I told that joke to Barnabas, who usually has a sense of humour. But this time he says to me, 'No, but Saul means it.' And I want to say, *I know he means it! That's the point*. But Barnabas is already galloping after Saul, the big man after the little man like a bear after the desert hare; so I take off too, the youngest man of all, barely keeping up.

$\mathscr{B}$arnabas

26

Judas Barsabbas said, 'I am a Jew.'

Saul shot to his feet. 'And I am not? I'm as Hebrew as anyone here!'

People in Jerusalem do not stand to speak. That's what the Greek rhetorician does. Rabbis teach sitting down. Jesus taught sitting down. So when Saul kept flying to his feet, he got attention, all right, but not the sort he wanted.

Saul pointed at Judas Barsabbas and cried, 'Are you an Israelite?' He pounded on his skinny chest. 'So am I!'

I reached up to tug at Saul's arm. 'Saul,' I whispered, 'Saul.'

Simon Peter spoke more boomingly from his other side. 'I can't wait to hear what you have to say, brother,' he called. 'I know how powerful your words will be. But listen first to shape them best. Please, Saul, sit.'

Saul sat down again between me and young Titus.

I declare it with praise for him and to God, that he shackled himself in spiritual chains then, and he listened. With praise for Saul, I say, and a little relief for myself, because we were here as ambassadors for Antioch, and I'd been put in charge, but my partner apostle had a habit of charging over everyone. Oh, I hoped he'd keep the shackles on. But he sat in a sort of a crouch, his narrow eye fixed on our opponent.

Judas Barsabbas: he had a long, scraggly beard which he stroked when he talked. He was a grey fellow, not much blood in him. So his excitements always seemed strange to me, like ice cracking.

'I am a Jew,' Judas Barsabbas said again. 'I was born a Jew, circumcised on the eighth day and named for the Maccabaean, that saviour of Old Israel who always, always, even under the severest circumstances, obeyed and honoured the Laws of God.

Like him I was trained to observe the Laws and, since the year of my own majority, have kept the feasts, have avoided impurities, have eaten nothing unclean, have rested on Shabbat, have meditated on the Law both day and night. I am a Jew. I was born an Israelite, one of the people chosen by God.'

The man paused to rearrange his robe. He said, 'But now, in the name of Jesus I am twice a Jew and twice the Israelite! And how,' he asked with a cold smile, 'can that be?'

We were sitting on long benches, some of stone built into the walls, some of plain wood in the rest of the room. The wooden benches gave out a faint smoke-scent, as if they'd been salvaged from a burned building. They were smooth with age. A room as large as this was unusual in the houses of Jerusalem, but my Aunt Mary had knocked down a whole wall in order to create a place for the assembly of many believers at once.

Judas Barsabbas sat on stone in the northern corner. 'And how can that be?' he said, turning his grey face this way and that, though he didn't look into our eyes. He seldom looked people in their eyes. He peered at our throats or the hair on our heads, and answered his own question: 'Because I have come to the Jew of Jews. Because I believe in the Israelite whom God the Father chose as last and best of all, the very fulfilment of Israel. For the God who chose Abraham; the God who chose Israel to be his people; the God who chose prophets to call the people back again; this same God, who cannot deny his own nature, has testified to that holy nature by choosing once more, for ever and for all. As the crown and the consequence of all his choosings, God has chosen Jesus of Nazareth to be his Son, his Beloved one, the Messiah. And what, brothers and saints, does that mean? Why, it means that we are an Israel *in* Israel! – and we ought, therefore, to be a leaven for the whole.'

Saul was listening. Every fibre in his skinny body vibrated almost imperceptibly, yet he kept his eyes fixed on Barsabbas.

James cast glances back and forth between the two Pharisees. Once he caught my eye and seemed to question me as to my feelings. I returned a pinched smile. I really didn't know what I felt. I don't like Judas Barsabbas. He's a contentious individual, unkind and un-humble. But I confess that his words were moving me, and all at once I discovered this vagrant thought within my heart: *how good to be home again.*

We had gathered in the house of my old aunt Mary, the

mother of my cousin, John Mark. There wasn't a better place in
Jerusalem. She kept a large courtyard just inside the street gate;
and this room, once it was enlarged, could hold thirty to forty
people. But for me, the house was a homecoming. After I had
sold my properties and given all my possessions away, it was Mary
who took me in and blessed me and fed me. The red paintings on
her walls, therefore, and the mosaics on her floors, the smell of
her bins and her baskets, the woven garlic, dried petals in a bowl,
the menorah carved in a ceiling beam with shofroth on either
side, the iron sconces, the pale blue lamps – these were the stuff
of comfort for me. *How good to be home again.*

And here were the people of that blazing Pentecost nineteen
years ago! Apostles and prophets, disciples and teachers and
friends whom I hadn't seen in a decade – the very same people
who, in the first explosions of the Holy Spirit, had thrown back
their heads and uttered tongues they'd never known before, nor
ever would know again! Here, in Mary's house on benches around
me, sat men with old scars, for we all, in those early days,
rejoiced to be beaten, rejoiced to be worthy to suffer dishonour
for the name of Jesus! Simon Peter sat behind my brother Saul;
James occupied a seat alone; John, the son of Zebedee, whose
brother was murdered for the faith, sat between his mother and
Mary Magdalene, now awfully thin and white-haired. All around
the room were the faces of those first days before the
persecutions scattered us. Grave, consoling faces: my old aunt
Mary and John Mark and Philip and Andrew and Matthias and the
young Rose, Rhoda, whose crooked nose I loved when she was six
and I was the man she knew best, a sort of a father. All these had
returned to Jerusalem one more time, for the sake of the unity of
the church. Oh, what a goodly company! *And how good to be
home again.*

Only one figure here in Mary's assembly room had not been
with us at the beginning. Not *with* us, I mean – though he had
lived in the city, prowling the streets like a Satan.

Saul of Tarsus, crouched beside me as tense as a cat, his red-
rimmed eyes fixed on Judas Barsabbas, his fierce black eyebrows
quivering.

'I know the Messiah whom God has chosen,' Barsabbas
was saying. 'I believe in Jesus: Lord and Saviour and the
Consummation of Jewish expectations. Brothers and saints, we
are Israel *in* Israel! For we have in Jesus the kernel of the nut! He

is the seed in the flower. The hearth in the house. In him we have more than the promises of God: We have the fulfilment of every promise! In Jesus the Law and the Prophets are made complete and are therefore more beautiful and more binding than ever. Believing in Jesus divides me not one whit from my people. Rather, he is the next word in our history, and the last one, too. Many have come among us claiming to be the Messiah, the Anointed of the Lord our God. The difference between them and Jesus is simple and singular: Jesus *is*.'

As if the Book of the Law had just been opened, some of the people murmured, *Amen, amen.*

Barsabbas twitched his moist eye to those that had spoken. 'And what else should the church say?' he asked them. 'What else need the church preach to anyone, Jew or Gentile? We declare that Jesus is finally the flower of a strong and ancient tree, and we who believe in him are its fruit. Why would anyone strive to cut that tree down?'

Several voices said, *No one wants to cut it down. Who wants to cut it down?*

Barsabbas said, 'It would kill the flower and the fruit as well!'

Now he lifted his right hand and pointed at Saul. 'But this man thinks the flower can live without the tree!' He spat the words in an icy logic. 'This man wants to plant an Israel *apart* from Israel, as if God would reject his people, as if God could deny himself! This man denies the need of the Laws of God for the salvation of the Gentiles!'

As if God could deny his own nature.

'But God,' Barsabbas raised his milky voice, 'sent Jesus as a Jew to the Jews, that we might love him and keep his name pure and *as Jews* invite the nations to come and to love him too! For by coming to Zion may every people be saved! God chose Jesus, a descendant of Abraham, that, *by Abraham,* as God himself says, *all the families of the earth might bless themselves*! And this is how they come to Zion: by keeping the Laws of Moses! And this is how they love Messiah: by keeping the Laws of Moses! And this is how in Abraham every family on earth can bless itself: by knowing and honouring and obeying and keeping the Laws of Moses.

'Circumcision,' Barsabbas intoned, 'is absolutely necessary for salvation!'

Amen! God has spoken! This is a prophet, indeed!

Pale Judas Barsabbas was done, but the room still echoed his sound and his sense, first in shoutings and then in personal conversations, head to head. It had been an argument empowered as much by cold anger and passion as by substance. But the substance was real, and people now chattered in passions of their own.

Rhoda the maiden, my little Rose, brought out flagons of wine which she had mixed with honey and water. She placed baskets of dried fruit around the room, scattered fresh mint leaves, then poured cups of the wine for everyone. She saved the prettiest cup and the shyest, most charming of smiles for Titus, who sat grinning like a split melon.

Under other circumstances I would have burst into laughter and teased the exchange – but I was preoccupied. Barsabbas' words had an obvious and positive effect on people. James and Peter and John had gone off to a corner, where they were locked in low dialogue. Other people munched and laughed with an easy confidence as if matters had already been settled. This was distressing. I was beginning to realize how much Saul and I were seen as aliens. We'd taken routes no one else was taking – and now we had come here to lay before them the truth of our gospel to the Gentiles, here, in the central and holiest place of the faithful. And Titus, himself innocent of the fierce histories of the Jews, had come as evidence of the rightness of our differences.

I looked at Saul. He did not look back. His huge head hung low. He seemed so sunken in private meditations that my anxieties increased and I felt faintly lonely.

Peter, James, and John – the 'pillars of the church', as Saul called them – returned to their places and sat down.

If I could have read their expressions, I'd have called them 'concerned', but that was too much like my own mood and I rejected it.

Peter said, 'Brother Saul?'

Others in the room reacted, directing their attentions to Peter and to Saul; but my partner didn't seem to notice anything.

Again Peter said, 'Saul?'

Saul jumped, as if startled. He raised his face and that beetling brow, and looked around the room with such a slow and kindly expression that the people fell silent in anticipation. Suddenly I knew that Saul had been fervently alert the whole while, only *seeming* lost in thought.

He spoke in a general manner, embracing the whole room, 'I can speak now? It is granted me to speak now?'

Peter smiled uncomfortably, as if waiting for anyone else to answer, then said, 'Yes.'

But Saul looked over at James and said, 'The things that we have done and seen in the name of Jesus – they can be presented now to the church?'

James nodded.

'Thank you. Thank you,' Saul said. He stood up with a precise formality, as short men are wont to do.

'Whether I need answer the… the charges of the brother who has just spoken, we will yet see. That time may come. Or the time and the need may never come. For my own part, I'd like to begin by introducing with joy my friend and my helper, Titus.' Saul gestured to the ruddy, innocent youth beside him. 'Saints, would you greet this new saint, Titus?'

In several languages the people did: *Shalom*, they said. *Eirene*. 'Peace be with you.' *Ave*.

'Thank you,' Saul said.

Then, as if the idea had just entered his mind, he said, 'And what if I should ask my young friend here to speak? What if Titus told you of our successes abroad in the name of Jesus?'

Poor Titus went as white as almond blossoms.

Peter strove to be jovial. 'Of course!' he boomed.

'Because the Holy Spirit is in this young man, you know,' Saul said, his enthusiasm growing. 'Titus is a Gentile filled with the Holy Spirit. Surely, that should give him leave to speak in this good fellowship, this body of broad repute. Surely, that should give us all good reason to credit his witness as truth – right?'

'Right, right!' boomed Simon. 'Anyone in whom the Spirit dwells is worthy to address us! We will listen.' Simon Peter and I are much alike: in tense situations we both want desperately to be agreeable.

'When we worship in the houses of Antioch,' Saul was saying, 'Titus worships with us. And whenever the Spirit blows through the congregation, young Titus also receives a measure of the Spirit. He takes part in the celebrations fully as much as Barnabas or I, though we preach. That's our sign of the Spirit, to preach. Titus has his sign, too, his own manifestation of the Spirit of God!'

'Good for you!' boomed Simon Peter. 'Ah, lad, we look forward to worshipping with you tonight.'

In Peter's wake a host of people smiled at Titus, murmuring praises to God.

'Indeed, indeed,' Saul responded, 'young Titus has faith in Jesus, for he confesses that Jesus died for his sins, and he declares that Jesus rose again for his salvation. Indeed, indeed! Young Titus is a believer like us, for he it was that brought his father to hear the gospel. This child was father of the man, and the gospel now shines in the parent's face!'

People began to applaud. Titus, too, was nodding and answering their praises with breathless pleasures of his own. His young eyes grew bright with thanksgiving.

Saul grinned and said, 'He walks in the light, though he is no Jew.'

The people said, 'Amen.'

Saul said, 'And this is the reason why Titus is here! He's a living example of the effect of our preaching, the gospel we preach to the Gentiles. We did not go out on our own, Barnabas and I. We were... chosen... by the Holy Spirit and sent by the church at Antioch as apostles. And this young Gentile, Titus, represents the fruit of our labours. He is but one of hundreds and hundreds who call upon the name of the Lord Jesus Christ. Titus! And isn't he also united with everyone here? Behold how he delights in salvation!'

The whole assembly began to clap. One or two let out whoops of good cheer.

I saw Titus' chin trembling with emotion. It caused me, too, suddenly to sob, because I understood: here in Jerusalem the church and the apostles themselves were receiving him, granting the lad both place and love at once.

Saul rode the noise of the people, as if they were the sea and he a ready boat: 'Behold how Titus delights in salvation,' he sang out, 'for it is with an unmixed gladness that he too anticipates the return of our Lord Jesus Christ.'

Amen, the people answered.

'And here is a sign of salvation and faithfulness,' Saul said, 'a sign as good as any: young Titus does not fear the coming of Jesus! He does not fear the judgment! He thirsts for it! He is like us. He, too, is hungry to see the face of our Lord!'

Amen, little brother! Amen!

A woman rose up and came to Titus and took his hands and caused him to stand, then she hugged him and kissed him in a transport of gladness, while others spoke his name, commending him ever more loudly to God.

I felt the gladness in me, too, like a deep wave of breathing, a huge and wonderful sighing. I began to rock and, deep in my bosom, to sing.

Then I saw young Rhoda, out in the courtyard, dancing round and round, lifting her arms like blossoms; and lo, the rhythm of her feet was the rhythm of my own internal song.

And Saul was speaking in his high voice: 'We venture to tell you nothing except what Christ has worked through us, to win obedience from the Gentiles!'

Amen! Amen!

'What Christ has worked through us,' Saul cried, 'by word and deed, by the power of signs and wonders, by the power of the Holy Spirit, by the preaching of the gospel of Christ!'

Hallelujah!

'Blessed be,' Saul cried, and spontaneously, Simon Peter finished the phrase:

'Blessed be the Holy Name of Jesus!'

Saul called out again, 'Blessed be!'

And this time all the people answered: *Blessed be his holy name!*

Suddenly my aunt Mary cried out, 'In the name of Jesus!'

And I myself knelt down in front of my bench. So did others, in spontaneous worship, kneel down.

But Titus spread his arms, and the woman that had hugged him did the same, face-to-face with Titus. Then he began to dance, two steps left, two steps right. He allowed his arms to droop, like hawk's wings on the air. He raised his face and closed his eyes – then the language fountained from his mouth. Fast, with force Titus cried, 'Bah-bah-bah! Bah-bah-bah!' There was, as always, an amazing authority in the tone of his voice. Laughter answered him everywhere. People raised their hands in grateful worship. Simon Peter was flushed and grinning. The wind of Pentecost was blowing again. And I sang more loudly now a whole new song:

> *Lo, how he pours!*
> *He pours out his Spirit*
> *Richly before our eyes!*

Lo, how in Christ
By grace he remakes us
Heirs of eternal Life!

Young, blushing Titus spouted his ecstasy, 'Bah-bah-bah! Bah-bah-bah!' and the room seemed brightened by fire.

Then, even as I was still singing, I saw Saul move to Titus. He put his arms around the lad and held him hard and long. Titus stopped speaking in tongues and soon was returning the embrace. They stood together in the midst of the people like a still and peaceful centre, until their steadfast silence became ours too, and we all in wonder ceased our noises.

'Jesus Christ is Lord,' Saul announced into the tangle of the young man's hair, 'to the glory of God the Father.'

Then to us all he said, 'You have witnessed the gift that the Holy Spirit has bestowed upon Titus. My friend speaks in tongues. And where the Spirit is, there is the favour and the presence of God.'

Saul paused. He stepped up on a bench and looked down at the faces turned toward him. In a gentle voice he said: 'Brothers, you wouldn't say we've run in vain, Barnabas and I, would you?'

He placed his hands on Titus's head as if in blessing, and said: 'Isn't this evidence that the Spirit works through us for the sake of the Gentiles, even as the same Holy Spirit works through Peter for the sake of the Jews?'

There was a marvellous murmur of agreement in the house. Simon Peter, husky with emotion, said, 'We've seen it with our own eyes. Yes, Saul. Yes, my brother. Yes.'

'Then, as a final proof that Jesus has entrusted me with the gospel to the Gentiles, I've one more thing to reveal before this assembly of the saints of Jesus.'

So quietly did the next words come that Saul seemed to be whispering them. But he pronounced them in perfect clarity, and the people leaned forward to listen.

'Titus,' Saul said, 'has not been, nor ever shall be, circumcised.'

Immediately, a hissing began to cut the air. A hissing, then a whistling, then we heard a fabric ripping, and I saw Judas Barsabbas in his northern corner, tearing his robe and clawing at his meagre beard, spittle on his lip.

No longer grey but white as death, his intensity was frightening.

It made Saul's revelation seem distressful even to me, though I had agreed with him. But things that are rightly kept separate had here been driven together, tender things with harsher things. It felt like a setup, and briefly I was blaming Saul for his trick and for taking control. We were not one single man come to Jerusalem! We were a delegation!

Judas Barsabbas was howling in pain. Other men lamented with him. Had they been burned by personal insult? Were these people genuinely grieved? I didn't know. The whole assembly seemed like a lake caught in crosswinds, confused, choppy, unknowing.

And then Barsabbas found his tongue, shouting sudden bursts of sentence: 'The Jews alone were chosen... A Gentile can be saved... only... if he becomes a Jew... through circumcision...'

Judas Barsabbas the Pharisee was standing. Not to teach. He would not stand to teach. He stood to accuse: 'Saul of Tarsus,' he barked, his throat thick with his wretchedness, 'you are striving to create a people of God... *outside* the people of God! Saul of Tarsus: you are overthrowing the Law by this 'Faith' in Jesus.

'Saul of Tarsus: you have therefore made the Lord Jesus an agent of sin, and all who receive your word are feeding on dust and death, while they think it is bread and life!'

Through the storm that broke in Mary's house, through the confusion of passions and loud antagonisms – and even under the high whine of Saul's belligerent voice – I saw one clear thing, and it broke my heart.

In the courtyard, standing barefoot, her hands hung down in helplessness, my little Rose was crying. It had begun to rain. Her face was tilted up to the clouds, but her eyes were closed and her mouth was rounded in a wolvish sorrow. I walked out of the house. I approached her. When I touched the maiden's shoulder, she jumped, and I saw in her eye the flash of horror. But then she recognized me and collapsed in my arms.

Someone was shouting: *Jesus didn't come to destroy the Law! He said it himself – the Law won't pass away till heaven and earth pass away!*

Someone shouted still louder: *He said that anyone who breaks the least commandment, and any who teach others to break it, will be least in the kingdom of heaven!*

Little Rose with the crooked nose had buried her face in the folds of my robe. Her body shook with sobbing. Even my tunic grew warm with her tears while my shoulders grew cold with the rain. I felt huge and clumsy and filled with apology that things should come to this.

James

27

In me there is a memory fixed, a single scene so stark and grave that whenever it seizes my mind, I gasp and grieve all over again. It signifies the beginning of separations within the church.

At the time of this scene's reality, however, I thought it but a passing problem – a serious problem, to be sure, one that could have elemental consequence if not solved, but solvable, withal, and confined to a small circle inside the church. In fact, I was more fearful of the broader assaults from without, both upon our people the Jews and upon the body of believers who bore the glory of Jesus *for* the Jews. This lesser rift within our fellowship I reckoned dangerous insofar as it weakened our unity in the face of these assaults. 'Solvable,' I said. Maybe it were truer to say 'dismissable'. My real effort, I'm afraid, was simply to get rid of the problem. I wasn't patient enough. I was angry. And my thoughtlessness led to solutions of terrible paradox: *Divide to unify; and to survive, divide.*

Here is the scene: Saul the anti-Pharisee is standing head and shoulders above everyone else in the assembly room in Mary's house, flapping his arms like a rooster, stretching his neck and crowing and crowing. He's standing on a bench. He's arguing with ferocity and a perfervid delight against other Pharisees in the faith who shout as loud as he does but failingly, since they are several and he is but one single, blood-red voice. And he's causing such outrage in his debaters, such emotional divisions, that other believers must be wondering whether choosing Jesus is only the first of a series of decisions.

Saul, that bandy-legged rooster, strutting on a bench like a cock-walk, crowing! This is the man I had honoured, once, a quick, convincing student of Torah. This is the one I thought would give Barnabas wisdom, stability, *gravitas*. Here he was,

the king of tumult, shamelessly turning good men into beasts!
That scene was troubling to everyone there, but to me it was
confirmation of disappointment, for I had heard of the changes
in him, but now my eye was seeing them.

I set my jaw, moved through the turmoil toward the northern
corner of the house.

'Barsabbas!' I said. 'Shut up! This is an iniquitous excess.'

He, his mouth caught open on some word, glanced at me.
I didn't wait for his obedience. I left him. I went first to Simon,
then to John, and asked them to follow, and walked out of the
house. I hoped that our departure would deflate the passions and
grant the people the right to go.

In a near corner of the courtyard I noticed the large form of
Joseph Barnabas. He was not inside the house, fighting on Saul's
behalf. He was outside in the grey of the rainfall, kneeling,
consoling young Rhoda. Come to think of it, Barnabas had not
even joined the debate! The great bearded Levite had drawn the
child to his bosom and was, I think, singing softly in her ear.

'Barnabas,' I said.

Simon and John paused behind me and looked at him.

'Barnabas, when Saul is able to hear you, invite him to Simon's
house. We are going there now and will wait for you. Come, talk
privately with us at Simon's house.'

We called it 'Simon's house' by habit, I suppose. Ever since he'd
escaped Agrippa's prison and fled Jerusalem, the church had
changed the use of the place. We made it an inn for pilgrim
believers, those who came to keep the feasts. We taught and
studied in small groups here. We shelved one room like a library
for our books, the scriptures, letters the saints had written from
abroad.

Nevertheless, when he entered the house that afternoon,
Simon Peter expanded as if it were still his home. And when Saul
and Barnabas arrived, it was Simon who led us into the dining
room, taking the host's position at the central table of three.
Saul went immediately to the table at Simon's right. Barnabas
followed him. John and I had no choice but to sit at Simon's left,
directly across from the Pharisee and the Levite.

We ate supper together.

Simon's wife served. He had not, as I had suggested, left her behind in Caesarea; but as things evolved, I was grateful to have her here. Her presence had a civilizing effect on Saul. Even as we were sitting down, the man restated his position with a lunging fervour, saying, 'There's no reason to circumcise Titus. If you demand it, you add to the gospel Jesus revealed to me, and if you add to his gospel, you judge it insufficient. But Jesus is sufficient. We will not circumcise Titus – '

Just then Simon's wife entered the dining room with towels and bowls of water, and Saul tripped in the midst of his speech. 'Oh!' he said. He gave the intruder a quick glance, almost turned back to talk, then peered closely at the woman behind him. 'It's *you!*' he cried. 'Peter, your wife is here!' The little man bounded to his feet, seized the bowls from her hands and set them on the table and, grinning like a boy, kissed her. 'How good to see you again!' He took the towels from her arms. 'Why, I haven't seen you in what? Fourteen years! Here in this very room, wasn't it?'

She smiled upon him with a kindly gravity – yes, exactly as if he *were* a boy. 'You're older,' she said, 'and battered, poor man.' She raised the tips of her fingers to the air above his brow. 'You have new scars,' she said, then she retrieved her towels, laid them each by a water bowl, and left the room.

Her gesture had a remarkable effect. When he sat down again, Saul's eye had turned inward, softening his face.

As for me, my eyes were opened: how could I not have seen the thick, wormlike welt at his hairline? And the lesser scoring of white scars across his temple and cheekbone? Suddenly I, too, was remembering that time seven and seven years ago when three of us had gathered here and eaten together, and Simon's wife had served.

John said, 'Where Peter goes, there goes Miriam.'

Simon said, 'Except to prison. Except to prison.'

The woman returned with a wide platter carrying clay bowls and a steaming pot of lentil soup. She set her service down at Simon's right. He watched as she ladled thick soup into Saul's bowl, then he said, 'I'm not going to fight you, Saul. Don't look for a fight from me. Maybe I'll argue with James instead.' He dipped his fingers in the water bowl and dried them on a towel. He looked at me. 'Saul may be the pressure on the haft, James,' he said, 'but the point was put to me several years ago – by the Holy Spirit. Saul's just driving home the will of the Spirit: that

God no longer shows partiality. Anyone who fears him and does what is right – no matter the race or the nation – is acceptable to him.'

I felt heat in my face. 'I know that,' I said. 'I've always known that. I'm not disputing that.'

Now Simon was receiving his soup at the hand of his wife. He said, 'I've seen the Holy Spirit poured out on others as it was on this boy today. On Roman folk. On the uncircumcised, James, and the Lord himself commanded me to reject no one.'

His wife moved to John, sitting at my right.

'Simon, listen to me,' I said. 'That is not the dispute. I am not rejecting anyone. I never have!'

She came to me, now, and began to ladle my soup. She smiled, but formally. It has ever been my station in life neither to seek nor to receive the more intimate friendships of women.

I nodded, acknowledging the greeting. I restrained myself, too, by the cords of formality. 'It's not the rejection,' I said, 'but the reception that's in question: *how* we ought to receive those whom we receive. Straightway by baptism? Apart from Moses and wide of the doors of Israel?'

Simon's wife walked softly from the room.

My voice rose a minimal degree. But my form and my countenance remained absolutely fixed. 'Do you want to allow that? And if you do, won't you seem to preach two paths to salvation? It's not only unreasonable; how can it be possible? What? You would make the Jewish Messiah into a 'Christ' for the Greeks? Simon, answer me: Is Jesus divided?'

While I spoke, he raised his hands palm-upward, likely to utter thanksgiving before we ate, but I kept talking.

'Saul refuses additions to the gospel that he preaches to the Gentiles,' I said. 'But there's adding, and there's taking away, too! It is written: *Give heed to the statutes which I teach you, and do them, that you may go in and take possession of the land. You shall not add to the word which I command you, nor take from it.* But Saul, the refuser of additions, himself does more than subtract some small portion of the Law: he cancels Torah altogether!'

Saul jumped on my word: 'For this one and for that one but not for everyone,' he said, looking me dead level in the eye. 'For Titus, for Gentiles, because the Lord Jesus Christ is all in all, and all-sufficient. But not for the Jews. James,' he snapped, 'you're the one who hasn't been listening! Listen to me: Torah is Torah, sound and good for the Jew. And Jesus is *both* Messiah and Christ, because Jesus fulfils *both* the Law and the screaming need of the world! No, no, Jesus is not divided. But if you require of Titus an adherence to Jesus and *also* to the Laws of Moses, then Jesus is diminished, and it is heaven itself that you have divided!'

Joseph Barnabas spoke. 'Saul. Eat something,' he said. He had himself been eating, but he set his spoon down now and looked at me. 'The works of God are proofs of the presence of God – and his approval,' Barnabas said.

I did not move. I set my jaw. I returned his look with my own most immovable look. He said, 'God has given Saul signs and power.'

How tired Barnabas seemed. But the man never had the tensile endurance of a good warrior. Too much fondness. Too much tenderness.

He could not sustain his gaze at me. He dropped his eyes, then looked at Simon and said, 'I remember when you and John healed a cripple, a beggar in the Temple gate. You said, *Silver and gold have I none; but what I have I give to you: In the name of the Messiah, Jesus of Nazareth, walk*. He did. The man leaped up and praised God. Peter, John: in the name of Jesus, Saul has done this very same thing in foreign lands. In cities where there are no synagogues. People are amazed. They listen. They believe. They glorify God. It's the same Jesus in Lystra as in Jerusalem, and the same salvation. It works. Saul is right. This gospel is sufficient.'

I said, 'Barnabas, look at me! Do you wish therefore to *abolish* the Law? It's been our fortress since Moses! Without it we would have perished a thousand times over, but *with* it we've survived Assyria and Babylon and Persia and Alexander and the Ptolemies and the Seleucids! And Rome. Abolish the Law and we will *surely* perish!'

Saul said, 'So what? The Lord is coming soon!'

'And the Lord requires his servants to *work* until he comes. Kill the Law, kill us *now*! But in fact we have no such choice: we must watch and strive for righteousness until that day when righteousness himself appears. No! We strive for righteousness *on account of* that great and terrible day of the Lord!'

Out of the corner of my eye I saw Simon's wife hovering in the doorway. I pressed my lips together. Suddenly Simon was shouting heartily: 'Eat! Eat what my wife has prepared – '

But Saul fairly flew over the table, crying, 'Strive, strive! Let *everyone* strive for righteousness! Beg everyone to walk in the light! But don't hinder my gospel or blame it or undermine it. I am called to preach to the Gentiles. I will not run in vain.'

Simon Peter picked up a small loaf of bread and, astonishingly, threw it at Saul. It hit his left ear, and the little Pharisee exhaled with the sound of an ox blowing. The woman in the doorway uttered a bark of delight then covered her mouth. Barnabas, on the other hand, sucked air and threw back his head and erupted in laughter, long and loud and sustained. The big man grabbed his sides to laugh. Simon beamed, pleased with himself.

John, to my right, giggled.

I held my peace. Simon is a spontaneous boor, and the people love him for it.

Simon said, 'Shut up, Saul. Eat your soup. Dip the bread in the soup, then wipe the bowl clean with it – and for once let someone else speak on your behalf.'

Saul cast a glance backward at Simon's wife, whose eyes were positively twinkling. Barnabas came forward with somewhat more appetite than he'd shown before. John picked up his spoon. And Peter, tearing off a hunk of bread and stuffing it into his mouth, began to speak:

'When Miriam and I were staying in Joppa, the day before we went to Caesarea, I had a vision,' he said. 'At noon I was on the rooftop praying. I got very hungry, then fell into a trance. I saw the heavens open up. I saw something like a huge sheet being let down to the earth by its four corners. When it landed, I saw all kinds of reptiles inside and birds and four-footed beasts, some clean, some unclean. And then I heard a voice say, *Peter, rise and kill and eat*. I said, *No, Lord. I have never eaten anything common or unclean*. But the voice said, *What God has cleansed you must not call common or unclean*. James, that happened three times. Three times the sheet came down. Three times I was commanded, and three times I refused to eat – on account of the Law. Then the sheet was taken back up to heaven, and I woke up, baffled by the vision.'

I said, 'Why are you looking at me? Are you telling this story just for me?'

Simon grinned. 'And here came the sense of that vision, straight from the Holy Spirit! Right away when I woke, there were three men knocking on the door below. They had come from Caesarea, from a centurion of the Italian Cohort who had been told by the Lord to come and get me. A Gentile, James. A God-fearing man, a Roman never circumcised – yet when we went to his house, and when I preached to him the news of Jesus Christ, the Lord of all, I knew that the Holy Spirit fell on his household, on everyone there, because they began to speak in tongues, praising God.

'James, that was no different from what Saul's boy did today at Mary's house. I couldn't forbid water for baptizing that Gentile and his people. There was no need to circumcise them. Why should I circumcise them? They had already received the Holy Spirit. All people,' Simon said to me sententiously. Moreover, the ox repeated the phrase: 'All people,' he said, 'no matter their race or their nation, are acceptable to God.'

'You think I deny that?' I said.

'Well, you have.'

'No, I haven't.'

'Yes, James. Yes, you do. You demand circumcision. You want to make Jews of those that aren't Jews! Only as Jews do you find them acceptable.'

'Simon!'

'What?'

'Is this your intent, to isolate me here?'

'No, not at all.'

'Then your intent must be to turn our Jewish traditions – the holy traditions which I uphold, which once that man there himself upheld – into trash.'

'No, of course not!'

'But that's exactly what you're doing, Simon!' I said with energy. 'And you're rejecting the intentions of the Almighty! The voice in your vision invited you to eat things previously unclean. Perhaps we should, therefore, receive people previously contaminated and impure. I will concede the interpretation. But,' – I was leaning forward to drive the point into this big man's mind – 'but that voice, the voice of the Lord, Simon, never invited you to *become* an unclean thing yourself! The Law, as it applies to *us*, is still the Law!'

'James!' Saul spoke. It wrenched my head to his direction. 'Where's the difference between us, then?' he said. 'What you ask of Peter, I beg of you. I allow Jews to be Jews. If Simon must keep the Law, let Simon keep the Law. Just don't demand that Gentiles become Jews too!'

Instantly, this answer shot through my head: *If Simon is eating with Gentiles, then Simon's not keeping the Law!* But I restrained myself.

I folded my hands and tucked my chin into my throat. I was suffering a sudden sense of panic. I needed time to reflect, because my mouth had outrun my mind. That last statement of mine had, in fact, shifted my position, and Saul had recognized the variance faster than I did. He had leaped on my words and changed the language to his own advantage. *The Law to us is still the Law*, I'd said, with stress on the personal distinction, *us*. It permitted Saul to extrapolate: *but not to Gentiles*.

Let Jews be Jews, the man returned my words to me with wondrous generosity, in order also to say: *and let Gentiles be Gentiles*.

In the gap of conversation, Simon's wife came into the dining room with a plate of cheeses and raisins and olives. She saw how little soup had been consumed, said nothing to break our silence, but withdrew, taking with her the plate still full.

At length, John spoke.

He had pulled an oil lamp to himself and was cupping the flame between his hands. Firelight played upward on his face. After the clamorous exchange, the man seemed subdued.

Well, and of course he would seem so: his first words gave good reason and laid caution to my own tongue.

He said, 'Four years ago my brother was executed outside the walls of this city. I am weak. I should not grieve his death. It was what the Lord had prophesied. He said that we, my brother and I, would drink the cup that he was to drink. But I think about him every day.

'And this, James, is what I think: why did Agrippa kill him? Because Agrippa was seeking support of the Jews – and he didn't see my brother as a Jew among Jews! He saw him as something different, though we are no different.'

John drew breath. His nostrils distended, but his mouth was solemn.

'James,' he said, 'that is the predominating problem today – both for us and for Jews in general: that Jews and Jews are divided. That we *seem* divided to the world, and we *are* divided internally.'

Again, he breathed, gazing into the lamp flame pink through the flesh of his fingers. He seemed to be seeking the best approach to his thesis. He said: 'What's happening in Antioch must not affect Jerusalem, nor should it seem even related to us in Jerusalem. For as greater and greater numbers of Gentiles join the company of believers, believing Jews are seen less and less as Jews.'

He looked at me. 'Do you agree?'

I didn't answer. Pity for his own loss nearly forced me to utter sounds of agreement. But my growing sense of isolation among these men, and a mistrust of my tongue, overcame pity.

'We should be known as Jews, shouldn't we?' John said, still looking at me, 'Not because my brother would not have died – though purely as a Jew he would not have died – but because that is what we are. Isn't that right, James?'

Simon, desperate at my silence, spoke for me: 'Of course! Of course, it's right. We *are* of Israel with a message *for* Israel.'

John turned his eyes toward Simon.

'Then we also ought to stand with our people – especially now, when they are everywhere under threat in the empire. Especially now when the favour of the emperor is so arbitrary and unstable. Now is not a time to divide and dilute the Jewish identity,' John said, 'but rather to unify and strengthen it.

'James,' he said, turning his eyes to me, ever and ever to me, 'you are right. The covenant Law has saved us alive for ages and ages, and the covenant Law must do so still today. Then let us purify covenant Law and make firm our Jewish adherence. By the same token, now is *not* the time to blur the Jewish face before the world.'

He paused. He returned his gaze to the lamp flame, again breathing, gathering his thoughts. John has enormous eyes. His manner is ruminative. If you interrupt his talk, you lose his talk. He falls silent. While his brother was alive, John was mostly silent.

Now, in a voice barely audible, he began to ask a series of questions: 'What happened to Israel in Alexandria ten years ago?'

Barnabas said softly, 'Pogrom.'

Simon said, 'Synagogues burned to the ground. Mothers and their children murdered. Fathers and husbands. It was more than a pogrom, Barnabas. It was a massacre. And the survivors were packed like cattle into ghettos.'

John's eyes glistened. The lamp flame showed in his tears. John of mortal sympathies.

'And what then?' he asked of the fire. 'Eight years ago the emperor wanted to put a statue of himself in the Holy of Holies of the Temple! The abomination of desolation was coming again. Saul, perhaps you heard the howls of Jews in those days. For six months we trembled in anguish here, praying, planning for war, committing our bodies to the death when that statue should actually come. The emperor changed his mind and changed it back, and we were saved from horrors only by his assassination. That was Caligula. Now we've got Claudius. And the whims of this one are no better than the whims of that. Jews,' John said, raising his gaze, 'must seem to be, and Jews must *be*, a visible blood unity everywhere in the purview of this present Emperor Claudius.

'Saul,' he said. 'Barnabas,' he said, 'do you know what happened this year, here, at the Passover?'

Barnabas, gazing at his own hands now, said, 'We heard that people died under the feet of other people, running.'

'Yes,' John said. 'Did you hear a figure? Do you know how many people died?'

'No,' said Barnabas.

John said, 'Peter does. How many died here, Peter?'

Simon responded to this catechesis also in a lowly voice and in a complete sentence. 'Twenty thousand pilgrims died.'

'Do you know why?' John asked. 'Do you know what created such a terrible stampede of humanity that twenty thousand people should perish at the Feast of the Passover?'

'No,' said Simon.

'James does.' John closed his mouth a moment. The trembling wet fire in his eyes had caused the water to rise in mine.

John said, 'James, why don't you tell them what caused the stampede? Show them the reason for Jewish solidarity in this Roman world.'

I said, 'The governor had stationed a regiment in the Temple courts to forestall rioting at the feast. It's not an unusual precaution. But this year one soldier, a pagan, uncircumcised, dropped his breeches and exposed himself.' I paused and sighed. 'The pilgrims were stunned at the blasphemy. They cried out with such rage that the governor thought a riot had begun. So he ordered the entire army to swarm the Temple mount. Our people fled in terror. And in the narrow streets of Jerusalem, Jews trampled Jews to death. The circumcised trampled the circumcised to death, while the uncircumcised laughed us to scorn.'

John's eyes were lost in flame again. He breathed quietly, then he said, 'And now comes the news from Rome that Claudius is closing synagogues. Roman religion is renewed. Rome detests the 'superstition' of the Jews. And the emperor, I hear, is threatening to expel the Jews – because of conflict among our people. Because of antagonisms made shamefully public. Antagonisms, so I hear, over Jesus. Lord help us, we are *inviting* the ire of the earthly powers.'

John said: 'It doesn't matter to Claudius whether some follow Jesus and others do not. Before Rome, Jews are Jews.'

Again, he turned his face to me. The rim of his cheek and jaw glowed orange from the single lamp flame. His eye receded into shadow.

He said, 'But Rome perceives a difference between Gentiles and Jews, and a Gentile is a Gentile whether he is circumcised or not. In the eyes of God, there is surely a distinction. Surely, James. But not in the eyes of Claudius. For the sake of the nation and of the faith, he must not see Jews fighting Jews over Jesus. On the other hand, neither must he lose sight of Israel among all the peoples, or we will lose place and privilege in the Empire. But I believe that the more Gentiles he sees inmixed with Israel, the less will he see Israel at all. James,' John said: 'Don't you agree?'

I nodded.

With a genuine mercy for me and with affection (which is most destructive of my reserve and my self-control), John placed his hand beside mine on the table and continued: 'Then you know, don't you? For our sake, for the sake of believers, and for the sake of Jews everywhere, we must let Gentiles both seem to be and *be* Gentiles – exactly as Saul has requested. Now is the time to refine our name, our nation, and our face in the world, not to undefine it. There is but one God and one Lord and one Jesus and one Messiah for us all. That is the union all believers have together, whether Jew *or* Gentile. Nonetheless, before a world that does not know the Spirit of the Lord, we faithful will appear divided. We can't change that. But we can turn it to our benefit.

'Saul, my brother,' John said, straightening his neck with a formality of his own. He had arrived at his thesis. 'Yes: Go forth with your gospel to the Gentiles,' he said. 'Go freely, unhindered and unrestrained. Establish churches separate from the synagogues. Likewise, we will keep preaching Jesus in the synagogues to the Jews.

'James, my brother,' he said to me, 'when the crisis and the collapsings come – and how can they not come in this world? – the divisions of the flesh would divide our people altogether. Jews would not trust Gentiles, even the circumcised Gentile, to sacrifice their lives for the Temple and for the Law. Suspicions and internal enmities would aid our enemies and defeat the chosen people – '

John stopped. He had run out of words. He touched the back of my hand without looking at me, then took his own hand back again. No one spoke. Barnabas had put his head down, laying his brow in the bend of his elbow. Saul was tapping the index finger of his right hand against his temple. I could not read the man's expression, though he must have recognized the effect of John's logic: the way was clear before him now. I would not dispute this final appeal, for I loved the Temple with all my heart, and I loved my people, the Jews.

I rose from the table and walked out to the tiny kitchen where Simon's wife was sitting alone in the dark, her hand upon her mouth, the cheeses uneaten beside her.

'Miriam,' I said, 'please bring us some wine. We're nearly done.'

She said, 'Is it well with us?'

I paused and said, 'It will be well,' then returned to the dining room.

No one had moved. I don't think anyone had spoken in my absence.

I approached Saul and Barnabas from behind, extending my hands to both of them. Saul rose and clasped my right hand in his right hand, smiling. Barnabas, gently for a big man, reached and took the fingers of my left hand in his right.

I said, 'It is done. Tomorrow we will speak to the whole assembly and assure them that, as Simon was given good news for the Jews, so you have been given good news for the Gentiles.'

I hesitated, not yet releasing Saul's hand. What was I not saying? What would I lose, losing this propitious moment in which to say it? Events had gathered speed today. I do not think quickly. My thought is circumspect and laborious. What might I regret tomorrow, not having said it today? Well, John's description of the trampling death of so many unfortunates rose to mind.

'Doubtless,' I said, 'there is wealth among the Gentiles. Would Antioch therefore remember the poor in Jerusalem? Would the churches in Antioch raise money for the survival of the saints in Jerusalem, and send it here to us?'

Verily, the man beamed with gladness. 'Oh, yes,' he said, and he kissed my cheek with a moist lip and a scratching chin. He had gladness. One ought not become too glad. It wasn't a victory. It shouldn't be seen as victory.

Barnabas remained sitting.

Simon's wife arrived with a nicely mulled wine. As she leaned forward to fill the cup of her husband, she breathed the question, 'Simon, what have we done?'

$\mathcal{R}$hoda

28

Abba Barnabas, you sang me my song again! After all these years you remembered my lullaby, and you sang it, and you made me feel so good again. I have never stopped missing you.

You found me crying, and I was surprised. I didn't know anyone was looking. Abba, you have a tender way! And such a kind voice in my ear.

'Rose, Rose,' you sang, just like when I was five:

Rose, Rose,
Do you suppose
I do not love
Your crooked nose?

I do, I do
Love all of you
From grin to gloom,
And head to shoe.

It's such a simple song. But it goes straight to my heart. You remember, don't you, how I would cry, frightened of the night. I was always so scared, but you would come to my pallet and kneel down beside me and rest your hand on my forehead and sing:

Rhoda Rose,
Your eyelids close
That I might kiss
The two of those.

And you did! Your big beard tickled all my face, and you kissed my eyes, and then, O Abba, how lovely you sang:

Sleep, sleep,
And do not weep,
The night is long,
The dark is deep,

But in my arm
I hold my rose
Safe from harm,
Until she grows
Too old, too old
And comes to know
What every Father knows.

I'm not too old yet, am I? I don't think I'm ready to bear the
knowledge of the fathers. Maybe I don't want to know.

Abba, you used to toss me so high in the sky that I would
hiccup for happiness. You made mushrooms in my tummy. You
made me fly. And when you caught me again, you laughed and
laughed like the thunder above me.

Why don't you laugh so much any more?

Titus

29

What a kick! What an honour! What a company, me and all the others walking home in a crowd, much slower than how we first raced down to Jerusalem, because then it was just the three of us, and Paul was grim about things, but now it's nine, and two of that is women, and they're in no rush, I can promise you that. But I mean, what a *company*! I look around through the rain of the day, and who do I see walking just in front of me? This is wonderful: it's Peter of the giant reputation, walking side-by-side with Paul, and you know by the looseness of their bones that they are happy, and I can't tell you how happy that makes *me* feel. I'm grinning. My cheeks ache. That I should be included, too! So Paul says something quick and fast, then Peter rears back and slaps him on the back, making the water fly, and I think he's going to knock little Paul forward on his face, but he's as quick with his feet as he is with his tongue. He skitters ahead, and soon he's ducking the swings of the big apostle. And that's the mood of almost everyone. We chatter and laugh together. Peter's wife is strolling behind me with another woman, and there's Philip, talking with John Mark. Philip's going partway back with us, as far as Caesarea on the Sea, but Peter and Miriam and John Mark and this other woman are going all the way to Antioch. Jesus, I want to sing! I want to shout praises to you right here on the road. When I saw Paul's face after that long meeting, that private meeting they had without us; when Paul came into my little sleeping room and woke me up with a candle flame and I saw his face – O Jesus, it was like sunrise in the middle of the night! He grabbed my hands and pulled me up and kissed me and said that I was his son! He said that I was his child and his brother, exactly the way that I was. He called me a saint, and he did a little dance with me. He capered barefoot on my pallet, singing, though he's got no voice for it. O Jesus, he picked up my heart and threw it to high heaven. And I flew. Because I am included, too.

So now I see Barnabas walking pretty much alone at the back of the group. So I stand still in the rain and let him catch up, and then I fall in step with him and give him a punch on the shoulder. 'What do you say?' I say, smiling. 'What do you think about it all?' I say. I can't help smiling. And he says, 'Well, it's a change, that's for sure.' And I say, 'For sure.' And then the words flow out of me. I feel so glad to be walking by him, that I pour out the major thought on my mind. I say, 'Barnabas, I'm going to give a feast.' And he cocks his head sideways and looks down on me, and I say, 'No, I really want to give a feast. Of thanksgiving. At my own house, my own food, my own money. Don't you think it's time?' But I don't wait to hear his answer. What can he say but *Yes*? I just chatter away, saying, 'I'm going to take my turn and invite the church to my place. Oh, Barnabas! I'm going to borrow embroidered cushions and good dishes and some wonderful silverware, and we'll have three courses! We'll start with salads and mushrooms and eggs. And we'll have meat better than goat's meat. Maybe mutton. Maybe some sausages of spice and quality. My father always says that a banquet of any importance wants sausages to prove itself. But I'll tell you what,' I said, punching his shoulder again – and this time I saw a grin hiding in his bush of a beard, so I slapped my thigh and went on with gusto: 'I'll tell you what! There's a dish rich Romans serve, a dish my father told me about called "The Shield of Minerva". It's the most expensive salad, greens and onions and artichokes, but then you add the livers of charfish and the brains of pheasants and the brains of peacocks and the tongues of flamingoes and the entrails of lampreys! Ha, ha! What do you think of that?'

And so here's the thing: I got Barnabas to laugh. We're walking along as wet as fish, and our friends are wet before us, laughing together. What a day! What a happy day!

So I say, 'Barnabas, what do you think? Will you come to my house for dinner?'

And he puts his big hand on my shoulder and squeezes it. 'Yes,' he says. 'Yes.'

$\mathcal{B}$arnabas

30

It wasn't a week after we'd been back when the word spread through Antioch and the whole region around that *Saul and Barnabas are preaching in Singon Street, by the Pantheon*.

Not altogether true. Half true.

Saul was preaching. I was there. But mostly, I attended him.

The crowds swelled day by day into multitudes. To hear him preach people travelled from Daphne, from Seleucia, even from as far as Aleppo. And why not? The various peoples of Antioch love a good speech. Your stolid Roman approves confidence. He wants a bold thesis backed up by rows of proofs as stubborn as stone. Greeks appreciate wit and a cunning tongue, words like foxes that can double back on themselves and surprise you by coming and going at once. If a speechifier argues one thing today and its opposite tomorrow, Greeks call that a triumph. Romans call it a lie. Now, your Syrian wants passion, a howling like wind in the wilderness. Egypt loves the low voice and the eye rolled back, the mystery of one who steals between the worlds invisible and visible.

Saul was all of these. Bold and cunning and boisterous and breathless with sacred vision – all of these, with never a previous plan to his speech. He just got up and opened his mouth and preached.

There's an elaborate fountain edifice on the northwest side of Singon Street, an open porch surrounding the pool on three sides, two levels of columns, pediments above, statues in the niches. The floor behind the pool is raised. That's where Saul took his stand to preach. The stonework cast his high voice starkly into the street.

One hour after sunrise, when servant girls had finished their gossip and borne the water pots away on their heads, Saul would come down the street bursting with energy and goodwill, seven or eight believers trooping with him. I, of course, would have arrived earlier in the midst of the gabbling water-maids, because Saul always wanted me to stand in his spot as a sort of notice to folks he was coming.

Saul and Barnabas are preaching in Singon Street, by the Pantheon.

I would preach before he arrived. And again when he left. And even while he was speaking I'd move among the people and watch for those who wanted the more personal and private word. I never blamed the arrangement. I'm a Levite. I'm a singer of songs. I'm a consoler, a comforter unencumbered by talent. What I did is what I do best. And Saul? Why he was Greek and Roman, Egyptian, Syrian, Jew; he was slave and free; unmarried, yet married to everyone; male and female, child and ancient; the drum, the trumpet, and the shepherd's pipe; a voice all full of force and conviction: a voice! Saul was a cosmic voice.

It was right that he should preach while I served the word that came from his mouth.

And I would have continued in that role gratefully, for ever.

But less than a month after our return from Jerusalem, the partnership was shattered, and Saul had left Antioch in a fury.

31

In those days Titus lived with his father. His mother had died during the terrible earthquake eleven years earlier, when the boy was only seven. His father had retired from the armies of Rome and was well off, though not rich. It was on the tide of his son's enthusiasms that the old man first came to us. He worshipped with us still. But he was a taciturn, reclusive man, grim, though uncomplaining. While she lived, he had been the opposite of his wife. Now he was the opposite of his son.

At an age when other Roman youths removed the *bulla* from round their necks, young Titus was sinking naked in the Orontes, in the wash-water of baptism; young Titus was exploding from the river with such a whoop I laughed out loud. An athlete! A tough, muscled body and a blunt mouth and a bright loyalty – happy in all the world was he. I liked him. I like Titus a lot. Even in the days of my confusion he could trick smiles out of me; and then he'd grin in victory and poke my ribs and slap my shoulder and cause me to laugh again in spite of myself. Titus was as innocent and as delightful as the tumbling bear cub. And perhaps as oblivious.

So when he asked me about the foods he should prepare for his 'Banquet of Thanksgiving', as he called it, I took pleasure in answering. Here was a simple subject, good for me.

Breads: Titus wanted the lightest, whitest bread, wheat from Egypt. He wanted 'the sweet *Siligineus*', he said. 'So which bakery is the best for me? Where should I go to buy it?' He wanted pastries baked with honey and filled with chopped fruits.

Meats: he had a notion to offer a mix of animal fleshes, poultry, hares, venison – 'No goat meat!' – partridges, thrushes – 'I wish I could get a mullet' – sausages, bacon, and beef. Beef, he said, because the occasion was so important, and we never could afford it. 'So which butcher shop is the best for me?' he said. The beasts should be slaughtered no earlier than the day before the banquet. The morning of was best, of course. But I didn't know the butcher shops in town. Not in the general market. I knew only the few Jewish shops under restrictions of purity, where the blood was drained completely, nothing killed by a twist of the neck, nothing sacrificed to some pagan god – even by the burning of a few hairs on a simple altar in a back room – and where only certain creatures were considered clean. Titus had to ask his father where *he* bought meat, and his father said, 'Lanius's, by the Aleppo Gate.' Done.

Well, and the young man planned to carve melons into buckets and fill them with cherries and peaches, with the jelly of quinces, with walnuts and filberts and almonds and poppy seeds and 'exactly seven seeds of anise' – his own variation.

'What a kick!' he kept saying. 'What a kick!'

Oh, he was giddy with planning: how the tables would be arranged, how many could come, where he would seat them, side by whose side, when to begin, how long to make it last. Simon Peter said he'd come with Miriam. Simeon Niger and Rufus and Alexander and the woman of the household all said yes. Saul, of course. Lucius of Cyrene, Timon, Gaius, a little Roman named Quintus...

'Barnabas, what do you think?' he said to me over and over, grinning: 'Will you come to my house for dinner?'

And I said, 'Yes.'

And he cuffed my shoulder for pure pleasure.

But then there was read among us the letter from James and the church in Jerusalem.

The letter. It had been brought to Antioch by Judas Barsabbas. A member of our church, Silas, accompanied him north.

But who knew they were even in the city?

In his own time, at his own choosing, Barsabbas popped up and reintroduced himself to members of the church by saying that he had come north with us, with Saul and me. Perhaps he really thought so, since he and Silas arrived soon after we did; and perhaps he *needed* to say so, since our names might make him more welcome to people he'd bullied the last time he was here. But before he made his presence known to us, he spent several weeks with Jews of the synagogues. And later I learned that he had gone to talk with Peter in private.

My own first hint of the trouble to come was finding Silas in Antioch. I noticed his face in the multitude. On the fourteenth morning of our return, I saw Silas near the fountain on Singon Street. I swam through the press of people and embraced him. 'Silas, you're back. I didn't know you were back,' I said.

'Yes, yes, I am,' he said, 'and with a mission.'

I drew him apart, to a portico on the far side of the street, but he kept gazing backward, shaking his head.

'What's happened to him?' Silas said. 'Look at these crowds!'

I smiled and shrugged. 'He's happy. No, he's jubilant. His heart is in his mouth. What mission, Silas?'

Silas has a slow momentum about him. He can't turn a corner quickly, whether walking or talking. Still watching Saul, he said, 'I've heard him preach for years, but this! His words are like... like grappling hooks. Barnabas, he takes my breath away.'

I, too, paused to listen and to gauge the change in Saul. He had begun to preach with something more than confidence, more than boldness. He was preaching headlong, with a kind of hilarity. It was as if someone had snapped the traces on a high-strung, explosive colt.

'Listen,' I said. 'Do you hear that? Do you hear the watery sound the crowd is making? It's giggles, Silas!' People smiled when they listened to Saul these days, and the multitudes *giggled* like skies full of sparrows.

And then I said, 'What mission, Silas?'

He looked at me and blinked and said, 'After you left Jerusalem, the counsel kept talking about matters in Antioch. I think they thought they had acted without consideration for all the consequences. So they've come to some conclusions. And they've written a letter with three or four instructions for the sake of peace in the whole church. James, you know – he chose the language. See, and they sent the letter by way of me and Judas Barsabbas. We should pay attention.'

Then Silas, very serious, asked me to help gather our people in one place, that the letter might be presented with explanations to everyone at once.

On the first day of the week, then, the congregation came together in Simeon Niger's house. I didn't see Saul. All through the meal I wondered whether Saul had decided to stay away.

After dinner we sang hymns and some prayed prayers, though no one prophesied that day. Nobody rose to speak in tongues.

At the time appointed for preachers to preach or teachers to teach, Judas Barsabbas himself went forward and took the seat in the centre of Simeon's atrium. He drew a slim roll from the folds of his robe and opened it high before his face: a single sheet of paper. Moist, nearsighted eyes; grey Barsabbas, his eyebrows arched in an ambassador's formality, his beard a miserable wisp of tow: He read his letter as cool as pewter.

From the brothers, both apostles and elders, in Jerusalem, to the brothers who are of the Gentiles in Antioch and Syria and Cilicia:
Greetings!
Since we have heard that some persons from among us here have troubled you with words, unsettling your minds, though we gave them no such instructions, it has seemed good to us, having come to one accord, to choose men and send them to you and our beloved Barnabas and Paul, men who have risked their lives for the sake of our Lord Jesus Christ. We have therefore sent Judas and Silas, who themselves will tell you the same things by word of mouth.
For it has seemed good to the Holy Spirit and to us to lay upon you no greater burden than these necessary things:
– that you abstain from what has been sacrificed to idols,
– that you abstain from blood,
– that you abstain from what is strangled,
– and that you abstain from unchastity.
If you keep yourselves from these, you will do well.
Farewell.

Judas Barsabbas rolled the paper slowly and tightly in two fists. Then he smiled and began to school us in these new proscriptions.

'It is James's intent,' he said, then paused for a humble tilt of his head, 'and ours as well, of course, that you Gentiles who have turned to God should not now nor ever in the future be troubled by us, by our ways and our fixed traditions. If you had been with me in Jerusalem several weeks ago, you would agree that brother Saul argued on your behalf with a wondrous rhetorical fervour, yes, yes. Indeed, he argued with such skill that Jerusalem was persuaded to release you from the mores of Judaism. You need not, on your own account, observe the feasts and the Law.

'On the other hand, though your church is mostly composed of Gentiles, there are Jews among you still. See? – there sits Joseph Barnabas and, beside him, his cousin John Mark. Near me here is one of the pillars of the temple of our Lord Jesus Christ, Simon Peter, the Lord's good rock. I see Manaen in the corner, a man who grew up in the courts of Herod. Yes, yes, I believe that fully a fourth of your congregation is Jewish. For their sakes we beg your indulgence: that neither should *they* be troubled by *you*.

'It is, we believe, a fair exchange.

'For the Law forbids that they consume an unclean thing. If you, Gentiles, serve what is unclean, then either you endanger the fellowship, should they refuse to eat, or else you endanger them, their souls, and their salvation. You endanger us as well, the faithful in Jerusalem, who can only suffer the loss of brothers and sisters beloved to us.

'Surely, love for those who brought you the love of Jesus will constrain you to honour these small requests from Jerusalem, to obey a few minor abstentions from pollutions of idols and unchastity and blood. Surely, no one would begrudge – '

Someone screamed, '*Anathema esto!*' Suddenly, in the greater house, a voice screamed: '*Anathema esto*! Damn your letter!'

Barsabbas stopped, his mouth open, staring.

Where he was staring, Saul appeared, limping stiffly toward the atrium.

'Reversals!' Saul cried. He was choking. The language was strangled in his throat.

He halted at the rail of the atrium, glaring at Barsabbas with eyes fire-red. All at once he leaped it, crying, 'Laws! Laws laid on the Gentiles!'

Barsabbas threw up his arms.

But Saul froze directly over the grey man. He lingered there a moment – a strange, dead inarticulate snarling in his mouth. His face was linen white, all his scars, orange and tough. His limbs shook violently. *Arrr! Arrr!* he snarled. Speech seemed impossible. His mouth kept working, but he couldn't put shape to the animal growling.

All at once, with a howl, poor Saul rushed toward the door and the darkness outside, leaving Judas Barsabbas trembling, though this ambassador's eyebrows were arched and his eyelids adroop, the picture of civil restraint.

I lowered my head and covered my face, my guts twisting within me. *Saul, Saul! Why must you drive us to such extremes?*

In my miserable darkness, I heard people approaching Barsabbas, consoling him, apologizing for the outburst, praising his kindness. Quickly their praises extended also to James and his efforts to make *them* kind. They honoured the messenger, begging Barsabbas to speak again. Clearly, the weight of persuasion was with him now, and he spoke. I raised my face and paid attention. He did not accuse Saul. He didn't even mention Saul or the embarrassment just enacted. Instead, with many words, he built up the church in Antioch. He strengthened the people, and they felt strong, and they rejoiced in his exhortation.

Finally, Simon Peter himself agreed. 'James and Jerusalem are right,' he said. 'Between love and pride, pick love.'

32

On the second day of that week, at about three in the afternoon, I walked alone to the house where Titus and his father lived.

The streets of Antioch are not like those in Jerusalem, winding and blinded. Here the streets are straight and wide. They cross each other at right angles, making squares of the blocks between. And the main street is paved in new marble. The surface sparkles under sunlight.

It was, in fact, a sweet springtime afternoon. The rains were past. The sky was kindly, clean and blue. The barley fields outside the city were whitening toward the harvest. The shipping lanes on the great sea had opened, so the streets inside the city were crowded with western merchants and fresh goods, and all the markets were buzzing like hives.

There was no need to carry a gift for Titus and his celebration. I did anyway. Tucked in a leather envelope I had a small silver pendant and an interlocking chain, so that Titus could wear the pendant at his breast, if he wished. I had purchased the chain. It was of a Greekish design. But I'd spent the previous night tooling the pendant myself. It's what I do, though not very well. I understand metals.

Even at a distance I could see that the outer door of his father's house stood open. Not wide, but not closed, either; neither locked nor attended by a servant. Open. I went through without a knock and closed it behind me. No one waited in the courtyard. No noises warmed the interior air.

'Titus?' I called his name softly, uncertainly. 'Titus? Are you here?'

I stepped through the doorway into the house. The entrance hall was dark, but I saw a figure in the far door, standing still.

'Titus, is that you?'

My eyes adjusted. I moved forward. It was young Titus, fighting tears.

'Barnabas?' he said. 'Come and see.'

He led me through a small passage into his dining room. The tables were polished. New pillows were on every couch. Flowers had been scattered everywhere.

One other human was here: Saul, pacing along the back wall like a leopard in a cage. Except for Saul, the room was empty.

Titus was searching my eyes with a childlike appeal. 'Barnabas,' he whispered, scarcely sounding the question: 'Where are they? Why haven't they come?'

Saul stopped pacing. The little man glared at me.

Helplessly I opened the leather envelope and drew out the pendant and chain. 'This is for you,' I said.

Titus wore a robe dazzling white. It had been to the fuller's. The nap was brushed and very soft. His hair had been oiled. The room smelled fresh and good.

He took my gift, the leather in his left hand, the pendant in his right. But I don't think he knew what he was doing.

I said, 'The chain is Greek. I didn't – '

Then Saul exploded. 'Answer the boy!' he yelled. 'Tell me too! Utter their hypocrisy out loud! Why *haven't* the guests arrived?'

'Oh,' I said. 'Well, I don't really know,' I said, now burning with a wretched news. I knew, I knew, but I whispered, 'Maybe they decided not to come.'

'Why?' Saul thundered.

Titus dropped his eyes. Saul's voice caused him to flinch.

'Don't be angry with me,' I said to Saul. 'I came.'

Saul was vibrating with anger. '*Why*, Barnabas?'

Titus received that *Why* like a blow. Tears spilled down his cheeks.

Gazing at him with a terrible pity, I whispered, 'Maybe they're waiting till he serves food which is clean, not… unclean.'

'And whose side are *you* on, Barnabas?'

'What? There are sides? Saul, there don't have to be sides!'

'Come with me,' the little man commanded. He was already in motion, springing forward on bandy legs. He grabbed Titus's wrist, snapped, 'Come with me,' then yanked the poor young man out of the room, out of the house, through the courtyard, into the street.

I followed, filled with dread.

Titus looked enslaved in Saul's hawkish grip. He kept pace because his body was able, not because his mind was willing.

After three turns on three different streets I knew where Saul was going. Everything in me hated this day. Sunlight was a mockery, and the blue sky was as false as paint.

Saul, why must you drive us to such extremes?

He may have been right. He may have been righteous. But rightness in him was a sunstroke on me.

Saul pounded on the door of the house where Simon Peter was staying. He did not stop pounding until it opened, revealing John Mark, then he drove straight in, Titus in tow.

John Mark stepped aside, looking at me. I shrugged and followed still.

Inside were Peter and Miriam and Judas Barsabbas and Manaen and Simeon Niger with his wife and two sons – in short, all the Jews whom Titus had invited and who had chosen not to come. They had gathered here instead.

Poor Titus kept his face bent down to the ground.

Saul's body was erect, his huge head was straight up, his red lips stretched with emotion.

'Who will apologize to the lad here?' he demanded. 'Is anyone ashamed in this place?'

Peter rose to his feet. He said, 'Titus, we love you – '

Saul interrupted with force: 'But suddenly you will not eat with him? You've eaten with him often enough before. What's changed? What breaks you? James writes a letter, and straightway Simon bows and becomes a hypocrite!'

Peter said, 'Strong language, Saul. These are simply matters of decency and fellowship – '

Saul cut through Peter's words like a saw: *'For freedom Christ has set us free!'* he cried.

Peter said, 'Then let Titus use his freedom to avoid offending the Jews. Let him *choose* to serve the clean foods only.'

Paul stepped to Peter, thrusting his face forward. 'If you, a Jew,' he cried, 'have lived like a Gentile, how can you now compel a Gentile to live like a Jew?'

'I learn. I'm enlightened,' Peter said. 'I'm willing to listen to faithful people. Let Titus do the same.'

'Not at your command!' Saul yelled. 'If you or Barsabbas or faithful James command it, it can't be freedom. It's obedience!'

Peter thundered back: 'Jesus, not me! *Jesus* commands our love for God and our love for the other.'

Saul's voice suddenly dropped. It coiled itself and came forth as tight and silent as a serpent. 'I am persuaded,' he said, raking everyone with his red-rimmed, glittering eyes, 'I am persuaded that in Jesus nothing is of itself unclean. It's unclean only for those who *think* it is unclean. You Jews are making your bound minds superior to the freedoms that Jesus gives us all. You're demanding Gentiles to live under the rule of your weakness. And now I know, and hereafter I will preach it wherever I go, that all who rely on the works of the Law are under a curse. Under a *curse*, Simon. For this is what the Law does best: it reveals the sin in us, the weakness in us, like the weakness I find in you right now. And it drives us to the promises and the righteousness we have in Christ Jesus, our Lord!'

Peter did not respond to that. No one did. The entire room had been struck dumb.

Even I myself, standing far back behind my old companion and partner apostle, felt a sort of horror at his words. For only a month ago, Torah was merely meaningless for Saul. He and I, we had said the same. Hadn't we all in Antioch said the same together? Yes, with laughter and with jubilation: *In Christ*, we repeated the refrain, *neither circumcision nor uncircumcision count for anything, but faith working through love.*

Now, though – now Saul had said another thing altogether. A new thing. A frightening thing. Not that Torah counted for nothing, but that Torah carried a curse.

How could anyone respond to such an enormity?

No, no, no, no, but he would not leave me the choice of a simple silence.

Saul read the room as a man reads the weather. I believe he recognized immediately the consequence of his proclamation. He had shut himself outside the body of believers here in this place.

The little man lifted his chin. He squared himself into a stance of a doorpost for wilfulness. I saw in his face the same expression I'd seen when he pulled himself from death, when he rose from the ditch outside of Lystra and walked back to town still bleeding at his brow.

Saul turned and looked at me.

'Barnabas,' he said softly, 'are you with me?'

It was then that my silence became my statement after all.

'Barnabas?' Saul repeated.

I lowered my eyes. I bowed my head. Only by tremendous effort did I stay standing. Oh, I wanted to crumple down and cry.

Still in his softer, more thoughtful voice, Saul said, 'Titus, what is the good of the gift of a stranger?'

In a moment I felt the fingers of the young man upon my

wrist. He lifted my left hand and filled it with crushed, sweaty leather. Into my right he dropped a warm chain and a thin silver pendant. Together, then, they departed. Just the two of them. I did not follow. I could not follow. I heard the door at the far end of the courtyard first open and then thump shut. I heard footsteps leave us. Someone dropped the bar into its metal brackets. It was that sound and that gesture – the locking of the outer door – that caused me to sink to my knees in sorrow.

33

Simon Peter remained in Antioch after Saul's departure. No one preached on Singon Street anymore. Instead, Peter began to preach in a large cavern under the rocky escarpment of Mount Staurin on the east side of the city.

He would stand at the back wall. People would fill the space inside even to its mouth. The cave was thirty feet wide, forty feet deep – and almost as high as it was wide. Peter's voice required the echoing stone. Too thick and soft, otherwise. You could hear the sound, but you couldn't understand the words without the rounded wall to magnify them.

There was a small spring inside that cavern. The water pooled in a stony depression where we baptized the Gentiles who believed in Jesus. In the months and the years that followed, the congregation in Antioch enjoyed a sense of concord. Of harmony. It grew in numbers. And Jerusalem was happy.

Regarding Saul, people said, 'Let him go. Our people and our synagogues are everywhere in the empire. How much can one man do in the face of an entire people?'

For my own part, I was too sad to stay. I had to leave Antioch for a while.

I went to John Mark and laid my problem before him.

I said, 'I wish the Lord would come back soon. Tomorrow. Today.'

I said, 'John, I feel like a sojourner here. I have no home except with Jesus.'

I said, 'Would you travel with me?'

I paused and gave thought to the implications.

I said, 'Don't let Saul worry you, John. He's angry at you, so he leaves with Silas. Well, he's angry at me too. He rejects me and takes a Roman citizen like himself. He's angry at everyone, John. At Peter. At Antioch. Jerusalem.'

I sighed.

'Travel with me, John. Let's go out preaching together, cousins and partners.'

And so it was that we set sail for Cyprus. The island where I was born. The first place Saul and I had stopped on our journey so long ago.

Part Three

CORINTH

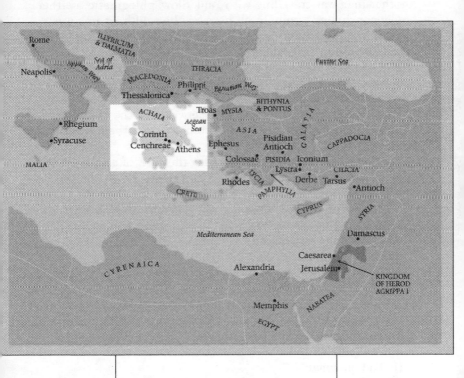

Timothy

34

In the nineteenth year of my age, the apostle Paul returned to Lystra once again, entered our house as if he had never left, and stayed with us a week. The jovial Barnabas hadn't come with him. I missed the grand fellow, his big laugh and his bigger beard. Another man was travelling with Paul. Slow, phlegmatic, neither kindly nor unkind, stolid in all his ways, he said his name was Silas. But Paul insisted on calling him Silvanus – the name they would not use in Jerusalem.

Paul told us that as soon as the winter snows had melted they had come through the Cilician Gates – the high, craggy pass over the Taurus Mountains north of Tarsus, north of Paul's hometown. He told us that they were making brief visits to the churches he had established two years ago, strengthening them by his preaching.

'How's your Hebrew?' he asked with the flick of a smile at his lips. He had taken my hand in his long fingers. He sat on the bench beside me. 'How's your Hebrew?'

'I can read it,' I said. 'I read to my mother every evening. She's learning the words too.'

'Can you write Greek?'

'I can. I always could. And Latin too.'

'Could you talk with the Romans in Rome?'

'Yes.'

'Timothy,' Paul said, the smile gone, his eyes locked on mine, his face thrust forward with a sort of urgency, that narrow blade of a nose foremost: 'What if you came with me? What if you came and travelled with me now?'

He had changed.

When first he came through Lystra, he used to react to the actions around him, quick as a sparrow, ready, learning, his expression swift to reflect the thing he'd seen, his words a rush of response.

Now Paul made his own path forward, straight as a sailing ship, expecting the world to react to *him*. Now the expression on his face arose from sources inside himself, and his words were meant – like the words of the Creator – to cause new things to be, to produce events, to invoke. So he presented his question like a gangplank by which to board his sailing ship: *What if you came with me?*

The scars from the stoning the Lystrans had given him were thick and pink at the hairline, a sort of raised astonishment. His clothing was poorer, rough unwhitened wool. And he carried two leather sacks when he travelled, one for food and clothes and pens and paper and personal goods, the other for the needles and knives and material of his trade. I had not known before that he worked in canvas and leather.

He said, 'I need an amanuensis.'

I said, 'Where would we go?'

'I am beholden to no one now,' Paul said, sailing his own waters. 'No people. No congregation. No authority, not in Jerusalem, not in Antioch. Only to Christ Jesus my Lord.'

He released my hand and lifted his index finger between us, as if on the tip of it were balanced a globe, an invisible sphere and mystery. He said, 'What I preach I received from Jesus. When I was a man of violence, he called my name, and I heard, and I came, and I became a man of peace. But long before I could hear at all – even from my mother's womb – the Lord God had called me, called me to preach in the strength of the name of Jesus. And then five months ago...

'Timothy,' Paul whispered, burning me with his eyebeams, 'no more than five months ago, while I stood bareheaded under the early rains, God tore back the blinds of the future and told me to go to Jerusalem. After fourteen years away, I returned to Jerusalem and I showed the apostles the gospel that Jesus had given me for the Gentiles. The apostles added nothing to that! – why should they? It is Jesus who sends me! This hand,' Paul whispered, spreading the fingers of his right hand, 'the pillars of the church took and shook this hand in fellowship.

'Timothy, take my hand. Come with me. Go with me to the nations.'

He extended his hand toward mine again. But I didn't know!

I did not in that instant know whether I should take it or not. I flinched, and he froze mid-gesture, though his expression remained unaltered.

He lifted his left arm and pointed backward, as though it were a wing stretched out. 'Where am I going?' Paul said in a fuller voice. 'That way, Timothy. Westward. Into the world. Into the great round world that encircles the sea. And this is the plan. We will preach in the cities. In the metropolises of the empire, where the paved roads cross, where Rome empowers rulers, and commerce reaches the regions around. In every city we will call forth churches, Timothy, even as I was called and you were called. And, like us, these churches will carry the gospel into the country-sides, to the towns and the villages, the hovels and huts. Before the Lord returns they will hear of him. They will believe in him *and* in his returning. They will confess with their lips that Jesus is Lord. They will believe in their hearts that God raised him from the dead – and so they shall be saved. Everyone who calls on the name of the Lord will be saved from the wrath which is to come.

'But Timothy, my son, my dear son, how can they call on him in whom they don't believe? And how can they believe in him of whom they haven't heard? And how can they hear without a preacher? Take my hand. Take my hand. Timothy, don your sandals and walk into the world with me. *How beautiful upon the mountains are the feet of him who preaches good news.* Come, publish the news of salvation with me.'

Singular man: he did not move. He didn't blink or switch his eyes till I dropped mine. My ears – my forehead, my face, my neck – were all on fire. And there was the man's right hand between us, palm open, the slender fingers lightly crooked and waiting.

Mother, don't cry. You mustn't cry. It was your training made me know the one true God. It was your praying taught me to hear his voice. The voice of our God has called me, Mother, and I have no choice but to go. Take care of your mother, my grandmother, now. There is so little time.

Paul and Silvanus – and I in my sandals – took to the road. Quickly we learned his strategies.

We stopped a few days in Iconium.

And then again, in Pisidian Antioch.

And though Paul pointed west from there to Asia, the Holy Spirit denied us that western route.

Instead we travelled north through Phrygia: twenty miles, twenty miles, twenty miles every day, Paul assaulting the road and the distances, Silvanus arriving behind us by an hour or so. We carried staves against bears and wolves and bandits. My father had taught me the use of the short sword, which I kept under my robe in a scabbard. Paul and his tongue, and I and my blade were weapons to protect us when we slept at night. Twenty miles, twenty miles, and the inns at the end of the day were filthy, brick-and-stucco accommodations grouped around three sides of a courtyard. Public rooms for food and drink on the ground floor; the sleeping rooms built over those, their midnight floors all crammed with strangers. Paul and Silvanus and I slept in a sort of circle with our bags in the middle.

Twenty miles, twenty miles, during which Paul seemed scarcely to breathe, so intent on the journey was he. But on the very day we entered the westernmost corner of Galatia, something snapped in him. Paul groaned then pitched forward on the gravelled earth, completely unconscious. He hit hard enough to raise dust on either side of his body.

Stolid Silvanus neither paused nor spoke. He gathered the apostle in his arms and heaved him bodily over one shoulder and started trudging eastward to the town of Pessinus. I followed. The town and the region are embraced by the Sangarius River.

In the village square I approached perfect strangers. I greeted them soberly in Greek and said, 'My father is sick. Will you take us in?'

They took us in. Though we were foreigners in Galatia, they did us no wrong. They neither scorned us nor despised us. They covered Paul; they warmed him and washed him; they massaged his arms and legs; and with their own mouths several Galatian women spurted fresh water into his throat, causing him to swallow. In the same manner they fed him, chewing the food first and transferring it to him as if by kissing. His peculiar illness tried their wisdom and their mercy. For five days he lay unaware on foreign sheets. But when he woke, it was mercy and wisdom that most overwhelmed him.

Paul awoke filled with affection for those who nursed him. And the love in him soon turned into talk. As they had fed him food from their mouths, so he served them the name of Jesus – and the Spirit of Jesus nourished their hearts. They rejoiced to hear the news.

And this to me was sacred proof that in choosing to follow Paul I had chosen rightly indeed: that the Galatians received him as if he were an angel of God, as Christ Jesus himself.

Luke

35

Paul attempted next to travel north into Bithynia, but the Spirit of Jesus did not allow it. So, passing by Mysia, they went west to Troas, where I met him with medicines of my own. His eyes suffered a discharge.

While we were in Troas a vision appeared to Paul in the night. He saw a man of Macedonia standing and beseeching him with the words: *Come over to Macedonia and help us.*

After he had seen that vision, we sought immediately a way to Macedonia, convinced that God had called us to preach the gospel to them.

From Troas, then, we set sail directly for the island of Samothrace, where we spent a night. On the following day we sailed to Neapolis, and from there walked ten miles along the Roman road to Philippi, which is the leading city of the district of Macedonia and a Roman colony.

We stayed in Philippi many days.

On the Sabbath we went outside the gate and down to the riverside, where we supposed there was a place of prayer. We sat down and spoke to the women who regularly came together there.

One particular woman listened most intently to our words, Lydia from Thyatira, a merchant of purple goods who worshipped God. The Lord opened her heart to the preaching of Paul, so that she was baptized with her entire household.

She said, 'If you have judged me faithful to the Lord, please come and stay in my house.'

She prevailed upon us.

Weeks later, while walking to the place of prayer, we were met by a slave girl who had a spirit of divination, whose soothsaying had made her owners rich. She followed us, crying, 'These men are servants of the Most High God!' Day after day, louder and louder the child shouted: 'They proclaim to you the way of salvation!'

Finally, Paul became so annoyed that he turned and said to the spirit, 'I charge you in the name of Jesus Christ, come out of her!'

That very hour, the spirit came out and left her.

But when her owners discovered that the source of their riches was gone, they seized Paul and Silas and dragged them into the marketplace before the rostrum and the rulers.

'These men are Jews!' they declared to the city magistrates. 'They are disturbing our city! They advocate customs unlawful for Romans to accept or practice!'

A crowd had gathered and now lent their more violent voices to these accusations.

The magistrates, therefore, commanded that the garments be torn from Paul and Silas and that they both be beaten with rods. The command was carried out. Lictors inflicted many blows on the backs of the accused, then threw them in prison and charged the jailer to keep them under the closest custody. The jailer took them into the inner prison, where he locked their feet in the stocks.

In the darkness of the night, Paul and Silas prayed and sang hymns so loudly to God that the rest of the prisoners woke and listened to them. At midnight an earthquake hit the city, shaking the foundations of the prison and flinging open all the doors. Everyone's fetters also broke open. When the jailer was roused and found that the doors were open, he drew his sword and prepared to fall on the point of it, certain that the prisoners had escaped.

But Paul cried out with a loud voice, 'Don't harm yourself! We are all still here!'

The jailer called for lights, then rushed in. Trembling with fear he first fell down before Paul and Silas, then brought them out of the prison and said, 'Tell me, tell me, what must I do to be saved?'

They said, 'Believe in the Lord Jesus, and you will be saved, you and your household.' Immediately they spoke the word of the Lord to him. He took them that same hour of the night to his house where he washed their wounds. Then he and his household all were baptized. He set food before them, rejoicing that he believed in God.

In the morning the magistrates sent police to the jail, saying, 'Let those men go.'

But when he heard the order, Paul said to the police, 'The magistrates have beaten us *publicly*, have beaten us uncondemned, have beaten men who are in fact citizens of Rome. They threw us into prison, and now they want to cast us out *secretly*? No! Let them come here themselves and escort us into our freedom, again, publicly.'

The police reported this to the magistrates, who were terrified to learn that they had beaten Roman citizens. They rushed to the prison and apologized and took Paul and Silas out themselves and asked them to leave the city.

So they left the prison and visited Lydia. They took the time to see all the believers in Philippi, exhorting them in the faith – and only then departed.

36

Now when they had passed through Amphipolis and Apollonia, they came to Thessalonica, where there was a synagogue of the Jews.

Paul attended the synagogue as was his custom, and for three Sabbaths argued with them from the scriptures, explaining and proving that it was necessary for the Christ to suffer and to rise from the dead.

Paul said, 'This Jesus, whom I proclaim to you, is the Christ.'

Some of the Jews were persuaded. They joined Paul and Silas, as did many of the devout Greeks and not a few of the leading women.

But others became jealous. With some wicked fellows from the rabble they fomented an angry crowd and set the city in an uproar. Together they rushed to the house of Jason, where Paul and Silas had been staying. They attacked the house, but when they couldn't find Paul there, they captured Jason himself with other believers and dragged them all to the city authorities.

'These men have turned the world upside down!' they cried. 'And now they've come here, and Jason has received them. They're defying the decrees of Caesar, proclaiming that there is another king named Jesus!'

Both the mobs and the city leaders were disturbed by these accusations. Though the leaders chose only to take a security from Jason and then to let him go, the general mood was bad enough that the believers went looking for Paul and Silas in order to beg them for their own sakes to leave Thessalonica.

By night Paul and Silas obeyed, travelling toward Berea.

When they arrived in that town, they went into the Jewish synagogue.

These Jews were more noble than those in Thessalonica, for they received the word with all eagerness, examining the scriptures daily to see if these things were so.

Many of them, therefore, believed. So did many Greek women of high standing, as well as men.

But when the Jews of Thessalonica learned that the word of

God was proclaimed by Paul at Berea too, they came there themselves, stirring up and inciting the crowds.

Believers again sent Paul off on his way to the sea, but Silas and Timothy remained there. Some people conducted Paul as far south as Athens; and receiving Paul's command for Silas and Timothy to come to him as soon as possible, they departed.

While Paul was waiting for his companions in Athens, he wandered through the city growing angrier and angrier at the number of idols he saw there. He argued with anyone and everyone: Jews and devout people in the synagogue; Greeks in the marketplace; Epicurean philosophers, Stoic philosophers, the trained and the common.

Some said, 'What a babbler! What a wiseacre!'

Others said, 'I don't know, but he seems to be extolling two foreign deities; one called Jesus and the other a consort to Jesus, Anastasis.'

'But it bears investigation,' they said.

All the Athenians and the foreigners who lived there occupied themselves in nothing so much as telling and hearing new things.

So they brought Paul to the Areopagus and said, 'What is this teaching of yours? Tell us. Enlighten us.'

Paul stood up and addressed them.

'People of Athens,' he said, 'I perceive that in every way you are very religious. In fact, as I passed through the city and observed the objects of your worship, I noticed an altar with the inscription, *To a god unknown*. What you worship as unknown, I now proclaim to you.

'The God who made the world and everything in it – the Lord of heaven and earth – does not live in shrines made by human hands! Nor is he served by those same hands, as if he needed anything. He himself gives all humanity life! And breath! And every other thing! From one man he made all the nations that live on the face of the earth. He has allotted the periods and the boundaries of their habitations, that they might seek God in the hope of finding him.

'Yet God is not far from each one of us, for "In him we live and move and have our being." So have some of your poets said: "For we are indeed his offspring."'

'Since we are, then, the offspring of God, we ought not to think that the Deity is like gold or silver or stone – something shaped by the imagination of minds that are themselves created.

'God overlooked the former times of ignorance, but now he commands everyone everywhere to repent, because he has fixed a day on which he will judge the world in righteousness by a man whom he has appointed – and of this he has given assurance to all humanity by raising that man from the dead!'

As soon as the Athenians heard of a resurrection from the dead, half of them hooted and mocked. The other half said, 'Maybe we'll listen to you some other time.'

So Paul fell silent and walked away from the Areopagus.

A few came to believe: Dionysius, himself an Areopagite, and a woman named Damaris; but Paul did not linger here. Soon he left Athens and travelled to Corinth.

$\mathscr{L}$. Annaeus Seneca

37

Seneca, with Nero and Agrippina at her villa in Antium,
   To Gallio, my brother in Rome,
   This ninth year of the reign of Claudius:

Greetings!

I suppose it may be considered an advantage of my office that
I, too, am bidden to avoid the chilly filth of the Roman streets at
the chilly expirations of winter. Spring comes sooner and sweeter
seaside. And this villa can make of the strongest Stoic an
Epicurean. *Mi Galli,* dazzling white walls, temple-elegance within
and without – Agrippina's retreat is perched on the very tip of
the promontory overlooking the sea. Marvellous sunsets rouge
these walls. We who stand on its veranda are set aflame. Even our
flesh grows ethereal. And all adown these hills are the steps of
colossi, terraced gardens, and marble porticoes shaded by thick
rambling roses.

In this place on the fifteenth day of December three months
and thirteen years ago, Agrippina gave birth to my present pupil,
Rome's future emperor: Nero. It was a breach delivery. Ruinously
difficult for the mother, an omen for others. Ominous. Gallio,
this boy is capable of cruelty. I've seen him, quick as a cat, with a
cat's detachment, thump the skull of his stepbrother Britannicus,
making the poor child mute with astonishment. And for what?
Last month Emperor Claudius concluded the adoption. Nero is
now his eldest son. Nero is 'Nero' completely. But Britannicus
neglects the adopted name and calls him by his birth name,
Domitius, for which the older, without a word, cracks the skull of
the younger.

'Nero' means *strong* and *valiant.* Perhaps. Or perhaps the name
should signify strong and extravagant. Already at thirteen he will

not curb his pleasures. And though an extravagant nature might one day give extravagant gifts, it could also apply extravagant punishments. Could, as well, delight in the torments of others. If ever this young lion tastes human blood, I believe he'll never eat grain again.

Yes, yes, yes – but I console myself with this, that having taken the cat in hand while still he was a kit, I may somewhat have shaped his majority. To some degree I think I've mollified his bestial nature, giving him reason, a rational mind, to bridle, to check, and to guide him. Ah, look: I just used the word 'bestial'. I should be careful in my comparisons not to impugn the beasts. Humans act by will and deliberation. The wild beast acts by instinct. *Instinctively*, animals treat each other with a natural civility. They do not bite nor maul their fellows. Where animals obey instinct, humans can only choose to obey reason. These two, defining the difference between us, do both function as restraints on violence. Disobeying *reason*, then, or lacking it altogether, humans out-beast the beasts by tearing each other apart. It is my hope that I have led the son of my responsibility into the long, cool halls of reason after all.

Maybe.

He's intelligent, Gallio. He's also oversensitive and spoiled by the purple flattery that greets him wherever he goes. Though shortish and thickish, faith in that flattery has given him the posture of an aristocrat. Already at thirteen this boy commands attention. He cannot be wholly unaware of that. His hair is richly, naturally curled and deeply burnished. His eyebrows are heavily arched. His nose is noble. But his manner muddies the aspect: he seldom smiles. His mouth tends rather toward a pout, and it is chiefly disdain that I find in his face. Strains of music and plain paintings can send my tender Nero into ecstasies, to be sure. And there are those who extol such emotions as evidence of a sympathetic nature. But I find them excessive. They reveal his soul's extravagance, and they trouble me, for these are not the signs of reason.

Nero Claudius Drusus Germanicus! Even while I am writing you now, I can see him sitting in sunlight above the sea, a flat and flashing object in the palm of his right hand. He is gazing long and longingly at a newly minted coin – a golden coin imprinted with the images of Claudius and his mother. Agrippina, the queen of the world! What does her son think, holding her in his hand? Agrippina, a woman of the highest designs for the future of her son. Agrippina, a mother who has already failed his past.

And if she has failed to train his past, what shall she have done for the future of the empire?

Do you see, Gallio, how up and down I go regarding my charge? How back and forth between hope and fear?

A better mother would have preserved the boy from the taint of pampering! Nothing encourages children to volatility and arrogance as much as coddling does. No restraint; every liberty; the denial of nothing his foolish heart desired! – these indulgences have produced a boy who cannot stand rebuffing. He *should* have been raised on truth, not praise. He *should* have been taught to fear. He *should* have been forced to respect his elders, rising humbly before them, and then he'd know how to judge and retain the respect *he* gets today. Nero should not have been granted the thing he demanded in anger. Instead, he should have received it when he was smiling again – as a gift and a reward, not a deserving. The child should have had sight of his mother's wealth, but not the use of it. He should have been reproved!

Nevertheless, I continue to make the effort, valiantly, with a philosophic strength, believing that the young will mimic the elder nearest them. There was a boy brought up in the house of Plato. When he went home he watched as his own father, for some silly reason, flew into a rage. 'Father,' he said, 'I never saw this in Plato's household.' Which of the two would that boy copy? Send him right back to Plato! Let him grow in the spirit of Plato! As for Nero, whom will he imitate? I'll keep him by my side, praying that reason may shape him more than the heartless, mindless calculations of his mother.

Forgive me, brother. I've spent the greater part of this epistle upon myself. But this last part, devoted to you and to *your* future, is by far the more important.

Gallio! I have persuaded the household of Caesar to elevate you in Rome to the office of consul! Your appointment begins within the month. That shall soon be evident.

Ah, but wait. Another gift follows! For I have received

promises, *mi Galli*, that one year from now you shall be raised yet higher, to the office of proconsul. You shall be given the governorship of Achaia, with a posting in the busy, busy city of Corinth.

Prisca

38

The winds of the sea blow eastward, mostly. Don't we know this, Aquila and I, from our own experience? We flew – it felt like flying – across the Adriatic at the start of our voyage to Corinth. But then we had to fight our way south down the coasts of Macedonia and Achaia. In the Gulf of Corinth our vessel took flight again, due east.

On the other side of Corinth lies the Saronic Gulf where the eastward wind blows stiff in spring and contrary to the westward traveller. About six months after we had come from the west, Paul the apostle wanted to come from the east. From Athens. The winter storms had finished their bluster. Ships were sailing again. But on account of the wind and the chancy seas, he chose to travel to Corinth on foot. He wanted the independence – to trust the trip to himself alone. He was anxious. Alone, he was; and lonely too, I think. He worried so much for his baby church in Thessalonica that he had sent Timothy north to look out for them. He was weak, too. Physically. The poor man had never quite recovered from a collapse he'd suffered in Galatia. Well, and the Romans had beaten him in Philippi. Some of these details Paul told me himself a long while later. Some I saw for myself when we first met in Corinth. Some I'm guessing. But maybe no one knows him better than I do, so I'm a pretty good guesser: I don't think Paul wanted to spend more than two days travelling.

So that first day out of Athens was a very long day. He took the Sacred Way to Eleusis, about fourteen miles, where he sat down and ate figs; then he followed the Saronic coastline another twelve miles as far as Megara. He slept on a leather sheet in a grove of olive trees.

Right away the second day, Paul had to go five miles on a

narrow track cut directly in the mountainside. On his left was a rocky drop straight down to the sea. On his right the mountain rose up lofty and forbidding. This particular stretch of road they call the Sceironian Rocks in memory of Scerion, a robber. They say that Scerion used to make lonely travellers kneel down and wash his feet; then, just as they were finishing, he'd kick them with his clean foot over the cliff. Paul walked that winding track, he told me, 'in a stinking sweat'. Not so much for fear of robbers – though they do still lurk in the rugged hills above – but for fear of the drop-off. Heights ruin him, he said. Heights cause in him a strange hankering to creep to the edge; to lean over; to lean till he goes off balance; to fall. His heart hammers at the possibility. That hammering is one part desire and one part terror that he might actually go and *do* the idiot thing. *I am two men striving for the soul of one.*

Now: I want to tell you as best I can what happened to Paul at his coming to Corinth. Or perhaps I should say, what Paul did. I don't really understand the story. But it feels heavy in my memory. I mean, it *wants* to be told.

As he approached the city that afternoon, even before he had reached the isthmus, Paul lifted his eyes and for the first time saw the Acrocorinth. It rose like royalty over all the land around. It shut his mouth. That singular rock, that grizzly rock a half-mile high, seized his sight and became for him a destination. Almost, I think, a destiny.

He travelled the isthmus like a ghost, unaware of anything except that mighty rock before him. Why should this be? I don't know. I don't understand it. These things, though, I do know: that there's a paved road called the 'Haul-across' which connects the two sides of the isthmus; that it goes four miles from the Saronic Gulf in the east to the Bay of Corinth in the west; that along this road drovers drag the cargoes of ships, and even the ships themselves, on large platforms from sea to sea – and that Paul crossed this road with its shouting men and its straining animals and its ships afloat on dry land, *completely oblivious*! In Corinth he couldn't recall a bit of it.

He recalled the Acrocorinth, that only.

He said that he came to Corinth trembling with weaknesses. Maybe weakness attached him to that immovable rock, the way a sick man fixes on a lamp flame in the dark. The rock drew him forward, that's for sure. It gave direction to his step.

There are walls on the crown of the Acrocorinth, a final refuge if ever the city's besieged. Paul, approaching from the east, watched as those high indifferent battlements caught fire from the dying sun. Then the mighty rock itself blackened into silhouette against the canvas of a deep green sky. As he entered the Isthmian Gate, now in the dusk of the day, Paul saw lines of torchlight ascending the rock on an incline. He couldn't see the bodies of those who carried the torches, but he saw the route that climbed the rock: a sweeping zigzag pattern. A girdle of fire at the waist of the Acrocorinth, which now seemed to him more massive than ever, a black dominion pressing breath from the earth. There are temples there: ten sanctuaries along that road that climbs it. Paul saw the glow of their fires, too, on the hillside. High up are ancient sacred dining rooms, stone tables and stone benches built for the feasts of Demeter. Highest of all, and hidden in the heights, is the temple of Aphrodite, small as temples go, but surrounded by the cells of votaries and expanded by subterranean chambers, one of which runs deep enough to receive the waters of a natural spring.

Paul lay down on his leather sheet in a vineyard at the foot of the rock. Perhaps he slept. If he did it was fleeting and restless, no longer than an hour or two. He brooded under the weight of the Acrocorinth. It sat, he said, like a throne upon his chest.

Hours before the dawn, then, he got up and folded the leather and hoisted his bags and began to walk in moonlight. All the city was asleep. He walked alone, his sandals grinding gravel.

Paul found the road that ascends the rock and began to climb. It starts its ascent on the north side amid a clutter of Corinthian buildings, then passes through orchards, then grows serious in the climb, sweeping long to the left, long to the right in the switchbacks that Paul had seen on fire before. There were no torches now. No people. He toiled alone. In the cold, he grew warm by climbing. In shadows he kept his feet upon the grooves the cartwheels carved. The land below him was watery-pale with moonlight, but the north side was the dark side of the rock, and he could not always detect where the edge of the road was, and the drop-off.

Finally the road ceased switching and climbed directly across the northern face to the great shoulder of the Acrocorinth and around to its western escarpments. Just before he made that turn, Paul saw firelight far off at the Lechaion port on the Bay of

Corinth. Then he lost the sight. He came round to moonlight and a sinking moon. He came round as well into a sudden howling wind, which tore at the cloak on his shoulders. It wanted to bear his bags away. It blew furiously and did not stop blowing. Above him the face of the rock gazed silver and black and impassive toward the white moon. Below him he saw a saddle of land that crossed to another, lower rock. Paul, panting now, tightened his right fist and hit himself on the forehead several times, hard, driving courage into his soul. He willed himself forward and upward, as if the climbing had become a combat. And his will, indeed, grew fiercer, and, yes, he climbed – but his skin raised welts of fright because he was so high, and the path was narrow and sometimes loose and often steep, and he could not hear his footfall. He could not hear his breathing. He heard only the roaring of wind in his ears. But he climbed.

There was a respite when he entered a passage banked on both sides by a higher limestone. And then he came over a final rise and found himself in something like a valley filled with shadow. The ground was humped and rugged, but more level than before, and the wind was broken by the higher rock around him.

Now the stars were dimming. The depths of the sky were losing their perfect blackness. In the east the heavens were growing grey behind the two highest summits of the Acrocorinth.

Paul did not pause in shadow. He made for the northern summit, the higher of the two.

He climbed. Pathless, now, on broken scree, he used his hands and feet together. He climbed, and the grey sky lightened, and the wind screamed up the shingle behind him. Who can understand these compulsions? Paul knew only that he wouldn't be done till he reached the top. Gasping a thin air, his muscles burning from the long exertion, he climbed.

On the topmost hummock of land was a heap of rough-hewn stones, built altarlike; and on that heap, a platform, space for one man standing and no more. Paul dropped his bags. He removed his cloak and weighted it down with the bags. He crawled up onto the platform, from knees to feet; he stood slowly upright; he lifted his eyes, then caught his breath and cried out in terror.

In the rude, red glow of the morning, Paul was the highest thing on earth. He said to his soul, *A storm is coming!* He was terrified of the sky, the place he had entered. Treacherous were the wind and the heavens together, assaulting his body. Down and down, on all sides round, he could see the world emerging from darkness, the patchwork pieces the farmers worked, vineyards, orchards; to the north, the Bay of Corinth and the Ionian Sea and ships at anchor; to the east, the Saronic Gulf and the Aegean laid flat on the earth; nearer, like pebbles at his feet, the city of Corinth itself. The wind blew. The wind kept blowing, still unbroken. *A storm is coming!* Paul was cold with a morbid sweat. He felt that idiot urge to pitch himself headlong from heaven to earth. But the wind preserved him!

So powerfully did the wind strive to throw him down, that Paul, enraged by the opposition, found the will to fight it. Rage external destroyed internal urges. He wrestled the wind, and the contest cleansed him, giving focus to his thought and purpose to his person.

Suddenly he threw back his head and began to howl.

'Jesus Christ! Lord Jesus, mercy, mercy on me! I want to know nothing but you! I want to preach nothing but you. Christ,' he wailed, 'I want to *be* nothing but crucified with you. Live in me! Live in me, Jesus!'

And immediately Jesus appeared in the wind and said, *Don't be afraid. I am with you. No thing shall attack you to harm you. And don't be silent. Go down and preach exactly as you say, for I have many people in this city.*

Paul's mouth was stopped. The wind scoured his nostrils with the terrible scent of divinity. Golden was the sky above, russet the rock on which he stood, and rose the tiny houses far below. The sun was about to breach the Aegean. In all the world, Paul would be the first to see it and to greet it.

39

'Prisca,' Aquila said, 'where have you been?'

On the day when I first met Paul in the marketplace – after the rain, after the crowds had dispersed, after the man had resumed his felling stitch to waterproof Timothy's tent – I said, *Can I sit beside you a while?* He paused and gazed at me. His eyes are the colour of polished walnuts. *Prisca*, he said. I nodded. *The wife of Aquila*, he continued, *leatherworkers from Rome*. I nodded again, unable not to look at him. *Why do you want to sit by me?* he asked, and I answered immediately: *Because you named the name of Jesus.*

I didn't say as well that I was grieving the death of my mother. I didn't name the comfort his previous words had granted me: *The dead in Christ shall rise first, then we who are alive...* He fixed his needle in a stitch and reached and took my right hand in his left and examined the pads of my fingers. With a callus on the edge of his right forefinger, he touched the similar callus on mine, then he brought my hand toward his mouth, causing me to step forward. *Sit*, he said. He kissed the tips of my fingers, and I sat. *We beseech you*, he said as he retrieved the needle. Timothy scrambled to moisten his pen in a newly opened ink pot. Paul bent down over his work and began again to dictate what Timothy wrote: *We beseech you to respect those who labour among you, who in the Lord's name lead you and admonish you. Esteem them, my friends, and love them because of their work.* A little man – just about my size. Intense, glowing like iron in a smithy's fire, his great head ruined with scars, the back of his neck no thicker than a sapling – yet the man had lips as soft as water, and he kissed my fingers with such a tenderness that I sat beside him weeping for the sake of my mother who would never kiss me again.

'Prisca,' Aquila repeated his question, 'where have you been?'

It was late in the afternoon. The streets of Corinth were deserted. Citizens rich and poor had betaken themselves to the bathhouses for their pleasure. I had wandered home in solitude. As I entered the door, my shadow fell across my husband's handiwork, causing him to stop and turn.

I couldn't answer.

Aquila stood up and stepped closer and peered into my face. He has weak eyes. He can't see things at a distance. All his motion is slow and infinitely cautious.

'Prisca, what's the matter?' he said. He put his knuckle under my chin and raised my face to his. 'Have you been crying?'

I patted the back of his hand and moved past him into the tiny workroom. 'No, but it's good news,' I said. 'We're not alone. Aquila, we don't have to be so lonely any more!'

I turned. He was a shadow filling the doorframe, darkening the room as I had darkened it before. He said, 'I haven't been lonely.'

I said, 'I've met two men who confess the name of Jesus. Here in Corinth. There's a third I haven't met. I'll meet him tomorrow. But Aquila! Aquila, one of these men is an apostle who has seen the Lord Jesus *alive*. After the resurrection! Oh, what better thing could have happened to us than this? And you should see the stitching he can do! Even while he's talking, his fingers fly – long fingers, perfectly accurate in leather. Canvas too, I'll bet. He owns his own tools. That's important. And the talk, Aquila! The language that comes from that man's mouth! The voice in him! I'll warn you, it's a sound to get on your nerves, but the meaning, Aquila, will ease your soul and comfort your spirit – '

My husband said, 'Drink this.'

He had stepped to the water jar and filled a cup and brought it to me. 'Prisca,' he said, 'drink this and sit down.'

I took two swallows. I didn't sit.

'But it's what I *did* that I need to explain to you,' I said.

I know I began to sound anxious then. Aquila paused beside the water jar and held quite still to hear me.

'I didn't plan it,' I said. 'I just did it. I think it was right to do it. Maybe the Spirit of Jesus did it through me. But I mean, we *really* aren't going to be alone any more. Because he's going to live with us. I invited him to live with us. And to share the business with us. Aquila? He said yes.'

Aquila set the cup on its little shelf. He came by me and sat on his stool. 'Prisca,' he said, 'go slower. Take me with you. What is his name?'

'Paul,' I said. 'He's a Pharisee. Or, he was.'

Aquila nodded.

I waited, saying nothing.

He said, 'This Paul has seen the risen Lord?'

185

'Yes. Truly. Maybe eighteen years ago. He's come here to Corinth to preach the name of Jesus.'

Aquila said, 'Those that came preaching Jesus in Rome brought trouble with them.'

'If this man brings trouble, it will be a holy trouble.'

'How do you know? How can you say that?'

'My heart says so, because it's what I feel. And my mind, because I heard him talk about the return of Jesus. Paul knows what will happen then – even for those who are asleep. Aquila, he knows what will happen to my mother. When the archangel shouts and the sound of the trumpet of God splits the heavens, my mother will rise up first. Before us. Paul said *first*, because we who are left alive will then be caught up *with* her to meet the Lord in the air. Aquila! Oh, Aquila! Those were tears of joy you saw in my face.'

'Three men?' he said. 'Did you invite all three to stay with us?'

My poor husband. My *patient* husband. Too often I run too fast and far ahead of him.

'Timothy and Silvanus travel with the apostle,' I said, 'but no, they won't stay with us. They sleep in the house of Titius Justus, beside the synagogue. Paul was there, too, until today. Well, and why I invited him is, Erastus, the Manager of the Markets, was threatening him. So I told Erastus that Paul had come to Corinth to work for us. I said that our market fees covered the costs of a co-worker. So Paul is our co-worker now. So then, my invitation wasn't just for a week or so. I asked him to live with us. As long as he's here in the city – '

My husband raised a finger which asked me to be quiet a while. He tapped the side of his nose with that finger, squinting out our doorway into daylight.

Finally he said, 'These little rooms are not enough.'

'But Aquila, I – '

'Prisca, we don't have space enough.'

'But I promised – '

'Whisht, whisht,' he whispered, advancing that finger. 'But the North Market still has shops for sale. It's well and freshly built. Good drainage in the square.' Aquila's tone grew murmurous, as if he were withdrawing to some private place alone. But I, his wife, now sweetly silent, was glad again, because 'murmurous' is how he calculates.

'More than forty shops in that market, and all their doorways

186

under a nice wide porch, and the porch runs unbroken around the four sides of the square. Yes, yes. The shops I've seen are thirteen feet deep and wide and high. Yes, and there are steps in the back to a loft above.

'So,' Aquila said, turning his nearsighted eyes toward me, 'you and I will sleep in the loft. Paul the apostle can sleep with the benches and the tools in the workshop below.'

40

Oh, Paul! How like sunrise is your coming into our lives.

Within days of our move to the new North Market shop, we, the three of us, fell into an easy routine.

The loft had a window we shuttered at night, Aquila and I. But it faced east, and the louvers could be cracked to admit the breezes and a little sky. Just at grey dawn, Paul would wake and awaken me by his stirring below. I guessed he was dressing. Jars bumped their wooden shelves. Water plunked against brass bowls. There was sighing – the low, grunt-sighing of difficult motion. Then through the window I would hear the crunch of sandal soles across the cold, and the shop door would open, and the door would close with a soft fall of the latch, and even before the songbirds sang, the murmuring voices of Paul and Timothy would raise a daybreak hum below. How like a cover kinder than linen were those voices under my dozy body! Daily, until he left with the letter for Thessalonica: daily, surely, devoutly at dawn, that lovely young man with his ringlet fall of honey hair arrived and exchanged nearly formal greetings with the apostle. But soon their voices would cease. A silence intervened, and then I would hear a sort of rhythmic movement and something like groaning. In my mind's eye I saw Paul and Timothy standing with their hands at their stomachs like two old Jews, rocking swiftly back and forth, and groaning wordless prayers to God. And so the red fires of the morning were kindled in the clouds outside the window, and Aquila would wake and rise and dress, and by then I could hear Paul whetting knives on a sharpening stone, while Timothy began to read the scriptures out loud – which was his morning's service. I alone still lay abed – I, on my back above, allowing my soul to float in the simple pleasures of company.

Aquila was probably telling the truth: *He* had not been lonely here in Corinth. But I had. For the last six months I'd suffered the loneliness dreadfully.

On account of the bitter divisions in Rome, we had decided to keep silent in the synagogue, my husband hidden among the men, I a grave suspicion to the women in the galleries above. Solitude may suit Aquila. But it feels like blame to me. I grow sad when I have no friends, and sadness turns into a wasting disease. Truly, I can't eat. I feel constantly close to tears. But then, in the spring of that year, my father... my father!

Oh, how can that man make such a dagger of his despisings? Does he realize the cruelty? My father used even the death of his own wife to punish me for my convictions, for the faith he refused to consider.

'Your mother is dead,' he wrote to me. And this is the whole of his letter: 'Your mother died of a broken heart not ten days after you left her alone in Rome.'

Father, I left her with you!

You abandoned your mother.

No, I didn't! I invited her, but she chose you.

You abandoned your mother.

So then I was suffering something infinitely more killing than loneliness. Anguish of the heart. Violent, physical spasms of guilt. Poor Aquila watched with a heavy-handed helplessness. Do you know? – I felt such sympathy for him in those days. And there was a part of me that wanted terribly to comfort him. But it was the smallest part. I couldn't help my husband either, could only cry, would not control my tears – causing him his own sort of loneliness.

But then, here came this skinny little man; this busy, bow-legged preacher; this cantankerous, compulsive, big-headed Voice, the daybreak sun of my life – and I said to Aquila, *I've asked him to live with us.* And my dear husband answered, *He can sleep in the workshop below.*

'The Lord be with you!' Paul sang when in the morning I finally descended the ladder from the loft.

'And with you,' I sang in return, bending for the water jar and walking out into the air.

The Lord be with you. Ah, me. What a music! You, O Lord, have put more gladness in my heart than barns have grain or vats have wine!

So this was our routine: Timothy read the scriptures. Paul and Aquila worked at their benches to fill the orders of our customers. And I walked to the fountain near the Lechaeum Road. On the way I stopped for simple purchases, filling my bag with smoked fish, dried fruit, yesterday's bread – which was always cheaper and quicker than fresh bread.

Then; always; as reliable as daylight: As I returned to the North Market I would hear from clear across the square that Voice, that high, insistent, nasal Voice wheedling, whipping, scolding, and calling to all the city of Corinth. From morning till mid-afternoon the apostle would measure the leather and talk; would cut the leather in perfect curves and talk; would punch and stitch and bend at the workbench, talking. Of sound and sense alone, he created a spiritual home, a dwelling place for my soul.

Talking, working:

If a woman in linen brought her belt to the shop for repairing, Paul would abandon the job at hand, beg her to sit, rush for a better thread, assess by the touch of his delicate fingers the damage done to her belt – and would all along, at the same time, be winning the woman's attention with questions. Once he himself was seated, he'd turn her answers into lectures and talk as long as she stayed in the shop.

'Good woman, what is your name?'

– *cutting, shaving the ragged edge of her leather* –

'Who are your people? Where were you born?'

– *punching new holes in old material* –

'Your husband's a soldier? From Cisalpine Gaul? Retired?'

– *stitching, stitching* –

'Well, and what war is your Fortunatus fighting now?'

'"None", you say? Ah, yes, "retired". Of course.'

– *stitching, tightening his stitches more slowly than was necessary* –

'Oh, certainly! I understand that the 'Peace of Rome', as you say, embraces all the world. Even with my own eyes I've seen how this wondrous Augustan Peace is still forestalling wars around the circle of the sea! So, then: is your husband peaceful therefore? Is he peaceful in his heart? Are you?'

– *biting the thread; breaking it between his teeth; finding a good oil with which to refresh the leather* –

'Listen: The *Pax Romana* may be good, but it is not holy. It can't be worshipped. And it will not last for ever. The peace of the world cannot outlast the world, now, can it? Right. Nor does it dwell in human hearts. Is your husband Fortunatus peaceful? Are you? Do you know what you will do when the world and its peace are destroyed? For they will be destroyed on the day of wrath, the day when God's righteous judgment will be revealed. For then the world will pass away. And there will be – ' *rubbing the leather, rubbing it with feminine hands, making it supple* ' – there will be tribulation and distress for everyone who does evil, but glory and honour and peace for all those who do good.' *Handing the belt back to the woman, smiling with soft red lips below his nose.* 'What war is your husband, the good Fortunatus, fighting today?'

All day long, day after day, people were drawn to the Voice as if to a long flag snapping in the wind. I was not alone. I inhabited a miracle. Small Paul seemed truly to grow in stature, his narrow nose becoming something noble to my sight, and his thick brow a battlement before the world.

Oh, Paul, how you shine when you are preaching! How like water you sparkle in the slant of sunlight!

By May, in spite of Timothy's departure, our shop was filled with people. They stood around the walls and sat on the floor. They spilled out onto the porch at our door. My dear Aquila worked silently, patiently, in ever decreasing spaces. He seldom speaks to anyone besides me. With Paul he was altogether mute – perhaps in admiration. Perhaps struck dumb by the apostle's ability suddenly to flood a room with language.

In the evenings when he had the workshop to himself, Aquila designed and built a collapsible workbench. I knew nothing of the project until the morning he carried it outside, arranged Paul's tools upon it, and set Paul's stool beside it. From that day forward, Paul both worked and preached at his bench on the porch, where greater crowds could hear him.

'You know the right. It is written in your hearts. You know the wrong, too, since to do it is to suffer the accusations of your conscience. To do it is to send your secret thoughts into a tumult. What is hidden from the world is not hidden to you. Nor is it hidden from God, who is about to judge all human secrets and punish the wrong. And how shall you be saved from punishment on that day?'

In everything you say I hear the Spirit of God. I, Prisca, sell

goods. I take orders in the shop behind you. I watch through the
doorway your busy form and marvel at the crowds:

'Idols can't save you from wrath.

'Anything made by human hands is less than human – which is
less than nothing before the living God.

'And nothing redoubles the wrath of God more than this: that
the humans he created would turn from him to worship the work
of *their* hands as if *they* were creators like him!'

Oh, Paul, how you hate to crouch while you're preaching. The
posture of the labourer – so demeaning. So slavish. Yet you have
chosen it. And in private you tell me it signifies that you are a
slave for the Lord. Yes, yes, of course: but I watch your eyes and
know you hate the bowing down.

Still, the crowds keep swelling. Women return with their
husbands. Husbands return with friends. Fortunatus brings a man
named Stephanas. Stephanas brings Achaicus, even to receive
your harsher preaching:

'There is the story of the people Israel, with whom the true
God established his covenant, whom God sustained by the food
and the drink of his mercy.

'When they were waiting for him at his holy mountain, the
children of Israel grew restless. They began to think that God was
delaying too long in silence. So they took matters into their own
hands. They cooked their bracelets, anklets, necklaces, all their
golden rings; and from the molten gold they formed a calf. They
said, "This is your god, O Israel!" To this calf they brought
offerings. And to honour it, the people sat down to eat and drink,
then they rose up to dance.

'What was that calf? A nothing. An idol! Corinthians, listen:
For their sins, three thousand people perished in a single day.'

As you tell that story, a man in the multitude catches my eye,
nodding in fierce agreement. You are hunched and cannot see; but
I gasp at the power of this gospel. Paul, the man is Crispus, the
ruler of the synagogue, persuaded to faith by your preaching!

'The story of that golden calf was written down as an awful
warning for us – because Israel represents all of us before God,
and it is upon us that the end of the ages is coming! Corinthians,
if God did not spare the people of his covenant, why would he
spare you?'

Here you clear the workbench and jump up to stand on it.
I rush out to steady the platform. You shout:

'I have climbed your Acrocorinth. On the way to the top I passed the dining rooms where people honour Demeter by their meals.

'Tell me: Who is Demeter? What is she?

'Goddess of growth, you say? Mother of rebirth in the spring of the earth? Absolutely not!

'Demeter is a demon! She's more disastrous than a thousand idols! When you worship her, you leave the living God for a thing that creeps and babbles below the earth! How can such an insult *not* enrage the God who is father of us all? And why would he spare you from his rage?

'Nevertheless, God *wants* to spare you! God has shown his love for you by sending his Son into the world to die the death you should have died.

'While you were living godless lives; while you kept intercourse with demons; while you were sinners and enemies of heaven – even then his Son, the Lord Jesus Christ, died on the accursed tree. Believe that! Believe it! And let your believing be based on this, that God also raised him from the dead – of which resurrection I, who speak to you today, am a witness!

'People – reject the demons! Turn to him who can save you from the rage to come! Turn to Jesus, the Son of God and the Lord of Glory. It is because he appeared to me that I have the authority to cry out, "Come!" Come to him who will make you righteous in the day of his returning. For it is written, "Blessed are those whose iniquities are forgiven, and whose sins are covered. Blessed are those against whom the Lord will not reckon their sin."'

Oh, Paul! How like the dawn is your presence in Corinth!

The North Market square isn't terribly spacious. The Corinthian Agora is four or five times larger. And I will freely admit that speakers spoke with no trouble in the Agora, that it was the one place in the city intended for crowds. Nevertheless, I blame Erastus for the tactics he used against Paul. They were excessive. They revealed – so I still believe – a particular resentment the Manager of Markets felt toward the apostle.

When there were seventy, maybe eighty people standing in the square, listening to Paul; when he was preaching from the shaky platform of his workbench while I held it steady in two hands, my face not far from his feet; when Aquila and Timothy had gone down to the harbour at Cenchreae, leaving us here at the shop alone – suddenly the mood in the market square and all its noises changed.

Paul snapped stiff and ceased preaching. I felt a drumming in the ground beneath me: a stallion's galloping. People at the back of the crowd began to scream. I wanted to see. I wanted to release the workbench and stand straight to see what trouble was coming – but I feared to let go. Paul might fall. I held on, hearing shouts and cursings, the clashings of metal, the thump of hard things on human flesh and bone, cries of injury. Then people were running, scattering everywhere, and here came a horse at a canter among them, and on the horse the florid, fat Erastus!

Around him, driving the people away with fists and the flats of their swords, came young soldiers afoot, helmeted, armoured and armed.

'Out! Out! Get out of here!' they were yelling. 'You're blocking the shops! Go home! Loiterers, go home!'

But Erastus had his eye on Paul. 'You try my patience, sir!' he announced, reining his horse directly in front of us.

Paul on his workbench, the Manager on his mount – they were eye to eye and high above me. My hair was coming undone, falling across my vision.

Erastus drew his sword with a flourish. 'Why do you insist on obstructing the commerce of my city?' he demanded. He pointed the weapon toward Paul's throat. 'Once,' he said, 'I was merciful. But twice is once too many for mercy from me.'

The horse beneath the magnificent Erastus was droop-headed and swaybacked. The poor beast was exhausted. Its rider wore two heavy robes over his tunic, rings and necklaces, and cross-gaitered sandals on his fat ankles. Yet, though his appearance was foolish, his eyes glittered with anger. Enmity. And his troops, now free of people and closing in on us, were cold, emotionless, dangerous.

Paul remained erect, gazing untroubled – gazing with a strange curiosity – at the Manager. From my low angle, it seemed his lips were struggling with a smile.

Erastus puffed his cheeks and looked away. 'It is within my power, sir,' he said, swinging the sword for emphasis, 'to remove obstructions. I do, sir, have that power and more: to punish impertinence, to strike contempt from the faces of the arrogant!'

Paul! Believe him and come down!

But Paul only scrutinized Erastus more closely, actually leaning forward and tilting his great head to one side.

Erastus the Manager caught the gesture. 'Bind him!' he cried. 'Bind him and drag him from the city!'

Three soldiers moved forward, one with ropes.

'Erastus,' Paul said in a soft voice and in wonder: 'I know you.'

Lightly he leaped from the workbench and touched the nose of the Manager's horse. 'I know exactly what you fear.'

A soldier reacted. He grabbed Paul's tunic.

'Wait!' I cried.

But another soldier threw an arm around me from behind. The miserable horse had not so much as shied.

Erastus was staring at Paul. His eyes were locked on Paul's face.

'My brother,' Paul said, 'you fear that you are a nobody. You fear you're a nothing in this city.'

The soldier yanked Paul's arms back and bent his elbows around a spear-shaft.

Paul said, 'And all because you are not nobly born. But I tell you, Erastus, God is choosing you!'

A soldier with ropes approached Paul, preparing to tie his wrists at the stomach. Erastus actually craned his head to see past the soldier to Paul.

Paul said, 'You were born in slavery, weren't you? And you bought your own freedom. You are a *freed*man, not a nobleman. And fear imprisons you, because those of noble birth have the power to scorn you. You strive, strive, strive for some standing in the world. O my brother – but there is no need, because *God* is choosing you now.'

Two soldiers each seized the ends of the spear-shaft and heaved it forward. Paul was pitched off his feet. The breast of his tunic tore. They lifted his little body, dangling from the shaft and grunting in pain.

But he bent his neck and kept his eyes on Erastus, and the Voice kept issuing from his mouth: 'Listen!' Paul said. 'This is the truth: God chooses what is weak in the world to shame the strong! Erastus! God chooses the foolish to shame the wise. God chooses those who are low and despised in society – chooses even those who are nothing – in order to bring to nothing those who think they are something – '

I believe that only the physical removal of Paul between two young soldiers finally broke the Manager's trance, reminding him of the order he'd given his troops.

'Wait!' Erastus cried. 'Where are you going? Bring the fellow back.'

I shook free of my own cold soldier, snatched a knife from the workbench, and ran to Paul. While his captors tried to understand the mind of their master, I cut the rope at Paul's stomach. He slipped to his knees, actually giggling. Why, the man had been enjoying this entire episode at some deep, interior level. His joy was an immediate sunlight on me, and my own soul soared. We turned together to see Erastus on foot, walking toward us in all his voluminous raiment.

There were hunger and an earnest appeal in the trembling of his cheeks.

'Please,' he said, placing palm to palm at his breast, 'which God is this?'

41

But then there came the dawning when what roused me was not the stirring of our co-worker in the shop below, but the sound of my own name.

'Prisca, Prisca,' I heard with a startling clarity and was immediately awake. Who – ?

'Prisca.'

Not Aquila. He slept heavily here in the loft. In fact, the whistle of his breathing made me know that the voice which spoke my name was not so near. It seeped up to me through the cracks between the floorboards.

'Priscilla... come down. I... need you.'

And dividing the words was that sigh, that grunting, sighing sound of difficult motion.

I descended barefoot, my hair unpinned.

Paul was leaning awkwardly against the edge of the worktable. His back and torso were twisted to an impossible angle. He seemed fixed that way.

'Paul?'

A single lamp flame burned on the table. It cut horrible scoops of shadow in the man's neck and throat and face. His head was caught at an extreme tilt, thrusting his jawbone out like that of a battlefield corpse.

'Paul?'

'Priscilla,' he said without turning or moving, 'I can't do this alone. Please. Be Timothy for me.'

Priscilla. No one had called me Priscilla before. *Little Prisca*, tenderly making me a precious thing.

'Let me lean on you,' he growled. 'Lower me, lower me down to the floor.'

I bowed beside him and felt his weight shift from the table to my shoulder. I knelt slowly down. He gasped and spit with pain, but when I had crouched on the floor, he rolled from me to his side.

'Paul?'

'Take,' he said, 'my tunic off.'

'What's the matter? What happened? Why are you in so much pain?'

'Oh, little Prisca,' he affected a chuckle, 'consider it my morning ablutions. Please remove the tunic.'

I did. He unbent himself. He turned face down on the floor and stretched his arms away, and I saw his back in the lamplight, and I couldn't help myself, I gave a tiny cry of pity.

Paul said, 'There's olive oil in the jar on the table.'

'Oh, Paul!' I whispered.

The flesh of his back was gouged, was shining white with old wounds and scars, with stripes and welts so dry that the whole expanse of skin had cracked like a wasteland.

'Please,' he spoke into the dust of the floor, 'pour the oil on my back. Then, as hard as you can, drive the heels of your hands into the bone and muscle. Please.'

Quietly I began to cry. I brought the jar from the table and tipped it and allowed the oil to flow onto his wretched flesh.

The cool oil caused him to shiver.

I knelt beside him, and touched him with the palms of my hands, and felt how ragged the whippings and beatings had left him, and began tenderly, tenderly to massage him.

'Push,' he said.

I did. I pushed harder, but it caused him suddenly to groan, and I snatched my hands back to my breast.

'Priscilla,' he commanded, 'you must push.'

I tried. I closed my eyes. Outraging every instinct in me, I leaned my bodily weight down through my arms upon the bones of his back. But this time he cried out, and I did too and froze.

A moment passed.

Then Paul said, 'If you don't do this, I will not be able to stand up straight today. And any motion could tear my skin. And I'll bleed into my garments. Little Prisca, I am so sorry – but I need your help.'

Another moment passed while I stared at my hands, glistening in the lamplight. Grey dawn was breaking outside over the city. I heard the first birds questioning the air.

Then Paul said, 'Erastus has invited me to live in his house. What do you think about that? He says he has more than room enough. He pats his chubby hands together and says it's the least he can do. I would, he argues, ennoble his name and his family if I moved into his house.'

Cunning Paul, the apostle of God! I lowered my hands again and slowly, slowly rubbed the rucked terrain of his back. He groaned. That groan gathered inside of me as if it were my own, but I pushed. I pushed harder and harder, while we both groaned together: *Ohhh, ohhh.*

Paul kept talking. For my benefit. As long as he talked, as long as I paid attention to his talking, I could not imagine the levels of his suffering.

He said, 'Priscilla.' He called me by that pretty name, *Priscilla*, and he said, 'I did not fear the Manager of the Markets. Neither sword nor soldiers can ever scare me. Push, push. From the very beginning I knew my word would have power over the minds of the Gentiles. You know that I saw the risen Jesus on my way to Damascus. Everyone who knows me knows that. But I have never yet told anyone what Jesus looked like.

'Push, child. Where is your strength? Push!'

I am a small woman. My hands are small. Rhythmically I massaged him, my whole body driving forward and forward. With such force I bore down on him that I could hear the teeth grinding in my head.

Paul groaned and chuckled, chuckled and gasped and groaned and said: 'Listen to me. When I lifted my eyes from the ground, the skies were torn asunder, and I gazed into heaven. Priscilla, I saw the dwelling place of God the Father.

'Yes, yes, you are doing well,' he growled like an animal. 'You are pushing very well.'

The lightening sky caused our interior room to seem darker than before.

Paul said, 'I saw a stormy wind, and a great cloud with brightness round about it, and fires flashing forth. I saw the firmament, shining like crystal. I heard a sound like roaring waters, and above the firmament there was the likeness of a throne, a sapphire throne, clear and blazing blue: there the Father took his seat while a stream of fire came forth before him. A thousand thousands served him. Ten thousand times ten thousand stood before him. And Prisca, Prisca! – on that great cloud, surrounded by brightness, came the Lord, the Christ, the Son of God. He sat down at the right hand of the Father, far above all rule and authority and power and dominion, above every name that is proclaimed in this age and the age to come – that all the peoples, all the nations, and all the languages of earth should serve him. His kingdom is everlasting. It shall never be destroyed.

'This is the one who called my name and sent me forth. He, the visible appearance of the invisible God.

'Adam once blazed with that kind of a glory, Priscilla. But he lost it, and all his children lost it too. Yet this is what I witnessed, that Jesus Christ has come to restore the glory again, first to the Jews and then to the Gentiles: for he is the new Adam, the radiant Lord of the cosmos, through whom all things and all people exist. It is *his* word in my mouth. Why would I fear any power on earth? I don't. I don't. I don't – except perhaps the wrath of Prisca, should I think to accept the invitation of an important official and leave her humble shop.

'No, no, my precious Prisca,' Paul sighed, raising himself upon his elbows, 'you can stop pushing now. The muscles are loosened. The skin is no longer on fire. I hear your husband above. It's time to go to work.'

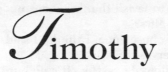

Timothy

42

'Look,' said Erastus, waving a thick arm toward five 'clients'
grinning in the atrium of his house, 'look what I can do for your
master.'

When I returned from Thessalonica, Erastus insisted that
Silvanus and I move into his house from the smaller one next to
the synagogue. Though the offer had been made grandly to all
three of us, Paul chose to stay in Aquila's shop.

'Look what joy it gives me to give my money away!'

Every morning when Erastus emerged from his tiny, windowless
bedroom, he was met by two servants, one who laid out his
clothes on polished racks in the hall, the other who brushed and
washed his body in preparation for the day. Arrayed, adorned, and
aromatic, having comforted himself with bread dipped in honey,
some dates, some olives, the Manager of Markets would then
proceed to his atrium, where six to twelve men, on seeing him,
would leap to their feet and cry out his praises. He gave them
coins. Or he signalled a servant to give them small baskets of
food. Sometimes he invited two or three of the fellows to follow
him on his daily rounds, performing small tasks as they occurred
to him.

'Look,' Erastus said, scattering money among the cringing
'clients,' as he called them: 'These men mean nothing to me.
They come no nearer my heart than my atrium. Yet I
accommodate them. But that Paul!' he shouted, sweeping open
his arms. 'Paul I love! Fearless Paul I honour! Who else ever
talked to me like him? Your master has a tongue like a shovel; he
dug the torment out of my soul. Oh, Timothy, you're too young
to know how wonderful it is to be sleeping again. Again? Why,
I've never slept so soundly in all my life. The vulture that chewed
at my liver – that vulture is dead! Oh, little brother, I want to

thank him! I want to lavish thanksgivings upon him! Why does he refuse me and my gifts?'

'It's a matter of conscience, I think,' I said. 'He chooses not to burden those he serves, Erastus.'

'No burden!' bellowed Erastus. 'It's no burden at all! I have a house of seven rooms. I lose nothing to give one away. I gain a guest. I gain the honour.'

'But Paul says the gospel is free. No one should purchase truth. No one can. *That's* the gift, Erastus, and it comes from God.'

'Little brother,' he declared, thumping the breath from my lungs, 'pretty Greek brother, Paul the apostle's as thin as a whistle! We've got to put some meat on those bones!'

And so it was that Erastus invited us daily to dinners – and not just us, but everyone he ever met in the company of Paul. There really had been a transformation in this man's life. As a friend and a benefactor he ceased to distinguish the high from the low (maintaining, however, his own height by his benefactions). Anyone who loved Paul, Erastus loved. Those who believed in Jesus before he did, he loved with even more voluble affections. And those (very few) people whom Paul himself had baptized, this city official adored with a purple extravagance.

By autumn, then, lamps and torches burned far into the night at Erastus's commodious house, since always a goodly number of people accepted his invitations and came. Even in the cooler air my host heaved about, sweating with happy contentment.

Happy Erastus! Poor Erastus – more tender than one would suppose.

'Timothy,' he said one evening when we were alone. 'Timothy, tell me.' He seized my hand with a blinking appeal: 'Did I offend your friend?'

He'd never been able to call Silvanus *his* friend because Paul's other companion was so laconic. Silvanus didn't talk. Neither did he respond to hugs or kisses. Erastus could handle the silence of those he commanded, but the silence of a house guest bewildered him. Stumped him. Some days he would pursue the taciturn Silvanus with a constant stream of cheerful chatter. Other days he tried to match him: two mutes moving through the same house. But then, just as the vineyards were starting to ripen, Silvanus absconded. He departed Corinth and the house of Erastus without a word. No explanation. Neither thanks nor farewell.

Erastus said, 'Did he talk to you? Did he tell you why?' Still holding my hand, my huge host drew me down till we were sitting knee to knee on the same bench. 'Was I too friendly for his taste?' Erastus asked. But his eyes unfocused and he answered his own question: 'No, a man can never be *too* friendly. It's always better to err on the side of friendliness.' Then he gripped me and drilled me again with his eyes: 'So what's the matter with Silvanus, anyway? Do you know? Does Paul? I'll bet Paul knows. Me too! Tell you what, little brother, I think the man is carrying a grudge against the world. Maybe he resents polite society. Maybe he never learned how to live in it – couldn't make the switch to independence the way some of us have and blames us for our success. In any case it's better this way. Best he go his way, and we look to the goodness of ours.

'Timothy!' He concluded the talk with another thump to my back: 'You're as clever a Greek as I've ever met!'

And who can describe the florid, bright-red delight with which this city official welcomed believers to his house for worship and the celebration of the Lord's supper?

We never stopped worshipping at Titius's house. Aquila and Prisca still shepherded believers in that place. But when Crispus – ruler of the synagogue next door! – came over announcing his new faith in Jesus, most of the God-fearing Gentiles followed him. So the synagogue was draining souls; Titius's dining rooms were flooding; and the dining rooms of Erastus, Manager of Markets in Corinth, now caught the overflow.

His was a completely genuine hospitality. In gorgeous dress he himself – not his servants – led slaves through his atrium and into the intimate halls of his house: slaves, whether educated or crude; day-labourers, beggars, sailors, bakers, bankers; people of no name, people invisible in the world, people inglorious – everyone.

He said, 'The Lord be with you,' to them all.

In the accents of the high-born, his full lips giving the words a luscious splendour, he said, 'The Lord be with you,' and then he kissed them every one, bearing for ever upon his brow the mark of apoplectic gladness.

This is the man who was ready to drag the body of Paul, bound and helpless, out of town behind his horse.

I watched the pleasure with which he dragged believers to his private apartments, and I grinned at the transition.

And still we grew. Still our glorious Lord granted increase to our preaching, so that by winter the leadership of those who worshipped in Erastus's house was bequeathed to me. We couldn't even fit in two houses any more.

Paul had found a man whose house was built at the base of the Acrocorinth. In fact, he found the man on *account* of the house. It was a mansion twice as large as Erastus's. Moreover, according to Paul that mansion sat at the very gates of idolatry. Paul had passed it regularly for nine months, since regularly, always alone, he climbed the road up the grim, colossal rock that can swallow our winter sun.

One afternoon, suddenly, he turned aside. He knocked on the outer door of the mansion and asked for the name of the owner.

'Gaius,' said a maidservant.

'May I meet with Gaius?' Paul asked.

The servant said that her master was at the baths.

So then my master and friend went himself directly to the baths east of the Lechaeum Road; and, still the Jew, wandered fully clothed through the room of tepid pools, into the room of steam and the hottest water, where he found Gaius stretched out under the ministrations of a servant who was scraping the sweat from his flesh with a curved blade.

Paul sat down beside him and said, 'Are you Gaius? Do you own the house between the city and the north foot of the Acrocorinth?'

In January, then, believers began to meet in that house, too. And so there were three churches in Corinth.

Though Prisca and Aquila shared the role, she was the more prominent shepherd in the church that met at Titius's. Her public prayers and her prophecy were the much more powerful, edifying the lowliest, encouraging the discouraged, consoling the disconsolate.

And though I was the ostensible leader for the church that met at Erastus's, it was the personality of our resplendent host that dominated. He was enchanted by the practice of speaking in tongues. Whenever anyone was moved to do so, Erastus raised his great arms and applauded approval. He prayed constantly that the Holy Spirit would grant him the very same gift – which, in fact, the Holy Spirit withheld until Paul and I had left Corinth; but that's another story for another time. Unlike the softer, more intelligible exchanges at Titius's, ours became a most clamorous body of worshippers.

But despite his noise and joy and his continuing hospitality, Erastus missed Paul's presence at the holy meal. Ever since Paul began to lead worship at the house of the man named Gaius – a man, incidentally, whose status had been received by inheritance, not earned by wit and work – Erastus had grabbed me for night-time conversations on his examination bench:

'How is Paul? How is the apostle? Does he like it at Gaius's place? How many people do you think are gathering there these days? Fewer than here, probably. It takes time for new things to grow.'

One balmy evening in March, Erastus came home from a dinner engagement at another house, his poor cheeks trembling with emotion. He took my hand and led me to the bench and sat and struggled for several minutes to talk.

'Timothy,' he said. The act of speech brought tears to his eyes. He covered his face with his fat hands. His shoulders heaved up and down. Then into the hollow of his hands he said, 'Paul the apostle. They told me tonight that Paul the apostle – he baptized Gaius. Yes, and his whole family. Timothy. Timothy, why didn't he baptize me?'

What happened afterward was altogether Paul's conceiving. I did nothing more than mention how dashed were the spirits of Erastus.

Four weeks later, in April, one month before the celebration of the Isthmian Games, early in the morning, as Erastus and I entered his atrium to meet his 'clients', we were surprised to find but one man standing there. My skinny friend. Meatless Paul of the moon-sized head – his lips sly with grinning, his small eyes laughing, his whole self directed at Erastus like a bee at a blossom. Beside him on the floor was an enormous canvas, folded.

'Erastus,' Paul announced, 'this is for you.'

The magnificent man at my side was dumbfounded. His cheeks were already trembling with emotion, though *which* emotion had still to be decided.

Paul said, 'A man as important as you must be given grand accommodations at the Games.'

'Me?' Erastus whispered.

'A man,' Paul said in the voice of announcements and instructions: 'A man as aristocratic as you must not, however, sit too long in the stadium sun.'

'Me?'

'Therefore, my dear friend,' Paul said, 'I have a gift for you. I've sewn an awning of the highest quality in order to shade you while you watch the Games, good and noble Erastus.'

Paul bent down and began to unfold the canvas.

Erastus followed the gesture so closely with his face and his breathless attentions, that he almost fell forward.

Paul said, 'A canopy better than any sail, for which Aquila has constructed a light wooden frame. And do you see? Can you measure it now?' He straightened up and stepped to the side. 'It's large enough to cover two persons comfortably.'

Now the spare gift-giver approached the gorgeous recipient. Paul put his hands on the heaving shoulders before him.

'Erastus,' he said, 'how grateful I would be if you would invite me to be that second person. What do you think, sir? Can I watch the Games beside you?'

Oh, what a boo-hooing broke forth in the atrium of the Manager of Markets that morning! What a marvellous slobbering of gratitude and gladness!

Paul did, you know. Paul loved Erastus as deeply as he did me.

'My child,' he said, bearing up the enormous person of Erastus, whose hugs were like the fall of painted walls. 'My dear child.'

43

Something in me yearned to stand at the starting gates. I wanted
to feel the stone sill under my foot. And to crouch, dropping my
right shoulder. To listen for the strings in their grooves below
me. A runner can hear them, you know. He can hear the strings
sing taut the instant the starter yanks them from his pit. Even
before the post-beams fall and the course is open before him, the
runner *knows* they're going to fall. The strings to the posts, the
strings to the gate-beams, they are cords straight to his heels, his
hips, and his heart. Oh, I wanted to experience that screaming,
complete attention again, when I am bent and at the ready, and
there are no people, no high encircling seats, no humans
anywhere in all the world except the men lined left and right of
me, and the only land in existence is the white clay of the track
stretched forth before me, waiting!

Several times that spring – always in the evenings when the
carpenters had departed and the stadium was empty under the
sky – I wandered over to the Isthmia alone, allowing memory to
overwhelm me. In those days the entire complex smelled of the
dust of fresh stone because the ancient Temple of Poseidon and
the stadium both had just been rebuilt.

But what to me were these pagan heaps of white stone? Well,
something. Something.

I confess, they stirred to life the spirit of my father. In the
sunset silence I walked to the pavement at the start of the
racecourse, already prepared with wooden posts, one for each
runner. I knelt and touched the long grooves that fanned from
the starter's pit to the posts. Eight grooves left of him, eight
grooves right: sixteen strings for sixteen posts for sixteen
athletes all in a row! Papa would have been astonished at that
number. I unbound my sandals and shuffled off my clothes and
approached a post newly carved with notches. I fingered the
notches and saw where the crossbeam would attach. When, at a
yank on sixteen strings, the beams all dropped, then the gates
would open and sixteen hearts would explode.

I turned my face to the course. I took a light stance, my bare sole on the stone sill. I dropped my right shoulder. I bent into that familiar crouch – and immediately my knees began to tremble. Until he died, Papa had been training me for this – this, precisely. Whether I would have loved the event for the race itself or for the sake of my father, I don't know. But I would have loved it. I'd have loved it like religion. I would certainly have honoured Melikertes, the child-god of the evening games who, as Papa told me, had been borne to these shores on the back of a dolphin. But for him, for my father, I'd have run like a votary, swift and devout, since he would have run within me. Ah, Papa! Oh, my desperate papa, all his motion cut short by coughing, his body made gaunt by sickness – to him my limbs and my speed had been as precious as life.

The Isthmian Games? Well, it could have been the Olympic, or the Pythian, or the Nemean Games at Argos. It didn't matter: I have no doubt that the man would have dragged his dry, flushed corpse to *any* site of sacred trial in order to watch me run – and to die, delighted, in my victory. But he died at home in Lystra, mere days before I became a man and before I could, as a man, enter the Games and save him. Then my mother made me a Jew. And the apostle made me a believer. And now I cannot take the vows required of every athlete. I cannot go down to the underground chambers and swear oaths to demons and idols. I cannot run.

And so it was that there, in April, in the Isthmian stadium, in the deepening evening, suffering the scent of olive blossom on the easy wind, and crouching by a starting post, I felt my knees begin to tremble. My stance alone, that posture of a racer's readiness, caused me to pant with longing and with sorrow. I thought I heard my papa call my name. I thought I heard, far east of me, the chuffing sound of his cough. But east of me was the gulf, and east of that the Aegean – seas too wide for sound to cross them.

ℒ. Annaeus Seneca

44

Seneca, in Rome,
  To Gallio, my brother in Corinth,
  This eleventh year of the reign of Claudius:

Greetings!

Are you well? Are you settled? Have you made your formal
appearance at the Isthmian Games? Have you, with grace and
Annaean charm, concluded the Great Round of Receptions,
Dinners, Theatrical Events – all the Canny Flatteries with which
a new proconsul is received into his office? What colour is your
face? Is the blush off my blooming Gallio yet? Surely Corinth
mimics Rome, where we've gone mad with flattery. Here, the man
who moderates his praise is not the truer but the cheaper!
Because, however gross the compliment, however fine our modest
denials, we hunger for the honey. Oh, don't we, though! Do you
remember Father's good friend, Crispus Passienus? He was
exquisite at naming and framing a natural fault. Well, Crispus
used to say we never slam the door on flattery; we nudge it shut,
like a man rejecting his mistress: if she nudges back, we're
pleased – and if she breaks it down, we rejoice.

Ah, Gallio, I'm joking with you. No one I know is more
indifferent to flattery. Indifferent and thereby protected, since that
part of oneself most open to praise is open as well to attack. But
you'll never be pierced with that daggery tongue. By its first word
you recognize it; before its second you have already cut it off.

I wish I possessed these two characteristics of yours: the charm
that deserves adulation, and the sense to reject it flat.

Wishes, wishes, O brother of mine: I wish manhood had
granted such grace and modesty to Nero, now entitled *Princeps
Juventutis*.

He has become a man, you know. Suddenly, a man. By fiat, by public acclamation, by whatever powers can countermand Time and the Seasons to force this boy into his majority two years sooner than any other true-born child – a man!

He has been in the world a scant fourteen years; yet in the evening of the seventeenth of March, the lad was dressed in a white tunic with saffron stripes – a sign in this palace of good omen – and put to bed so clothed. In the morning he was roused before sunrise and led to the household altar, where he accomplished several sacred acts; he consecrated the beautiful, delicate gown of his boyhood to the *Lares*. Nero conducted himself with a suitable solemnity. A genuine solemnity, I will admit, though thin, because his love for ritual is really a love for things theatrical and dramatic. Solemnly, then, he took from his neck the golden chain and the golden *bulla* that had protected his younger vulnerabilities.

Next, an entire train of imperial attendants escorted him to the Capitol. In the ancient Temple of Jupiter, our little Nero made offerings and sacrifices as if he were already *pater* of some rich and recognized household. Then the priest brought forth the white. And Nero bowed his head. The high priest whirled the white before him, behind him, around him, enwrapping his form in a toga whiter than the flying clouds. When Nero Claudius Drusus Germanicus lifted his head, and when he brought this right hand across his chest to grip the folds of the *toga virilis* – that robe as radiant as *gloria* – the boy had become a man.

Gloria left the temple, then.

Gloria descended to the Forum, where the multitudes roared to receive him. All of Rome delivered itself to celebration then. The day of Nero was also the day of Bacchus, the Bacchanalia. Priestesses, their heads enwreathed with ivy, were frying little cakes at every corner, and dipping them in honey and selling them to those who wore masks, who danced and sang in the streets. Measures of wheat were given away for free. Soldiers received bonuses in silver. The Circus Maximus threw open its gates to one hundred thousand people – and there was Nero, raised up in his gleaming triumphal dress, for the first time taking his place upon the Imperial seat.

Now, then, Gallio: There were two voices in the ears of the boy-man that day. Which do you think he will heed?

One of these voices was mine. Early in the day, as our

procession moved with sober deliberation from the palace to the Capitol, I, walking beside and a half-step behind him, had time to deliver the personal sermon I'd fashioned in advance. 'Our souls are in the image of God,' I said, 'or so they should be.

'Nero, the natural reason which controls the world – that is the will of God made visible and available to human study. But the dearer, more intimate reason living within us – that is the very mind of God. Avail yourself of that mind. Make it yours. Child, you cannot know a durable happiness except it come from the peace of a pure conscience. By the mind of God, master your passions. By the divinity of reason within you, master your passions. For our sakes, Nero: master your passions.'

The boy kept doggedly walking a half-stride ahead of me. I cornered his left while his mother strode directly beside him on the right. Claudius was borne foremost in a divan on the shoulders of six servants.

'One day,' I said to the boy, in the hearing of his mother, 'this procession will carry you to the throne of all power. Into your hands they will place the life of the empire, the destiny of the world. Upon your back shall fall the terrible weight of greatness – for you will be given the role of God in human affairs. In that day,' I said, 'for the sake of the earth, for the sake of the *orbis terrarum*, your soul must be in the image of God, that all your deeds be godly.'

That was my voice, the one that released him to manhood.

The other voice received the man he became. Loud, brutal, multitudinous, and mightily persuasive, that second voice roared in the Circus Maximus, thundered in the streets wherever he went:

'Nero Imperator!' it declared, though he was not that, yet.

'Nero Caesar!'

Wild with glee and swollen with flattery, that voice bawled: 'Nero *Divinus*!' Already, you see: divinity.

Wishes, wishes, *mi Galli*. I wish Nero, like you, were unaffected by such screaming, self-serving mendacity. For when it's an emperor who opens himself too much to praise, that part of himself most open, then, to attack is *ourselves*, the people dependent upon his wisdom and his goodwill.

Emperor? 'Nero Imperator'?

In my judgment, that day cannot be far away. Ridiculous Claudius is old, old. He always did shake. But now it's a farcical doddering. He's senile, his brains as cogent as a pillow-cushion. But that wretched body of his, Gallio, however bulging and porcine, still shudders through its appetites! He eats and drinks and whores now more than ever. It must kill him soon. He goes daily to the banquet rooms attended by four women: a blonde Syrian, a huge Nubian with purple lips, a slim Jewess who makes him savour cruel caresses, and a bronze Egyptian. When he eats, the ceiling drops roses and perfumed water. Naked slaves serve – and dance while serving. And when the blowzy emperor begins to sink nose-first into his dishes, here come two more dancers to accomplish before him the union of Psyche and Cupid to the shrieks and the scrapes of flutes and lyres.

I watch Agrippina who watches these feasts. She comes and does not eat. Neither does she touch her husband any more. But he is oblivious to her presence.

I watch her watch with the blinkless, glittering eye of a serpent.

So how is the Achaian weather affecting your health? Your lungs, *mi Galli* – can they inhale that Greek humidity and not drown?

Write me. Divert me. Describe Corinth. Our nephew Lucan greets you. Write.

Titus

45

Okay, I'm on my way. Practically running. What do I mean 'practically'? I *am* running. The weather's good. The dates are in harvest. The sun is high and dry. My legs are strong, and I've got about a thousand reasons for speed, some in my head, some in my heart. But here's the thing: I'm going to take to the sea as much as I can. There isn't time to walk it all the way. So when I get to the port at Seleucia – still today, I've only the sixteen miles today – I'll try to find work. A stevedore, maybe. Sailor'd be best. It'll get me on board and gone. I can learn. If I absolutely have to, I'll pay for the first passage. I've got a little money in my scrip. Otherwise, I'm doing this thing on my own, totally alone – though I hinted to Barnabas he ought to come with me. He wouldn't. He says he's got no heart for travelling any more. Says he wouldn't find a true home anywhere on earth. Too old. Too tired. Looking for Jesus to come. Says his last trip to Cyprus was his last for ever. That's more than two years ago, the same time Paul took off with Silas. Actually, I think Barnabas isn't sure if he wants to see Paul again. I want to see Paul again. It's one of my thousand reasons for going.

Who knew when he left he wasn't coming back? Not me. Peter knew. Barnabas knew. A lot of people knew. Not me. I must have been too young to see the signs. Like, that Paul left angry. And that (so everyone has told me since) he lost the fight. What fight? There was a fight? I thought he was just being good to me and scolding folks for hurting me by skipping my banquet. But it was a *fight*. Hum. So that made me wonder what side *I* was on. Then Judas Barsabbas was preaching that Paul was destroying the kingdom of God, and people were agreeing with that opinion, so I began to feel like a stranger. And the Holy Spirit took away my gift of speaking in tongues so that I'm a lump when we worship.

And I began to miss Paul, who had danced with me one night in Jerusalem and had told me that I was fine. Fine. Just fine the way I was.

So that's a heart-reason for going now on my great adventure. A pretty strong reason, loneliness. And love.

But this other reason's the kicker. It's the one that made me make up my mind. I didn't even think about it. I got the reason yesterday and today I'm running and tomorrow I'll be on a ship.

Last year autumn, Silas showed up in Antioch. Silvanus. He says Paul calls him Silvanus – and he hates that name. Well, when he came he said they'd been as far away as Corinth. Said he decided to come back to make friends with his friends again and to 'cast his lot', as he said it, with Peter. In worship at old Simeon Niger's house, then, he talked about the churches he and Paul had started on their travels to Corinth. Churches first in Galatia, and then in Macedonia, then in Achaia. I'll tell you what: it *dazzled* me to hear these things. My friend, my Paul, was busy still in the distant places, huffing and puffing and preaching Jesus. Hoo, I was gladder than I'd been for a year!

But the same news did something completely different to Judas Barsabbas. He got very grim that night and very pale, which I remember on account of, the next thing was: he disappeared. I mean, the next *day* – one month before the winter set in – Judas Barsabbas was gone. And who am I? No one told me where he went. Well, and I didn't think to ask, either. Things change.

But yesterday good old Barnabas came knocking on my father's door. To see me, not my father. A private meeting, he said. Between two men. So I led him into the dining room, and we sat down, and he laid a soft leather pouch on the table in front of himself, then he folded his hands on top of the pouch and bowed his head so that his huge beard got smashed against his chest. He's going grey now, is Barnabas. He's got the bird-grips of wrinkles in his face, and his nose is bigger, reddish, and I can't remember the last time he laughed.

'Titus,' he said. He raised up his big shoulders and then blew out a whistling sigh through is nose. 'There is news,' he said. He turned and looked at me with dribbles of wrinkles around his eyes.

'Judas Barsabbas writes us from Pessinus in Galatia, where he has been preaching for half a year. He is triumphant. I am,' said Barnabas. He turned away again and he looked down on his folded hands like they were dead fish. White. Useless. 'I am,' he said, 'worried. Pessinus, Palia, Orcistus – Titus, do you remember these names? Silas first told us about them. They're the towns where Paul planted churches. Now Judas Barsabbas writes that he is succeeding in teaching them Torah. They are – 'with joy and gladness', he writes – preparing to be circumcised. Barsabbas counts fourteen men already committed, and another twenty whom he is sure will be circumcised sometime this winter – while the rest of the believers, he writes, give praise to God for the truth.'

So then I'm sitting there, me, Titus – staring at the big, sad man, half-wondering and half-knowing why he's telling me these things, and already my stomach is twisting with fright and delight, both feelings at once.

Barnabas pulled his hands apart and opened the leather pouch and began to take things out of it.

A sheet of papyrus, written on both sides. 'This is a copy of the letter Barsabbas sent, word for word, though the penmanship is mine.'

A handful of money. 'This could get a frugal traveller – if he knows how to bargain patiently – as far as Attalia. If he also knows how to work, and if he isn't proud, that same traveller can get himself the rest of the way to Corinth. In five weeks. Maybe six.'

Finally, a pretty interlocking chain. And attached to the chain, a pendant made of silver.

'This was a gift,' Barnabas said, stringing the chain between his fingers, allowing the pendant to touch the table. 'I gave it once to my friend, but my friend gave it back to me. I wonder,' he said, not turning, but staring at the disk of silver: 'I wonder if it can become a gift again. And if my friend might keep it this time. Because I love him. And I fear I will miss him tremendously.'

That was yesterday.

So today I'm running as fast as I can. Good sunlight, good stout legs, a thousand good reasons for going. I'm dashing the deep road, cut through rock, descending, descending – the easiest part of the day. Seleucia's above me on terraces. In a minute I'll turn a corner and see the bay and the warships of the Roman fleet and the docks. I'll find work. It's too soon to spend the money Barnabas gave me.

risca

46

'Hi-yah! You! Woman! Stop!'

I had just stepped out of Titius's house into a blinding noonday sunlight. My eyes were adjusting. I couldn't see the man who screamed, though I thought I knew the voice. He seemed enraged.

'Stop!' he screamed. 'Wife of Aquila, Jew from Pontus – I have something to say to you!'

He meant me. I stopped. I shaded my eyes and strained to find him, but it only made my vision swim in tears. People filled the sunny street, passing to and fro. Carts moved slowly behind their oxen, wheels grinding the deep grooves of the pavement.

'Yes, you! – walking with your outstretched neck! You, mincing forward on tinkling feet!'

I blinked the water away. There he was. Coming along the street-wall of the synagogue. Sosthenes, the head of the synagogue himself, shuffling sideways, one eye on me, his face askance like a four-legged beast.

'Whore!' he screamed.

I turned to knock on Titius's door. But who would hear me in time? I turned again and hiked the hem of my robe and started to cross the street, calling over my shoulder, 'We have nothing to do with each other!'

Sosthenes broke a brick from the wall that joined the synagogue to Titius's house – and suddenly I knew who had been throwing bricks at us when we worshipped.

The synagogue sits on the north side of the Cenchrean Road, but its door and façade face east, straight at the western wall of the house of Titius Justus. While Titius attended the synagogue, this, his wall, was praised as protection. The space between was cultivated as a little Judea. The man himself was beloved for fencing this 'little Judea' from the street by constructing a brick wall between the corners of the buildings, a beautiful gate in the middle.

But then they banned Paul from the synagogue.

Immediately Titius the Gentile left as well, inviting the apostle to preach in his house.

Next, marvellously, the head of the synagogue – Crispus! – followed Paul to the house next door. For a while he worshipped in both places. But people blamed him for 'limping between two opinions'. They begged him to abandon Paul. He wouldn't; so he, too, was clean cut off.

That cut caused a wondrous bleeding. Gentiles began to flow from the congregation of the Jews to churches in the houses of other Gentiles, Titius Justus, Erastus, Gaius.

There emerged – there *had* to emerge – a new head for the synagogue; but this was a man of angers: Sosthenes, swearing he'd heal this wound to their membership.

He couldn't. He didn't. And maybe the failure drove him crazy.

Lately someone had been throwing bricks at Titius's house while we were worshipping inside. I always assumed it was children – till now, seeing Sosthenes break that brick from the wall and come at me.

'Whore!' he cried. 'Whore! – and worse than a whore: *adulteress*!'

I quickened my pace. I leaped the sewage in the middle of the street. It was noonday, bright and busy! I had to weave through scores of people, but no one would pay attention.

'I have nothing to do with you!' I cried. 'You have nothing to do with me!'

'You're the woman,' Sosthenes screamed, 'who forsook the companion of her youth! You've forgotten the covenant of your God! Your path leads down to death!'

I was running westward toward the Julian Basilica, toward the marketplace. I ran like a slave, my bare legs flying free.

Suddenly, right behind me, the man barked, 'The blood in you – '

I shrieked and shot forward.

But he grabbed my tunic, yanked it, spun me around.

'The blood in you is Jewish,' he yelled, driving me down to my knees, 'even if the heart is not!'

Sosthenes, his face inflamed, his hair a horror of knots, lifted the brick above me.

'Bad enough that you stand among men when they pray,' he screamed. 'But you! I have heard what else you do!'

The brick grew huge in the sunlight. I felt a wild tingling in my scalp where it would hit and split the skin. I threw up my arms.

Sosthenes caught both my wrists in his right hand and twisted them. I cried out.

'With my own ears,' he hissed, bending me backward before him, 'I've heard you disgrace the nation!'

He was directly above me, black as a storm. The rough pavement was cutting my knees.

Sosthenes hissed: 'I have heard you pray, woman – *pray* out loud, pray among the *men*! Through open windows I've heard you utter instruction to men as if *your* authority were greater than theirs! Oh, woman – '

He rose up and the brick rose higher to hit with a harder fall. I dropped my head between my shoulders. Sosthenes began to whip me left and right from the wrists, screaming, 'Show your face! Show your shameful face – '

Then he said, 'Oof.'

Somewhere in the spaces above me, Sosthenes said, 'Oof,' and released me.

I collapsed.

At the same time I heard the round *thump* of a good-sized body hitting ground, not mine.

A lovely fragrance enveloped me, then – the scent of clean flesh. Strong arms slipped beneath my back and my knees, and I was lifted lightly into the air, lifted as if I were a baby; and like a baby I started to cry.

'But I cover my head,' I sobbed.

The man who held me said, 'What?'

'I never prophesy,' I kept sobbing, 'without covering my head.'

'Well, of course not, of course not,' he said. 'Now, where do you want us to take you?'

I looked. I saw Sosthenes sitting in sewage, his legs stuck out like rake-handles, his mouth wide open, striving for air, his face as purple as the seat of Solomon. The brick was still in his left hand, forgotten. But his eyes were not oblivious. He saw the people passing by. He saw their expressions. He saw the good man holding me.

'Where do you want us to take you?'

My saviour was black, a Nubian.

'I can walk,' I said, but I sobbed while I said it. 'I can... walk home,' I said.

'Of course you can. But my mistress would never hear of it.'

'Mistress?'

'There. Awaiting you. See?'

I looked and saw a woman smiling at me through the parted curtains of an expensive litter. Seven strong men – all the same height, all dressed in the same red livery – stood by the long poles that bore the beautiful box. The man who carried me also wore red.

'She heard your cries,' he said, striding toward the litter. 'She sent me to knock courtesy into that round fool on the ground. And she now begs your company.'

Indeed, the woman pulled the curtains wide apart so that the Nubian could hand me into her compartment and set me beside her on pillows.

'Ah, my poor dear,' she said receiving me. She had delicate laugh-lines at the corners of her eyes, lines of smiling around her mouth, a prominent cheekbone.

As they closed the curtain, she offered me a shining linen cloth.

I stared at it, at the tiny weave of the piece.

'For your tears, my dear,' she said, 'to wipe them.'

But I couldn't take it, couldn't soil it, so the woman leaned forward herself, braced my neck in the crook of her wrist, and dabbed my eyes with the cloth.

A child, a child: I was nought but a child that day, brought down by an angry man, raised up by a slave, and delivered into the care of a woman I'd never met before. An angel, I think, whom I loved immediately.

'What shall I call you?' she said. She had grey eyes. Her voice was like doves. She cooed.

'Prisca,' I said.

'Well then, Prisca,' she said, moistening the linen with saliva and cleaning the cuts on my knees, 'call me Phoebe. I live in Cenchreae. But I'll take you to your house before I go to mine.'

'I can walk,' I said – though I confess, I was melting under the woman's touch.

'Where do you live?' she said.

And I said, 'In the North Market.'

She cracked the curtains. Sunlight fell inside. 'Marcus,' she called, 'carry us to the North Market. Oh – and pull that poor man from the middle of the street. It's indecent to leave him there.'

Well, and if I was fast to love Phoebe, she was equally quick to love Aquila. Already that afternoon she took him to be a man both grave and wise – she, in whose manner I saw gravity, wisdom, and grace, all three.

(Actually, my husband's sobriety comes as much from physical caution as from mental deliberations. He's frightfully near-sighted, you know. But who was I to ruin impressions?)

On that first day of our meeting, Phoebe spent the entire afternoon with us in the shop. When I told Aquila the tale of my attack, she heard of Sosthenes and the synagogue, and it caused her to ask questions: why was the man so antagonistic toward us? Aquila answered. He was genuinely grateful for the woman's intervention. He was moved, too, I think, by her interest, her civility, her listening – for nobility had come to our humble shop. Aquila answered, yes, and with a deeper feeling than I'd heard before. His answer brought more questions: but why did we leave the synagogue in the first place? Why would those nearest us hate us the most? How could we maintain this 'peculiar joy', as she called it, 'in the face of human abuse?'

And whom, she asked, did we worship in the house next door?

Aquila then began to talk about Jesus. As slowly as the motion of the sun, he described the righteous life of our Lord, while the grey-eyed woman peered at him and listened, drinking his words like water. He described the awful suffering that Jesus sustained, and the death he died for human sin – so that those who believe in him might be freed from sin and made as righteous as Christ himself before God the Father. I cooked a great pot of porridge. Enough for everyone. Timothy came in. Neither of us said a word. What was happening here in our little shop was purely a wonder to both of us. Silently we served the slaves outside the door, both porridge and a mulled wine. And we listened, all of us.

In twilight Aquila declared that on the third day Jesus Christ was raised from the dead; death, therefore, had lost its power over us, and nothing could grieve us any more, no, nothing could kill us as once we might have been killed.

'That,' said Aquila, my sober husband, solemn in tone and doomful in aspect, 'that is the reason for our joy.'

Joy, said the man, nodding like a donkey at a funeral. He said *joy* – and I, standing in the doorway, lost control. I glanced at Timothy, saw the same delight in his bright eye, and burst out laughing.

Lady Phoebe looked at me with a half-smile, questioning.

Timothy couldn't help it either. Giggles crinkled the young man's face – then he gave up and threw back his head and roared.

'Oh, Aquila!' I cried. His joys are never frivolous, never giddy, seldom productive of smiles. Joy in such massive solemnity strikes me as silly.

'Oh, Aquila,' I cried, 'you are so... wonderful!'

'Yes,' said Phoebe. 'You are, sir, a wonderful preacher.'

So then he lowered his nearsighted face and grinned truly, on account of the blush that was burning the rims of his ears.

And I loved this woman from Cenchreae more and more, for she had defined precisely the pure wonder that had moved both me and Timothy before: My silent husband, wordless Aquila, had spoken. Indeed, indeed – he had preached indeed, and the Spirit of God was upon us.

Phoebe said, 'I will come back tomorrow. You must show me more of this joy tomorrow.'

She kissed Aquila. Oh, my heart – she kissed me too and wrapped the precious linen round my neck. Then she went outside. The slaves lit torches and bore them high in their free hands. The poles of the litter they slipped into straps on their shoulders and quietly walked away, their blessed burden between them.

Then we three sang hymns together. We sang till the lamps died out, and the city was dark, and the fires on the Acrocorinth began to collapse on their ashes.

47

Timothy remained with us that whole night through. He slept in the shop, ready to unbar the door when Paul returned and knocked for entrance. But Paul didn't return; so Timothy, when he left the following morning, promised to watch for him and send him back for a fuller account of this lovely woman, Phoebe from Cenchreae.

About midmorning the great and gorgeous Erastus processed into the North Market. He circled the shops anti-sunwise, then paused by ours and rapped on the collapsible workbench Aquila had built. He had come to hear his dear friend Paul, he said. We told him that Paul wasn't here. He said he was sorry to have missed the apostle, but glad, he said, knocking the workbench with his heavy finger-ring, glad to hear that Timothy had slept well – even if not in his usual room in the house of the Manager of Markets. Surely Timothy would this night exchange the rough quarters of a market shop for the soft pallet of a private domicile.

Oh, and would we let him, Erastus, know when Paul was ready to teach again?

We said we would.

He thanked us and careered onward.

Six or seven others were lounging outside our door. I told them I wouldn't be surprised if Paul didn't come at all that day. They said they'd wait.

In fact, he didn't show.

Well, autumn was here, lengthening nights and shortening days. The greater number of those who regularly gathered for Paul's teaching were spending their daylight hours in the orchards and the vineyards, harvesting dates and the sweeter fruits, treading grapes. Slaves and servants, merchants, smiths, artisans, shopkeepers – even the bankers who financed shipping during these last weeks of the moderate seas – everyone was more occupied than usual. In summer and in winter people had time for talk and the instruction of their souls. In autumn they bent to their labours.

And last year at this time Paul had diminished his public

teaching in order to train a few people privately, preparing us to teach as he taught. I assumed he was doing the same again this year. Last autumn he had selected five of us: me, Aquila, the mild Stephanas, Titius Justus – Timothy, of course, and Silvanus, until that one vanished. Paul declared that he wouldn't be staying in Corinth for ever. He wanted to leave teachers behind. He wanted to send teachers and preachers out to the surrounding cities and villages. Well and he had excellent candidates for the same training this year, Gaius, Crispus, a freedman named Tertius who could write as well as Timothy, a slave they called Achaicus – and Phoebe. I was already thinking great thoughts for that wonderful woman named Phoebe.

So there was no reason to be troubled if Paul were absent for a day. I assumed that he, like any farmer in the fall, was harvesting what he'd sewn in spring: preachers to preach the gospel.

But neither did he return that evening, not to the houses that often fed him, not to the shop for sleeping.

By nightfall Timothy came by, but without news. Erastus, true to his word, had gone around the city asking after Paul. When he discovered nothing on his own, he'd sent a swarm of his clients out of the city, to the 'Haul-across' road covered with cargo and foreigners, to Isthmia in one direction, and to Lechaion in the other – but these, too, failed to find the apostle. Erastus had grown uneasy. He suggested that Timothy spend the second night with us, ready to run and comfort his anxious heart the minute that Paul appeared.

I lay down in darkness and did not sleep. Aquila did. He slept as soundly as ever. Timothy, too, on a pallet downstairs, soon filled the shop with a moist and peaceful snoring. He had consoled himself by recalling Paul's fierce independence.

'Really, Prisca,' he'd said as I stood at the ladder, a lamp in my hand: 'it's his nature to be solitary, beholden to no one.'

I said, 'But who will massage him in the morning?'

Timothy looked at me with a sudden, searching scrutiny. Then he smiled his beautiful Grecian smile. It turned his cheeks to wreaths and sealed the kinship between us. We had a shared ministration.

'Go to sleep,' Timothy said. 'Paul knows his limits as well as he knows his friends.'

I climbed the ladder and doused the light. But I did not go to sleep.

Paul knows his limits. Ah, Timothy was so young, such a sunny boy. He could have the heart of a son or a brother, surely – but not the heart of a sister to Paul, nor the fears of a mother. I agreed Paul knew his limits. But I never believed he'd choose to live within them.

I lay listening to the wind outside, gazing through the cracks in the louvres. It was a starry, cold autumnal night. I rolled to my stomach, sighing. *No, but Paul defies the limits!* I could not keep my mind in the loft. I kept wondering if he was even then exposing his flesh to the elements, endangering himself.

There were whole nights when he would climb the Acrocorinth alone and not come down till morning. Even for only one night, the practice frightened me. What would cause him to linger for two?

He told me of the scent of the pagan shrines he passed, of his own convulsive loathing of the goat smell, his bright hatred for the guttural utterance and the worship of demonic shadows. I don't pretend to understand his motives, why he was drawn toward things he despised, why he would hazard the lairs of the enemy, why he put his body to tests of such severity, the climbing, the cold, the winds that tore at the top, height to a man afraid of heights. *No, Paul assaults the limits!* He told me that high on the northern summit of the rock he would pray out loud, would shout his supplications into the teeth of a screaming wind. Encircled, he told me, by the pale populations of the heavens, he would watch and wait, wait and plead for Christ to come – in whose gaze all would be still, and all would be sweet, and all would be warmer than the wings of the hen who gathers her chicks together. But his uncontrollable yearnings, he told me, and his very pleadings shamed him for the sake of the nations below, unto whom he had not preached. *Come, Jesus! Don't come yet!* There was so much, so much left to do. Paul told me these things with water in his eyes, with a look so distant and mysterious that I thought him caught in a vision. He was seeing with spirit-eyes things I could not see. It scared me, because one of us no longer seemed to inhabit the truer world. One had been transported, and one had been left behind, and I didn't know which of these was Paul and which was his little Priscilla.

What, I wondered in the dread of my midnight waking, could have kept him exposed on the rock for *two* nights running?

What might consume him there? And what would he be when he descended to us again?

Or would Jesus come and pluck us one by one? Oh, that would be the cruellest harvest of all!

I waited for the night-time knock, but no one knocked, and Timothy's slumber continued unbroken.

Timothy

48

'They're arraigning him! Midday! At midday they'll make an official complaint!'

It was one of Erastus's personal servants – acting now as a crier – who alerted us to the crisis. We tumbled from Aquila's shop into a cold, cold morning.

'Arraigning who?' We blew clouds with our talking.

'Paul! At midday! In the forum!'

'Why? What charge?'

The crier didn't know.

'Who's making the charge?'

That the crier did know: Sosthenes, on behalf of the synagogue.

'What do they want?'

The crier didn't know.

'I mean what *punishment* do they want?' This was Prisca, wild-eyed. 'To beat him again?'

The crier shrugged.

'To *kill* him this time?'

The crier looked distressed.

'Where is he now?'

The crier didn't know.

Prisca wailed, 'Who *does* know?'

Erastus, perhaps. Ask Erastus. The poor fellow before us was only a servant who got the news from Erastus, and this is all Erastus told him.

'I'll go,' I said. Prisca's eyes had darkened, making her face so small, her bones so crushable. 'I'll try to find Erastus.'

Immediately I took to my heels and ran. If I lost breath, I can't recall it. My feet were silver. I ran to Erastus's house. He wasn't there. To his offices, next. He wasn't there either, but a scribe told me he'd gone to the Roman proconsul, Gallio, seeking an audience before the arraignment should take place. Erastus thought he might use his civil influence to persuade Gallio not even to hear the charges at all.

God bless Erastus!

On the chance he was awaiting audience among members of the City Council, I sprinted south through the forum, past the bema, through the pillars of the southern portico, to the door of the Council Chamber itself. Gallio had established formal meeting rooms hard by the Chamber, and Erastus was well recognized by those who administered the city.

Yes, several of the magistrates had seen him earlier. But no, they couldn't say where he was now. Nor were they interested in pursuing the matter further.

Paul of what? Tarsus? Never heard of him.

Nor had they heard of the morning's formal charges.

The synagogue? Who knows what they do in that synagogue?

No, no: It'll do no good to try the proconsul's residence. They've already shut the doors to the public.

Sorry. Can't help you. Be patient. Wait till Gallio takes his judgment seat, and all will be known.

Now I was breathless. That fruitless exchange was more exhausting than hard running. I walked west of the portico, panting as after a race, tasting salt in my mouth.

Who was holding Paul? Where should I look? There was a prison beneath the proconsul's house.

If I'd been travelling, if I'd been back in Thessalonica, I could not have felt farther from Paul than I did then. I wouldn't have felt so *helpless*.

Then, by the merest accident, I saw Erastus leaving a tavern where noble Romans dip sweet breads in wine in the morning.

'Erastus!' I cried. 'Erastus!'

He raised a face all full of tragedy and started to walk in my direction.

'What did the proconsul say? Will he cancel the arraignment?'

The man walked right past me into the southern portico and kept going, distracted, heavy with dejection.

I fell in step beside him. We went two hundred paces, all the way to the end of the portico, then he turned, and we retraced the same track back. Erastus was talking – as much to himself as to me.

He had not seen the proconsul – no, not seen Gallio at all.

Even though he had sent no servant in his stead; even though he had gone in his own person to make request for an audience, they – all of them servants themselves! – would not so much as carry his name to the proconsul. Erastus hadn't the bloodline! Erastus was nobody, nobody, and they dealt with him still as a slave.

He slapped his thigh as we walked: 'Impotent! Impotent!' His shaven lip glistened with sweat.

What *had* his reputation earned him? Well, he'd spent the entire last hour sitting in the tavern with a lisping factotum, an undersecretary who took his money for the food, but who refused his suit.

There would be an arraignment, Erastus said, nearly in tears. And once that proceeding began, no one – surely not the impotent Erastus – could intervene. Gallio would hear arguments. Gallio would judge. Gallio would utter punishment. Paul might be granted the right to speak on his own behalf –

'But how,' Erastus wailed, throwing his hands in the air, 'how can Paul prepare a decent defence if he doesn't know the accusations in advance?'

I said, 'Erastus, where is he? Where is Paul?'

He stopped walking.

'In a guest room,' he said. Suddenly he was giggling. 'Oh, my! Oh, my!' Erastus began scraping his face with his fingernails, giggling still: 'In a guest room!' he howled – then he broke into soft sobbing. 'I'm sorry, it isn't funny, it's horrible,' he said, looking at me. 'Paul's locked in the synagogue, in one of the rooms prepared for weary travellers – '

But I knew that room! I'd slept in it myself! Paul was not in Roman custody; he was in a familiar place. All at once he seemed so close to me!

'Can we see him?' I said. 'Let's go talk to him!'

'Little brother, I'm sorry, I'm sorry – we can't.'

'Can't? Why not?'

'They're angry at you.'

'At me? Erastus, at *me*?'

'At Jews who rejected them and went after Paul.'

'That's nothing new!' I cried. 'Ever since Crispus left they've been angry.'

'But something else is new.'

'What?'

Erastus shook and shook his woeful head.

'Insult,' he said. 'Two days ago the manager of your synagogue, Sosthenes, was humiliated by one of Paul's people. A woman. He says that she commanded eight slaves to beat him before a thousand people in the city streets. He says the woman was our little Prisca – '

'Prisca?' I gasped.

Erastus turned fully toward me, his shoulders and eyebrows raised in a grievous appeal: 'I don't believe it,' he sobbed. 'Prisca couldn't hit anyone. It's a lie. It's a damnable lie!'

'Prisca,' I whispered. *So that's why you speak of beatings and killings. That's why your eyes are dark with terror!*

'Don't worry, Timothy,' Erastus said, reaching to embrace me. 'They won't punish little Prisca. It's Paul they're after – '

'Erastus! Listen,' I said, seizing his hands before they seized me: 'The woman with eight slaves is Phoebe from Cenchreae. Do you know her? I know her. If anyone was attacked two days ago, it wasn't Sosthenes. It was Prisca herself!'

Erastus's face went slack at the news.

'It's happened before. It's following us,' I said, panting again, overwhelmed by the evil wherever we went in the world. Maybe the race would never be won.

'Paul was attacked in my hometown and beaten so bad we thought he was dead! He was beaten in Philippi. He was imprisoned in Philippi. They tried to beat him in Thessalonica. They tried to beat him in Berea – '

Oh, what a *child* I was! I wanted to cry for Paul. I wanted to weep for my own helplessness. I wanted the sweetness of plain rage. I wanted to throw stones at the synagogue.

'Erastus,' I said, still holding his hands in mine. 'Erastus, can you – ' I said, casting about for a word, an act, a wall to stop things, a wall against my anger and our enemies. 'Erastus – can we fill the marketplace? When they arraign Paul, can we crowd the forum with people? Our people, yes, yes – but others too? Corinthians, servants, sailors, strangers, anyone, everyone? A thousand times *more* than Sosthenes has friends? Can we do that? Is there a way to do that?'

Erastus didn't ask why. What would I have answered? – that I want a wall?

Instead, the big man lifted up our hands till we formed a tent together, under which he shuffled his feet. He danced. Among the pillars of the southern portico, Erastus began to lead me in a silly, skipping dance.

'Little brother, prophet of God,' he announced, 'you have given me back my powers again. Yes!' he bellowed. 'We can do that!'

He let me go and clapped his hands and turned to the first liveried slave who passed by. 'Here! Come here!' he shouted. 'Whose man are you?'

The slave stopped and said, 'I belong to Annaeus.'

'Good. I'll pay Annaeus for your time and you for your service. I am Erastus, Manager of Corinthian Markets. Do this for me: run among the shops announcing that they must, every one of them, cease trading at noon today. By my express and sudden command, all commerce shall be halted for the pleasure of the people – all commerce, that is, except for that of bakeries, whose bread I shall buy myself, which bread I shall distribute in the forum. At midday! Announce that there will be bread in the forum at the middle of the day.'

Prisca

49

*But you said, O Lord – you said it to Paul – that none would
attack him to harm him! Jesus, keep your promise! Keep your
promise!*

I wanted to see Paul when he came out. I wanted to be close
to events. This was not a choice. It was the pressure of my heart.
I hardly knew, then, how I kept moving forward through the
crowds toward the bema and the judgment seat.

I am a light and little woman. All Corinth is taller than me.
I slipped through gaps among the people. I lost Aquila. I arrived
alone at the platform built in front of the bema. I put my toes
right at its bottom step so that no one could stand in front
of me.

*O God and Father of my Lord Jesus Christ, comfort Paul,
comfort your servant and my dear brother in his affliction!*

The bema is twice as high as I am and long both left and right.
It's like the rostrum in Rome – both of them podiums for
speaking, for meetings and proclaimings. Or judgments. There
are rooms on the ground level at either end. Paul was in one of
those rooms, waiting.

The platform between the bema and me was empty. It was
three steps high with a rail around the edges.

No one stood in the space that divided the platform from the
bema. No one could, during the hours of judgment.

I watched as servants brought out Gallio's chair – wooden,
carved, magnificent with armrests and a back.

Crowds milled everywhere in the forum, laughing, shouting,
enjoying the flush of noonday wine and bellies full of bread. They
had gathered to eat. But the appearance of the proconsul's chair
signalled the judgments to come and gave focus for their woozy
interest.

The man beside me yelled, 'Who's accused? Who's going to bleed?'

I recognized the voice. I took a quick sideways glance and saw Apelles, the irascible shoemaker who had despised Paul from the very beginning. His body stank of a sour sweat, but I would not move and lose my place at the platform.

Kyrie, eleison!

A door in the wall at the back of the bema opened. Four soldiers emerged and took up positions left and right of the chair. A scribe, next, with his writing kit, moved toward a low stool and sat. Several secretaries appeared, then came Gallio himself.

He was tall and lean, his spine bent somewhat forward. The wind caught at his toga. When he gathered the cloth in his hand, I could see how sunken was his chest. Where was there space for breath in the man?

His motion was courtly. He acknowledged the crowds by inclining his head – but he frowned faintly and, at the back of his hand, whispered something to one of the secretaries, who looked at the people and shrugged.

Gallio lowered himself into the chair. His knees beneath the folds of toga were painfully sharp. He coughed into a linen cloth, then nodded.

The scribe called out a name in Latin. Not Paul's name. Not the name of anyone I knew. *Patience, patience, Prisca*: while prayers kept flying from my lips.

At the crying of that name, a small, round man came bustling out of the room to the left of the bema. He was followed by three others, two with weapons and one in shackles, a tall, rawboned fellow with long, blonde hair.

'*Adsevero!*' the small man shouted in Latin as he stomped up the steps and through the railing to the platform. He carried a tablet on which these exact words were inscribed, but he probably couldn't read. 'I assert,' he declared, 'that this slave belongs to me in virtue of the law of the Quirites!' Nervous, angry, pointing at the man in shackles: 'This one! This barbarian slave! They found him in Thrace, posing as a *grammaticus*!'

Gallio leaned forward. To the blonde slave he said, 'You can read?'

The round man screamed, 'So he can read! So what? What's that got to do with anything?'

People closest to the platform clucked and whistled their contempt, but whether for the anger or else for the reading, I couldn't tell.

'And you,' Gallio said to the owner, 'I suppose you have proofs of ownership?'

'Purchase documents! Bought him young! Insolent, lazy – '

The proconsul ignored the rest of the round man's outburst. He leaned left and said to the scribe, 'The action has been initiated.' It was a formal pronouncement, which the scribe wrote swiftly upon his tablets. 'The issue before us,' Gallio said, 'is ownership which, if proven, condemns the slave for the theft of his own person. In that case the *fugitivus* will be flogged and branded on the forehead with the letter F.'

People in the forum produced a smattering of applause.

Apelles the shoemaker shouted, 'I train slaves!' He reached over the railing and slapped the white slave on his buttocks. 'Good sir, rich sir,' he laughed, 'let me train your hairless slave!'

At the same time the proconsul was naming an adjudicator for this case and setting a date for arguments. He looked at the plaintiff below, who said, 'Yes, yes, yes.'

'Clear the stand,' a soldier commanded. Master and slaves left by that narrow pit between the platform and the bema.

Then the scribe stood up to call another name.

The instant he rose, my heart raced. I hadn't seen Paul in two days. What had they done to him?

But again, it wasn't Paul. It was a stranger's name.

Two Corinthians appeared to argue over a piece of property.

As they mounted the platform, one said loudly – as much to the judge as to the other – 'I summon you to justice.' He said, *'In ius te voco,'* to place himself and his cause under official authority. He'd brought a lump of earth as symbol for the land he said he owned.

Gallio uttered formal words.

The men began to state claims and counterclaims. Money was pledged on both sides, security against the final verdict.

I wasn't listening. I was shifting my weight from foot to foot. I was looking around for Aquila. For Timothy or Titius or anyone whose familiar face might comfort me. *Jesus, keep him safe. Jesus, keep us all.*

High behind the bema, passing among the pillars of the south portico, I thought I saw the form of a woman: Phoebe –

But then the scribe stood up and called out in Latin, 'Let Sosthenes approach on behalf of the synagogue of the Jews.'

Sosthenes!

My ears filled with a rushing sound, a waterfall sound, the roaring of my own blood.

From the room at the right of the bema five men stepped out into sunlight. There he was! Paul! Paul was in the midst of them, his wrists in ropes.

They walked toward the platform, where they were joined by six more men. So these had been waiting in the crowd around me. How could I have missed them? All ten were members of the synagogue, and I knew them. I mean, I recognized their faces. Grim, solemn men!

O save him! Save your servant, Paul!

Was it my anxiety that made him look so pale? Was he always so pale? That black eyebrow gave his head a moon-white pallor. His eyes were redder than usual. Irritated. His neck was thin. I could see the cords and the vessels in his neck. He was wearing nothing but a tunic, like a slave on an errand. He didn't turn and look at the people. He didn't see me. I wished he would speak so I could hear his Voice. I know Paul best by his Voice.

Nine of the men on the platform formed a semicircle, their backs to the railing. The tenth man stepped centre, a papyrus rolled up in his left hand. He was facing away from me, but I knew him. I knew Sosthenes by his hair. I hated that hair, tight knots and furious curls.

Sosthenes, the head of the synagogue, raised the papyrus like a wave offering toward the bema, the chair, and the judge in the chair. He bowed and began to unroll it, at the same time announcing in Greek: 'By Gallio's permission, and begging his indulgence, we will read and present a complaint – '

But Gallio raised a languid hand.

He coughed. In Latin he said, 'Why is that man bound?'

The interruption confused Sosthenes. Or perhaps the question did. He glanced at Paul, who returned the look unblinking.

'Well, he, that is, Paul,' Sosthenes began, still speaking in Greek, 'this same fellow, Paul of Tarsus – '

'*Solve eum!*' Gallio said.

Sosthenes stumbled into silence. He cleared his throat. 'Excuse me?' he said. 'What did you say?'

Gallio smiled. In Greek he said, 'Unbind the man you've

brought before me.' He spoke in a manner most urbane, as if he were cajoling kindness from a child.

Sosthenes squared his shoulders. 'No, but the law allows it.' He tapped his temple, quoting: '"If the adversary resists" – so states your law, your own law, proconsul – "if the adversary resists, the plaintiff can use force, but always in the presence of witnesses." Look: we have ten witnesses – '

Gallio raised a slender finger and switched it left and right. 'Unless your charge regards some vicious crime,' he said, 'there is no need to keep him bound.'

'But it does!' Sosthenes replied immediately. 'The charge specifies a savage bodily – '

'Cut him loose, Jew!'

A rough voice behind me shouted, 'Cut him loose!'

People began to laugh, though there was no humour in it. They moved closer to the platform. The sour-smelling Apelles was pressed against me. My mouth was dry. I kept trying to swallow.

'Cut him loose!'

Sosthenes turned and shot quick, nervous looks at the crowd.

Paul, my Paul, stood silently by, gazing at Sosthenes with curiosity. No, with something more than that: with an intense interest. He was watching no one else, nothing else, but Sosthenes.

Suddenly that head of the synagogue drew himself up to his full height and faced the proconsul above him on the bema. 'Sir,' he said, 'if you will allow me to read the accusation and to adduce the testimony of even a single witness, you will hear how vicious are the crimes that have been done in this man's name.'

He raised the papyrus to read it.

Again, Gallio interrupted, smiling. 'My friend,' he said, leaning forward and beckoning Sosthenes to step nearer, nearer, and nearer still.

Blinking, walking stiffly, Sosthenes obeyed.

'My friend, I want to save you from further embarrassment.'

The proconsul's tone was intimate, implying that this present matter involved no more than the two of them. But we could hear him. Everyone could hear him. The crowd grew hushed in order to listen, and silence fell upon the forum.

The silence scared me. My mouth kept trying to swallow. I looked toward my Paul in his thin tunic, bound at the wrists by ropes, pale and perfectly calm, watching Sosthenes.

Gallio said, 'If your charge concerns an altercation which you experienced the day before yesterday on the Cenchreaen road, a physical altercation in which you received a blow to your own person, I suggest you withdraw the charge or else revise it – '

That was me!

My face flamed at the public recognition. That 'altercation' concerned *me*! How many people were staring at Prisca now?

Sosthenes cried, 'Why?' He stamped his foot and cried, 'Why are you persecuting us? Why should we withdraw the charge?'

Lowly, lowly, the crowd began to growl.

Gallio paused and coughed. 'Because you, Sosthenes,' he said with a cold articulation, 'were the aggressor. You, sir, initiated the altercation.'

'I, I,' Sosthenes choked. He shook the papyrus like a stick at the judge and cried, 'I initiated nothing!'

'Careful, careful,' the proconsul said. 'Say nothing more till you've met every witness to this unfortunate event.' He rose and turned to the door behind him. '*Veni huc,*' he called. 'Come hither.'

The language invited one person only, yet two came through the door.

The first was a Nubian – *the* Nubian, in fact! I went up on my toes with gladness. Here was the marvellous black man that had caught me when I thought I was going to be beaten. *Marcus! His name is Marcus!*

And immediately behind him – moving without a tread, smoothly floating toward Gallio on the platform – came Phoebe, my radiance from Cenchreae! The courtly Roman took her hand and led her forward with a dignified stride.

Oh, Paul, this is the woman I want you to meet. You will love her as much as I do.

Suddenly the day was going well, and very well indeed!

Gallio looked down on Sosthenes. So did Phoebe look down – but at me! I think she was looking at me!

I beamed right back at her.

'Never again, sir, accuse me of persecutions.' Gallio curled his lip with patrician contempt. 'Accuse me instead of truth. This particular witness brings a disinterested testimony, you see. Nothing to gain, nothing to lose. And she is of the highest repute. You would be a *damn* fool to contradict her.

'Now then, Sosthenes of the Jewish Synagogue,' Gallio said,

stepping backward and giving his voice the ring of a rhetorician: 'If your accusation regards no vicious crime, you will immediately unbind this "fellow", as you call him, this Paul from Tarsus, and let him stand freely on his own.'

Sosthenes wiped his mouth. He glanced at Paul. He twisted round to the men behind him, seeking some word, some counsel, I think. There was a wild bewilderment in his eyes, and in that instant I did not hate him. None of his company responded. They shuffled and stared at their feet. Only Paul continued to gaze at the poor man with an unwavering attention.

'Cut him *loose*, Jew!' The yell in my ear – the yell made me jump. Apelles the shoemaker screamed, 'Noxious Jew-roach – cut him loose!'

Somebody else cried, *Loose!* Others chanted: *Loose! Loose!*

Sosthenes acted. He crushed the papyrus and threw it down and pointed toward the bema, shouting: 'We too have laws!' There was a stubborn conviction in him. The man was unclosing his soul! 'Ours are the laws of life and death, laws greater than your human codes, because these are the laws of heaven!'

'Cut him loose, poltroon! Cut him loose, you grovelling Jew!'

Scorn and laughter, catcalls, hooting, whistling filled the forum like the crackle and the flashings of a coming storm.

At the top of his lungs, Sosthenes roared: 'This man is persuading others to worship God contrary to the laws of heaven!'

Gallio gathered the folds of his toga close to his body. I couldn't hear his words. I read his lips. He said, 'Since this is a matter of your own law, see to it yourselves.'

He swept the toiling multitude with an impassive glance; then, taking Phoebe's hand, he led her to the back wall and out the door. Soldiers, secretaries, the cringing scribe all followed –

'CUT HIM LOOSE!'

All at once, Apelles the shoemaker launched himself. He leaped past me, over the rail and onto the platform. I saw a round-edged knife in his left hand. With one stroke he cut the rope that held Paul's hands, then, whirling round to the right, he struck Sosthenes in the cheek with a backward crack of his elbow.

Sosthenes stiffened. He opened his mouth. But a second hit to the side of his head sent him tumbling down into the space between the platform and the bema – and then the great storm broke.

Men surged forward, breaking the railing and swarming the platform. They plunged down where Sosthenes had fallen, swinging and screaming an animal anger. They formed a wall, a circle concealing their violence.

The nine men of the synagogue had vanished.

I stood with my hands over my ears, wailing for my blood kin, my fellow Jew.

But then, louder than the multitude, piercing my hands, my ears and my head, cutting the air like a knife blade, came the high cry of a single Voice!

'*Meeeee!*' it sang on one note, snapping like a banner under heaven: '*Hit meeeeeee!*'

I knew that Voice! Nasal, whining, outcrying every other sound! The Voice belonged to Paul!

And all this happened in a twinkling:

I saw Paul on the bema, at the front edge of the bema, just before he leaped.

I watched as he threw himself down into the violence and was swallowed up.

And I began to run. I climbed the steps in front of me. I drove myself forward through people and over people, until I could see down into the stone pit between the platform and the bema, at the bottom of which was Sosthenes, unconscious. But there, too, was Paul!

Paul, my Paul, had stretched his body, belly up, over Sosthenes, his arms flung wide to cover the other completely.

Between me and Paul there crouched the shoemaker Apelles, the knife in his left hand cocked, ready to drop and slash. Paul was looking straight at the shoemaker, pleading with him, 'Me! Hit me! Apelles, hit me instead of him!'

'Give me the reason!' Apelles barked. 'Fight me!'

Paul said, 'No.'

'Take a swing at me,' Apelles yelled.

Paul said, 'I can't. I won't.'

Suddenly Apelles drew back his right hand and struck Paul in the mouth, crying, 'Fight me, dammit!'

I gasped.

Paul squeezed his eyes shut for an instant, then looked up again at Apelles. He nodded, as if with enormous pity. 'It's okay,' he said. Blood threaded the lines between his teeth. 'Apelles, don't be afraid.'

The shoemaker screamed into Paul's face, 'Fight me, you bastard! Stand up for yourself!'

Paul didn't move. The ropes like bracelets still circled his wrists. 'It's okay,' he said. 'Everything is okay.'

Apelles lunged. It was a false start. With a yell, then, and with redoubled force he struck Paul on the forehead, splitting skin to the white bone.

I started to sob. No one else made a sound.

Paul's eyes were closed.

'Bastard!' Apelles screamed. 'Spineless Jew!'

Suddenly the wound filled up and overflowed with blood. Blood poured over Paul's brow and into his hair. He opened his eyes. He didn't move his arms. He blinked several times and focused on Apelles and cleared his throat and smiled. 'Don't worry,' he said in his nasal voice. 'Everything is okay. Because I love you.'

Apelles recoiled as if stung. 'What did you say? Don't say that!'

'There's no reason for you to be afraid of me, Apelles,' Paul said. 'Because I love you.'

The shoemaker threw his weight forward. He brought down the knife in his left hand, pressing the edge against Paul's throat and whispering, 'I am *not* afraid.' Whimpering, 'Goddammit, I am *not* afraid, because who can kill who here?'

'Only God can kill,' Paul said. 'But God knows your name, Apelles. God is calling you by name. He is speaking to you through me.' Now Paul lifted his head. He raised himself, his thin chest, to his elbows, causing the shoemaker to take the knife backward, causing the blood to rain forward down his own face, causing Sosthenes to stir beneath him.

Paul spoke dead-level to Apelles. He said, 'It is God who speaks. It is God who says, *I love you, Apelles. I have loved you all your life long.*'

A perfect stillness fell upon the world. I was not sobbing. I was holding my breath. But then I heard a grievous moaning: 'Oooo. Oooo.' It was Apelles the shoemaker, rocking back on his heels. His lip was trembling. His whole expression was crashed. 'Oooo. Oooo.'

Paul said, 'Be at peace, Apelles, beloved of God. There is no reason to be afraid.'

Because he was afraid. I too saw the fear in the shoemaker's eyes.

'Oooo,' he wept. He stood up. No one pressed upon him any

more. People had fallen away. He dropped the curved knife and began to walk backward over the platform. He turned and went into the forum, northward, moaning as he went.

And so the storm was over.

No, but the storm had *been* over. I just hadn't noticed. The crowds had dispersed. People moved through the marketplace in the regular boil of business again, merchants and soldiers and children running. The masons made their hammers ring on rock. Shop doors were open. Dogs pawed through the trash of the people, crumbs of bread, dusty meat, grains of salt on the ground.

And here was Aquila, quietly standing behind me. How long had he been there?

I gestured toward the pit between the bema and the platform. Aquila nodded. We stepped down and knelt beside Paul and Sosthenes, two men wounded and leaning against each other.

Sosthenes was confused. His tight, neat hair glistened with mud and sweat and blood. It was Paul's blood – though I don't think Sosthenes knew who held him now, whose arm embraced him, whose cheek was by his cheek.

The fountain from Paul's forehead had laced both men's faces in red.

'Here,' I said. While Aquila took Sosthenes' elbows and heaved him to his feet, I untied the precious linen cloth from round my neck and handed it to Paul. 'Here, use this,' I said.

He gave the cloth two folds and bent his head and laid it to his wound.

Aquila led Sosthenes like a drunken man away.

Paul sighed.

'Priscilla, Priscilla,' he whispered. 'My little Prisca, how good it is to see you again. But I knew you would be here.'

Then he raised his eyes to me and began to chuckle through a cock-eyed grin.

'The reason I didn't lie face down on Sosthenes,' he said, 'is that I'm tired of getting beat on the back. My back can't take much more. I thought I'd offer the smiters a fresh part of my flesh. But look,' he chuckled. He removed the linen and brought his forehead within inches of my sight. 'Priscilla, look and tell me: didn't the shoemaker pop that old scar open again? The same old scar?'

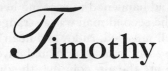

Timothy

50

And then we were gone.

In the time it took to sell the leather shop, we gave away what we'd been gathering for eighteen months in Corinth; we kept the necessities, for which we sewed new bags from old material; Paul dictated, I wrote and we dispatched a letter to be read in several Galatian towns, Pessinus, Palia, Orcistus; we tucked the shop-money in belts and bound the belts around our bodies; we bid farewell to a hundred friends, weeping, eating one last supper, commending each other to God – then we walked to Cenchreae. We were a goodly company on the road: brothers and sisters of all three churches, Crispus and his family, Erastus and Gaius each with his servants. Nearly twenty people altogether, laughing, sighing, singing hymns. That night Phoebe housed everyone in her villa – 'Because of my love for Aquila.' Paul preached, promising to return. In the morning six of us boarded a boat for Ephesus in Asia, where we would divide into two parties of three. Aquila and Prisca and Sosthenes planned to establish themselves in Ephesus while we – Paul and Titus and I – sailed all the way to Syria. Paul wanted urgently to get to Jerusalem.

It was Paul's anger that had driven us so swiftly from the city.

And it was Titus, or rather the news young Titus brought, that had ignited the anger in Paul.

On the day the apostle was arraigned before Proconsul Gallio – in fact, during the arraignment itself – two men found me high above the forum, on the hill of the ancient Temple, where I could watch the multitude and the dumb show at the bema, both. The first man I recognized as a regular guard at the Cenchreaen

Gate. He said he had happened to spot me here. Did I know where Paul was? The second man was a stranger to me, a vigorous youth, well muscled, ruddy and healthy and blooming.

Yes, I knew where Paul was. Why should anyone have to ask? There, I said, stabbing the air, pointing: the one tied up, the one accused of a crime, that's Paul.

The youth followed my line of sight and grew suddenly very red. His skin began to quiver, like the flank of a warhorse.

The guard said he had to get back to his post. He said that this young man had travelled all the way from Syrian Antioch looking for Paul. The lad's name was Titus. Would I, the guard asked, take young Titus to Paul whenever it was convenient to do so?

'If,' I said, 'they don't jail him or kill him first.'

The youth shot me a horrified look.

'Kill him? Kill Paul?'

The guard thanked me for my willingness and left.

I felt suddenly sorry for having flashed with anger. The young man was too tender to it. And he seemed truly concerned about Paul.

'Well, not *kill* him,' I said.

I tried to explain the circumstances as I knew them, the accusations, the synagogue, the head of the synagogue, Sosthenes – but we both kept staring down at the forum, growing increasingly nervous. The crowd had formed a tight ball at the bema, was crouched and growling, like a beast approaching its prey. The proconsul was standing, a woman at his side. Her face was too distant to identify. Her posture looked familiar. He turned and departed by the back door. Everyone on the bema – everyone, the soldiers too – followed him. Then with a hoarse, sustained roaring, the whole crowd converged on the stand in front of the bema, and Paul and Sosthenes both disappeared, as if the sea had drowned them.

I began to run. So did young Titus. He would have outdistanced me, but he didn't know the way. We had to go west to get east, back toward the well of Glauce.

By the time we came into the northwest corner of the forum, the multitude had changed directions, was scattering outward and blocking our progress. I saw Erastus mounted on a horse. There were four or five others cantering among the people and crying, 'Break it up! Break it up!'

I had no idea where Paul was.

Only after the forum was normal again did I see a familiar face: Aquila at the eastern end of the forum, helping someone ascend the broad steps past the Peirene Fountain. I ran and caught up with him and was astonished to discover Sosthenes in his arms – Sosthenes, stunned and covered with blood.

Aquila told me it was Paul's blood.

He said that Paul was by the bema.

I turned and ran – and this time young Titus, whom I had forgotten, flew by me as if he had wings.

Then occurred a silly scene.

Just as Titus arrived at the bema, so did Erastus astride his steed, calling, 'Paul, Paul, what happened to you?' He began to dismount.

Paul, sitting on the platform face-to-face with Prisca as if they were having a picnic; Paul, bloody, the front of his tunic crimson with wet blood – Paul turned to see Erastus, but noticed Titus instead.

He screamed. Paul the apostle screamed and leaped to his feet and threw his arms around the young man. 'Titus! Titus! Titus!' he screamed, and the young man was grinning with strong white teeth, and suddenly Paul sagged. He bumped down to sitting on the platform, his head drooping forward. Everyone rushed toward him, reached toward him, but he shook his head and looked up, smiling.

'Dizzy,' he said. 'Just dizzy.'

Erastus announced, 'Why, the very reason for which I've brought my horse, soft-saddled and ready to carry you home, Paul – to my house, Paul, where we can heal you.'

Erastus bent low, as if to pick up the apostle, but Paul's attention wasn't on Erastus.

'Titus,' he said. 'O Titus, come give me a shoulder to lean on. Come show me your love, sweet Titus of mine.'

So the two of them moved off through the forum, Prisca beside them, and I heard what sounded like three puffs of wind, and I looked, and I saw great Erastus reduced by emotion. It had been a difficult day.

At the shop that evening Paul would not be comforted. He paced up and down the small room, spitting fury, dictating a spew of words which I strove to transcribe on fresh papyrus. But it seemed that the man had lost more blood than he would admit. At odd moments he would slump down, pale and fainting and suddenly still. No matter: as soon as his senses returned, he rose up again, pacing, raging.

'*Kuno-tharses!* Hateful! Deceitful! Foes of the freedom of Christ! Timothy, they gave me the right hand of fellowship! Titus remembers, don't you, Titus? No one required you to be circumcised. Nothing was added to me. Nothing! But now they want to destroy the gospel of Christ!'

Young Titus had brought us the copy of a certain letter by a man named Judas Barsabbas, a letter in which Barsabbas was thanking God that fourteen plus twenty men were likely to be circumcised by Passover. The letter had been sent to Antioch, but its place of origin was Pessinus in Galatia – the same place where Paul had fallen ill two and a half years ago, the town where Paul and Silvanus and I had preached and established a baby church.

'Circumcised?' Paul howled. 'Circumcised! The dogs are pursuing us, stealing God's children as if they were sheep, cutting them bloody, casting them under the Law, casting them straight to hell!

'*Circumcised*! Oh, let them lay the blade of the knife on their own most tender parts – and slip! I wish they'd castrate themselves!'

The sea would be shut to shipping in less than a month. Then snow would close the mountain passes. Time for travelling was limited.

Paul wanted to leave for Jerusalem in five days: Jerusalem first; then Antioch – and then, when the Cilician Gates were open for travel, to Galatia before the Passover. Titus and I agreed. We said we'd be ready tomorrow.

Aquila and Prisca had been subdued that whole evening, part of which they spent alone in the loft above the shop. I thought Paul's wrath was troubling them, or else that the day itself, its fights and its triumphs, had bewildered them. But I was wrong. The cause of their quietness was closer to loss.

In the darkness, in the approaching cold, they descended the ladder and softly disclosed their hearts to us: 'Paul, please, take us with you.' They knew how to live in tents, they said. They had already moved once, leaving everything behind, and were prepared to move as often as necessary for the sake of the gospel of their Lord Jesus Christ.

Paul stopped pacing. His agitation vanished. He picked up the oil lamp and went to Prisca where she had remained in the back by the ladder. He lifted the lamp beside their two faces, rimming their cheeks with a bashful light, his a hawk's glare, hers uncertain. Distinctly, soundlessly, he whispered, 'Priscilla?' He called her 'Priscilla'. I'd never heard the name before.

Prisca bent her head and looked at the floor between them. Her dark eyes sank into shadow. Her hair was pulled tightly back to the nape of her neck, so that she presented Paul with a straight white part from brow to crown. Almost imperceptibly, she nodded.

And Paul said, 'Yes.' Then he put the lamp down and pitched himself again into his restless pacing. He wondered aloud: Could Aquila sell the shop in less than *ten* days? Paul would wait ten, he said, but no more. It would kill him to wait longer.

Yes, Aquila could sell the shop in less than ten days.

Good, good.

And what about this, Paul asked: What if the two of them travelled just halfway with us? – to Ephesus, stopping there while we went on? Paul said that Corinth should be a model for their next metropolis. Let Prisca and Aquila find living quarters and set up another workshop and win friends in Ephesus, just as they had in Corinth, and so prepare for Paul's arrival there at a later date. Because he was coming back, he said with vigour. Oh, yes, he was returning to continue his mission among the Gentiles, just as soon as he took care of business in the east.

No, he said: this time we wouldn't travel on foot. We would ship eastward. 'The winds will be with us, sudden and strong,' he said. And God must be with us too.

There were two advantages to our waiting the full ten days:

First, Paul had time to regain his strength – though when we went forth toward Cenchreae, walking, the bow-legged man did not scramble ahead of the pack, as once he would have done. He had aged, Paul had. His body was tired. And his back tormented him more than anyone knew. He walked in a sort of drop-shouldered pain.

And second, Paul had time to talk with Sosthenes. Two men of intensities, they debated in the marketplace, argued in the streets, quarrelled beside the synagogue, and shouted so loudly in Little Judea, I thought they'd pick up bricks to knock each other down.

In the end, Sosthenes put money in his belt and came with us.

Paul

51

Paul, an apostle – not from men nor through man,
  but through Jesus Christ and God the Father,
  who raised him from the dead,
  To the churches of Galatia:

Grace to you and peace from God the Father and our Lord
Jesus Christ!

How can you do this? How can you so quickly desert the one
who called you in the grace of Christ? — desert him for a different
gospel? No, no, no: there is no other gospel. But there are
different people, different preachers, those who are among you
right now, troubling you, trying to pervert the gospel of Christ! I
tell you, if anyone – even an angel from heaven – should preach a
gospel contrary to the one we preached, let him be damned to
hell. Do you hear me? Shall I repeat it? If anyone is preaching to
you a gospel contrary to that which you have already received, *let
him be damned to hell*!

For the gospel I preach is not some human thing. I did not
receive it from man or woman. It came through a revelation of
Jesus Christ! And it was accepted by the whole church!

You heard about my former life in Judaism, how violently
I persecuted the church of God, trying even to destroy it. You
heard how I advanced in Judaism beyond many my own age, so
zealous was I for the traditions of my fathers. But when the God
who had set me apart before I was born, the God who had called
me through his grace – when that God was pleased to reveal his
Son to me so that I might preach him among the Gentiles, *I did
not confer with flesh and blood*! I did not go up to Jerusalem! I
did not listen to those who were apostles before me. I went away
into Arabia. I preached in Damascus. And only after three years

did I finally go to meet Peter. Did I stay long? No! I stayed no more than fifteen days with him in Jerusalem, seeing no one else except James, the Lord's brother.

Listen to me, I'm telling the truth! Before *God*, I am not lying!

I went from Peter straight into the regions of Syria and Cilicia where I preached the gospel Christ had given me. I planted, and the Spirit gave the increase. Churches began and people believed, exactly as happened for you in Galatia!

It was only after fourteen years that I went again to Jerusalem, this time with Barnabas and Titus. I went to lay before the pillars of the church the gospel I preach to the Gentiles. I went by a revelation. And I went because false brothers had been spying out the freedom we have in Christ Jesus, planning to bring us under bondage.

Listen: those pillars of repute added *nothing* to me! Even Titus, born a Greek, was not compelled to be circumcised! On the contrary, when they saw that I had been entrusted with the gospel to the uncircumcised, just as Peter had been entrusted with the gospel to the circumcised, and when they perceived the grace that was given to me, James and Peter and John gave me and Barnabas the right hand of fellowship, that we should go to the Gentiles and they to the circumcised.

Listen. Are you listening to me? I myself, a Jew by birth and not a Gentile, have believed in Christ Jesus in order to be justified by faith in Christ, and not by works of the Law, because by works of the Law shall no one be justified. No one, neither Jew nor Greek! Through the Law, I have died *to* the Law, that I might live to God. I have been crucified with Christ. It is no longer I who live, but Christ who lives in me; and the life I now live in the flesh I live by faith in the Son of God, who loved me and gave himself for me.

But *you*, you brainless Galatians! You, who had that model in me when I came preaching to you! You (oh, I fear I've laboured over you in vain) – you: who has bewitched you now?

You had a picture painted right before your eyes of Jesus Christ dying on the cross! Nothing could have been plainer!

Let me ask you this: did you receive the Spirit by works of the Law? – or did you receive the Spirit by hearing with faith? Well, then you've lost your brains in the meantime, because you started in the Spirit, and now you want to end with the flesh. You experienced *God* by the Spirit and in miracles, and now it seems that your experience was all in vain.

But scripture says that Abraham 'believed God, and it was reckoned to him as righteousness'. Don't you see that the real children of Abraham are people of faith? Scripture foresaw that God would justify you Gentiles by faith; therefore already to Abraham scripture preached the gospel which includes you, saying, 'In you shall all the nations be blessed.' Everyone who has faith is blessed with Abraham – who was himself, first and foremost, a soul full of faith!

In Christ Jesus you are all children of God, through faith. For those who have been baptized into Christ have put on Christ. There is neither Jew nor Greek! There is neither slave nor free! There is neither male nor female – for you are all one in Christ Jesus. And if you are Christ's, then you are Abraham's offspring and heirs according to God's promise.

Listen: as long as they are children, heirs are no better than slaves, even though they might legally one day own the estate. Children are under guardians, trustees, tutors until the date set by the father for their inheritance – exactly as Jews were under the tutelage of the Law while they waited for the fulfilment of the promise. But when the right time had finally come, God sent forth his Son, born of woman, born under the Law, to redeem those who were under the Law, so that we might receive adoption as children. And because you are children, God has sent the Spirit of his Son into our hearts, crying, *Papa! Father!* So through God you are no longer slaves, but children and heirs.

In the past, when you didn't know God, you were in bondage to beings that by nature are no gods. But now that you've come to know God – and now that you are known *by* God – how can you turn back into slaves again? – slaves of the weak and beggarly elemental spirits?

Please, please, I beseech you, brave Galatians, be like me again – as I have been like you. You did me no wrong. Surely you remember how I happened to come to you: I was sick. Yes, and though my condition tested you sorely, you never scorned me. You never despised me. In fact, you received me as an angel of God – as if I were Jesus himself! You were so happy in those days! What happened since then? There was a time when you would have plucked out your eyes and given them to me. Am I the enemy now, just because I told you the truth?

FOR FREEDOM CHRIST HAS SET US FREE! You must stand fast. You must never again submit to a yoke of slavery.

Listen to me! I, Paul, tell you this: if you allow yourselves to be circumcised, Christ will be nothing to you. I'll say it again: if anyone is circumcised, he's bound to keep the *whole* Law! And anyone who wants to be justified by the Law is clean cut off from Christ. You would fall from grace! It is through the Spirit, by faith, that we wait for the hope of righteousness. For in Christ Jesus neither circumcision nor uncircumcision count for anything, but faith working through love.

Little children, you were running so well. Who hindered you from obeying the truth? The man who's troubling you, whoever he is – that man will get his comeuppance. I wish, I wish he'd mutilate himself!

And I have confidence in the Lord that you will see things exactly as I see them.

But far be it from me to glory except in the cross of our Lord Jesus Christ, by which the world has been crucified to me, and I to the world. For neither circumcision counts for anything, nor uncircumcision, but a new creation. Peace and mercy be upon all who walk by this rule, upon the Israel of God.

Henceforth let no one give me grief, for the scars on my body are the marks of Jesus.

The grace of our Lord Jesus Christ be with your spirit. Amen.

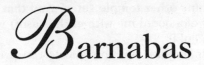

Barnabas

52

Saul left angry. Saul came back angry. Oh, Heavenly Father, forgive me my weariness; I could not abide the anger again. Not his. Not anyone's. I didn't have the heart for another dispute.

I know, I confess: I probably caused it myself. I'm the one who sent Titus to Corinth with the news that Barsabbas was ploughing Saul's fields. But that was a matter of right and wrong. I had no choice *but* to let him know. And I think I thought he'd go *there*, if he went anywhere. To Galatia. It didn't occur to me he'd rush all the way back to Jerusalem and then come storming north to Antioch. Why should I have expected him in Antioch?

But he came roaring like the lion, so I shut my door against him. I refused to see him.

Dear obedient Titus visited me straightaway. He sat and ate with me in my little room. Bold young Titus, suddenly grown into a man, travel-hardened and independent: it brought true warmth to these old bones to look upon my friend again. And that, too, I discovered I had not anticipated, that Titus would return – at least not any time soon. Corinth is so far. Only the rich or the royal go back and forth so quickly.

Titus talked all breathlessly of sights and cities. For example, he asked me if I knew that the bronze gates outside the Temple in Jerusalem – the gates called 'Beautiful' – had been made in Corinth?

Yes, I said. I knew. 'But you are the more fortunate of us two,' I said, 'because I've never actually seen the foundries in Corinth.'

And did I also know, Titus continued, eager as a ferret, that Corinthian bronze was the finest bronze in all the world? Praised by Caesar Augustus and loved by Tiberias?

Nope. Nope, didn't know that.

Well, did I know that the gates called 'Beautiful' were worth more than the nine other temple gates? And that *those* (he half stood; he nearly clobbered me with enthusiasm) were plated with silver and set in gold?

I found myself laughing with my guest, a surprise to me and a pure delight. When was the last time I had laughed?

'Nope,' I said. 'I had no idea of the value.'

Suddenly Titus was serious.

'Barnabas,' he said.

I stopped laughing. 'What?'

'Why won't you see Paul?'

Titus used the Greekish name. I think it was thoughtless. I mean that there were no hidden messages in his choice of name. But it made me feel estranged, and for this I need forgiveness too, that I envied the friendship of Titus and Saul. It seemed new, deeper than before.

Titus said, 'Why won't you sit and talk with Paul?'

I took the flagon and poured wine into his cup. 'Did he send you to me?' I asked. 'Are you speaking for him?'

'No. He doesn't know. He'd holler at me if he knew.'

Too bad. Another insight into myself: I half wished that Saul *had* sent Titus.

I poured wine into my cup.

'Maybe we can talk about something else,' I said.

'But I love him, because who else stood up for me when Peter wouldn't eat with me?' Titus said, earnest, innocent, as young as grass. 'And I love you, because you *are* the someone else that stood up for me,' Titus said, suddenly cutting me to the heart. 'And before I believed in Jesus,' he said, 'when I was just a boy, I believed in you two, I mean in your friendship. I was so happy to see you together, and Paul would be talking and you would be laughing, and those days were perfect, Barnabas. Those days were so perfect. Why won't you see Paul now?'

I pretended to drink a little wine. This was, in fact, the best wine I had. I was celebrating Titus.

'Where is he staying?' I asked.

'The same as before. At Simeon Niger's house.'

'Is he angry?'

'I think so.'

'Was he angry in Jerusalem?'

'Oh, yes, for sure.'

'What did he do there? Why did he go there?'

'To yell at James,' Titus said.

'Were you close by? Did you hear what he said to James?'

'Yes. On account of, he didn't wait to be in private. He started yelling right away.'

'Ah,' I said.

Oh, Father in Heaven, I am so tired, so tired. And yet I pressed the young man, my guest. 'What,' I asked, 'did he say to James?'

'He said he's fighting the devil already,' Titus said.

Titus bent his face down to the table. He dabbled his finger in a puddle of spilled wine and began to make circles on the tabletop.

'Fighting the devil,' I said.

Titus shrugged and continued: 'Yes, well, "fighting the devil", he says. And then he says he's already fighting "principalities and powers". He says he's been stoned and robbed and flogged and covered with scars, the marks of Jesus. Then he yells in James's face, 'So why do I have to fight my own people, too? And why do my people lay waste the work I do for Christ?' That's his exact words: *Lay waste the work I do for Christ*. Next he opens his pouch and pulls out the letter you gave me to give him, and he shakes it under James's nose, yelling, 'Call off your dogs! They're biting,' Paul yells, getting pinker and pinker in his face: 'They're biting, devouring Gentiles! Or if you didn't send them out to circumcise, then control them, James. Control the men that look to this place for authority!' James asks, 'When have I been able to control anyone?' And Paul says, 'You know you rule in Jerusalem.' And James, as smooth as you please, says, 'We asked you, sir, to persuade the Gentiles to observe four plain rules for the sake of the Jews. Remember?' And James says, 'How can I rule anyone, if I can't rule you?'

'Barnabas.' Titus lowered his voice, remembering. 'I got scared then. I thought punches were coming for sure.

'When James says, 'Can't rule you,' Paul has a purple fit, and screams, 'Only Jesus!' raising his hand up like he's going to bring it slap down on something: 'Only the Lord Jesus Christ rules over me!' James doesn't act scared. He says, 'And how do you know that Jesus doesn't rule Judas Barsabbas too?' Paul makes a gargling sound. I think he's choking. James says, 'Are you the only one with the truth?' James says, 'Does the whole judgment of right and wrong rest only with you?' James says, 'What? Are *you* the Law, now? Have you taken the place of Moses?'

'Now I'm watching Paul and I'm worried. That hand is still up in the air. He's shaking. The tiny eyes in his big head – they're crossing, and he's baring his teeth, and he's saying, *Arrr, arrr*, like he's swallowed his tongue, and either he's going after James and I have to grab him, or else he's going to pass out and I have to catch him. I've never seen anything like it!

'And then what happens is just as strange. He just quits. Paul, I mean: he gives up. Suddenly he lets out a little sigh, and it's over. He blinks, he clears his throat several times hard, he turns to the side and rubs his forehead, then he's looking at James again, and in his usual voice he says, 'I am going to Galatia for the saving of Gentiles. And look here,' he says, 'I'll go for the saving of Jerusalem too. Do you remember mentioning a collection of money for the poor in Jerusalem?' James nods. I can't tell what James is thinking now. His eyelids droop and cover his feelings. But he nods and says, 'I do.' So Paul says, 'I will honour your request. Starting with the churches in Galatia, I'll take a collection from all the churches I have planted, from Gentiles even as far as Macedonia and Achaia.'

'Barnabas, what does a collection have to do with anything?'

Titus stopped speaking. I didn't answer his question, though suddenly I, too, was remembering that James had spoken about the poor of Jerusalem. The wonder is that Saul recalled it. Till now, I'd completely forgotten the suggestion.

Titus took a little sip of wine, then looked at me. 'I don't understand these things, Barnabas,' he said, 'but that's what happened. What else should I tell you? There's nothing else to tell you. Why won't you see him? It could be that Paul is – I don't know – what? Sad? Can a person be sad and angry, too? Why won't you see him, Barnabas?'

The scene that Titus had just described was exactly the sort of thing I could no longer abide. Saul fighting, Saul being fought, and no one near can walk away, but everyone has to choose one side or the other. And the scene was extreme. Saul must have gotten worse in the west. Only once before had I seen him lose control, lose his speech, at any rate: when Barsabbas read the four decrees in Simeon Niger's house.

'Because I'm old, Titus,' I said, 'and tired. Look at me, son. Look at the back of my hand. What do you see?'

'Veins.'

'Blue veins. Snaking swollen veins. The brown blotches of age. What colour has my hair become?'

Titus flashed a quick grin. 'Silver, my father! As silver as my pendant.'

He lifted the gift like triumph between us.

Ah, Titus! I smiled at the gesture. I smiled in sudden gladness that a young man wore an old man's gift.

'Silver on you is precious,' I said. 'Silver on me is age.' I raised my cup. We both sipped wine.

I thought about the Titus interpretation: Sad? Could Saul be *sad*? I had never perceived that emotion in him. Never. It seemed likelier that the man was brooding. There are, I thought, as many changes to anger in Paul as weathers upon the sea. Trust none of them. Even a calm might suddenly swamp you.

Titus gave me a light punch on the shoulder. 'Why won't you sit and talk with your brother, Barnabas?' he said.

This time I answered. 'He yelled at me, too, Titus,' I said.

'But that's what he does,' the young man said immediately. 'He yells.'

'I know, I know. I just couldn't carry the burden one more time. Ah, Titus,' I said, 'the man came looking for me. He found me on Singon Street, preaching to a group of women. Even from a distance I heard his voice, but it was no greeting. He yelled: 'And did you write him *too*, Barnabas?' I looked up smiling, glad to see him. But he was bearing down on me, with questions that felt like accusations: 'Did you send someone to Pessinus when you sent Titus to Corinth? I hope so! Did you condemn Barsabbas for his treachery? He has, you know, betrayed the Lord!' Saul yelled. No *excuse me*. No *Peace be with you*. His first words were furious – and these are the exact words, Titus. In the street, in front of the women, Saul threw up his arms and yelled, "Barsabbas has been sending Gentiles to hell! Gentiles are dying the death because of Barsabbas!"'

Quietly, Titus said to me, 'I know those words, those exact words. I heard them, too. I was there.'

'You were in Singon Street?'

'Close behind him.'

I gazed at the young man beside me. 'Then you can understand, can't you, Titus? All at once I knew how tired I was. How tired I am. I didn't answer Saul. I couldn't. I couldn't say anything at all.

I turned and walked away. I walked back here, to my little rooms, and I shut and I barred my door.'

Titus, this young man of energies and gladnesses, seemed to sigh. He took a moment, then said, 'But it was then that I think I saw the sadness in him, Barnabas.'

James

53

Saul has a sister! I confess I was astonished to discover that Saul has a sister – living, moreover, an easy walk north of me, in a house by the wall at the tower gate. A sister in Jerusalem! One should not be astonished to learn that any man born of family and bred in family *has* a family. But I was. At the same time, I took a private cheer in the knowledge. It diminished the man, somehow – the force of the man, his visible presence – to imagine attachments and encumbrances upon him. The fighter wasn't as light on his feet as he had seemed to be.

And the fact that Saul had not, during his first two visits in Jerusalem, either mentioned her or, so far as I know, *gone* to her; the fact he had an attachment he wouldn't acknowledge – a secret to keep, perhaps, a something to hide – diminished him the more.

It was during his third visit that he unwrapped the matter before me. He had a request, he said.

After we two had debated, and after a remarkable display of weakness on his part (the man is prone to debilitating emotion), and after I had drawn the line, so to speak, that contained him, he meekly asked whether I might talk to this sister on his behalf. He explained – again, full meekly – that they had not spoken together in more than twenty years. The separation was by mutual consent, for she was still as zealous for the God of Moses as he had been before he switched his allegiance. And would I myself be the one to go, he asked, since his sister despised believers in Jesus, but my reputation even among the Pharisees was honourable. I was James the Just, he said. James the Gate.

By then the *Sicarii* had begun to roam Jerusalem streets. So the Romans call those fiercest of Jews who conceal a thin knife, a *sica*, in the folds of their robes, who, when they pass the unwary enemy, kill him with quick slits of the knife and then keep walking undetected, never breaking stride while the dying man slumps down behind them. Those whom the *Sicarii* kill are temporizing Jews, rich collusive Jews whose hatreds of Rome zealots consider neither passionate enough nor public enough. Though Saul had no wealth nor status, he seemed too much in love with Rome – and to go personally to his sister's house could be disastrous. Saul explained that her husband was violently zealous for the Law, the purity of the Temple, and the freedom of Jerusalem: He loathed those who cooperated with Rome, interpreting that allegiance as idolatrous. *No lord but God!* he swore with murderous intent.

Saul told me he needed something from his sister – and would I, he asked in perfect, planned, articulate Aramaic, help him get it?

During the single day of his brief sojourn in Jerusalem, Saul astonished me on three counts. This was the second: not that he needed something from someone, but that he admitted the need as well as his inability to fulfill the need. He needed something of her; and he needed me to get it.

'It' was a small wooden diptych which his sister had received from their father. The diptych was a legal document. Its waxed surfaces preserved the certification and the signatures of witnesses to the fact that Saul is a Roman citizen. He had, he said, been arrested in Philippi, had been beaten and imprisoned there. It was only after his suffering – and God's intervention by means of an earthquake – that the magistrates accepted his word that he was a citizen. But if he'd been carrying the proof upon his person, he might have avoided the rod and the shackles in the first place.

Saul needed me, and I agreed.

I went to the house of his sister and discovered that she had a son. Saul had a nephew also living in Jerusalem! His family *was* a family.

A pretty young man opened the door to me: a rich, red complexion and a violent shock of black hair. When I gave him my name and asked to see the woman – his mother? – he left me at the door and disappeared.

Saul's sister never appeared. A man did, a tall man with high cheekbones, an even brow, and a grey-eyed, smoky gaze, a man remarkably handsome, clearly the father of the pretty youth and the husband, I supposed, of the household.

He said nothing.

I spoke without invitation. I made my request – Saul's request, actually, naming Saul as a brother-in-law – while the tall man stared down on me with lidded scrutiny.

When I was done he said, 'I've heard of you. I have no quarrel with you.'

I thanked him for the approval and apologized for the lack of his name. I wished, I said, to call the man by his name.

He gave me no name. He merely stared at me.

So I repeated Saul's request with variations.

The man said, 'There is no such thing in my house.'

I said, 'Perhaps your wife knows. Perhaps she has the written certificate, since she, too, lived in the family of Roman citizens...'

The man said, 'There is, sir, no *Roman* thing in this house, living or dead. And if some Roman thing entered this house living, he would leave it dead. I would kill him with my own hands.'

He closed the door without farewell.

In general, the man was a sign of the state of the city. Jerusalem was a nest of suspicions. Anger hummed in every house. But I had no doubt that in *this* house there existed a particular, personal, and murderous despising of Saul himself for reasons beyond my knowledge.

When I returned to him, I told Saul that his sister knew nothing of the diptych and that it were best to avoid her family altogether.

He nodded and probed no farther for details.

Let me also record my third astonishment during his brief visit: that Saul thought a leader of the Jerusalem church could exert leadership abroad. Not once in our discussions did I give outward expression to the series of amazements he produced in me. I have learned by long necessity to keep composure. But this was the deepest of the three: Saul asked me to control Barsabbas and other preachers in Galatia! What a remarkable concession to the reach of my authority – though I verily believe he had not thought it through. It came as a passionate utterance and an unstated premise. I, of course, could not – and therefore did not promise to – comply.

If only it were true, though. If only Saul himself had a bone of obedience. If only there might be, by the leadership of one for all the churches, no dissension among the churches at all. If only we were everywhere united in the same mind and the same judgment.

I offered Saul these sentiments before we parted.

And I offered him, too, condolences on the grim refusal with which his family had met his request.

He said, 'My house is in no earthly city.'

Timothy

54

Between Jerusalem and Antioch, Paul's physical afflictions weighed heavily upon him. His ruined back caused him to limp and to labour like a larger, older man. He sat and rested more frequently. I carried one of his two leather bags. We could no longer walk twenty miles a day, as once we had when we left Lystra a lifetime ago. Fifteen miles, maybe.

But when we entered Antioch, the man was transformed. Paul's step was brisk, his mouth set, his body taut, strong, erect. He went ahead of us down a wide boulevard called the Street of Herod and Tiberius. He sprang forward on his bandy legs, not the first sign of weakness in him.

'Where is he going?' Titus said.

But Titus knew the city. I didn't. He didn't expect an answer from me.

Paul turned into a narrow cross-street. Titus brightened. 'Singon Street,' he cried, 'near the Pantheon!'

The young man quickened his pace to keep up with Paul.

I struggled under the luggage behind them.

Paul didn't enter Antioch by the gate. He struck it like the bolt that drops from heaven.

By the time I turned into the narrow cross-street both he and Titus had left it for another broader avenue. Nevertheless, I could already hear his voice above all the common city sounds. Not what he said, but how he said it: I recognized his saw-blade whine of a cry as aggression, questioning.

When finally I caught up with them, Paul was standing near an elaborate fountain watching the back of a big-shouldered man who was walking away.

'Barnabas?' Paul said. 'Barnabas?'

The big man shook his head and kept on walking.

Young Titus stood speechless, shifting his glance from Paul to the departing figure. His cheeks looked slapped, burning.

Very quietly, he spoke to Paul. 'I think he's sad, now,' Titus said. 'I think you made him sad.'

Neither one of them noticed my arrival.

For just an instant Paul sagged as if some internal string had been cut. Then he straightened and demanded: 'Titus, where do the believers meet? Where would they be meeting now?'

'In a cave,' Titus said. 'A grotto. I'll show you.'

So then we were walking through the city again, though somewhat more slowly this time. Titus said that Peter had started preaching in this cave after Paul had left Antioch: 'Preaching and baptizing too,' he said, 'on account of, there's a little spring inside the cave.'

We went by straight streets to the east side of the city.

'There,' Titus said, pointing toward the rocky face of Mount Staurin.

A crude stone wall had recently been built to enclose the mouth of the cave. From windows high in the wall we could hear the voices of men and women singing the refrain of a hymn – no hymn I'd ever heard before, but it named Jesus as Lord, and it caused Titus to glance at Paul and to grin.

'Home!' he said. He cuffed Paul on the shoulder, mischievous, teasing. 'Our people,' he said. 'Makes me feel good to be home again!'

The young man had never been away from his hometown before. Titus fairly skipped to the wooden door in the wall and threw it open and beckoned us in.

We entered, Titus preceding, then Paul in his strength again, and finally I myself.

It took a while for my eyes to adjust to the darkness. The people were shadows before me. Their singing faltered.

Titus threw back his head and cried out, 'Look who's here! It's Paul!' – and the singing halted altogether.

The living shadows shuffled their feet. But no one said a word. I began to see individuals, all standing, all having turned to look at us, but I couldn't read their faces. Strangers! Strangers to me, to be sure; but they seemed strangers to Paul as well. I felt as if we were trespassing.

Titus, the grin still clinging, said, 'I went to Corinth and I brought him back. Look, it's Paul – I mean, *Saul!*'

Paul's knees were bent, his weight on the balls of his feet. I recognized the posture: a racer's readiness. It made my heart trip with a fearful anticipation.

He took a step forward. 'Church in Antioch!' he announced abruptly. 'I have something to say to you.'

His tone offered no greeting; it promised a scolding, and the group's reaction was something like a flinch.

But one man immediately shouted, 'Is that you, you troubler of Israel?'

Quick as a flash, Paul answered: 'I have not troubled Israel.' He was quoting scripture, Elijah's answer to the accusations of Ahab – and the rest of the quote is: *But you have.*

No, they weren't strangers. They knew each other. So what was going on here? Why was Paul so wary? Why should these people be wary of *him*?

The man said, 'What? What?' – and I picked him out, tallest among the people, long-necked and completely bald. 'Have you come to blame us again?' he shouted.

Titus raised a plea. 'Wait a minute! Wait a minute!'

But Paul ignored him. Paul overrode him, saying, 'Do you deserve blame, Manaen? Does the church of Antioch deserve to be blamed?'

A woman said, 'It is the Spirit who knows our hearts! Not you!'

Paul said, 'Hearts are made manifest in action.'

'Yes, and what about *yours*?' a new voice called. A man stepped forward, wearing the knee-breeches of a soldier. 'I've seen you act,' he declared, raising a fist. 'You're a madman, Saul.'

'I'm a free man!' Paul said. He spread his arms to include the whole group of worshippers. 'Antioch, O Antioch,' he said, 'I learned of freedom here, from you. You taught me that all things are lawful, and I believed it. Do *you* believe it still? Or have you sacrificed the very freedoms for which Christ Jesus set us free?'

Several people started to speak at once.

'It's you who tied us in knots,' they said. 'Peter relieved us!'

'We can't feel free and guilty too!' they said.

'Saul, Saul, why have you come back again?'

Paul cut through the clamour. He raised that sharp, remarkable voice and uttered the theme that had driven us here from Corinth: 'If anyone in Antioch still honours the perverted words of that perverting prophet, Judas Barsabbas, you *ought* to feel guilty.'

'Oh, leave us alone,' they said. 'Jesus is our judge, not you.'

But Paul had gained momentum. He had already begun to preach. 'I will show you a shame,' he cried. 'This is a shame, having once been free, to choose for oneself the yoke of the Law again. But worse than a shame,' he cried, 'I will show you a sin and a treachery – '

The people were muttering, 'Go away, go away,' but Paul wasn't listening.

He cried, 'This is a sin worthy of damnation, to persuade others to exchange their freedom for the bonds of the Law. O Antioch!' Paul cried – even as the people now started to walk away from him toward the back wall of the cave – 'Antioch, are you ashamed? Is it shame that you feel? Have you surrendered your freedom?'

At the back of the cave the tall bald man bent and entered a narrow cleft in the rock. Others followed him into a tunnel that must have led to a second exit.

Paul kept preaching, even to the backs of the people: 'Or is it something worse than shame that you feel?' he cried. 'Do you support the treachery of those who proclaim a false gospel, who destroy the souls of Gentiles? Do you approve the damnable sin? Are you supporting Judas Barasabbas – '

But the people were leaving. The people were gone. Paul's voice echoed in the hollow rock: ' – as once you supported me?'

He fell silent.

For the first time I could hear the gentler sounds of the cave. I heard trickling water. There was a pool in hewn rock in the middle of the floor. Ah, that's what Titus had talked about, the spring where Peter baptized. I glanced at the young man and found him gazing at Paul, again with a visible anxiety.

Paul himself had allowed his eyes a dreamlike gaze at the back of the cave.

Tonelessly, as if thinking aloud, he said, 'Then we'll have to take care of the matter ourselves.'

A second gentle sound now came from shadows, the odd click-and-tread of an old man walking. Apparently, one worshiper had not departed with the others. He emerged from a dark corner and hobbled toward us: a black man with white woollen eyebrows, leaning on a walking stick. *Click! Click!*

Though slow, his tread was directed toward Paul alone, and Paul could see, and Paul was watching him come: warily, it seemed to me.

'My friend,' the old man said, 'come, stay in my house again, just as you did before.'

Paul didn't answer. He frowned. He opened his mouth and rounded his lips on silence, as if silence itself were a word.

The old man came to a stance in front of Paul. Once he would have been a full head taller than my friend. But now, since age had bent him down, both men's eyes were on a level.

Slowly the black man opened his arms. 'Come, Saul,' he said. 'Be my son again.'

With a cry, Paul fell upon his neck and kissed him and embraced him.

The walking stick clattered to the floor.

And I heard the old man whisper: 'It's not too confining, is it, to be my son?'

Paul shook his head, incapable of language.

'My love, Saul,' the old man whispered, 'it isn't a yoke, is it? It doesn't cancel your necessary freedom, does it?'

The men were cheek by jowl. Neither could see the face of the other. But I could. I saw Paul's chin quivering. I saw his nostrils flare, and his eyes so tightly shut.

The black man whispered still into his ear: 'Or that you should love an old fool like me – surely, that is a law that will not kill you, will it?'

$\mathcal{B}$arnabas

55

O Jesus, I'm tired. I'm old. I'm older than I ever thought I'd be. And heart-sick and sorry and scared for the world since we should be preaching your name, but we're failing, failing, and falling apart...

Christ, where are you?

What are you waiting for?

Whenever will you come back again?

Why didn't you return when we were all so noisy in our joy? Oh, how good were those days! Everything was new, the food and our feelings and the Holy Spirit! And I used to laugh. The gladness lived like a tickle in my chest, always ready to burst forth. Nothing stopped my laughter then.

And the whole world seemed as fresh as creation. All things were possible. I heard the stories. I heard the marvels: how the earth shook when you died, and the rocks split, and tombs opened up, and the saints came walking into Jerusalem. Or else how those who lied to the Spirit fell dead at Peter's feet. Or how, in a single day not two months after you rose from the dead, three thousand people were baptized and added to the church. Three thousand!

Weren't we ready then? We were good. The preaching was good. Jesus, Jesus, in those days we devoted ourselves to the apostles' teaching and to fellowship and to prayers with such light hearts and gladness. We owned everything in common. I wasn't the only one who chose to sell my land and give the money to the church. All of us gave as were able, and all of us got as we had need. Daily we attended the Temple. Daily we broke bread together in our own houses. Daily we partook of food, praising God, enjoying the praise of a smiling world –

Why didn't you come back *then*?

Tell me, Jesus: What good has your waiting accomplished?
Is strife a good? Are we better for the trouble among us?

No, no, I never wanted to be an old man. No. And now that
I am I find it worse than ever I had imagined.

When the church was young, I thought of your kingdom as a
garden, rich and sweet and green, fruit for the eating, grasses for
running swift as gazelles, a golden air for breathing and shouting
and laughing. Now I think of the kingdom as a couch in the
darkness, a bed to rest on, no more pain, no more sorrow, no
more tears. It used to be I thought that things would *start* in
heaven. Now I only hope that things will end.

You have delayed, and the world has grown heavy with regret.
Peter's gone. He and Silas and John Mark left Antioch for Rome.
I'll never see them again. I miss my cousin.

Saul, on the other hand, has come, peevish and angry. The
Holy Spirit should console us. But when Saul's around the Spirit
reproves and convicts. The Holy Spirit judges and divides us.

What do we have in common now? What is the good of your
Word among us? Why do you wait?

Why couldn't you have come yesterday? Even just *yesterday*?
Before the angel of death came down to Antioch and entered the
house of Simeon Niger, the man that carried your cross?

O Lord Jesus Christ, if you had been here yesterday my
brother, my dear friend Simeon Niger would not have died!

Ah, forgive me, forgive me. Who am I to be blaming? I'm losing
sense and goodness and self-control. I'm old, and I am so tired.

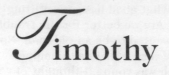imothy

56

In the middle of the night a wailing awoke me. A long, beseeching wail caused my stomach to seize and me to sit up, shivering. The voice was the voice of my mother. I leaned forward on the pallet, cold, convinced I was a child in Lystra, and that my mother was wailing for my father.

In my heart's distress, I cried: *Mama, Mama, where are you?*
She didn't answer me.

My father was dying, for hadn't I heard the wail of death's discovery? My mother was watching the bright fountain of blood which rose from my father's throat and which, flowing down his bed like a crimson covering, was the flow of his visible life away.

A second time I heard the wailing, this time with words distinct through the doorways. 'Simeon! Ohhh, Simeon!'

No, I wasn't in Lystra. I wasn't a child, though that baby sorrow lingered in me.

'Paul?' I whispered. 'Paul, did you hear that?'

But the air in our bedroom was dead. I couldn't hear his breathing.

I reached over to wake him and found his pallet empty.

I stood up in the absolute blackness and crept toward the door.

The whole house seemed to expand, like lungs inhaling, and then the wailing was everywhere around me, sourceless, 'Simeon, take me with you! Simeon, I want to go with you!'

Simeon: the old black man that leaned on a stick and invited Paul to stay with him.

Outside the bedroom I saw a faint light round a farther corner.

Barefoot, filled with the grief of my father, I walked on carpets toward that light.

I turned the corner.

In a bedroom no larger than ours, but lit by oil lamps on

stands in the corners, I found my friend and teacher, Paul. He was kneeling at the left side of the bed, his tunic torn, his head larger and heavier than ever. Simeon's wife knelt at the right side. Simeon lay between. She was caressing her husband's dark forehead, leaning forward to kiss his face, pulling on his hand, pulling it in strengthless anger, bowing her head, burying her eyes in the palm of his hand.

And Simeon was pliable to all her tugging. The force of will was not within him. His jaw was slack. His black skin had taken on a chalky pallor, especially at the lips. Simeon Niger was dead.

I came carrying sorrow, and here was sorrow to companion my own. We were a family bound by sadness. Simeon's wife was the wife of my father, my own mother. Both women sang the same song, so that time collapsed and all death everywhere had become this one death. My friend and my teacher, Paul, was mute. Thoughts may have been roaring in his great head, but his eyes were fixed on Simeon, and his lips were pinched; his lips were bloodless, white, and pinched.

I, too, knelt down. I touched the soles of the old man's feet. The toenails were thick and ridged. His ankle flesh was barky. He was a black man in whom I saw the image of my father, and I let the grief flow out of me. I began, as women do, to hum high in my nose, in a flutelike falsetto to utter my lamentation.

My humming increased. It caused the old woman to nod. She slumped low by the side of her husband and delivered herself to tears unhindered.

But then I heard something like the cracking of sticks in angry rhythm with my music, and I saw that Paul was rocking to and fro, striking his bare breast with the flat of his hand.

'Ah, my father!' Paul said. *Crack!* His eyes were red-rimmed, dry, as hot as an oven. 'Ahhh' – *Crack! Crack!* – 'my father!'

His father, too!

'This was a good man!' Paul said. He raised his voice as if accusing someone. 'A good man! The best of men! This is the man who carried the cross of Jesus. This is the man who carried,' Paul dropped his voice to a whisper, 'who carried me.'

Then the room was still.

Both mourners had pulled Simeon's arms toward themselves, stretching them wide apart, Paul the right arm, gripping it, Simeon's wife his left arm, weeping upon it. They looked alike, Paul and the woman. To my sad sight they seemed like angels

269

about to break for heaven, bearing the body between them.

But finally I spoke. 'Woman,' I said, 'where are your sons? Has somebody gone to tell your boys that their father is dead?'

Paul looked at me with incomprehension. 'Rufus,' he said, as if I'd asked for their names. 'Alexander,' he said.

'Where do they live?' I said. 'How can I find their houses at night?'

The poor widow lifted herself and extended a hand toward me. I rose and took her hand. 'Thank you, Timothy,' she said. The tenderness in her voice unmanned me. I could hardly stand such merciful kindness. Her husband was black. She was fair. And together they were the picture of grace in old age. Why couldn't they have died together, like Baucis and Philemon?

She said, 'Take our maid. She sleeps by the kitchen door. She will show you the way.'

So I was the bearer of unhappy news to men I'd barely met, and a little girl led me. I was the one who frightened people by knocking on doors in the night. Alexander, when I told him of his father's death, went in to wake his family. Rufus had no family to wake. He didn't even shut his door. He dashed through the streets as fast as he could to his father's house.

By the time the maiden and I returned, Paul and Rufus had moved Simeon's bed onto the marble floor of the atrium, near the fountain. The sheets had been stripped. The bare wooden frame held the dead man's body, also stripped of its outer clothing. A loincloth covered its nakedness.

Simeon's wife was washing the poor bony corpse with water and sponges. The old man's white, woollen eyebrows glistened with droplets.

As soon as he saw us enter, Rufus asked the maid to bring fresh sheets and clean cushions and Simeon's best robe.

Paul fluttered around, like a leaf on the breezes. 'Where is olive oil?' he said.

He said, 'Incense? Do we have incense? And myrrh?'

He said with force, 'We will not grieve!'

Paul repeated this thought, though to no one in particular. 'We must not grieve as those who have no hope,' he said. 'Jesus died and rose again. Simeon Niger will rise again!'

Piteously Paul said: 'Rufus, can we find myrrh at this time of the night? Does someone we know have aloes?'

But there was myrrh, already mixed with unguents, already in flasks and handy. It was applied directly by the hands of Simeon's family, giving his old black flesh its gloss again. It darkened the chalky pallor. It filled the air with a pungency that caused my nose to run – and again I was reduced to the child in Lystra who stood confused by his papa's body.

Rufus lifted his father in his arms so that his mother could pull the clean tunic over the dead man's head. The bed frame was covered with clean sheets now. The body was arranged with the arms at its sides, its head on a cushion, its feet toward the door.

And the people began to arrive. Not just Alexander and his family. Others.

The word had spread abroad. Believers came in weeping. Two women sat down in a corner and blew on flutes, the melody weaving sadness in the air, piercing our souls. Flowers torn to petals were scattered around Simeon's bed, on the white and black squares of the marble floor. The fountain flowed with fresh water.

And dawn was lighting the sky above the atrium. Morning was coming down to earth.

As more and more people came into Simeon's house, I withdrew to the wall beyond the atrium, to a corner farthest from the entrance hall. In grief we yearn community, truly. But the same grief cuts us off. We know both things at once: love and isolation. I can't explain it. It's like drunkenness. Like floating above the people, above dear friends who are also strangers with featureless faces.

Suddenly Paul was beside me.

He seized the flesh of my upper arm and pinched it painfully.

'We're running out of time!' he said swiftly, softly, precisely, earnestly. He wasn't looking at me. His small eyes were fastened on Simeon Niger, lying black on white sheets in the atrium. Paul's shoulders were rounded with intensity. Beside me he seemed monkey-like, crouched smaller than usual. 'Timothy, we have so little time! Not that Christ is coming soon. But that we're *dying* soon. If ever I had a home on earth, this was that home. But look at him. Look at him. Oh, Timothy, *look* at him. Simeon Niger is dead.'

The tall, bald man who had berated Paul in Peter's cave now entered the house by ducking his head. He joined the line of mourners that filed into the atrium. I was surprised to see tears. When he looked down on Simeon's body, his chest heaved and I felt a sudden sympathy for him.

Paul pinched my arm.

'Simeon was there when the Lord Jesus died,' he said. 'This is the man who made me understand the cross of Christ. By Simeon's eyes I saw the tree and by no other way. Look, Timothy. Look at his face. His eyes are closed. His seeing has become a dust. O Jesus, Jesus,' Paul said, pinching so hard I gasped, 'the time is short, the world is wide, and I am weak. I am so weak.'

Titus entered. The man beside him I took to be his father. That man joined the sad processional, but Titus saw Rufus and ran through the crowd and fell upon his neck and howled. So then Rufus was patting Titus and saying, 'There, there, Titus. There, there.'

People were sitting on benches, on cushions, on the carpets that covered the floor. They were standing in the dining rooms, kneeling in various groups side by side, sitting even on the dining room tables, waiting; both alone and in close company, waiting; some of them singing under the keening of the flutes, most of them silent, heads bent down, waiting as if something were about to happen; waiting, keeping vigil.

All at once Paul let go his pinch and snapped erect beside me. His head went up and down on its narrow neck like a crane that wants to see better.

'Oh, no,' he said to himself. He was shivering. 'Oh, no.'

His face was white, the scars at his hairline gone hard and orange, his little eyes blinking rapidly.

'Oh, Barnabas,' Paul whispered. 'No, no, no.'

The great-shouldered man, the hugely bearded man whom Titus called 'sad', had just entered the house. Sad, indeed! He approached the atrium with tremendous slowness, as if he were a mountain loose, uprooted, lonely, and forced to move from one place to another.

I heard a quiet convulsion in Paul's throat. I looked and saw that he had begun to cry. His mouth was open like a child's, his brow raised in a hopeless appeal, his chest panting.

He started to walk forward.

'Barnabas?' he said, questioning.

I think he was unconscious of himself. He held his arms away from his sides, simian-like and empty. He didn't walk directly forward, but first to the left and then to the right, like an animal approaching with fear.

'Barnabas?'

The big man turned and saw the small one coming. He froze.

Everyone in the house seemed suddenly aware of these two only. The flutes ceased. The crowd around Barnabas backed away. A path was formed behind him. He could turn again and escape if he wished.

But Paul was crying. Unbeautiful. Wretched. Paul was bawling noisily, publicly, shamelessly. This was no Paul I'd ever seen before. This was no imposing figure, no threat to run from.

The big-shouldered man did not run. He regarded Paul with a squinting, shocked bewilderment.

'Barnabas, my brother,' Paul wept, now barely moving forward, honouring some invisible wall between them. 'Barnabas, please: forgive me.'

Barnabas produced an audible gasp, doubling somewhat at the stomach.

Forgive me?

Paul went down to his knees.

'I am weak and weaker than I knew.'

He raised his hands, palms empty. His face, too, he thrust upward to the mountain-like Barnabas, and all the water on Paul's face streamed backward to his ears and neck. 'I am grieving, brother Barnabas,' he said, 'for the dying around us, grieving. I am grieving like the faithless! I am grieving like those who have no hope! Because weakness *murders* hope! And I need... I need... I need you – !' Sobbing overcame the apostle.

But his was the only sound in the house now. No one spoke. No one interrupted. Astonishment had fallen upon the entire congregation. Faces everywhere gaped and watched, while feet crept forward, closing again the path behind Barnabas.

Ah, Barnabas: the eyes in his great grizzled head, still fixed on Paul, had begun to glitter. His nose and his forehead were turning a blotchy red. He was shifting his weight from foot to foot.

Paul forced his words past the choke of his sorrow: 'We're running out of time,' he said. 'There isn't time for divisions. We have to be one. There must be one mind among us, the mind of Christ. And the humility of Jesus.' He folded his hands and crouched down, bowing his head and making his small body smaller still.

'Barnabas,' he spoke down to the carpet.

In response the big man lifted his hands and stopped moving.

'Barnabas,' Paul uttered his words so softly that Barnabas turned an ear. 'For the sake of the Lord Jesus Christ, forgive me. Please forgive me. I lacked humility. I lacked any incentive of love. I judged you, my brother. When I had no right, I – '

It is, perhaps, a good thing that Paul had averted his eyes and could not see the great disaster about to befall him.

With a trumpet sound. With an enormous bellow, Barnabas the mountain threw open his arms and stumbled forward and dropped to his knees and embraced Paul. The smaller man vanished, but his voice rose up in a sweet and keening cry. They boomed and wailed and wept, the two of them together. They came up for air. They gave each other humid kisses. They looked each other squarely in the face, and they burst out laughing, laughing – Paul, his silly *Tee-hee*, and Barnabas his trumpet blast like the coming of the kingdom.

Titus was clapping his hands. He ran over and began to beat them both on their backs, laughing and praising the Lord.

There rose a general, chirruping hubbub throughout the house, tensions breaking, a fluid movement returning again, sighs and smiles and breathings.

And then a new focus presented itself, another softer drama to draw the attentions of every person:

Simeon Niger's widow left the side of her husband's body. She followed the path that Titus had made, but this time Paul and Barnabas saw the approach. They gripped each other in order to stand. They stood, big man, little man, side by side, and watched her coming.

As she walked, the old woman spread her arms. Spontaneously both men bowed their heads as if for a blessing.

She paused in front of them. Then, with the edge of her thumb, tremblingly, the widow drew two lines on Saul's forehead, one line down from his brow to the bridge of his nose, the other line crossing from temple to temple. Paul shuddered. The woman reached her full arm high and marked Barnabas with the same two lines.

'I am the wife of the man who died,' she said. 'And I am your mother, Saul; your mother, Barnabas. For I am the prophet through whom the Holy Spirit first sent you out from Antioch.' She gazed at them, her eyebrows working in their thousand wrinkles. 'They gather,' she murmured, as if to herself. 'My sons have come from afar. Oh, see how my sons have come home to me!'

Everywhere in Simeon's house the people breathed, 'Amen.'

'Saul,' she said, 'Barnabas, will you with Rufus and Alexander bear the bier of my husband from here to the grave where he will wait for Jesus? Will you?'

They were not bowed now. Each man had lost himself in the looking of this good woman. Not bowed, I say – but neither did they speak.

'I would be grateful for the service,' she said. 'Saul,' she said, 'I would be proud to see you share that burden with all my sons together. Will you?'

Someone behind her said, 'Say yes!' It was the tall man, the bald one, surprising himself.

Simeon's widow, quick as a sparrow, stood up on tiptoe in order to kiss Paul's face. She took it in her two hands, brought it to her lips, and kissed the scars at the hairline, one after the other with accurate pecks and tenderness. When she released him, then; when the woman withdrew and the apostle raised his face to public view, we were ourselves struck into a preternatural silence. His skin was shining! Paul's countenance was white with a wonderful fire – and now he spoke, and the words that he spoke were as radiant as his face.

'Let no one say,' he said, 'that there is no resurrection from the dead!'

The widow turned to us. She held up both her arms again, this time to signal our sitting.

We sat. We understood. Paul was about to preach.

He walked into the atrium. He stood by Simeon's glistening body and said, 'If there is no resurrection of the dead, then Christ has not been raised. And if Christ has not been raised, then this my father is dead for ever. If for this life *only* we have hoped in Christ, we are of all people the most to be pitied.'

Ah, my teacher – back again! And how limber he looked. Healthy, weightless, flying!

Suddenly Paul sang out: 'But in fact Christ *has* been raised from the dead! The firstfruits of those who have fallen asleep! For as by a man came death, so by a man has also come the resurrection of the dead! In Adam all die. In Christ all will live again. And this is the order of risings: first, Christ Jesus; then, at his coming, those who belong to him; finally, the end, when he will destroy every rule, every authority and power, and will deliver the kingdom to God the Father.

'Somebody asks me, "But how will the dead be raised? What kind of body do they get?"'

'Saints, what a silly question!'

Oh, Paul was merry now. He wriggled and twisted and bounced on his stick-thin legs – and we all took the mood, and we all were glad.

'Listen,' he said. 'Seed can't live unless it dies. And the golden wheat that springs from it is nothing like that little seed!

'Simeon's body is the seed. His resurrection will be like the wheat. So will yours. So will mine. What's sown is perishable. But what's raised up – why, that is *im*perishable altogether.'

Paul looked down into Simeon's black face. With the backs of his long fingers he stroked the cheekbone, the lips, the throat. 'Do you see how quickly the dead flesh fades?' he asked.

I thought of my papa in Lystra, whose lungs had faded and failed him even before he died. *Yes*, I said in my heart. *Yes, I see.*

'Do you see how helpless the old bones are?'

Yes.

'How strengthless the corpse becomes? It is sown in dishonour,' Paul said. Then he looked up and grinned and shed a more marvellous light. 'But it is raised in glory!' he cried.

'It is sown in weakness. But it is raised in power!

'It is sown a physical body. But it is raised a spiritual body. First the physical, *then* the spiritual, because that's the order of things. The first man was formed of the earth, but the second man came from heaven. So we who carry the image of Adam, what do you think will happen to us? Why, we will soon carry the image of Christ in heaven!'

Suddenly Paul jumped up on the railing round the atrium, little eyes flashing, red mouth split with grinning.

'Lo!' he cried. 'I tell you a mystery. We shall not all sleep, but we all shall be changed! In a moment! In the twinkling of an eye, at the last trumpet. For the trumpet shall sound, and the dead shall be raised imperishable! And we shall put on immortality!'

Barnabas stood up. Barnabas *shot* up like a fountain, then rocked to some internal rhythm.

Paul turned and directed the bright darts of his delight straight to his mountainous friend.

'In the day when the perishable is made imperishable,' the apostle cried, half laughing. 'In the day when mortals become immortal,' he said, '*then* shall be fulfilled the saying that's written, *Death is swallowed up in victory. Death, death, where is your victory? O miserable death, where is your sting?* The sting of death,' Paul cried, clapping his hands to the beat of his words, 'is sin! And the power of sin is the Law. But thanks be to God! Who gives us the victory! Through Jesus Christ our Lord!'

And immediately Barnabas was singing! A luscious baritone, rich as ginger, killing me, killing me: heaven was in it.

'The Lord to my Lord says,' he sang – and all of the people rose up and answered him, chanting: 'Down, down, my Son; sit down!'

Oh, what a morning! Oh, what a congregation surrounded me now.

Barnabas sang again, 'The Lord to my Lord says!'

The people stood up and repeated, 'Down and down, sit down!'

And Barnabas let flow his beautiful verses:

Sit down, down at my right hand
    Authorities meek
    Beneath your feet.

My Son, sit down and take command
    Powers and rules
    Become your stool.

And which was the final enemy?
    Which of your foes
    The last to go?

'Death!' cried the people, everywhere leaping to their feet. 'Death is the last to go!'

Barnabas roared:

Death's swallowed down in victory!
    Pitiful thing,
    Death's lost its sting...

Taller than everyone else, that bald man now threw back his head and bellowed, 'Thanks be to God!'

A maiden cried, 'In the name of Jesus!' and immediately people dropped to their knees, in unison answering, 'Amen! Amen!'

'In the name of Jesus,' the maiden cried again, and I became aware that someone had not kneeled down with the others. I heard him first. Then I looked and saw him: Titus! Young Titus was uttering sounds in a swift and feral refrain: 'Bah-bah-bah! Bah-bah-bah!' And he was dancing, moving his muscled, flowing frame as if it were a girl's, two steps left, two steps right, 'Bah-bah-bah!'

Barnabas, grizzled, grey, massive in shoulder and thigh, seemed now to be swimming through the congregation toward the atrium. No, it was to the atrium's *railing* that he swam, to Paul still perched by a pillar there.

And Paul – smaller now, crouched, exhausted, pale – saw him and waited while the big man came.

What had begun in mourning, in funeral tears and a vigil sorrow, had turned to dancing after all. All the house was bright and loud with jubilation. Surely, the Holy Spirit was here.

But in the midst of things, as if they two were completely alone together, Paul and Barnabas met with a gentle searching of their eyes.

Is it well with us, Barnabas? Is it truly well?

The big man hooked his hands beneath the little man's arms and bore him down from the railing and took him into a private embrace.

Oh, Paul, I love you. It is well with us for ever.

I saw it. I, Timothy, witnessed the miracle. I have it still in my heart, this healing of estrangements.

O Jesus, the water that springs from forgiveness: how sweetly it slakes us, reviving our love. It is the life between us, the life of the church, and here we are one body again, and you are the head, and you are the fountain, for you are the fullness that fills us all in all.

Luke

57

After spending some time in Antioch, Paul departed and went from place to place through the region of Galatia and Phrygia, strengthening all the disciples and the churches as he went.

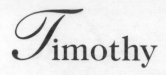

Timothy

58

After Antioch – after the only visitation I've ever made to that city – we moved by slow steps through that great gorge, the Cilician Gates, and then overland toward Ephesus.

Titus, his muscles shivering like the flanks of a colt, set a pace impossible for Paul. The glad young man kept rushing forward, kept dashing back with grins and apologies.

Paul's steps had become stiff, cramped. His little body seemed, by the slouching trudge of its motion, to be burdened by a much greater weight of flesh.

At every city where Paul had established churches in the past, we paused. He preached. He renewed his affections and their convictions, and he persuaded people in every place to begin a collection of money for the poor in Jerusalem.

As long as we moved in the midst of these congregations, Paul showed no sign of his physical afflictions. None. He stood straight. He talked strong. He walked with snap and energy.

But when we took to the road again, a nameless threesome in the busy streams of travellers, his body drooped and grew crippled. I watched him. I watched his eyes. I am convinced that he was oblivious of this difference between the public and the private Paul.

In Lystra we learned that my grandmother had died. Lois, the mother of my mother, her only companion and all her family since I had left them three years earlier.

She hadn't known where I was, my mother. She couldn't send the news to me. She had mourned in solitude for more than a year, and now my sudden appearing seemed only to renew her grief, for she said, 'You've come home only to go away. And I think I will never see you again.'

I, too, was filled with sorrow. For my grandmother. For my

poor mother, living alone. And for my father.

I said to Paul, 'You preach of the resurrection of those that fall asleep in Jesus. This means my grandmother, and I'm comforted. But what about those who did *not* fall asleep in Jesus? Paul,' I begged, 'what about them?'

On the day of our departure from Lystra, my mother clung to me.

I said, 'I will be back.'

'No, you won't,' she said. 'I know whom you serve. I will die before you return. My home is not your home any more.'

Then she said, 'Take these. I have no need of them.'

She went round to the back of the house and brought forward two gifts for us: the cart that had been my father's and the donkey that had been my grandmother's.

After that we travelled at the speed of Titus.

We spent most of our time among the Galatians. Paul's energies burned brightest there, cajoling, scolding, preaching, pleading, calling back to his gospel the men whom Judas Barsabbas had led astray.

They had received our letter.

Giants, these Galatians, blonde and battle-tough and happiest in combat, they had nevertheless been reduced by that letter to the misery of little children chastened.

They were desperate for Paul's affections again. And for his forgiveness.

Forgiveness he had in abundance, now. And soon he discovered how much he loved to give it away. It renewed him. It empowered him, not least because it caused in the grateful Galatians a more willing obedience than ever before, proving Paul's to be the greater authority for them.

Judas Barsabbas was bested! Judas Barsabbas departed. Paul followed him to the city gate in order to watch him go. 'Jawbone of an ass,' Paul said to me. 'Lugubrious, whitened, gaunt and hollow jawbone of an ass.' It was a cold, unsmiling pleasure he took in the departure of Judas Barsabbas, as if he were, with the chisels of his words, carving the man's sarcophagus.

But with the Galatians Paul was positively avuncular.

'Show your thanks,' he said to them. 'My children, having been forgiven, make your thanksgivings manifest. I will be leaving soon for Ephesus. After I'm gone, let the elders among you gather money from the churches of your villages, then carry the collection to Jerusalem. Carry it to the saints who live in poverty and worship at the Temple there.'

By summer we finished the circuit of our travels.

Aquila and Prisca welcomed us to Ephesus in Asia, where a little church had already sprung up, worshipping in their house.

Part Four

EPHESUS

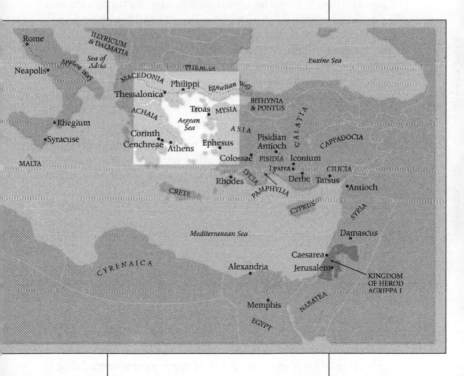

$\mathcal{L}$. Annaeus Seneca

59

Seneca, in Rome,
　To Helvia, my mother in Cordoba,
　The first day of the reign of Nero:

This, Mother, is how the wheel turns, how fortunes rise and
fall – and rise again. I am the same man that languished in
exile nine long years. Yet tonight, not five years since returning,
I have received a golden gift from Agrippina, the mother of the
princeps, a gift of personal thanksgiving from the mother of
the emperor of an empire as round as all the world.

Shall I love fortune better now than I did on Corsica, that
pitiless rock?

It is done. Nero is, as his mother had intended, *imperator*. The
Senate has embraced him. The city receives him like springtime
after endless winter. And I am saddled with the twin tasks,
onerous and honorous: first, to advise him; second, to write the
words he utters before the world.

I am no mean man in the empire now. Am I also *fortunae filius*,
her fair-haired child? Fortune's favourite? And should I therefore
offer sacrifices to her whirling will?

Lo, how I am the tongue in the mouth of power:

Today, in the red cloak and gilded armour, Nero was carried
to the troops outside the city, where he greeted them grandly
with... my words.

Next he was carried to the Senate where, in the plainer toga,
he declaimed... yes, my words, noble and good.

Would they were also his thoughts.

If my duty obliges me to make decisions, rest assured that
I shall think only of the welfare and the happiness of Rome. I
recognize, the child spoke as I had written, *my inexperience, my*

youth, my ignorance. But surrounded by the wisest of counsellors,
I will set myself the noblest of examples... And so forth and so on.

When he was done, the Senate thundered approval. And why
not? I put good pledges in his mouth: *I pledge an absolute*
separation between the State and my person. A citizen among
citizens, as the first among them I must also be the most loyal,
the most respectful to Law and Country.

So tonight the city is buzzing. Behold what I have accomplished
with my less evident power, conceiving the words another utters:
Nero's speech is deemed wiser than any since the days of
Augustus. The praise means much to Nero, who is sitting up
with friends, repeating over and over bits of the speech.

I myself, less glad for praises, have retired here to my own
apartments.

But at twilight Agrippina found me and expressed her more
personal thanks in the form of a gift, a golden page-scraper –
by which I might remove old words from parchment in order to
inscribe my new ones there. *What of the soul, m'lady? Will it*
scrape old words from the younger soul? She kissed me where my
head is bald. She smiled. The woman is beautiful. She polishes
her beauty as a centurion does his shield – or the headsman his
sword.

So I have scraped a page and trimmed a wick and taken my
pens in hand. What new words shall I write on this old sheet,
Mother?

Well, let me see: why don't I describe to you how beautiful and
how cunning is the face of Fortune, and then you'll know why she
shall have no sacrifice from me.

Days ago, mere days ago, Agrippina murdered Claudius.
There's the long and short of it. She killed the king to make her
son the king. So turneth the wheel: up goes down that down goes
up – and the hand that cranks it round is more lovely than tough.

But why blame the woman alone for a practice that has such
precedence in Rome? Caligula murdered Tiberius. Soon Caligula
himself was murdered, and the timorous Claudius became
emperor.

It was Claudius's turn.

He had begun to show too little love for Nero, too much for
Britannicus, his own blood son. And his advisors had grown bold
in their opposition to Agrippina – Narcissus bolder than most.
In front of a crowd of courtiers, Narcissus rushed to young

Britannicus and embraced him and cried: 'O disinherited child, when will you have the courage to drive your pretenders from this place? God protect you,' Narcissus continued, 'until you surround yourself with good people, souls disgusted by incests and prostitutions and treasons!' That maundering display did not go unnoticed by Agrippina.

Moreover, Claudius in his cups had uttered gloomy warnings, saying that it was his destiny first to suffer, then to punish the sins of his wives. And in his wife's presence he'd grumbled about presenting Britannicus to the people of Rome, that they might at last 'have a real Caesar'.

Shortly thereafter Agrippina attended one of his excessive banquets – unusual for her, though it did still please the old king to see her there. She came in grace and beauty, with surprising compliance. *All is well*, her sitting said. She smiled.

A dish of mushrooms was brought to the table, Claudius's favourite mushrooms.

Halotus, the imperial taster, sipped some of the sauce, then with his own hands presented the dish to Claudius.

Agrippina nibbled on a few of the smaller mushrooms set before her. She smiled again and nodded to indicate their goodness. She pointed to the largest ones.

And Claudius ate the largest ones – ate them and asked for more.

An hour passed.

Suddenly the emperor was seized with shivering. His face went white. He grabbed his enormous stomach in both hands and bellowed like a bull.

It was time to call the court physician, Xenophon.

He was, of course, the second and not the first to be called. Earlier that day Agrippina had called upon the services of Locusta, the court poisoner, who had sworn that the poisoned mushrooms would work almost instantly. But the old man's body must have been inured to foreign intrusions. Not only was the poison slower in him, it was weaker as well, causing strong evacuations and little else. Claudius stopped bellowing.

Agrippina rushed out and intercepted Xenophon in the hallway. They entered the banquet hall together.

Xenophon examined the great *corpus* of the king, and said, 'Sir, it's a minor indigestion. Let me tickle your throat with a feather. You'll vomit and improve immediately.'

Claudius agreed. The feather triggered huge heavings of food, and for a while Claudius thought he might return to eating.

But the cramps came back with violence, cutting the king in two.

It took four slaves to bear him bodily from the banquet tables to his own rooms.

Rome never saw Claudius alive again.

The feather had been dipped in poison. There was no other physician at work that night, except Xenophon only.

And Fortune had no other face than Agrippina's.

The empress sat by the bed of her husband for two days together. He would groan and chatter, but he could not speak. He retched constantly but brought up nothing but a thin, viscous bile; any motion flattened him with dizziness.

Agrippina ran her hands down from his throat to his chest to his swollen abdomen, where she felt a terrific lump the size of a human head.

Finally the old man expelled a foul air and, under the examining hands of his wife, died.

So Nero has become the emperor.

And your second son is as powerful as any in the empire now.

Mother, I wrote you once that the lowliest hovel can be as furnished as the richest: with *virtues*, I said – remember? 'Justice and temperance make room for grand companies of friends,' I wrote. I have not forgotten my old words. 'Wisdom and righteousness are chairs and tables. The knowledge of God is food and drink indeed. And lo,' I said, 'how a hut is a palace after all.'

But the wheel turns.

And here in this letter I have written the same thing, but inverted: lo, how a palace for *want* of virtue becomes a hovel, a shack, a rat-hole, a stinking bone house. This is where I live.

The wheel turns, and I cannot tell whether I am presently up or down of the axle.

No, I have never loved Fortune. I do not love her now.

risca

60

I wish I had been seen at the city gates to greet my friend when
he arrived, to embrace him and tell him how lovely it was to see
him again. But I wasn't. I didn't.

I wish – though I know I have no right to wish it – that he had
come looking for his Priscilla. I wish he had sought me swiftly
and found me with gladness and said to Aquila, *Now, this is a
home worth waiting for.*

Often during the nine long months of his absence I had
allowed my heart to trouble me with foolish imaginings. On any
day I might, just before turning a corner, be overcome with the
sense that he was standing on the other side, smiling, waiting to
greet me with his quick eyes, the colour of polished walnut, his
dear head balanced on that stalk of a neck. Always there was only
disappointment on the other side; but the sweet and melancholy
sting of anticipation lingered the day long. And in the darkness
before the Ephesian dawn, lying half awake on my pallet, I would
hear him call: *Priscilla, Priscilla, come down. I need you.* The
sound of his voice was like fragrance to me, a pervasion of my
senses.

When in fact he did arrive, however, he did not seek me out.
And I felt silly for my anticipations.

He came in a cart which was pulled by a donkey.

He came with books and parchments, now more precious to
him than the tools of his leatherworking trade.

He came surrounded by a small crowd of men, listeners,
talkers, labourers, all of whom were strangers to me – all except
Timothy.

Timothy, who appeared in the doorway of our house with his
beautiful fall of ringlet hair, his straight, pagan smile, and his
soft announcement, 'We're back.'

And what Paul did in Ephesus after his arrival was to spend his attentions *outside* of Ephesus, on Asia abroad.

The men that he gathered (and kept on gathering) he trained as preachers and teachers, travellers, 'partners with me,' as he called them, 'in the gospel'. He rejected the term 'disciple'. He laughed much in their boisterous company, laughed his squealing giggle more than I'd ever heard before. This brave squad of hearty 'fellows' must have fulfilled some need in him.

Paul rented a schoolroom in a columned building on the south side of the Harbour Road. The man who owned the building, one Tyrannus, let him have the room for a pittance because Paul chose to teach in the heat of the day when the rest of Ephesus dozed.

There he taught the whole year through, and the second year too.

And from Ephesus he sent forth a stream of his 'fellow-workers for the kingdom of God', his 'fellow-servants in the Lord', 'fellow-soldiers with him', 'fellow-helpers', *fellows* like Justus and Tychicus and Demas – like the man named Luke, whom Paul called his 'beloved physician'. His *fellows*, then, went proclaiming the name of the Lord Jesus Christ north in Smyrna and Pergamum, northeast in Philadelphia and Sardis, east in Magnesia and Tralles.

One example of the men at the beck of the apostle will do. Let me describe Epaphras, born in Colossae. This is the fellow who had led the donkey that had pulled the cart that had brought the busy Paul to Ephesus. A vigorous, take-charge sort of male was Epaphras. Paul sent him farthest east, back to his hometown in the valley of the river Lycus, there to start a church. Delight, delight, and giddy praise met Epaphras when he returned seven months later, for not only had Epaphras succeeded in planting a church in the house of a man of means named Philemon, but he had also preached in several cities besides Colossae, Laodicea and Hieropolis – *and* he brought to the schoolroom new men to be taught and to be sent, such as Archippus, who two years later was leading a church in Laodicea.

Paul had extravagant things to say about the eager Epaphras. This man prayed much. This man prayed constantly and ever for others. This man was 'our beloved fellow servant', and 'a faithful minister of Christ on our behalf', and 'a slave of Christ Jesus', which Paul had said of no one else but himself.

But Aquila and I – *we* had been faithful! *We* had been uncomplaining labourers. With the help of none but Sosthenes (whose knowledge of the Lord was limited) it was Aquila and I who had established a church in Ephesus, and we did it when we were strangers in this place. We weren't born here. Aquila is from Pontus!

But who are we, after all? What worth in all that boiling energy? Not *fellows*, that's for sure. My husband is a man of silences, nearsighted and stolid and shy to the point of extinction.

And me? I'm but a woman.

I'm wrong. Forgive me.

It wasn't just men whom Paul taught, not men only whom he sent forth preaching.

I'd been with him, of course, in the summer and fall of his arrival at Ephesus. He worshipped in our house often enough and preached when he did and ate in the midst of the community; and we were welcome, surely, among his mobile company.

But because he never gave me the sweet greeting of my anticipations, I too withdrew. I watched him from something of a distance, fighting my feelings as if they were a sickness.

Oh, Paul! Not only did you come riding instead of walking, you came older. Your poor bones seem to be dragged down like the limbs of the ancient olive tree. How can I look on you and not try to help you?

And I see it, Paul. Despite the headlong energy of your labours, I see that something's distracting in you, something dearer and deeper than these fierce administrations. Your drive is no longer spontaneous; it requires concentration and a will, now, doesn't it?

If, during worship, he seemed to glance at me, my heart failed. I fought a sigh. I fought the flush and the smile that rose to my lips. I turned away from him, his strong skull and his drilling eye, because he hadn't, really. He seldom glanced at me. I knew it was only my yearning that made it seem as if he had.

So I drove hope away with anger. I protected my heart in a case of anger.

And then the apostle Paul took that away, too – the anger,
I mean.

Early one morning in July, when Paul had been a twelvemonth in
Ephesus, he sent Titus to our house asking whether I would
prepare a dinner for our people. 'Four,' Titus said, winking, 'if
Aquila will be present. Three if not.'

I was sensitive to things like winks. I noticed them, but I never
understood them, and I did not ask.

Four. Aquila would definitely be there.

I chose summer fruit and goats' cheese and bread baked from
Egyptian wheat and pigeons.

In those days we lived in a house completely enclosed by
other houses, walls to walls, our doorway found through narrow
passageways, stairs up, stairs down, and darkness. We had one
room with high windows for light in the daytime. But everywhere
else we lived with lamps and a continual smoke.

I thought that Titus was to be the other guest.

Just because he begged the meal, I guess.

But I was wrong. I was wrong about many things.

Because Paul's companion, when they arrived at the door of
our house, was a woman.

I led them to the only room of windows, where the table
was already set. As they entered the room I saw how Paul held
this woman's elbow, gently, intimately, with more gallantry
than I'd ever thought him capable. And she responded to the
touch with more than her mind. There was a bond. There must
have been a history. She was, I thought, two or three years
older than Paul, though she did not need to lean on him. She
had long hair, iron-grey, combed and piled after the manner of
the Macedonians. Her clothing was rich and simple, her eyes
both cautious and intelligent, her body heavy with an old
strength.

Aquila entered last.

I invited my guests to make themselves comfortable on the
couches round the table. It was my intent to leave them and to
serve. Aquila sat at the foot of the table. I prepared to go.

But Paul sank to a knee in order to seat his companion, then
rose and approached me, truly looking at me, searching my face,

my eyes. He reached, and for the first time since leaving Corinth eighteen months ago, he took my hand in his.

'Prisca,' he said, 'this is your mother. But she hasn't come for honour, or admiration. She's come to learn from you.'

James

61

Crosses fill our land, and corpses hang on them. There is a stink among us, and the grief of the people screams to heaven.

In the year since his appointment as the Governor of Judea, Antonius Felix has sent his legions bloody through the countryside, catching and killing the bands of men that hide in the hills.

He classifies them as 'bandits'. Perhaps they are. They steal. They make travel a dangerous enterprise.

'Insurrectionists', Felix calls them too, and that they are for sure. They hate Rome. They hate the Roman tax. They hate the rich who grow fat in the shadow of Rome. They hate every Jewish collaborator – for those who serve Rome, they say, serve a god besides God.

But the poor, the peasants, the lowest orders of priests; the broken in our land, the crushed and the hungry – these believe what the 'insurrectionists' say. Poor Jews know in their bones the afflictions of Rome. They send their sons to join the bandit bands and their sons are crucified.

I have heard it said of Felix that he exercises authority like a king, but blinks and cringes like a slave. When we are ruled by obsequious dogs, there is no honour anymore. There is a stink, and nothing is sure.

Oh, let the rich man weep! And those who make friends with the world, let them howl because of the miseries soon to befall them! For the friends of this world are the foes of God! And riches rot, and gold will rust, and the rust will eat their flesh like fire!

This is what I say: I say that those who live today in earthly luxury are larding their hearts for the slaughter tomorrow.

This morning I walked outside the city by way of the Garden

Gate. I walked with my eyes cast down, my whole mind filled with solemn thought. But then I became aware of a rapid panting, and I looked and saw that I was passing Golgotha.

On that little hill there are stout posts planted, each awaiting the crossbeam and the body that will die on it.

But one post already had its beam, and from that beam hung its body.

The panting I heard came from the breast of a young lad crucified.

A boy, bleeding from the Roman scourging, his blood baptizing the post, his thin arms bound by thick rope to the crossbeam, his head pressed back against the wood so that his mouth hung open, panting – a mere boy, his throat a column of ivory purity.

I went and stood in front of him and began to pray in a low voice.

Soon the panting stopped and I paused in prayer.

The lad had rolled his head to the side. He was gazing at me with stricken eyes. I returned his gaze and was caught, locked eye to eye and bound to sorrow. No longer could I be a bystander.

'Who are you?' I said. 'Tell me your name, and I will lift it to the Lord.'

At first he only looked at me. But then he said, 'I know you.' He closed his eyes, then opened them again and murmured, 'James the Just, you are. My father always loved you.'

The lad contrived to smile. He smiled at me and performed another endless blink of his beautiful eyes.

He knows me? How does he know me? When have our two paths crossed?

I said, 'What's your father's name?' I waited, then I said, 'What is your name?'

Slowly the boy drew breath. Smiling still, he whispered, 'We watched when that Roman soldier was tearing sacred pages of Torah.' He breathed a while, then said: 'We watched when he threw Torah into the fire. We pledged our lives, my father and I...'

'Please,' I said again, 'what is your name?' I feared the speed of time and the dying, the immediate dying: the lad was leaving me! I pressed my hands together and begged: 'Please, child, tell me your father's name!'

Once more he laboured to draw breath, causing the blood on his stomach to glisten. Then, as that difficult wind escaped his lips, he whispered, 'Patience, James. The Lord is coming.'

The boy lifted his beautiful eyes to the horizon and smiled a welcoming smile. His face bloomed with the smiling, and suddenly he shouted: 'See? Can you see him? Oh, James, the Judge is standing at the doors!'

While he still was smiling, the flames in his eyes were extinguished, and he died, and he did not breathe again.

I took his feet into my hands. I laid my face against his young and unencumbered ankles, and I wept.

$\mathcal{P}$risca

62

Paul's voice had changed. I mean, his whole manner of speaking had changed. That snarling, aggressive, supercilious whine – that nasal screech of his – had softened into something almost introspective. He breathed more. He preached with less violence, less drama, less – what should I call it? – gesticulation. He announced his themes at the beginning of a proper talk, then he would pause now and again to collect his thoughts. The apostle was teaching now, leading people in a planned path, adhering to a self-conscious strategy.

When had the change taken place? I don't know. Whether it happened while he was gone from us or else in the year of his return, I really don't know. I didn't become completely aware of the difference in his voice until the evening when he escorted Lydia to our house for dinner – not until the moment he took my hand and said, *This is your mother.*

My mother! For one blink of an eye, I suffered the impossible thought that this *was* my mother, suddenly restored to life, suddenly in my home again.

Paul must have seen the shadow flit over my face. He squeezed my hand for attention and said, 'Priscilla, your spiritual mother. The mother of your calling. It is because of this woman that you pray and prophesy in public.'

Now he did for me exactly what he'd done for his companion: He knelt in order to lower me onto my own cushion, side by side with the older, larger woman.

But the food, the dinner…

As I was brought low, speechless, to the table, Aquila rose and quietly left the room.

Paul took a seat facing the two of us. He smiled.

'Prisca,' he said looking at the woman beside me, 'this is Lydia, my steadfast friend and beloved to me – one of my dearest partners in the gospel since I entered Europe and travelled to Philippi.'

Lydia looked at Paul with complete familiarity, as if she were receiving some interesting pieces of information.

Paul said, 'Lydia trades in a splendid cloth dyed purple in the vats of Thyatira. She's on her way to that city now, to make purchases – and to preach. It's her hometown, Prisca. She wants her people to know the news.'

Lydia nodded agreement, aristocratic, content to be praised. So *that's* why her robe was so expensive and so elegant.

There was a bump at the door and Aquila entered the dining room with my pigeons still in the baking dish, grease gurgling and spitting with heat. I doubted the meat was thoroughly cooked, but I kept quiet. My humble husband knows nothing of the sequence of meals and proper presentation, yet he had chosen to serve and I determined to be as proud of him as if he were a lord of lands and lakes and magnificent holdings.

Paul said, 'Lydia's a Jew, like you. But unlike you, she's unmarried. In Philippi there is no synagogue, nor were there men enough to lead in prayers and readings and worship. So what did you do, Lydia? Tell Prisca what you were doing when I first met you.'

The woman beside me said, 'You tell it much better than I.'

What a low, thrilling voice she had! Big as a bed, warm as a blanket: *You tell it much better than I.*

Paul grinned.

Aquila left the room.

'Prisca,' Paul said, 'Lydia led the worship herself, meeting on every Shabbat with other women by a stream outside the city. And after I baptized her, the good work that the Lord had begun in her did not cease. It will not cease until it is brought to completion in the day of Jesus Christ.

'Until Philippi, I never thought that women could or should utter sacred words in public places.

'But there in Philippi I found the Spirit already working in this woman, working with power. How could I contradict the

Spirit of God? How could I refuse to admit the evidence before my eyes? God chose the woman, not me. I had to accommodate myself to God.'

Something crashed in the kitchen. There followed a silence, and then I heard the slow, dragging strokes of the bramble broom as it pushed potsherds into a pile. The sweeping made a slushy sound. Yes, it had been the wine flask, alabaster, irreplaceable.

I said, 'So then it was not you, Paul... but God... who chose me to prophesy?'

He looked at me. 'God: yes. To prophesy: yes.' Paul spoke in a studied, tutorial tone. 'To practise that spiritual gift, upbuilding the people, encouraging them, consoling them – yes, Prisca. God chose you to edify the church.'

O Paul, but I always thought it had been you. I thought you had approved of me, selected me, prepared me to join you, preaching.

'This is more than I knew,' I whispered, 'and less than I felt.'

'Prisca,' Paul said piercing me with his red-rimmed eyes, 'Prisca, what does that mean?'

Lydia, too, turned toward me, mildly reflecting his question, sublimely expecting an answer.

I blurted, 'But *you* are the one who told me to cover my head! Why did you tell me to cover my head?'

Aquila came into the room with three brutish clay cups already filled with wine. I noticed the lees turning and turning in mine.

Then he sat, my husband did, as if the meal were spread and ready.

I was not going to ask for bread. I was not going to mention the water for washing. Aquila had taken a seat by Paul. He was squinting hard in my direction. He who cannot see knows not how much he can *be* seen.

In that moment I loved Aquila almost to tears.

Paul spoke again in that schoolish tone – having missed completely my deeper meaning. 'In this created world,' he said, 'your head declares your source, and your face is the glory of *that* source and *that* authority. Your "head",' Paul said, 'is like the headwaters of the river. Being comes from it.

'So it is in the order of creation: the head of every man is Christ; the head of a woman is her husband; and the head of Christ is God.'

Paul paused to bethink himself. Oh, my smart apostle – deaf

to the sense of the heart – he began to roll the rough clay cup between the palms of his hands.

'But when you pray, Prisca,' Paul said, staring into his wine, 'when you prophesy, *that* act jumps the order of creation. The source of that gift is the Spirit of Christ. Its practice must give glory to none *but* Christ and God the Father, whom the angels make present in our worship. No glory to Aquila. None to your husband. It would dishonour him and offend heaven if anything signified that the prophecy came from him. So you must hide that which declares Aquila to be your source. You must cover him up, as it were. You must cover your head, Prisca, which signifies your earthly "head".'

Smiling, mild and undisturbed, Lydia of Thyatira now raised her hands and pulled out the pins that held her hair in place. She rolled her shoulders, she bent her head left and right – and, as if it were a cloud of rain upon the mountain, her hair fell thick and beautiful. It covered her head all round.

'My veil, Priscilla,' she murmured from behind the iron-grey rain. 'Or if I wanted to deny the veil, I might as well shear this off and go bald about the country, showing my head and my face in full.'

And what, Lydia, I said in my soul, *does THAT mean?*

She called me 'Priscilla'.

No one ever had called me 'Priscilla' before, not even Aquila – just Paul. Paul only. In the mouth of this woman, wealthy and powerful, the name lost all its tender affection. It became to me a great diminishment. *Little* Prisca. Prissy.

Paul smiled at me. Paul, his own large head seeming loose on his narrow neck, grinned at me, cracking the flesh around his moist, red mouth. He said, 'I've told Lydia all about you, Prisca. She loves you. She's as proud of you as I am. It was her suggestion that we eat together before she leaves for Thyatira. She wants to learn from you. She wants you to teach her everything you know about the edification of the church – for though she may be your mother in ministry, you are the more mature, having practised it the longer.'

I, too, smiled. I smiled at Paul. I smiled at Lydia, as she divided the hair from her face, reappearing strong and jowlish.

But, on a sudden impulse I rose to my feet and went to Aquila and knelt down behind him and draped my arms around his neck and kissed the hair on the crown of his head.

Now, how can I explain this? It was during that summer's eve in Ephesus, at table with Paul and Lydia and Aquila, that I experienced a new and complete release. No, I can't explain it. I don't understand it. But it is true, and the truth has lasted.

When I rose to kiss the head of my husband, I could feel neither the bone nor the flesh of my legs. There was no weight in me. I floated. I soared and learned laughter again. I felt, in fact, freed from bonds I hadn't known were binding me, and by plain instinct recognized that I would be equal to every task the Lord might send me, present and future.

I knew that we, Aquila and I, would someday return to Rome.

I knew that I could indeed teach Lydia the public gesture and the faithful word that would build a church in Thyatira.

And I knew that I was free of Paul to like Paul very much again, a friend, a fine man and a foolish one, audacious, imperious, insolent, short – and a slave of Jesus after all.

Lightly I floated from Aquila to Paul. Lightly I knelt and lightly kissed the wispy hair on the top of his own huge rucked moon of a head. I plucked up his right hand, selected the long forefinger, laid it beside mine in the light, and showed Lydia how the apostle and I had the self-same callus in the self-same place because we did the self-same work in leather and tents.

'Equals,' I said.

Paul blinked.

Lydia let out a glad whoop – and so we began. We ate the pigeons first.

Luke

63

God accomplished extraordinary miracles through the hands of Paul. Cloth that had touched his body, handkerchiefs with his sweat, aprons he wore while working, were carried to people suffering sickness, and the sickness vanished, and evil spirits came out of them.

There appeared in Ephesus seven travelling exorcists who sought to use the name of Jesus in their craft. They were Jewish, the sons, they said, of a high priest named Sceva.

One day they entered a small house and gathered around a man possessed by an evil spirit.

Together they all said, 'I adjure you by the Jesus whom Paul preaches...'

But the spirit answered, 'Jesus I know, and Paul I know; but who are you?'

Suddenly the man with the evil spirit leaped on the seven sons of Sceva, beat them, stripped them, and drove them naked, bruised, and wounded from the house.

When this became known to the residents of Ephesus, both Jews and Greeks were filled with fear, and the name of the Lord Jesus was praised.

Moreover, many of those who had become believers now revealed and repented their own magic practices. They brought out their books and heaped them in a public place and burned them. And when the value of the books was calculated, it added up to fifty thousand silver coins.

So the word of the Lord grew in Ephesus and prevailed mightily.

James

64

Where is Saul? No one knows. No one here in Jerusalem knows. He might be anywhere in the empire.

Where has that itinerate freedom-monger gone? We know where he *was*. After Antioch he spent time in Galatia – but that was nearly two years ago, and we didn't receive that piece of information until last month. Where is he now? I wish I could send him a letter. I want to warn him away from Jerusalem. He mustn't come here.

It's not just that tensions are intolerable, hatreds both external and internal ripping the people apart. Saul can live with tensions. Saul sports in tension like Leviathan in the sea. It's rather that Trouble cries his name in the street and seeks his face particularly. There are certain men here, Pharisees and zealots – and believers too, if the truth be told – who will arrest him on sight. Or kill him, whichever person or mood prevails.

Last month, unprepared for, unexpected, five men arrived in Jerusalem from the northern regions of Galatia. They had travelled by land and by sea and by land again, fighting all along the way, dispatching thieves and pirates and bands of robbers – engaging in combat, it seems, with high delight and a whooping exultation. Two of the five are giants with long ropelike arms, yellow hair, a worm-white skin, and frozen eyes. I mean that their eyes are like chips of blue ice. And their mouths are filled with enormous blocks of teeth. All five entered Jerusalem armed, bearing that gross leather shield, the brutish pole, the heavy long-bladed sword of their kind.

That – their appearance, their weaponry – was enough to draw attention: Gentiles striding the sacred streets, men of threat but of no status either Rome or Judea recognized.

But then they practically begged attention and pleaded for an official scourging.

They walked straight to the Temple.

Booted and brazen, they entered the outermost court and began to stroll all gladly through the columns of the Porches of Solomon... giving money away! Every time they came upon a beggar begging, they filled his hands with a heap of coins, crying out in a loutish Greek: 'For the poor of Jerusalem!'

They had bags of the stuff, three bags full of mammon! That, apparently, had been the cause and the object of all their fighting southward.

The beggars, of course, jumped up and ran to the tables of the money changers, because the coin the Galatians brought was Roman, stamped with images. As long as they dispensed the money in the porches, they may have been boorish fools, but they were not yet sinners.

On the other hand, as soon as the white giants left the porches and entered the Court of Gentiles; as soon as they came to the Nicanor Gate, an entrance to the Court of Women; as soon as they poured forth their graven images upon the beggars sitting there, that coin became a horror and a blasphemy.

A cry of outrage went up. As if against an evil wind, women clutched their robes to their throats. Old men tore their hair and began to scream. Priests ran thither and yon like ants in an anthill kicked apart. And one man in particular took specific, effective action.

It is nearly certain that this man – a zealot of calculation and cool ferocity – had been watching the Galatians from the moment they climbed the Temple Mount. He anticipated opportunity and had prepared.

For now he came running with a large company of the Temple Guard, thirty or forty men with knives and spears, battle-ready, trembling with the hatred of these times: those who despoil the Temple need no trial. Kill them on the spot!

Seeing the attack at hand, and the man who led it levelling his sword toward them, the Galatians piled their bags on the pavement and formed a circle, all of them facing outward, the giants foremost. They started to bellow, a gleeful bull-like bugling, a dreadful sound to hear.

The Temple guard wilted.

The man that led them felt the shift. He turned. He picked out one young man who was shrinking backward, commanded him to attack and, when he did not, slashed his neck so that blood spouted out while the poor man stood there, confused.

The leader announced, 'I am Mattithias! Those who will not serve the Lord must be destroyed before the Lord destroys us all!'

Two Galatians burst out laughing, filled with admiration for the gesture.

When Mattithias turned back to them, he discovered that an advocate had interposed himself between them and him.

Barsabbas! Our Judas Barsabbas, bold in the breech after all!

'Mattithias,' he said, speaking with as much hauteur as the zealot before him. 'No one questions *my* zeal for the Lord. I have invited hardship for the sake of the Lord. I have travelled to distant regions to teach the ways of God and the Laws of Moses!'

A hush descended upon the courts of the Temple. Indeed, Barsabbas was known as one who strove to preserve Israel.

Mattithias himself now halted.

And the Galatians broke their own ranks. They ran to Judas Barsabbas. They would have thrown their arms around him. They would have crushed him with love, except that he snapped an order in Greek that stilled them.

To Mattithias he now spoke Aramaic. 'These men have never meant any harm. They are not sinners, Mattithias; nor are they enemies of Israel. They're just stupid. They don't know the traditions. Their skulls are as thick and their minds as slow as turtle shells, but they are men of goodwill. I know. I taught them in their own city. If you will release them to me, I promise, I will make them more than friends of Israel. I will make them sons.'

Mattithias considered this.

He is a man of remarkable beauty, a Benjamite, tall as the first king, Saul.

Finally, quietly, Mattithias said, 'You saw me kill young Eleazar.'

Barsabbas said, 'I did.'

Mattithias said, 'He has a wife and two children. That did not stay my hand. There can no longer be mercy among us. Mercy will abolish us. Even as I killed Eleazar, so will I kill you if any one of these men shows contempt for God or threat for Israel.'

He turned on his heel and departed alone, leaving the temple guard to gather the body and clean up the blood of their dead companion, while the white giants began to beat on Barsabbas until he grew angry and scolded them in Greek.

Roughly, clamorously, the Galatians explained to Judas Barsabbas and to me that the notion of collecting money for the poor in Jerusalem had come from Saul. They called him *Paulos*. They had loved the idea from the start.

'Yes, yes, *Paulos*,' Barsabbas said with a sigh, 'the wretch who turned your heads and hearts against me! He never thought to teach you – did he? – that the poor are not those who sit in the Temple and beg. I would have told you that. They are the *Anawim*, people who attend the Temple in piety and righteousness, people who do not trust in their own strength but place every confidence in God. They are distinguished by their faithfulness, not by their physical condition.'

Judas Barsabbas is frightfully thin, as if he eats air, but as long as a Temple candle. He stared at the white giants a moment, then said, 'Look at me. Do I look beggarly? Yet I am one of the Anawim. Look at me: We put oil on our heads and wash our faces and fast in private. We are the remnant of the remnants of Israel.'

With guttural barks of recognition, the Galatians heaved up their bags of coin, and carried them to Barsabbas where he sat. They were just about to pour them out at his feet, when he howled, 'No! No!' and leaped backward as if the money were fire.

'I don't want it!' he cried. 'We can't take it! It's tainted!'

The Galatians were stunned to silence. No greater blow could have been delivered to them than this blow to their generosity, their conviction, their purpose, their good hearts.

Still holding his bag, the blondest and biggest of the men gazed at Barsabbas, blinking back a sudden spring of tears.

I knew what Barsabbas meant, of course; but I thought his response was overdramatic, unnecessary – until he offered the Galatians a shrewd solution to their dilemma.

'Here in Jerusalem,' he said slowly, with an air of thinking aloud, 'here in the sacred City of God,' he said, 'Gentile money is an abomination, a corruption and a corrupter too. The Anawim especially would rather go hungry than touch it.' Now Barsabbas returned the gaze of the weeping giant and spoke directly to him:

'But you have come a long way, haven't you?'

The giant nodded like a miserable child: a very long way.

'Sir,' said Barsabbas, pointing toward the bag of coin, 'if you were not a Gentile, this would not be Gentile money, would it?'

The giant shook his head.

'Then this is what you must do: cease to *be* a Gentile. Become at one with us.'

Let me attest to the truest intentions of Judas Barsabbas: he was not a greedy man. Though the money would be useful to the *Anawim* – those who chose poverty and those who had poverty forced on them, the sick, the downtrodden, widows, orphans – it was not the money that Barsabbas was after. It never was. He had, as he believed, a deeper, more godly design.

In thick Greek the giant said, '*Ti me dei poiein?* What must I do?'

And Judas Barsabbas answered, 'Be circumcised.'

Yesterday, as we walked passed the Antonia, Judas Barsabbas pointed to a tall man with raven black hair bound in leather cords, falling down his back – a strongly handsome head.

'I need to speak with that man,' he said.

I recognized the face immediately, but I couldn't recall a name. 'Who is he?' I asked.

'That's Mattithias the zealot. I want to tell him that the Galatian men have all been circumcised.'

It was then that I realized who this Mattithias is: he's the man I met at the house of Saul's sister. He is her husband, the despiser of her brother. *If some Roman thing enters this house living, he'll leave it dead. I'll kill him myself.*

'Judas,' I said, 'does he know Saul? Do you think he has ever met Saul?'

Barsabbas looked at me. 'Why did you mention Saul just now?'

'This Mattithias is his brother-in-law,' I said.

Still Barsabbas looked at me, as if considering his answer. Then he said, 'Twenty-three years ago they travelled north together, to arrest believers in Damascus. It was then that Mattithias discovered the treachery and the wickedness of Saul. Moreover, Mattithias actually witnessed God's judgment on the man, for God struck him blind. Mattithias has made a vow to kill

Saul on sight. He says God will not blame him to take Saul's life. Rather, God will blame him if he has the chance and doesn't.'

'Barsabbas!' I whispered. 'You share these sentiments?'

'Not,' he said, 'to the death. But I will confess, it was our mutual loathing of Saul that caused us to talk in the first place.'

Saul, this is James:

If I could find you, I would write you.

Not out of admiration, though twenty-three years ago I did admire your grasp of Torah.

Not out of love, though once you kissed me and stirred that coal in my heart.

I would write you for the same reason that I clothe the naked and feed the hungry: evidence of my faith and love for the Lord of the both of us.

Saul, I would say: avoid Jerusalem. Live the rest of your days anywhere else in the empire. Not here. God bless you for remembering the poor in this place; but send every further collection, don't bring it.

You would be in too much danger here.

Don't come.

James.

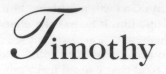

Timothy

65

There was trouble in Corinth. Paul sent me to fix it.

While they were visiting us in Ephesus, some of the slaves of Chloe's household told us there were divisions among the people there. Corinthians were quarrelling over which house-church possessed the greater spiritual wisdom. It seemed that believers in the syncretic city had slipped back to their old Greek ways, attaching themselves each to the one that baptized them, exactly as neophytes of the mystery religions attach to the *mystagogue* that initiated them. Corinthians were arguing over which baptizer had the higher insight into the mind of God.

By that spring, we'd spent nearly two years in Ephesus, which Paul had come to recognize as a hub in the wheel of all his far-flung churches. To keep the many connections alive, he would delegate responsibility, sending ministers constantly and everywhere in his stead.

It was no surprise to me, then, that he asked me to travel to Corinth to help heal the situation.

'Tell them what I always told them,' Paul said, instructing me: 'Nothing – no wisdom, no deed, no person, no *thing* – is important except it's attached to Jesus Christ and him crucified. Tell them that all we who preach and baptize are equally servants of the Lord. Tell them,' Paul said, 'that God alone is the source of their life in Christ Jesus; that God made him to be our wisdom, our righteousness and sanctification and redemption.'

Thus my assignment; thus my message. But then Paul bethought himself of the universal need of this particular truth, and he said, 'Timothy, take the route we took when first we entered Europe. Remind all the churches of the cross and Christ alone.'

Paul was cheerful when I left him, filled with thanksgivings to God, convinced that his plans for the world were working.

'You have beautiful feet, Timothy,' he said, grinning, 'because of the news that you preach!'

When problems arose in his churches, he wasn't so much aggrieved as glad for the chance to think and write. He said that in solving problems, the Spirit taught him things he hadn't known before.

'Tell them I give thanks for them always because of the grace of God which they have in Christ Jesus, who will,' Paul said, 'sustain them to the end, guiltless in the day of our Lord Jesus Christ.'

From Ephesus I walked to Thyatira. There I met with Lydia, who had spent the last eight months gathering goods for her trade and souls for the Lord. From Thyatira to Troas we rode together – she and I and fifty bolts of purple material – in a four-horse, four-wheeled, well-covered carriage. Lydia is a woman of *gravitas*. She has a weight both physical and grand. It moves on wheels more easily than on foot. And then it takes to the sea with majesty. Graciously, she paid passage for both of us to Samothrace and Neapolis. Then we took the carriage again to Philippi, where I stayed for two weeks, preaching.

It is the cross, Timothy! Tell them that the word of the cross – which the world scorns because the world considers it a hideous failure – is for us the power of God!

I walked again, alone again, from Philippi through Amphipolis and Apollonia. At Thessalonica I paused to preach. Next I went to Berea and preached there, too.

Jews demand signs. Greeks seek wisdom. But we preach Christ crucified, a stumbling block to Jews and lunacy to Gentiles, but to those who are called, both Jews and Greeks, Christ the power of God and the wisdom of God. For the foolishness of God is wiser than the human mind, and the weakness of God is stronger than all the forces flesh can muster.

Finally moving south with speed and intention, spanning the miles on my own legs at something like twenty-five in a day, I got to Thebes in a week and Megara in nine days. The closer I came to Corinth, the more I smiled; and the more I smiled, the faster I went. It felt like a homecoming. After Megara, skirting the Saronic Gulf, I lifted my eyes and saw that marvellous massif, that monument of deities dead before our God: the Acrocorinth.

That afternoon I crossed the road of boats: I made my way through the shouts of straining men and ropes and the great wooden grindings of the ships they were hauling overland between the Bay and the Gulf. I passed the stadium of the Isthmian Games, and then I raced like an athlete truly. I put my face into the wind and felt the flume of my hair behind, and I sprinted the last six miles to the city.

'Erastus!' I cried, reaching my friend's house under the sapphire skies of the evening. 'Erastus, it's Timothy! Timothy! I've come to stay a while.'

And there was Erastus, that friend of mine! There was he, emerging from his door like an entire ship of state with all flags flying. Gorgeously dressed, oiled and jewelled and pink with good living, he spread his mighty arms and burst into a boo-hooing of tears.

'They said you were coming! I didn't believe them,' he wept. 'But it's Timothy true and for sure!'

Erastus has hands as big as hams. The great man threw his arms around me and crushed me with huggings and kissings. He rained his gladness all over me, then pushed me back to see me clearly.

'Oh, look at my little brother grown older,' he wept. 'Look at his hair all scrubbed by the sun!'

'Who said I was coming?' I said. 'I didn't think anyone knew.'

Erastus began to pop his moist, magnificent mouth. 'And look at these lines in my pretty boy's forehead. Timothy, Timothy, what causes such frowning?'

I smiled. 'No frowning!' I promised. 'Not in the house of the grand Erastus, could he offer board and a bed to a tired traveller.'

'Ah, yes, a bed. Well, well – a bed. Hum.' A cloud darkened his features for a moment, then he beamed: 'Yes, yes, I know the bed for you. But until then, come. Come in. Let me refresh you with water and washing and something to drink. Oh, Timothy,' he cried, turning to the house, 'wonderful things have been happening to me in these last weeks. Come! I'll show you!'

He pulled me almost like a little wagon through halls and his atrium, into a dining room where the table still held the remains of a meal.

As we entered the room, three men rose as silently as shafts of shadow. Erastus clapped his delight, but they stood solemn and unsmiling.

'These men,' Erastus giggled, 'these holy, holy men – all three and each my guests for as long as they wish – these preachers,

Timothy, are the direct cause of the wonderful things that have come to me!'

Erastus bustled out of the room. His guests put their hands behind their backs. They were clothed like nobility, the folds of their robes causing each to seem a statue of some ancestral figure, the studied blankness of their eyes like carven marble.

'So,' said the foremost, speaking toward a point above my hair, 'you are Timothy.'

'Yes,' I said. 'The peace of the Lord be with you.'

'So,' he said again, 'you are a companion of the man named Paul – '

'Yes,' I said – a little too quickly, I fear, for the guest repeated: 'a companion of that man Paul, who calls himself an apostle.'

'Well, yes,' I said, with some hesitation.

A silence fell between us.

Then Erastus rolled into the room at the head of a procession of servants.

'Sit!' he cried. 'Recline! Lie down, lie down, and talk with me. Let's talk about gifts and the Spirit and the things breaking forth among us now. Timothy, you first, since you're the last to come. Timothy, dear friend, what do you have to say?'

Suddenly servants were washing my feet and fitting them with silken slippers from India far in the east.

Servants were laying a meal for me, wine with purple beads at the brim.

Servants were massaging my shoulders, my back and buttocks, thighs, and calves. They massaged the three guests too, whose robes the servants had removed.

Servants were bringing perfumes and oils and combs –

Remind them of their calling, Timothy – that not many of them were wise according to worldly standards, not many were powerful, not many of noble birth. But God chose what's foolish in the world to shame the wise; God chose the weak to shame the strong; God chose the low and despised, even the things that are not, to bring to nothing things that are – so no human can boast in the presence of God.

In fact, there was no bed for me in the house of Erastus. His present guests – 'apostles', he called them, men who travelled with rather more baggage than I – occupied all his rooms, all his hospitality, and most of his heart as well. 'Timothy, their spirits are closer to the Spirit of Jesus than anyone else I know.'

Erastus dispatched a servant to lead me to another lodging.

'Stephanas is the one who told me you were coming. Stephanas is prepared to receive you, Timothy.'

Stephanas welcomed me in quietness, with no more exuberance than the embrace of brothers and gentle signs of peace. Very few lights were lit in his house, and he seemed himself to hold his soul in darkness.

'How did you know I was coming?' I said.

'Paul told me.'

'You saw him? You were with Paul?'

Stephanas unrolled a soft leather pouch and pulled out sheets of papyrus. 'Yes,' he said softly. 'And look. He sent a letter back with us.'

A very long letter indeed. It wasn't for me. It was for the churches here in Corinth; but twice this letter begged the churches to receive me. I, Paul's 'beloved and faithful child in the Lord', should be put at ease, Paul wrote; and no one should despise me.

Why would someone despise me?

Now my soul entered as well the quietness and the occlusions of Stephanas's mood, and though he strove to put me at my ease, I was not at all easy. I was sorry.

With one lamp lit between us, measuring his words, Stephanas explained the present circumstances.

With many sighs, he told me his story.

During the recent winter, certain questions had arisen among the Corinthians which, they felt, required Paul's assistance and his answer. Therefore, as soon as spring brought calm to the seas, the churches deputized Stephanas and Fortunatus and Achaicus to sail for Ephesus with a formal list of the issues that most wanted response.

I too had begun my travels with the better weather, so the deputies arrived in Ephesus several weeks after I had left: arrived cheerfully, Stephanas said, rejoicing to see their teacher again; arrived as a pure surprise to Paul, who kissed them and laughed and stroked their faces and kissed them again.

But when the four of them sat for discussions face-to-face, things changed, and it came to pass that they had borne more than a public letter to Ephesus. Under Paul's urgent inquiry, pressed by Paul's strong desire to know the state of the churches in Corinth, Stephanas began to tell truths no one had asked him to tell.

Members of the churches were involved in extreme sexual immoralities. Members were bringing lawsuits against other members. Members frequented prostitutes. Members delivered their bodies to debaucheries –

Paul interrupted Stephanas. 'But you,' he said. 'How do you know these things?'

Stephanas shrugged. 'Why, everyone knows them,' he said.

Paul gaped. 'Everyone? All the churches? Don't the sinners cloak their sinning?'

'It's public,' Stephanas said. 'It's what they do. It's how they *live* – ' Stephanas paused, beginning to view things from a distance, objectively. Paul's presence cast new light on the behaviours in Corinth. Stephanas swallowed and said, 'And there is no guilt in what they do.'

'Surely the churches have spoken that guilt,' Paul said. 'Surely the leaders condemn them.'

'Well,' Stephanas murmured, growing more and more abashed, 'no.'

'What?' Paul leaped to his feet. 'Are people *afraid* of a sinner these days?' he said. 'How can he learn that his act *is* a sin till others address it out loud?'

'No, but they *have* addressed it, out loud and in public too!' Stephanas said – and immediately he felt a panic; for Paul said, 'What did they say?' and all at once Stephanas was brought to the most difficult disclosure of all.

He began to rub the back of his neck.

Paul repeated the question: 'What did the leaders and the sinners among them say?'

With his head down, Stephanas answered: 'They say that you would approve.'

'That I would... that I would *what*?'

'Approve. At least, that you would not condemn them. And I myself,' Stephanas whispered, 'I wasn't sure what you would do.'

The room in which they were talking became as still as the air before a storm. Paul was fixed and mute, unreadable; Stephanas saw no sign for what to say next. He had to proceed by his own conceiving.

He said, 'You were the teacher. You are our teacher still.'

Stephanas folded his hands and strove to speak with a grave articulation. 'You taught us it was for freedom that Christ had set us free. You urged us to stand fast and never again to submit to slavery under the Law. Freedom,' Stephanas said. 'Freedom. You gave us the wonderful gift of freedom. And when the churches discussed the behaviours of some of these members, many people reached the conclusion that all things are lawful. *All things*, they said, *are lawful for me*. And the leaders did not disagree. And even if most could not go through that door, we didn't close it either – because it seemed, you know, it was opened by you. But some grew angry, very angry, saying, *Paul has un-sinned sinning.*'

Suddenly Paul came back to life, calling loudly, 'Sosthenes! Sosthenes, bring your reeds! There's something I want you to write!'

He ran from the room.

Stephanas, Fortunatus, Achaicus – none of them saw Paul again till the following day, when he came and embraced them with a solemn strength and gave them the long epistle which now was lying on the table between us – between Stephanas and me, I mean, under one lamp in his little house, in the dark of a dismal night.

Paul's letter covered everything: the divisions that Chloe's slaves had reported, the formal questions of the congregations, the sins of some Corinthians, the actions others should take.

Stephanas was miserable.

This was not a letter of concessions. It neither praised much nor excused at all. It was the teacher teaching, the preacher exhorting, scolding, but seldom consoling. It was the apostle exerting authority, issuing instructions to the whole community, sometimes requiring kindness for others, sometimes demanding the rod – and Stephanas, who had brought so much of Corinth to Paul, now had to bring Paul to Corinth.

It was his obligation to read this letter aloud to each of the churches, in all of the houses where congregations gathered, beginning with the house of Erastus, the Manager of Public Markets.

*P*aul

66

Paul, called by the will of God to be an apostle of Christ Jesus,
To the church of God which is at Corinth, to those sanctified in
Christ Jesus, called to be saints together with all those who in
every place call on the name of our Lord Jesus Christ, both their
Lord and ours:

Grace to you and peace from God our Father and the Lord
Jesus Christ.

I do not write to make you ashamed, but to admonish you as
my beloved children. For though you have countless guides in
Christ, you don't have many fathers. I, however – I through the
gospel – became your father in Christ Jesus.

I urge you then, my children, be imitators of me.

You see before you Timothy, my beloved and faithful child in
the Lord, whom I have sent to remind you of my ways in Christ,
as I teach them everywhere in every church.

Some of you are showing arrogance, as if I were not coming
to you. Don't worry! If the Lord allows it, I'll come to you very
soon, in order to test not the *talk* of the arrogant ones, but their
power. For the kingdom of God does not consist in talk. It
consists in power.

Which do you wish, then? That I rush toward you with a rod,
or that I come with love and a spirit of gentleness?

It is actually reported that there is immorality among you, an
immorality like nothing found among pagans! A man is living
with his father's wife. How can you be arrogant about such a
thing? You ought to be *grieving*!

Let that man be removed from among you.

For though absent in body, I am present in spirit and, just as if I were truly present, I have already pronounced judgment in the name of the Lord Jesus on this sinner. Now it's your turn: while you are gathered in a body, by the power of our Lord Jesus you must deliver this man to Satan for the destruction of the flesh – in order that his spirit may be saved in the day of the Lord Jesus.

Your boasting does you no good. Don't you know that a little leaven leavens the entire lump? Clean out the old leaven that you yourselves might *be* a new lump, truly unleavened. You are that. You can be that. For Christ, our Passover Lamb, has been sacrificed. Therefore, let's keep the feast not with the old leaven, the leaven of malice and evil, but with the unleavened bread of sincerity and truth.

You say: 'All things are lawful to me.' I say: but not all things are helpful.

You say, 'All things are lawful for me,' but I myself – I refuse to be enslaved by anything.

You say: 'Food's for the stomach, and the stomach for food' – yes, and God will destroy them both together!

If the only thing you take from my teaching is freedom, mere freedom, you haven't taken enough.

If you think that holy living involves your spirit alone; if you think that this mortal form, your body, has nothing to do with goodness or with heaven, then you think like children! You think no better than babies who splash at the edge of the ocean while breakers are forming offshore.

Listen to me: The body is not meant for immorality but for the Lord, and the Lord is for the body! And God, who raised the Lord, will raise us up as well. Your bodies therefore – your *bodies*, beloved – are members of Christ! Shall you take the members of Christ and make them members of a prostitute? Never! Don't you know that he who joins himself to a prostitute becomes one body with her? Because, as it is written: *The two shall become one flesh*. But those who are united to the Lord become one body with him.

Shun immorality!

Every other sin which a person commits is outside the body; but the immoral man sins against his own body.

Don't you know that your body is a temple of the Holy Spirit within you, which you have from God?

You are not your own!

You were bought with a price!

So glorify God in your body.

I commend you for remembering me in everything and maintaining the traditions even as I have delivered them to you.

But in the following instructions I cannot commend you, because when you come together, it is not the Lord's supper that you eat. For some of you go ahead with their own meals, and some are drunk, while others go hungry. What? Don't you have houses to eat and drink in? Or do you so despise the church of God that you will humiliate those who have nothing? What shall I say to you? Shall I commend you in this? No! No! Absolutely not!

For I received from the Lord what I also delivered to you, that the Lord Jesus on the night when he was betrayed took bread, and when he had given thanks, he broke it and said: *This is my body which is for you. Do this in remembrance of me.* In the same way he took the cup after supper and said, *This cup is the new covenant in my blood. Do this, as often as you drink it, in remembrance of me.* As often as you eat this bread and drink the cup, you proclaim the Lord's death until he comes.

Whoever, then, eats the bread or drinks the cup of the Lord in an unworthy manner will be guilty of profaning the body and blood of the Lord. Let all examine themselves, and so eat of the bread and drink of the cup, because those who eat and drink without discerning the body eat and drink judgment upon themselves. That's why many of you are weak and ill, and some have died. Listen: if we judged ourselves truly, we should not be judged. But when we are judged by the Lord, we are chastened so that we may not in the end be condemned with the rest of the world.

So then, my beloved, when you come together to eat, wait for one another, lest you come together to be condemned.

Now, then: concerning spiritual gifts, I don't want you to be ignorant...

Timothy

67

While Stephanas was reading Paul's letter to the congregation in Erastus's house; while some folk disputed the letter as if Paul himself were present; while others moaned or hooted or clucked their tongues, I began to notice that several voices were stronger than the rest. These were voices of power, thrown upward from the lowest parts of the chest, voices rich and deep and musical.

They said, 'Who is this Paul?'

They said, 'By what right does this man utter such things? Why should you good people imitate him and not another?'

They said, 'This hard man! This taskmaster: did he ever bring letters of recommendation to you? Is he approved by anyone, *anyone* else besides his own bluster, his grim self-righteous blather?'

And then they said, 'Look at us!'

Stephanas kept reading Paul's letter aloud – *though absent in body, I am present in spirit* – yet the rich voices repeated themselves, saying, 'Look at us!'

I did. I turned around and saw the same three guests whom Erastus had called 'apostles' standing as they stood before: perfectly erect, the folds of their expensive robes as smooth as flowing candle wax. They showed no exertion in their rhetoric, no uncontrol nor emotion, yet powerfully they seemed to be discoursing with Paul, of whom they demanded proofs that his spirit was, as he wrote, *really* here.

'Paul! Paul!' they thundered. 'Can you truly leave your body behind, or are you strong in letters only?'

And they cried 'Silence!' to people still gabbling: 'Silence! Let's see if Paul will answer us!'

Stephanas resolutely took no notice. Into the sudden and watchful silence of the house, he laboured on with the words of

Paul: – *boasting does you no good. Don't you know that a little leaven leavens* –

The guests, these luminaries, affected to laugh. They said, 'Do you see a Paul? We see no Paul. We feel no presence of a Paul-ghost. But look at us, watch us, turn your eyes here to us, not to that whining, mindless interlocutor!' They were referring to Stephanas, who never ceased reading.

'The words of Paul come on paper,' they said. 'The ghost remains in his body. But we are able to leave our bodies behind and ascend as living spirits to the heavens and into the heaven of heavens! We! We have seen the blinding face of Christ, his two bright eyes like lightning, his golden breastplate red as a furnace. We! We have heard that voice roar like a waterfall. And we have returned again to impart his messages to people bound by their bodies below, to those still gross with corporeal weight. Now then, can anyone say that our word lacks authority? Who has the brass to dispute our supremacy? – for our glory comes from the mouth of the Lord!'

The house was fixed on this noble triumvirate. Faces shined like lamps; blood and expectation brightened the flesh.

Erastus began to approach the three men as if drawn by cords. There was a stunned, wondering expression in his eyes. He was smiling. At his motion, the rest of the congregation, too, began to crowd closer to these 'apostles'.

'Or do you want for proofs of our own?' they sang in rich voice. 'Does the wise Corinthian want evidence he cannot contradict, the witness of his eyes?'

Erastus nodded vigorously – though it seemed to me a formal thing, a ritualized response.

Stephanas was a low drone behind us all.

Whispering now, the foremost eminence of the three said: 'Watch!'

The other two stepped to his sides, while he raised his face to the ceiling.

The church held its breath.

Stephanas read; Paul said: *Now then, concerning spiritual gifts, I don't want you to be ignorant* –

Suddenly a trembling seized the body of the central guest. It grew in force till the excellent white teeth in his head began to clack together, and his eyes rolled back to blankness. He must have bitten his tongue, because blood liquored his lips and dribbled at the corners. I watched with a helpless fascination. I think it was the weird disparity between the body's seizure and the man's composure. He'd lost control; yet he was in complete control! He was quivering, writhing with remarkable disinterest and calm.

Paul was saying: – *led astray to dumb idols. You must understand. No one speaking by the Spirit of God ever says, 'Jesus be cursed,' and no one –*

The man in pale ecstasy suddenly sucked a great lungful of air and blew it out his nostrils with a violent mewing sound. Vibrating, he began to fall like a hard board backward, but his companions caught him and laid him flat on his back, while the human fence, the Corinthians around him, started humming and singing.

Paul was saying: – *and no one can say, 'Jesus is Lord' except by the Holy Spirit –*

Several people had begun in rhythm to shake rattlers, music makers, the clattering castanets. There arose a strong smell of sweat in the room. Those who had the space turned round and round with their arms extended, faces gladly upward.

Paul: – *varieties of gifts, same Spirit. Varieties of service, same Lord. To each the manifestation of the Spirit for common good, for common good: apostles, prophets, teachers, miracle-workers, healers, helpers, administrators, speaking in various kinds of tongues –*

Now, like the midnight cry that stops your heart, the apostle on the floor emitted a wild, wolvish howl.

Erastus reacted. He shot straight up.

I mean that literally: Erastus flew up and out of his slippers, which stayed side by side on the floor. He somersaulted backward, legs flying uppermost. He landed so hard on the back of his shoulders that his jaw was driven into his chest. I was on my feet, running toward him. I thought he'd broken his neck. But before I got there, he had reached his two hands high and begun to clap – *two, three, four* – and, light as a child, the fat man leaped to his feet. Clapping, clapping – *seven, eight, nine* – and jabbering loudly in some indecipherable tongue.

I watched him and I thought, So *this* is the wonderful thing he told me about. Erastus has learned to speak in tongues.

Paul: – *but earnestly desire the higher gifts, and I will show you a still more excellent way –*

Music and dancing, Erastus sweating, the room all full of

whirling bodies, uncanny jubilations, while Stephanas alone by the door kept reading, reading: – *Though I speak in the tongues of men and angels, but have not love, I'm a noisy gong, a clanging cymbal. Though I have the gift of prophecy and understand all mysteries, though I have faith to move mountains, but have not love, I am nothing. Love is patient and kind. Love is not jealous or boastful. It is not arrogant or rude. Love does not insist on its own way –*

It was then that I, Timothy, withdrew.

I was being torn between the poles of some tremendous dialogue. For there, to the east of me, was Erastus babbling and happier than I had ever seen him before. And here, to the west, Stephanas small and still, reading with his head bowed down, and dropping tears upon the pages.

– love bears all things, believes all things, hopes all things, endures all things. Love never ends –

I withdrew to a quieter place inside myself where my spirit and I might hide. For the rest of the evening, I allowed all sound and motion and odour and light to wash my body like a blurring rain; but it did not wash my soul.

At some point the apostle of cool enthusiasms rose up and stood, his garments returning to their rich, unwrinkled state. His rising signalled the rest of the church likewise to halt, and he spoke in a reasonable voice, unaffected by any exertions. He affirmed that he had, indeed, just soared to the heavens, where he had received the blessing of Jesus both upon himself and, through his person, upon the others assembled here. The whole congregation then, subdued, walked past him person by person, allowing him to touch their foreheads. When they had been touched, they departed into the night.

In the door of the atrium, his face still hidden, Stephanas still was reading Paul's words:

– tongues will cease. Prophecy and knowledge will pass away. For knowledge and prophecies are imperfect. When the perfect comes, the imperfect must go.

When I was a child, I spoke like a child; I thought like a child; I reasoned like a child. But when I became a man, I gave up my childish ways.

For now we see through a mirror dimly, but then we will see face-to-face.

Now I know in part; then I shall understand fully, even as I have been fully understood.

So faith, hope, and love abide, these three. But the greatest of these is love.

Make love your aim –

On and on the long epistle continued, until there was no other voice left speaking in the house, nor any other ear left listening but my own alone:

– for God is not a God of confusion, but of peace –

*P*risca

68

Never again after the sweet green days of Corinth did Paul ask me to lay my hands on his back. I know I am no healer, either by training or miracle. But I have been a comforter, both by the gift of the Spirit and by the model of my mother. I have, therefore, missed the intimacy.

Timothy, too, had lost that office by the time we lived in Ephesus. He, however, didn't miss it. He loved Paul deeply; but he hated to witness his pain, hated even to see – or worse, to touch – the scars that were evidence of cruelty and his previous punishings.

In fact, Paul had found a better healer than either of us, crude bumpkins that we were; and that was a matter for rejoicing.

'Beloved! Beloved!' Paul called this new physician, because his ministration truly did relieve the apostle's wretched body.

Luke knew what to do.

Below the State Agora, at its northwest corner, Ephesian doctors can practise their healing arts in three small halls, each hall divided into tinier rooms for patients and surgery, bleedings, evacuations, skull cuttings, tooth pullings – that sort of thing.

I don't know whether Luke talked Paul into a little surgery of his own, or whether the pain persuaded the patient without Luke's urging – or whether (this is a real possibility!) Paul thought to honour Luke by trusting his back to the knife in the hand of his friend.

I myself find it hard to believe that pain alone would have caused Paul to accept Luke's suggestion.

Well, he said often that he carried the death of Jesus in his body, so that the life of Jesus might also be manifest in his body. For 'death' I think Paul meant the suffering of the severest pain;

and for 'life' the glad endurance of that pain. Two sides of the same coin. Paul *liked* these holy conundrums, these human impossibilities, contrarieties that baffled the world, because it was Jesus alone who made them possible: 'to be struck down', for example, 'but not destroyed. To be punished to death and yet not dead.' Or, as Paul cried out in the street one day: 'We're dying, dying! And behold, we live!' If a cripple can act like an athlete, he argued, or if a man of afflictions is also a man of genuine joy, no one can doubt that the transcendent power belongs to God and not to that particular man.

On the other hand (always with Paul there's this other hand, three or four other hands) he didn't *ask* for pain. He didn't like pain. And I heard him once, with a hissing disgust, curse Satan as the source of his pain.

So, then – whatever. For whatever motive, Paul entered the doctor's rooms with Luke, and Luke cut the back that Timothy and I had massaged with more love than knowledge. They did this four times in four different regions of his back, removing something and creating four new scars, though these were stitched to thin lines where once there had been knots and cruel lumps.

Moreover (and this tickles me whenever I imagine the details), Luke talked Paul into taking up a daily pagan practice: bathing. They went together every afternoon to the public bathhouses. They moved together among naked pagans from room to room, warm room, hot room, cold room, and Luke took upon himself the servant's role, washing, scraping, massaging, and oiling the meatless body of our little apostle. Here again, the motive is somewhat ambiguous. That the massage was therapeutic, there is no doubt. But neither is there doubt that Paul emerged from the bathhouse with a dreamy, contented expression on his glistening face, under his few hairs combed slick on his scalp.

One might almost, with sober proofs and private assurances, record in some future history of the apostle that he *liked* it! He liked to be primped.

On one such occasion I heard Luke say, 'Wait till we get to Thermopylae and experience the sulphur springs in *that* place. You'll bend like wheat fields in the wind.'

Paul said, 'Hum. I'm thinking of a journey to Corinth again. I want to direct the collection for Jerusalem. Hum. Maybe we'll take the long way round.'

Timothy had taken the long way round during our second year in Ephesus together. He had left at a lazy pace early in the spring. But at midsummer, even on the day Paul mentioned his own trip over, Timothy was sailing back to Ephesus by the fastest route possible.

Still while the ship was docking, Timothy leaped ashore and raced the Harbour Road straight to our house, Aquila's and mine. And when Paul too had arrived, Timothy faced him with visible anguish and said: 'The trouble in Corinth is worse than we knew, worse even than Stephanas said! Oh, Paul, a corruption has entered the place. Men who call themselves 'apostles' are charming the hearts of the churches, and you, Paul – ' Timothy swallowed and ran his hands through his hair. 'You,' he said, 'are held in the highest contempt.'

Paul

69

Paul, an apostle of Christ Jesus by the will of God;
   To the church of God which is at Corinth:

   Grace to you and peace from God our Father and the Lord
Jesus Christ.
   So somebody thinks I lack authority, does he? He wants to see
letters of recommendation displaying past proofs of the worth of
my work, does he?
   Well, tell that man of slanders to look around – if, that is, he
has the eyes for truth. He is surrounded by more than a hundred
such letters, but they're not written in ink on paper, nor etched
on tablets of stone.
   Dear Corinthians, *you* are the letters that recommend me. You
are letters from Christ, delivered by me, written with the Spirit of
the living God on the tablets of your hearts! Where you go, there
go my letters, to be read by all humanity! – by anyone not
blinded to the truth.
   Such is the confidence we have through Christ toward God.
   Not that we are competent of ourselves, as if anything came
from us. No, no, our competence comes from God. *He* has made
us competent to be ministers of a new covenant. And since we
have this ministry by his mercy, we do not lose heart!
   For the man who scorns our work scorns God.
   We ourselves, *we* have renounced disgraceful, underhanded
ways. We refuse to practise cunning or to tamper with God's
word, but by open statement of the truth we commend ourselves
to everyone's conscience in the sight of God. This is how *we*
teach and preach. And even if our gospel is veiled, well, it's veiled
only to those who are perishing! In their case the god of this
world has blinded the minds of the unbelievers, to keep them

from seeing the light of the gospel of the glory of Christ, who is the likeness of God. For what we preach is *not* ourselves! It is Jesus Christ as Lord, with ourselves as your slaves for Jesus' sake! For the God who said in the beginning, *Let light shine out of darkness*, this same God shines in our hearts to give the light of the knowledge of the glory of God in the face of Christ.

But we have this treasure in earthen vessels to show that all transcendent power belongs to God and none to us. We are afflicted in every way but not crushed, perplexed but not driven to despair, persecuted but not forsaken. For while we live we are always being given up to death for Jesus' sake, so that the life of Jesus may be manifested in our mortal flesh. So death is at work in us, but life in you.

Neither should you lose heart, then. Even though our outer nature is wasting away, our inner nature is being renewed each day. If this earthly tent in which we live is destroyed, we know we have a building from God, a house not made with hands, eternal in the heavens. Yes, yes, here we groan. In this tent we sigh with anxiety, because here, at home in the body, we're away from the Lord; but we long to be away from the body and at home with the Lord. Nevertheless, beloved, we are always of good courage, able to walk by faith and not by sight, because he who has prepared our heavenly dwelling is God, who has given us the Spirit as a guarantee.

In the end we will all appear before the judgment seat of Christ, so that each may receive good or evil according to what each has done in the body. For this reason, knowing the fear of the Lord, we preach and persuade. It is the love of Christ that drives us, because we're convinced that one has died for all; therefore, all have died. And he died for all that those who live might nevermore live for themselves but for him who for their sake died and was raised.

Those who are in Christ, therefore, are new creations. The old has passed away; behold, the new has come! All this is from God, who through Christ reconciled us to himself and gave us this ministry of reconciliation – that is, in Christ God was reconciling the world to himself, not counting their trespasses against them, and entrusting to us the message of reconciliation.

So we are ambassadors for Christ. God is making his appeal through us. We beg you, on behalf of Christ, be reconciled to God. For our sake he made him to be sin who knew no sin, so that in him we might become the righteousness of God. Please! Corinthians, please: do not accept the grace of God in vain!

God says, *At the acceptable time I have listened to you, and helped you on the day of salvation.*

Well, now is the acceptable time!

Now is the day of salvation!

You must – you must in your conscience – know that we do not and we will not put obstacles in anyone's way. No fault shall be found in our ministry. But as servants of God we commend ourselves in every way: through great endurance, in afflictions, hardships, calamities, beatings, imprisonments, tumults, labours, watchings, hunger; by purity, knowledge, forbearance, kindness, the Holy Spirit, genuine love, truthful speech, and the power of God; with the weapons of righteousness for the right hand and for the left; in honour and dishonour, in ill repute and good repute. We are treated as imposters! And yet we are true.

Our mouth is open to you, Corinthians. Our heart is wide open. You are not restricted by us, but you are restricted in your own affections.

Open your hearts as well to us.

We have wronged no one. We have corrupted no one. We have taken advantage of no one.

I don't say this to condemn you, for you dwell in our hearts, as I said before, to die with us and to live with us.

I have great confidence in you.

I have great pride in you.

I am filled with comfort.

In the midst of affliction, I am overjoyed.

Give Timothy cause to bear good news to me again.

The grace of our Lord Jesus Christ be with you.

Amen.

$\mathcal{L}$. Annaeus Seneca

70

L. Annaeus Seneca, advisor to Imperator Nero, in Rome,
   To Marcus Antonius Felix, Procurator of Palestine, in Caesarea:

I write to caution you. If you are wise, you'll use the
information contained herein to temper your arrogance and
serve with a better judgment. If not, you'll suffer what judgment
you will.

As the imperial treasurer – and more significantly, as a
favourite of Agrippina, the wife and the mother of emperors –
your brother Pallas has been a political force in Rome.

It may not be common knowledge – but *we* know, don't we,
Felix? – that you received the governorship of Judea and
Jerusalem by means of his influence.

It is *very* common knowledge, however, that Pallas has used
his position to serve himself: selling offices, extorting bribes by
threats, bringing charges against rich men whose estates he
covets.

And presently it is knowledge known to no one (though soon it
will be common to all) that the Emperor Nero is about to remove
your brother from his office as treasurer.

This is the information which wisdom will consider and folly
will ignore. For when M. Antonius Pallas departs this palace,
though he will remain a shamefully wealthy man, his force and
his influence must diminish.

Your Roman boat is springing leaks.

Henceforward, Felix, you neglect wise governance at your own,
your personal, peril.

Yesterday we received the prisoner you sent from Judea, one Eleazar, son of Dineus, whom your written dispatch defines as the 'leader of a great company of robbers' – robbers, you write, who 'torch the villages and steal the goods of their own people'.

Surely, a robber is not to be trusted, least of all when he's defending himself. Nor could I ever abide the behaviours of passionate Jews. The less religious they, the better it is for me.

Nevertheless, Felix, Procurator: I find a certain credibility in the man, intelligence, articulation, a balanced mind. And his version of his arrest contradicts yours significantly. He says you seized him by treachery. He says you promised him safety, if he would come to you to discuss the causes of Jewish unrest. He says that when he did come, relying upon your word, you drew him into the courts of the praetorium and trapped him, surrounding him with more than forty soldiers; that you bound him, imprisoned him, *then* sent him to Rome.

He also says that, far from suffering violence at the hands of his company, the poor people of Judea *are* his company, joining him more and more, the more and more you, Felix, with indiscrimination, crucify them.

He says that this is how you govern, by killing your subjects, the good and the bad alike.

Whom shall I believe? The procurator or the robber?

Before you answer that question, be advised of a final fact: that your own centurion, in whose custody the robber was brought to Rome, agrees completely with... the robber.

One word to a wise man is sufficient. But look: I have given you two.

Prisca

71

Oh, my! Look at this crowd! I can't see the house for the people. Every believer in Corinth must be here. Did Paul do this? Is this truly his doing?

'Excuse me,' I say. I lower my head and push past elbows, buttocks and backs like the paddle-footed mole past roots underground. 'Excuse me, excuse me.' I have a light and little frame, quick as a child. 'Excuse me, I'm looking for Paul.'

Less than half of these people are familiar to me. Those who know me nod, kindly but not warmly, I fear. The gladness of last week's reunion and the vigour with which they welcomed us back cooled as people discovered the reason for Paul's headlong trip from Ephesus.

Corinth likes its new apostles very much. What they preach – yes, and what they do – flatters Corinthian tendencies. But Paul calls them 'super-apostles' with an unsmiling scorn.

Beside me a big man growls: 'Inside.' His body smells of a sweat so sour, it raises the roots of my hair.

'What?'

'Inside,' he growls. 'Paul's inside. They all went inside. No thought for the plain and honest folk that might want to get a listen.'

I can't see his face, but I think I know this plain, honest folk-person. His stink is familiar. And I've heard that voice before, screaming, *Cut him loose, Jew*: Apelles, the shoemaker.

'Listen to what?'

'Fights. A good fight,' he growls.

The entry room is as mobbed as the street. So are the halls, where the air is already thick with human breath, suffocating after the blue snap of the autumn day outside. I admit, the size of this crowd disturbs me; the mood makes me feel alien.

Why 'fights'? What sort of fights does Apelles expect?

Three of us have come by sea from Ephesus, Paul and me and Sosthenes. Sosthenes begged to share the voyage because he yearned to fix the friendships that broke at his sudden departure four years ago. Why Paul asked me to accompany him, though, I don't know. He never offered a reason. Perhaps I'm a public example of something. He does that sort of thing. Or perhaps my gentler nature and my love for the believers here was supposed to tenderize his, Paul's, purposes. He said, 'Prisca, come with me.' He said, 'When Corinth told Timothy I should leave them alone, I had no choice. This time I have to go in person to purge the church.'

If his 'purging the church' meant that he might wound a soul or two, then maybe I am the balm.

As soon as we landed at Cenchreae, Sosthenes walked west by himself to Corinth. Paul went to work right there in the port-village. We accepted an invitation from my good and gracious friend Phoebe to stay the night with her. She had servants prepare a large meal; she sent servants through the village to bring believers back 'for food and for talk'. She produced a small congregation. Paul didn't eat. Instead, he questioned the people intensively about these 'arrogant super-apostles'. What did they teach? What did they do? Where did they come from? What sort of lives did they lead?

That, I soon discovered, would be his pattern every day of our sojourn here, even to yesterday.

We visited all the houses in the Corinthian region where believers gathered to worship – all the houses but one.

At the house of Titius Justus I experienced two distinct pleasures. This is the building that shares its wall with the Jewish synagogue. Sosthenes had never set foot inside it. He'd thrown bricks at it instead.

But there he was, roundish body, flipperlike arms, that tightly knotted hair, and all his face aflame with gladness and with family feeling. For sitting at table with him were Titius Justus, the neighbour Gentile he had despised, and Crispus, who had been the ruler of the synagogue before he turned to Jesus. Now all three sat in the union of the Holy Spirit, grinning.

That pleased me more than I can say, as did this other thing: that privately I heard my own voice ringing through the rooms. I heard in memory the first praying I ever did out loud, the first prophesying I ever did in public, for this is the place where the Spirit moved me to speak. This is the cradle of my baby ministry.

So then, all four of us shared the wordless pleasure and sweet communion – until Paul arrived, until Paul began to pace the room and to drill both Justus and Crispus with questions concerning the super-apostles. That changed the atmosphere. We got down to business, as it were, and no one smiled after that.

In fact, for seven days now Paul has been doing nothing *but* business. I myself have taken the time to walk the city, revisiting the places Aquila and I once knew together, where we lived, where we worked. Two days ago, I grew so reflective that Paul noticed and interpreted my mood for me. He said I was feeling the 'sting of the world'. I said, no, it was rather the pangs of nostalgia. But he said that even sweet stings can poison the blood, and that I should be careful of too much attachment. Has this man never smiled at a sunset? Would it crack him to quit for a single day?

He planned first to learn as much as he could about the situation in Corinth, first to take the measure of these interlopers, apostles who declared that they were better than he, and then to gather the entire church together in one place, there to deliver certain pronouncements for change.

Only one house in Corinth is spacious enough to accommodate the whole church at once. Gaius's house, at the foot of the Acrocorinth.

Yesterday morning Paul and I went there seeking permission to use his rooms. This time Paul didn't have to initiate the questions. Word had spread. Gaius knew what Paul was doing and offered his thoughts unbidden.

He said of the new apostles: 'They ask for things quite easily. It's refreshing, frankly. They're not afraid to ask.'

Paul said, 'What things?'

Gaius said, 'Food. Rooms. Raiment. Money. They want letters that tell of the marvellous things they've been able to accomplish in Corinth.'

'Money?' Paul said. 'They ask for the coin?'

'Yes.'

'For the poor?'

'For themselves. To maintain their ministries.'

Paul nodded. He rubbed his jawbone, murmuring, 'Of course the best of the best of all the apostles must be paid.'

Abruptly he said, 'I'll do as they do. I'll ask a thing of you. Gaius, could we use your rooms? I want to call the whole church together to meet in your house.'

Gaius said, 'It's too late.'

Paul frowned. 'What?'

'Has no one told you?'

Paul didn't answer that.

Gaius said, 'The apostles have already sent out a request for the church to gather with them, in the place where they are staying. Tomorrow,' Gaius said, 'at the house of Erastus.'

That was the single house we had not yet visited. The house of Erastus. But I'm visiting it now! Me and this mob. I'm crushed and suffering a strange alienation.

Paul is somewhere farther inside, but I'm stuck in the hallway between large people. Oh, yes! The second part of Paul's plan has come to pass, with or without his instigation. He has his crowd. But I'm not sure he has the reception he wants. Nor can I guess who is really in control.

'Coming through! Coming through!'

It's the hard barking of soldiers. The crowd tightens and heaves around me like a sea swell.

'Out of the way! We're coming through!'

In fact, it *is* the military. Here comes an armed guard driving a path through the midst of the people. I count six men. Well, well, and there's the gorgeous Erastus in the midst of them, smiling, greeting people as he passes.

'Don't mind my men,' he says. 'It's for safety and order, the safety of my guests, order in my house. All's well! All's well!'

Oh, how fat Erastus is! What great mountains are his shoulders now and his rolling hips and his face as red as a pomegranate. Ah, but he smells deliciously of cinnamon and cassia. Hoo, what a man! He drives by like a four-horse carriage all covered with brass and bangles.

I take advantage of his passage, slipping behind his soldiers and letting them make a way for me.

A whiff of sour sweat announces that I'm not the only one caught in the wake of Erastus.

But suddenly my spirit flies out of myself. All sound in the house goes dead. All people fall from my vision...

I see Paul.

My friend, my friend, he's standing alone in the far left corner of the atrium, his right hand high, his mouth open upon some word.

The soldiers take up positions at six points around the columns of the atrium. Erastus bustles through to the three men standing directly across from Paul. He kisses them one by one, fatly on their cheeks. The Manager's breathing, wiping his brow.

But he's late. Clearly, he's late, and so am I: some sort of debate has already begun.

In his daggerish voice Paul is saying, '*Define* the differences! For the people's sake, define the *differences*, sir. I have never peddled the word of God. But I, as a man of sincerity commissioned by God, and in the *sight* of God, I preach Jesus Christ the crucified.'

Erastus has taken a seat at the far end of the atrium, between the contending forces. He glances left and right, still wiping his forehead. One of the three men is already answering Paul, a tall man, aquiline, of a royal bearing, with clothes as rich as the robes of Erastus.

That man is saying, 'Nor do we peddle the things of heaven. We do nothing more than follow the custom. All who serve the Lord are *rightly* fed by the churches where they serve – all except you. You seem to seek the hard life, sir, going about in blight and poverty on purpose. It's almost as if you're proud to be poor.'

A hundred heads turn from this grandiloquent man to Paul: short Paul; pale Paul; skinny and bunched and losing his hair and dressed in a threadbare tunic, Paul – while these most upright three wear a fine and healthy flush in their countenances, and dark beards wonderfully oiled.

Paul says, 'I never chose poverty.'

The royal apostle responds immediately, 'Yes, you did! And you do! Every time you refuse a gift you choose a nothing over a something.'

I hear a *thwack* in the atrium. People jump. It was Erastus slapping his thigh at what he considered a palpable hit. He's grinning and blinking.

Paul persists: 'Indeed, indeed, you tell the truth! Why, the Spirit himself must be roaring through you today, because I agree with you. This is the difference between us: I am proud of poverty, while you are proud of your successes! Mighty men, you soaring *super*-apostles, great in your good offices! If ever I boast,

I will boast of the cross of Jesus Christ, his suffering and his death – '

'Right!' he interrupts Paul. 'Right! And in what state did your boasting leave the churches here? These good Corinthians surrounding us now, what did your wonderful humility require of them before we came? Misery! Gloom, laborious toil, pain, and shameful treatment. You yourself wrote of afflictions and perplexities and persecutions and strikings down and death besides. But we have released the Corinthian people from your melancholy millstone of a Jesus! We are making them lightsome and cheerful again, for *we* boast of a triumphant Christ and victory!'

'You're throwing them back to the world,' Paul cries, his voice rising, his eyes flashing. 'You're making them children of hell! I boast of the cross, the salvation of God. I preach the cross, which the world rejects as failure. You boast of things the world finds dear and delightful: triumph, success, and personal power. You preach what you yourselves desire: elation, self-celebration, a glorious name. If the Corinthians find your preaching dear and delightful too, then they are of the world, and they are *perishing*!'

'Perishing? Perishing, Paul? Fool, we give them life and a direct connection to Christ.'

'Through *yourselves*! Through your ecstasies, as if you were *yourselves* the mediators between earth and heaven.'

'No, sir! No! Through the Holy Spirit. We have moved on, Paul, and you are left behind on a dark and dreary ground. We've moved with Christ out of the past and into the future, out of this clay-life, out of this cloying earthbound life, and into the life of the Spirit. Haven't you heard? Christ *overcame* the cross. He is now the Exalted One, whose Spirit blows through the church to lift it to himself. You did good here, but you didn't do enough. We're finishing your work. The cross was a good step, yes: but to what? Why, to the Holy Spirit and to a very present heaven. This is what we do: we leave our bodies behind and fly straight to Christ in heaven. Those who cannot do the same, those who cannot take these steps, cannot, cannot be true apostles! You, Paul! You are not an apostle!'

Oh, what a sword in the heart of my friend. This is the worst to be said.

There follows a moment of absolute silence. The people freeze. No one moves. My flesh is tingling. Even from here I can see bright red splotches on Paul's forehead. The bridge of his nose is ivory white, as if the bone were breaking through. His eyes are stretched and rimmed with fire.

Softly, softly, he breathes through his teeth, 'Yours is a different Jesus.' Through lips drawn taut he hisses: 'A different spirit. A different gospel – '

Suddenly Paul is walking. With stiff steps he walks toward Erastus. He draws a hot breath and says, 'Send these men away! Erastus, tell them to leave your house right now.'

Massive Erastus, surprised by this turn of events, starts to rise. 'I... can't!' he yelps. 'I won't!'

'Throw them out of the house!' Paul says, dead earnest. It's a command. 'Drive them from the city!'

Erastus is on his feet now, raining perspiration and trembling with emotion. 'Who do you think you are?' he whines. 'You have no right to order me around.'

'Erastus, listen to me.' Paul stands directly in front of the man. He pokes him with his forefinger. 'These self-important super-apostles are the death of faith and a danger in the church. If they stay, people *will* begin to perish.'

But Erastus has found his own words. Jowls flapping, his fury pure white, he cries, 'You are the one who hurts people, not them.' He grabs Paul's finger and twists it backward: finger, hand, and arm. Paul's eyes widen. Erastus is full of conviction now: 'When I offered my house, you refused it. When I offered my goods, my support, my horse to transport you, you refused them, insulting me over and over!' Erastus advances. Paul buckles at his knees. 'These men accept what I give,' Erastus says with a grand authority, the Manager of Markets in charge. 'They honour me. They taught me to speak in tongues, but you' – he looms like a hillside over Paul – 'you' – he can't find the words – 'you!'

'Erastus, how could you?' Paul groans; he collapses backward. His head bounced on the floor.

Immediately a shrieking splits the atrium. A man leaps past me and rushes Erastus, his fingers crooked to kill.

Oh, my heart! It's Apelles the shoemaker, screaming, 'Fight me! Fight *me*, you bastard! This man's too good for you!'

Erastus, raising his face in a sudden terror, yells, 'Guards! Guards!'

The house erupts. People bellow and press each other, crushing the breath from me. I am borne backward on a slow stream of mindless humanity, and I lose sight, and I lose consciousness, and I think I almost lose my life.

Who is waking me? Who is chafing my hands? I'm lying in a little room – a little guest room I think – with a small menorah painted on the wall. Who is the good man above me? Ah – Sosthenes, watching my eyes.

Sosthenes is singing a lullaby psalm.

But roughly my memory returns. I sit up and beg him for information. He tells me that two men were arrested in the melee at the house of Erastus, both of them bound and thrown out of the city.

We must find them, he says.

Who are they? Who are those men?

Apelles the shoemaker.

And Paul the apostle.

72

The wind howls in the lanyards. The ship heaves and creaks and casts a long white wake behind us. Only a small foresail is raised, but one is enough. We're running with the wind.

O Lord, we should not be on the open sea – not now, not in this season. The winter's descending with death in his wings. Jesus, Master, save us.

But Paul refused to bide the winter in Achaia.

He found a last ship out and boarded and hasn't spoken since. He sits with his back to the gunwale, taking the sea spray on his poor unhousled head. He sits with his knees drawn up to his chest, his chin low and extended. That silent, vulturelike crouch has spooked the sailors. They've told me that if we run into storm, they will not lash him down. If the waves want him, say the sailors, let the waves take him.

There are three of us here, three of us mad as shearwaters, skimming our graves. The third, however, is not Sosthenes. He chose to remain in Corinth. The third is Apelles the shoemaker, who also raises the sailors' suspicions, for he is filled with the joy of danger. On the other hand, he gladly does the most perilous tasks, so they tolerate him in their company.

I myself, I am sick at heart.

My friend, my Paul, is mute.

Paul

73

I, Paul, in prison,
To you, the churches at Corinth:

Grace.

I beg you, I beg you by the meekness and the gentleness of
Christ, to open your eyes and see what's right in front of you.
If someone among you says he's of Christ, so am I! But the man
who commends himself is not acceptable to God; the man whom
the *Lord* commends – he is!

Bear with me in some foolishness. Please, bear with me! I feel
a divine jealousy for you because I'm the one who betrothed you
to Christ exactly as a pure bride is betrothed to her one true
husband. I fear there's a serpent among you. The serpent that
lied to Eve, he's leading your thoughts away from the pure
devotion to Christ. I've seen the effects! Someone preaches
another Jesus from the one I preached, and you submit!
Someone brings a different spirit, and you receive it! Look at
yourselves: You've accepted a different gospel from the one you
got from me, as if these preachers were better than me. They're
not! Nor am I in any way less than your super-apostles coiling in
Corinth now! Do they say I am weaker in speaking? Well, but I'm
stronger in knowledge!

But what do *you* say? Did I *sin* by humbling myself so that
you might be exalted? Did I sin by preaching the gospel of God
without a penny's cost to you? I'm like a soldier, robbing some
other church in order to fight for you. When I was in Corinth and
hungry, I troubled none of you, not one of you! – since my needs
were supplied by friends from Macedonia. I won't be a burden. Do
you hear me? I will never be a burden to you! In fact, I'm going
to boast about my humility wherever I go in Achaia. And why?

Do you think it's because I don't love you? God knows I do!

But I will continue in poverty – yes! in *poverty* – to prove the truth of my apostleship. I will continue to labour in sacrifice – yes! – to show how false are those who claim to be apostles like me. They lie! It's a disguise! They learned the game from their real lord, Satan. Even as he pretends to be an angel of light, so his servants pretend to be servants of righteousness – and as they live, so shall they die!

I repeat, don't think me foolish.

Well, but even if you do, then *accept* me as a fool, that I might do a little boasting of my own. (This isn't from the Lord's authority; this comes from a fool; but since others have boasted of worldly things, it's my turn now.) And why shouldn't I? You people have gladly borne with fools, no matter how wise you are! Open your eyes and look at yourselves: you bear it when someone enslaves you, when someone eats you out of house and home, when someone takes advantage of you, or puts on airs, or strikes you in the face. Oh, shame on *me*! I was just too weak to treat you with that sort of boldness.

But whatever anyone dares to boast of (I'm speaking as a fool) I dare to boast of it too.

Are they Hebrews?

So am I.

Are they Israelites?

So am I.

Are they descendants of Abraham?

Me, too.

Are they servants of Christ?

Well, I'm the better servant (I'm talking like a madman) with far greater labours, far more imprisonments, countless beatings, often left for dead.

By the Jews I've been whipped to the legal limit – how often? Five times.

By the Romans I've been beaten with rods – how often? Three times.

I was stoned once.

Three times I've been shipwrecked, adrift a night and a day at sea.

Travelling, I've been in danger from rivers, danger from robbers, danger from my own people, danger from Gentiles, danger in the city, danger in the wilderness, danger at sea, danger from false brothers. I've suffered toil and hardship, spent many a sleepless night, gone hungry and thirsty for lack of food, exposed my body to the elements.

Daily my spirit groans for all the churches.

With the weak I suffer weakness. When somebody stumbles, I fall.

If I must boast, I'll boast of the things that show my weakness. The God and Father of the Lord Jesus – he who is blessed for ever – knows that I do not lie! At Damascus the governor under King Aretas guarded the city in order to seize me; but I was let down in a basket through a window in the wall, and escaped.

I must boast. There's nothing to be gained by it. There never was. Nevertheless, I can speak of visions and revelations with the best of them.

I know a man in Christ who, fourteen years ago, was caught up to the third heaven – whether in the body or out of the body, I don't know; God knows. This man experienced very Paradise – whether in the body or out of the body, I don't know; God knows. This man heard things there that cannot be told, ineffable things that no one can utter. For *this* man I will boast, but for myself I will not boast... except about my weaknesses.

If I really wanted to boast, I wouldn't be a fool in fact, because I'd be speaking the truth. But I'll refrain so no one may think more of me than what can be seen or heard.

For to keep me from being too elated by the abundance of all my revelations, a thorn was given me in the flesh, a messenger from Satan to harass me. Three times I begged the Lord to remove it, but he said, *My grace is sufficient for you, for my power is made perfect in weakness.*

Therefore, I will all the more gladly boast of my weaknesses, my weaknesses, my weaknesses – that the power of Christ may rest upon me. For the sake of Christ, then, I am content with insults, hardships, persecutions, and calamities. For when I am weak, then I am strong.

Oh, I have been a fool!

But you forced me to it.

I should have been *commended* by you! I am not at all inferior to your super-apostles, even though I'm nothing. Corinthians, open your eyes and see as once you saw. Surely you remember: the signs of a true apostle were performed among you in all patience, signs and wonders and mighty works! In what way were you less favoured than the rest of the churches, except for this, that I chose not to burden you? Well, forgive me for wounding you.

If I love you the more, am I to be loved the less?

But you say I was crafty and got the better of you by guile.

Really? Did I *ever* take advantage of you? Did anyone whom I sent to you ever take advantage of you? Did Titus take advantage of you? Didn't we all act in the same spirit?

All right, stop!

What do you think is the purpose of this letter? What do you think I've been doing here – defending myself?

No, dear ones, that's not what I'm doing. In the sight of God and speaking in Christ, I've been building you up.

I'm scared of what I might find when I return to you. I'm scared that God may humble me again, making me mourn over many who sinned and haven't repented. Oh, Corinthians, I'm scared I'll find quarrelling, jealousy, anger, selfishness, slander, gossip, conceit, disorder.

If I come, it'll be the third time. Any charge you make then must be sustained by the evidence of two or three witnesses. I said it once when I was present; I'll say it again in my absence: If I come I will not spare the sinner, and you shall have your proof that Christ is speaking in me. He is not weak in dealing with you. He's powerful in you. For he was crucified in weakness, but lives by the power of God. For we are weak in him, but in dealing with you we shall live with him by the power of God.

Examine yourselves to see if you're keeping the faith. Test yourselves. Don't you know that Jesus Christ is in you? – unless indeed you fail to meet the test! I hope you will find out that we have not failed.

What we pray for is your improvement.

Dear ones, farewell. Mend your ways. Heed my appeal. Agree with one another. Live in peace, and the God of love and peace will be with you.

Greet one another with a holy kiss.

All the saints greet you.

The grace of the Lord Jesus Christ and the love of God and the fellowship of the Holy Spirit be with you all.

$\mathcal{P}$risca

74

The winter is cruel this year. A salty wet wind off the sea. All
things are chill and moist. Nothing is dry or warm or comforting.
Every surface sweats and stinks of mildew. The days are grey from
dawn to darkness. We cast no shadows because we walk in shadow.
There is no consolation any more.

Paul is in prison.

A letter was waiting for Paul when we came back to Ephesus.

It had been sent from Philippi. Lydia's seal.

Aquila and I were both with Paul when the letter was read to
him.

Unhappy news.

Lydia had finally met the man whose name is Simon, whom
Jesus called Peter. He and his wife and another man ('most
wonderfully gross and slow,' she wrote – it could have been no
one but Silas) were travelling the Via Egnatia west toward Rome.
They stopped in Philippi. Lydia offered them room in her house.
They talked.

Conversation turned to Paul.

You know where the man is staying now?

How is his health?

Does Jesus give him the increase?

Then Peter sent one piece of information to Paul on purpose.
'Tell him James thinks he should never return to Jerusalem. The
mood of the city is murderous. He won't survive.'

Paul snorted a humourless joke. 'When am I not in danger?' he
said.

Peter was also the source of a second piece of information, but this he dropped by accident, like seed on the wayside. Chitchat. Lydia plucked it up and sent it to Paul with audible sighing.

It regarded the men of the churches in Galatia.

They had all been circumcised.

Paul gaped at that news.

'What?' he said as if Lydia were in the room with us. 'What did you say?'

Nobody answered. Nobody spoke for Lydia or for Peter. Nobody spoke for the men of Galatia.

'What did you say? What are you telling me?'

Paul was so deeply moved that he went out and walked through the city, weeping. His motion was frail and stumbling. 'O my churches, my churches,' he said. 'O my dying churches.'

What a wretched winter this is!

Never were days so dreary.

The heavens are heavy as pewter. No god can live in such a sky. And children can't breathe beneath it. The clouds are a gravestone, cold and grey. I pile blankets on me at night. I draw near my husband – and still I shiver as if I were sick.

'Aquila,' I say.

In the middle of the night. Neither of us is sleeping.

I say, 'Aquila. How can we get our friend out of prison? What can we do for him?'

Luke

75

About this time there arose no little stir concerning believers in Ephesus.

There was a silversmith named Demetrius who made silver shrines of Artemis which brought a great deal of business to the craftsmen of the city. This man gathered the craftsmen together with all people whose occupations similarly depended upon Artemis, and said to them: 'Friends, you know that from this business we have our wealth. But now you can see and hear that not only at Ephesus but almost everywhere in Asia this Paul has persuaded a great number of people to turn away from us by saying that a god made with hands is not a god. Now there's the danger not only that *our* trade might fall into disrepute, but also that the temple of the great goddess Artemis itself might count for nothing. Why she could even be deposed from her magnificence, she whom Asia and the world worship.'

When they heard this, craftsmen, workmen and all were enraged. They cried out, 'Great is Artemis of the Ephesians!'

They filled the city with confusions, rushing together into the theatre, dragging with them Gaius and Aristarchus, Macedonians who travelled with Paul.

Paul wished to go in among the crowd, but the disciples wouldn't let him. Some of the Asiarchs too, friends of his, sent word begging him not to venture into the theatre.

Now some cried one thing, some another; for the assembly was in confusion, and most of them didn't know why they had come together.

Some of the crowd prompted Alexander, whom the Jews had put forward, to speak. So Alexander motioned with his hand for silence, wishing to make a defence to the people. But as soon as they recognized that he was a Jew, with one voice the multitudes cried out, 'Great is Artemis of the Ephesians! Great is Artemis of the Ephesians!' This went on for two hours, until one of the city clerks took the stage and quieted them.

'People of Ephesus!' he said. 'Who does not know that the city of the Ephesians is the temple keeper of the great Artemis? Who in the world doesn't know that the Ephesians are the keepers of the sacred stone that fell from the sky? Seeing, then, that these things cannot be contradicted, you ought to calm yourselves. There is no need for rash action. For you have brought these men here who are neither sacrilegious nor blasphemers of our goddess. If therefore Demetrius and the craftsmen have a complaint against anyone, the courts are open, and there are proconsuls: let them bring charges against one another. But if you seek anything further, it shall be settled in the regular assembly. For since there is no cause to justify this commotion, we're in danger of being charged with rioting today.'

When he had said this, he dismissed the assembly.

Timothy

76

Paul sits in prison, blaming no one.

I'm the one who feels a bitterness. I'm the one with blame in my heart – God forgive me – for if Aristarchus had left well enough alone, nobody would be in prison now. But after the riot in the theatre, after the city clerk had forced the silversmiths to release him, Aristarchus followed the clerk's advice (as though the clerk had been talking to *him*) and immediately brought formal charges against Demetrius.

This infuriated Demetrius. It also persuaded the silversmith to attack Aristarchus – and Paul – less publicly, under cover of darkness.

I'm convinced that even this situation wouldn't have landed Aristarchus and Paul in prison. If it had been just the two of them, they might have been beaten, but they'd still be free. However, when Demetrius and his gang of longshoremen surprised Paul and Aristarchus in a narrow street in the night, they were not alone. Epaphras was with them.

Epaphras made the difference.

This man fights like one of those bear-shirters out of the frozen north, screaming, kicking, striking, biting all at once. There's no time for surprise in him: touch him and he's already pounding you.

And so it was that night. Demetrius and one other man accosted Paul and Aristarchus and Epaphras face-to-face in the narrow space between stuccoed walls. The five of them, as it seemed, were at an impasse, blocking each other's way.

But Epaphras detected the slightest motion behind them, felt the slightest breath upon his neck, and went crazy.

Three more men were lurking there.

In a flash Epaphras was a street-dog fighter, a blur of terrible speed, bellowing, cursing, causing longshoremen to cover their heads as if the bees were stinging them. Epaphras delights in the smacks of bone on flesh. In him there is no honour. He'll hit anywhere, tear anything, scratch like a cat, drum and drum a human skull till its brains are porridge, and all the while he'll produce such a savage hullabaloo that the poor fool who attacked him thinks the sky is raining devils.

All but one of the longshoremen fled. That one lay bleeding on the ground, scarcely breathing.

Demetrius, too, was immobile with pain. Fingers on both his hands were broken. Craft had been wrenched from the silversmith's hands and would never return.

When soldiers appeared, dispatched from the praetorium to investigate what beasts were screaming in Ephesus, Demetrius, filled with pain and fury, finally got his wish: Epaphras and Aristarchus and Paul were all taken to prison to await trial, possibly for murder.

These days hatred has swelled in this city for Paul in particular. *The blood of the innocent, shed in his name!* says the rabble, the gossiping population. All at once Ephesus is convinced that Paul has been busy creating a subversive, secret sect among them: *a thousand here, ten thousand in Asia!* they say. Everyone knows him by sight. You can't miss the man. They read his character in his skinny form, and having heard of his imprisonment, they say, *I knew it!* Sometimes I think that fewer people would detest my friend if he were a prettier man, as tall and strong as that other Saul, that other Benjamite, the King of Israel. And if he spoke with a honey-er tongue, how then would the gospel fare in a world that judges by the eye and the ear alone? But his voice grates on the ear like the rims of cymbals rubbed together. People don't forget the effect of little Paul preaching, whether or not they stop to fathom the language.

But because some people *do* stop, *do* understand, and do *follow* this little ferret of a preacher, Ephesian detesting has turned to downright fear. What magical powers does he possess?

So it's more than the craftsmen who hate Paul; and more powerfully than the common citizenry, it's the priests of Artemis themselves: they fear him as a sorcerer able to suck the very soul from their votaries. And they fear a sect of people so heedless of the Artemisian traditions that, growing in size and might, it could jeopardize their authority, their financial affairs, their banking ability, their keeping and lending of monies.

Paul sits in a windowless cell, blaming no one.

His wrists are manacled, chained to the wall. He can neither stand fully upright nor lie down flat. All the other prisoners move about together in a greater room; he is the only one bound alone in a single silent cell.

In the lowest regions of the praetorium, Paul sits on the stone floor of his cell without blame – and without joy.

I serve him. I bring him food. I take dictation for his letters. I strive to console him, but I fail.

He wept while he uttered an angry letter for the churches at Corinth. When, as a portion of that letter, I wrote the words, *A thorn was given me in the flesh*, I wondered whether his *flesh* were the thorn, this physical *form* of his that so offends the world.

Titus is carrying that letter of tears the long way round to Achaia.

Daily Paul says to me, 'Is there news yet? What's the news? What have you heard of Titus? What does he say of the Corinthians?'

I serve Paul. The guards recognize me. They allow me to come and go. I bring Paul the news. I tell him that the man struck down in the streets, the longshoreman whose head Epaphras had cracked – that man is dead.

Paul sighs and rubs his eyes with the heels of his hands and heaves a yet more heavy sigh. Not because the charge has changed to murder; but rather because a man is dead.

'Oh, Timothy, how do you think it goes in Corinth? What is my letter doing to them now? We lost the Galatians. How could we lose the Corinthians too?'

Paul sits in prison utterly, unbearably crushed.

To me it seems that he is despairing of life itself.

$\mathcal{L}$. Annaeus Seneca

77

Seneca, in Rome,
  To Lucan, my nephew studying in Athens,
  This second year of the reign of Nero:

Cave, Fratris Filie! Beware, my gentle nephew! Oh, beware:
great Nero is in love with you.

Forgive me, I'm making a joke – but only half a joke.

The emperor is calling you home from your studies in Athens.
He knows your natural force with language. He admires you,
Lucan. Nero sees himself as an artist among artists: he wants you
to join his intimates, his little gang of orators, poets, musicians –
and how can you not accept? Of course you will come, and you
will become a familiar in the palace on the Palatine, and it will
comfort my soul to see you now and again, laughing in the
hallways, making public recitation of your verses.

Nero can do much for you. He can magnify your voice. What
you sing in Rome, and what you say on her rostrum, will echo
through all the great cities of the provinces, and a piece of you
will never have left Athens.

But nephew, how old are you now? Seventeen? Eighteen? I beg
you, bring caution with you when you come. Bring an old man's
wisdom. When you are in Nero's company, be more politic than
poet: for though he wears the lion's mane and the lion's might,
he has but a tomcat's heart.

For your own sake, pretend to be callow if you are not; affect
innocence; chose carefully what parts of your life you will give to
Nero, always reserving the greater portion for yourself. Do not
accept his every invitation.

At night this emperor surrounds himself with riotous fellows –
friends no better than thugs – and roams the streets disguised.

They insult the women, they threaten men, they break down the doors of the shops and steal the goods for the plain pleasure of lawlessness. Worse than that: ever since several shopkeepers fought back (I saw the bruises on the lion's face the following morning) Nero has commanded a band of gladiators to follow at a distance, ready to use their weapons. Attacks on his person have very different conclusions now.

High spirits, say the courtiers, giggling at the antics of their 'bronzebeard', their darling. He's a young man, they say, playing with his power like a boy who is suddenly rich, and all his wishes are granted. It'll pass as he matures, they say – and I don't disagree with them.

Do I sound prudish to you, young Lucan? – grim and narrow-minded?

Well, it isn't certain; I may be wrong; I hope with all my heart I am wrong: but when these 'high spirits' pass away, I fear that the mightier spirit to take their place shall not be different in kind, but only in degree, in boldness, in the scope and the complexity of its malicious influence.

You heard that Nero's stepbrother Brittanicus died last year – him whom you yourself praised as 'the poet of the future': lean, dreamy young man, always quiet, content in seclusion, never seeking public power, never blaming Nero or Agrippina for having stolen the throne from him.

You heard as well, I'm sure, that shortly after his death Nero published an edict bewailing the loss of his brother's support, that he refused to keep the estate of Britannicus, the houses and villas, for himself, but distributed them among the gravest and most honoured of his friends.

But did you also hear in Athens the rumour that Britannicus died not of a severe epileptic fit? That he was murdered?

In public this is only a rumour of pale force. I know of no one who feels offence.

In fact, however, it is more than a rumour. It is the truth.

Locusta, whose poisons killed Claudius, still lives, dear nephew. She is guarded and *under* guard in her dismal little house, kept by a tribune whose name is Julius Pollio against the day of her usefulness.

It was to be expected that Agrippina would feel neglected and out-powered by her son, once he was the emperor. Well, she did, and she began to fight to renew her influence. But on the day she

uttered a public threat, announcing to Nero that she was
switching allegiance from him to Britannicus, 'who is,' she said,
'the rightful heir to the throne' – on that day she went too far,
and the son proved how closely he'd watched his mother's cold
manipulations: Nero called for Locusta.

Pollio brought the old woman with her bottles and potions
to a little room in the emperor's personal apartments. There
she mixed and tested various poisons on a succession of small
animals. In five days she produced a mixture that killed a pig in
a minute, and Britannicus was invited to banquet with Nero that
night.

The redoubtable Agrippina attended the banquet, too,
reclining, as she requested, at her son's right side instead of his
left. Face-to-face she holds a fearsome power over the boy. But
heart to heart she's weaker than she knows: that night, while
she burst grapes against her palate fine, Agrippina was sweetly
oblivious of plots and plannings.

A cup was passed to Britannicus's official taster. The wine was
so hot that it burned the taster's tongue. Otherwise he called it
'faultless'.

A little water was poured into the cup to cool it, and
Britannicus drank.

Instantly the young man stiffened and fell rigid to the
cushions, his mouth open on a soundless cry.

Horror ran through the hall. Some people rose and ran out.
Others kept still, watching Nero to know what to do. He took a
sip of his own wine and then spoke with an easy indifference. 'He
often suffers fits like these,' Nero said. 'My brother will be better
in the morning.'

Agrippina herself never moved. She held her body fiercely
composed. But I watched her, and I saw in her face the dawn of a
terrible knowledge. This was no boy beside her now, and scarcely
a son – except in the legacy of murders.

That knowledge, Lucan, you too must learn. Learn it deeply,
learn it now, even before you enter the service of your new
benefactor, so that you may never be taken by surprise: kindness
is but one of Nero's capacities.

They had to crack the rigor to close Britannicus's mouth. So
violent had the poison been, that it blackened the flesh around
his eyes. They covered these ruptures with creams, though only a
handful of people would ever actually view the corpse, for it was

carried out that same night to the Campus Martius. There the unfortunate lad, your 'poet of the future', was burned and buried. No speeches. No ceremony. Haste.

On the other hand, I must tell you that the very first time a sentence of death was submitted to Nero for his written endorsement, it caused him a moment of morbid woe. In my hearing he said, 'I wish I didn't know how to write.'

And goodness has come to the government now. There is lawfulness in Rome and prosperity generally throughout the empire. Nero countenances my policies. In fact, he presents them as his own both to the Senate and to the public. And though I write the speeches he delivers, I believe he understands them – insofar as he is able.

There. I have acknowledged both sides of the lion.

He loves you. If you tread with the step your uncle can teach you – more politic than poet, as I say, Lucan, and prudent rather than passionate – he will roar approval, and the world will know your name.

Timothy

78

Prisca asked me, 'When do you visit Paul? What hours in the day?'

'In the evening,' I said, 'when the city sits home eating supper.'

Prisca said, 'You must take me with you.'

'I don't know,' I said. 'I don't think the guard will let anyone else in the cell but me.'

'Timothy, don't say no. I'm going to enter his cell with you.'

'Why, Prisca?'

'I'll tell you only this, and this is what you will tell the guard: that I go to give him a massage. Say that the man will die before his trial unless I can lay hands upon his back.'

'But Luke can do that better than you.'

'Luke's too big,' she said. 'Besides, Luke has other work to do.'

'What are you saying? What do you mean?'

'And this time when you visit Paul, we must go a little later than usual. We'll go as the day gets darker.'

'Prisca, what are you telling me?'

'Come to my house at sunset. Wear heavy clothing, whatever the weather. I'll be waiting.'

In fact, the weather has been balmy all day long. A lovely day, a zephyr day, one of the first true days of spring, and now the sun is sitting on the edge of the sea, gazing back at me. He lays upon the water such a hard gold path that I imagine walking to him and going home for good.

The passing of winter makes daydreams in me.

In spite of the vernal warmth, I'm wearing a robe of coarse wool, as Prisca requested.

In my robe I turn the corner to her house – and just as I approach it, the door opens and Prisca stands before me, grave, mysterious. She's dressed in something like a Roman toga. The *sinus*, the fold that usually drapes the shoulders, is pulled over her head as a pagan priestess might cover herself to offer sacrifice. Prisca's face is in shadow. Aquila steps into view. He puts his own face into the shadow of her hood and kisses his wife. He looks at me a long moment, spontaneously kisses me as well, and vanishes indoors.

Prisca has a supple leather pouch in her hand. I assume it contains the lotions for massage. I have a scrip with bread and dry fruit and a leather flask of thin wine.

'Come,' Prisca whispers as though no one should hear her but me, and we set out for the praetorium.

Neither of us speaks. My heart has begun to pound in my breast. Nothing is common right now. Something enormous is rising tonight – but I can't see it to name it. I'm walking in darkness.

At the back of the praetorium I lead Prisca down a narrow stone staircase into the dank basements of the place. We enter a hallway which ends at a heavy wooden door with a grate and a binding of steel bands. I pound on the door. One of the interior guards puts his face to the grate.

'Timothy,' I say, 'bringing supper to Paul.'

The guard is chewing something. He has a gap between his front two teeth. He grunts and unbars the door from the other side. It swings on an iron post that turns in sockets of stone.

We enter.

The guard closes and re-bars the door, then turns away from us and goes to a stone bench where two other guards are sitting and eating. The room is narrow, long to the left and the right. The ceiling's low, all its beams and stonework blackened by the smoke of bad oil and open torches.

'Timothy,' I repeat myself, 'bringing – ' But the captain of the guards raises his arm without getting up.

'You,' he says through saliva and a mash of bread; he nods and thrusts his thumb toward his left, our right. He means me. He's granting me passage to the cells. 'But not you.' He aims a fisted arm at Prisca. 'And why the hell are you hiding your face? You got something you're ashamed of?'

I grin and fawn and bow a bit. 'Listen,' I say, 'it's a woman.

She's only a woman, but she's come for good reason. Listen,'
I say, 'your prisoner could well die before his trial. I mean, he
could die on your watch, sir, if you don't allow my friend here to
minister to him. She will work his joints and the infirmities of his
back. It's a massage,' I say.

All three guards keep chewing and staring at us – at Prisca,
really, a woman.

The captain says, 'What you hiding, woman?'

I say, 'How often have you found your prisoner unconscious in
the cell? He does that when he's in extremity. He passes out and
nearly dies – you know that. This shows the need for my friend's
healing. Please let her pass with me.'

'Shut up,' the captain commands me.

Oh, my heart is charging like a horse in my breast! I'm not
succeeding here.

'Woman, speak for yourself,' he says. 'Show me your face!'

Prisca, in a timid halting voice, says, 'Please don't ask that.
Because you're right. You are right, sir, I am ashamed.'

All three guards are interested now. The captain narrows his
eye and leans forward.

'Ain't nobody passing me here,' he drawls, 'whose identity
I don't know. Either drop the hood or get out.'

Slowly Prisca raises her right hand to the hem that hangs at
her brow. She lifts it. She draws the cloth backward – and I gasp!
Tears sting my eyes. 'Prisca!' I breathe.

Her hair is shorn. Chopped off, so that patches of scalp show
through and the skin has been cut; the skin has scabs. Oh, her
whole face looks so tiny now, so pinched and miserable!

The gap-toothed guard says, 'What the hell?' and starts to
laugh. 'Gel, you're butchered, you are!'

The captain barks, 'Shut up!' To Prisca he says, 'Who did that
to you?'

She answers: 'My husband.'

'Prisca!' I hiss. '*Aquila*?'

'Why, for God's sake?' the captain demands.

'Custom, custom,' Prisca sighs with sadness. She lowers her
eyelids and stares at the floor. 'I wronged him. He has the right.'

Oh, how I want to take the mournful woman in my arms right
now, to hold her and comfort and protect her.

The first guard says, 'Damn, I'd like to hear tell of that
partic'ler wrong.'

'Please, sir,' Prisca says to the captain, her voice, her whole being drooping like the willow, 'now that you've seen me, can I cover my head again?'

He wipes his mouth with the back of his hand. 'His name's Aquila, hey?' the captain growls – and I die for my mistake. 'I'd like to meet this brave Aquila. Cover it.'

Prisca has never let go of the cloth. She pulls the hood slowly over her ruined skull, then reaches into the leather pouch and takes something from it. With a graceful motion, with the carriage of nobility, she steps forward to the captain of the guard – and as I watch her I realize that events have passed me by. I am no longer leading. I'm following.

Prisca extends her hand to the captain.

She says, 'I have another request, sir. Just this once, just for this visitation, would you be kind enough to unshackle the prisoner? He must stretch out on his stomach, or my hands can do him no good.'

She opens her palm. She is offering him seven pieces of gold, fresh Roman coin stamped with the head of Nero.

The captain grunts and accepts the gift.

He takes a great swallow from a clay jug, then stands up, grabs a smoking torch from its sconce, and walks down the narrow room to his left. He limps as if his joints are stiff. All the other prisoners are locked on the other side of this wall. We can hear murmuring, muffled motion, but we pass on. Paul's cell is at the end of the hall.

'Stretch out,' the gap-toothed guard behind us is making a joke. 'Stretch out,' so's her hands can do him good! Well, I got a mind to do some stretchin' out too when she comes back. Shear a woman once, she's sheared for ever – '

Paul sits on the floor of his cell, his back to the wall, watching as the captain enters and approaches him and starts to unlock the manacles on his wrists. We enter, too.

In the light of the torch, Paul's face is meatless, gaunt, and drained of emotion. He asks nothing of the captain of the guard. His wrists are raw from the metal. He rubs each one as it comes free, but grimaces. Rubbing itself is a torment.

The guard retires and leaves us alone, and only then does

Paul raise his eyes to indicate he knows there are two of us here.

I think I see the ghost of a smile.

And then my teacher and friend amazes me, for in a croak of a voice he greets Prisca while still her face is hidden.

'Priscilla,' he says, 'you've come to see me.'

'I've come,' she says.

'She's come,' I announce, feeling giddy at our success, 'to give you a massage!'

Prisca turns and scolds me: 'No, Timothy! No! That's not my place any more.'

'But you said – '

'I said what you needed to know to argue the guards with sincerity.'

She turns back to Paul and kneels down in front of him, 'Not to give you a massage,' Prisca says, gathering his hands in hers and laying them against her lips. 'I've come to give you my clothes.'

Paul, so thin and wasted! Emotion begins to twist in his face. His black brow rises in question and, I think, in gratitude to the woman whose kisses are warming his hands. But his body is unused to strong feeling, and it trembles: his arms and his great head tremble as with a palsy.

Both of us speak at once, Paul and I.

I say, 'What? Your clothes? Prisca, what are you talking about?'

While Paul says, 'No. I don't like it. I refuse.'

Prisca says, 'You have no choice. Everything has been arranged. If you don't go now, you leave all your friends in the lurch.'

'And if I do go,' Paul says, withdrawing his hands from hers and balling them into pitiful fists, 'I leave you in danger of losing your life! I can't do that.'

For my part, I don't understand. I'm holding my peace. The air in this dark cell seems to spark with tension and matters unspoken. If I say one more foolish thing, something will crack like thunder.

'It's too late for objections!' Prisca says. She seizes Paul's hands a second time and draws them to her brow. She lifts her chin. The hood falls backward, and she places his hands palm-flat upon her wretched scalp. 'You see? Things have already begun. Your freedom is my gift to you. When you go out of here in my clothes with your head covered, no one will ask you to uncover it.

The captain will not shame me twice. And he won't shame you the first time.'

'But why,' Paul croaks, 'should it be *you*?'

'Oh, my brother,' Prisca gives a little cry, 'have you never noticed? We are the same size!'

Paul, his great head loose on its hinge, gazes at her a while longer. His eye moistens. I think he is seeing the scenes in his mind: a future too disturbing to bear.

Suddenly he begins to struggle. 'No, Priscilla! No!' he says. 'You will not take my place!' Paul puts his hands on the floor and pushes – a terrible, failing struggle. It isn't immediately clear, but soon I realize that he's trying to stand up. His limbs are sticks. His chest is a cave. He has no strength.

'Timothy, Timothy, help me,' he says. His weakness tears me to pieces.

'Prisca,' he orders: 'Get out of here!'

And 'Guard?' he calls. In a desperate voice, '*Guard*!'

Prisca speaks his name in grief. 'Oh, Paul!' she says. Then, with the flat of her hand, she slaps him in the face.

Paul slumps to the ground in a dead faint.

'Timothy, look away,' Prisca says.

I do. What can I do but obey? Paul called for help. I didn't help him because Prisca is in control. Prisca, courageous and undismayed.

I hear the rustling of cloth behind me. Even in this stony cell I catch the scent of womanskin, and I swallow.

Prisca speaks as she handles the body of the apostle: 'Timothy, pay attention: Luke, Demas, and Justus are waiting at the Magnesian Gate. Get there as fast as you can without drawing attention. There's money in my pouch. When you leave, give two more coins to the captain of the guard and ask him to wait before he shackles the prisoner again. Tell him Paul's unconscious. And tell him that the poor woman on your shoulder passed out from sorrow at the sight of her friend – her lover.

'Timothy,' she says sharply, 'look at me!'

I turn and look. She is wearing Paul's filthy tunic. Her breasts are small. They scarcely break the fall of the cloth. Her head, uncovered, looks thorny and torn.

'Oh, my brother,' she says softly to me, 'don't cry, don't cry. I will be well. Aquila will come asking for me. Here,' she says, taking a piece of charcoal from her pouch. 'Black my face. Black my scalp. I will be Paul as long as I can. Black my shoulders, my arms, and my legs – '

I do. And while I do, I find I can't stop weeping. It seems to me that I'm preparing her body for burial. Oh, her lovely arms! – destroyed by this kindless begriming. Oh, her gentle, watchful face, that looks back at me while I shroud it! Oh, her white neck, the twin wings of her shoulders!

Paul, all hooded in Prisca's toga, lies beside us, helpless.

And she sings softly while I paint her in the colours of the grave.

She sings, 'There is one mind among us – '

She sings for me and for herself and for Paul, for Aquila and all who risk their necks in service to God:

'Hush, hush, and strengthen your knees,' Prisca sings, 'for this is our mind, the mind of Christ, who gave up power and took a body, who humbled his body to dust and to death – who died the death,' she sings as I rise and take Paul's weight upon my shoulder, 'Who died the death of deaths,' she sings, 'on the cross.'

Part Five

JERUSALEM

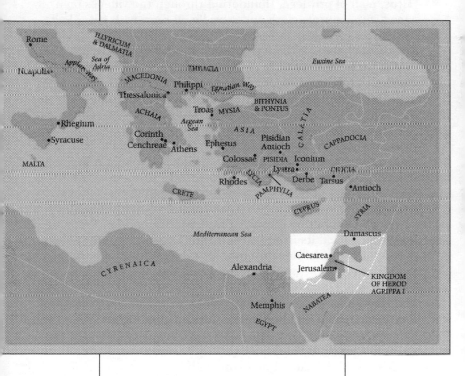

itus

79

So here's the thing: I'm riding a horse! *Ai-eee!* – I'm Titus on horseback, galloping hillsides through orchards and vineyards, galloping toward Thermopylae (Paul, Paul, your healing baths, and what will you think of my news?). Look out! Here comes Titus, man of privilege, thundering through the villages on a steed with a purple cloth and a bridle all sewn with silver bells. Oh, he's a royal one, is Titus!

No, but I mean it: *Look out!* I'm prone to fly off this creature, which turns or stops without my how-do-you-do. I got my two feet stuck out to either side, on account of I'm trying to squeeze its ribs with my thighs, which is how Erastus said I should stick to the beast. 'It's not a stool you're sitting on!' he said. 'Don't bend your knees! Sit like standing, straight-legged and tight. You'll do fine. You'll be all right.' So he told me, but he didn't tell the beast, which goes from a walk to a trot when I don't ask, bouncing me, bouncing me sideways till I just drop to the ground. Well, but if I try to hang on by gripping the leather straps to the horse's mouth, it snorts and shoots forward, and all at once we're tearing through the vineyards, and I'm wrapping my arms around its neck and screaming to farmers along the way, 'Not my fault! Not my fault!' I've never ridden a horse before! There's the problem. And I said that exact thing to Erastus when he brought the creature out to the fields with me, the three of us alone. 'Give me a donkey,' I said, 'on account of I've never ridden a horse before.' But he put a finger first to my lips and then to his, shushing me and shaking his chins at the great solemnity of things.

'It's a gift!' he said. 'I'm giving a gift.'

Erastus wants to give away the absolute best mount in his stables. He has no horse, he tells me, finer than this.

'Titus,' he said full serious, looking me dead in my eyes, 'Titus, you must take my gift to Paul and tell him I love him. Say that I love him. I love the man with all my heart – '

Here Erastus lowered his head, heaved his shoulders, and blew a stream of air through his lips like whistling. He was fighting his feelings, I think, which took the fight right out of me. How could I ask for a donkey now?

So then he squared himself, soldier-formal, tough and official, and said, 'You must lead this rich grey horse to the apostle Paul and say to him these words: "Here, Paul, is a gift from the man who hurt you. In God's name, he is sorry for what he did. He begs your forgiveness. Truly, truly, he did not know you could be hurt so deeply, or that you could be so sad."'

I have the words by heart.

I'll say them to Paul exactly like that – if ever I get to Macedonia before one of us, me or this 'gift', kills the other.

And when I repeat Erastus's piece, I'll add a thing or two of my own, so Paul gets the whole picture. I'll tell him what happened when I read his letter in the house of Titius Justus to some of the people that Sosthenes gathered. How quiet they were. How nobody argued. How I wondered if they were even listening. But when I got to the part about Satan and the thorn in Paul's flesh and God's big *No*, no, he would not take the thorn away, and when I read God's announcement about who was strong and who was weak, someone hit the floor and howled. Someone couldn't control himself. Someone blubbered so loudly that I read the letter at the level of shout or no one else would hear the rest of it.

Well, and you know who blubbered. He'd been lurking near the door of the house. I hadn't seen him, didn't know he was there till he fell down and started to cry. Yep. Erastus.

So, there it is. This is the news I'm bringing Paul at lickety speeds on the back of Erastus's four-legged, bell-ringing gift. *Gift*? No sir, a trick and a torment is what it is! A hairy affliction! The flesh inside my thighs is raw. My butt is beaten, my backbone's jolted, my body's snapped and shaken like a mother's rug, my arms hold the throat of this hellion – and my plan: to choke it till I win!

I'll bring it to Paul, all right, in a bag or in obedience.

And to everything else I tell him I will add this:

'Paul,' I'll say full serious, looking him dead in the eyes, 'Erastus is waiting – and dying, I think, till he hears from you.'

Timothy

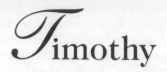

80

It took us a night and a day and a night again to carry Paul from Ephesus to Smyrna. Forty miles, the first fifteen in grim haste despite a sheeting rain and lightning in the night. Fog shrouded us the following morning, and still we did not stop. Good to be cloaked, if someone was chasing us. Good to be ghosts on the road.

The four of us, Demas, Luke, Justus, and me – we bore Paul along on a piece of leather he'd cut himself. Luke had thought to cover him with it, but when the others saw that the apostle was as good as dead, we lashed short poles into a narrow frame and sewed the leather around it. Me. I did the sewing with an awl and some cord from Paul's tool bag. I used a basting stitch of which no one would be proud, but I'd only learned it by watching Paul, and I had neither the time nor the light to do a proper job.

We drew Prisca's toga over him, then clutched the rude litter at the corners and ran.

He didn't wake the entire time. At least, I don't *think* he woke. Now and again I saw an eyelid open halfway to the daylight, but the pupil was blank and his head rocked in rhythm with our going as if it were as mindless as a melon. His arms fell out. His poor, wasted arms dropped out of the litter. I kept tucking them under his sides, but I couldn't unball his fists. His jaw was locked. This seemed a sleep too mortal, and I worried. I watched him while we drove forward, scared that the man was dying.

My papa told me once that Homer was born in Smyrna, that blind old seer, the singer my papa loved. Then he threw back his head and laughed. The laughter turned, as it always did, to coughing and a pinkish foam. *They claim him, they claim the man as their own*, Papa said when he got his breath again: *but they don't know a damn thing about him!*

In the grey dawn of the second morning we slipped into Smyrna exhausted, but travelling still as quickly as we could go. We feared that four men with a fifth on a bed between them would draw suspicion. In Smyrna the streets are so perfectly straight, so perfectly parallel east and west, that the sea breeze blew unbroken from the harbour while the sunrise raised a blister in the east, and we were caught between.

Two miles north of Smyrna – rushing toward Pergamum, now – my stitches ripped, and Paul fell through the pole-frame hitting the road below.

'Oh, *no*!' I cried, frightened for Paul, furious with myself. I dropped to my knees and for an instant thought I saw life in the body, or else the draining of his life: Paul rolled to his side and drew his knees to his chest.

'Paul? Paul, are you all right?'

No answer. None.

His right temple was wormy with a blue vein and pale as ivory; his nose was too prominent, his eyelids so thin as to seem translucent, the eyeballs crossed beneath them.

And his jaw was locked. And his fists were balled.

'Paul?'

We stopped where we were. We carried him into a low enclosure of stone, where the other three fell asleep while I re-stitched his narrow bed, watching him, watching his tight, unconscious body on Prisca's beautiful robe.

Oh, Paul, I'm so sorry.

When I had finished a tighter stitch – a seam stitch this time – I woke Luke and asked him to watch while I ran back to the city.

I bought my friend a pillow. I ran back and placed a little cushion under his head, and then I collapsed.

I cannot remember the falling asleep.

I see Luke pouring water onto Paul's lips as if the two men were great clouds bowed together in the heavens, and then I see nothing.

81

On the third day Paul woke up. Just at noon, suddenly. And began quietly to cry.

We were about halfway to Pergamum, skirting high ground on our right. The day was bright, the sun behind us and warm on our shoulders, the breezes more earthy than salty here, and the air made moist with the breathings of a vernal soil.

I was walking at the back of the litter, the left side, considering for the first time in a month that this was the season of the Passover. I wondered at myself – at all of us, really: how could we have forgotten the feast? Were we forgetting our heritage? Had the festivals begun to fall away from us, even without our noticing? Ah, but immediate events had been so consuming that we had no time for anything else: Paul's imprisonment, fear of the trial to come, fear for his *life*, I mean, and the failure of the Galatian churches, and the horrors of Corinth, Prisca's heroic sacrifice…

When was the Passover? Which day? I truly didn't know. Justus was Jewish, more Jewish than me since his father had not been Greek.

I asked him, *Which day is the day of the Passover?*

Without looking around, he answered me. *The night you brought Paul to us – that was the start of the Passover.*

Who had celebrated? Had my mother found a family to share with her the bread, bitter herbs, the lamb and the wine and the story? But Lystra's Jew-less.

Surely that man in Jerusalem, solemnly, had sat at table with others like him, a host of others, I suppose. That man whom Paul knows. James.

Had Barnabas?

But we didn't. Didn't even think about it. Didn't feel the world change, didn't hear the ancients call us or accuse us.

I said to Justus, *Did you miss it?*

And he said to me, *Miss what?*

I walked mechanically. I walked all full of thought, abstracted from the world around me, allowing my eyes to settle without seeing.

But slowly I became aware that my eyes had settled on Paul, on his face in the litter before me.

And then the seeing turned electric: Paul was looking back at me! He was awake! He had woken from his deadly sleep – and there were tears leaking from the corners of his eyes, smearing his temples.

'Paul!' I squeaked. The word stuck in me. I coughed. I cleared my throat hard and cried, 'Stop!' to the others. 'Look! Paul's here! Paul's awake!'

Swiftly we lowered the bed to the ground and turned, all four, to look down on him, down on my dear brother, my friend, whose eyes were shining, whose brow was lifted in childlike questions, whose bottom lip was trembling gently, and who gazed up at us, one by one and each by each.

'Who gave me a pillow?' he said. His voice was thick with emotion, and at his speaking the tears rolled down in a greater flow. 'Who,' Paul begged, raising his hands and spreading his fingers as if to hold some delicate bowl in them, 'was so kind as to put this pillow under my head?'

82

Paul could not walk the rest of the way to Pergamum. But he took food and water in small, continual quantities, and by the time we set out for Troas he could manage a mile or two afoot before he had to recline on his bed again – which kindness on our parts, as he termed it, still caused him tears of gratitude.

He asked about Prisca, whether Prisca was safe; had she perished saving his life? We couldn't answer. We didn't know. Nor could we speak of Aquila, nor of anyone or anything in Ephesus.

No news. It silenced him. I think, too, that the love of his friends stole his language, stilled his voice.

In time he asked about Titus and Corinth. To this I could respond, but oddly.

'You told him to meet you in Troas, Paul. Don't you remember?'

He gazed at me as if the memory might be found in *my* face.

'I did?' he whispered. 'When?'

'When you gave him the letter to carry to Corinth.'

'But I was in prison!'

'Yes, yes, and that's the wonder. I tell you that I myself marvelled when you told him Troas, because there were no prospects of freedom then, no plans to get you out. It seemed impossible to me.'

Paul blinked at me. 'It couldn't have been me,' he said.

'Who else?' I said. 'Who else was in that cell but me and Titus?'

He frowned. He set his elbows on his knees and cradled his chin in his hands.

'Jesus,' he said.

He looked forward to Troas after that. It gave him focus – one touchable thing in his future. And once we were in Troas, he looked forward to meeting Titus again – but with a yearning uncertainty. He wanted to know. He needed to know. But he feared to know what was happening in Corinth, because as long as he *didn't* know, the news could still be good.

Paul never mentioned the Galatians again. But I believe he thought about them all the time. I think his greatest anxiety was that he might be losing churches in the east and the west at once.

A month passed. Another, and as he gained strength, Paul rose up and did what he always did, wherever he went, for this was the *who* that he was: he began to preach the name of Jesus and the cross of Christ in Troas. All over again he began to establish churches there.

'We are the true circumcision,' he preached, still dividing the old and the new that the people might come to the new, 'we are the children of God, we who worship God in spirit, and who glory in Christ Jesus, and who put no confidence in the flesh.'

As much for us as for the baby souls surrounding him, Paul preached: 'Whatever gain I ever had, I count it as loss for the sake of Christ! Indeed I count everything as loss because of the surpassing worth of knowing Christ Jesus my Lord. For his sake I have suffered the loss of all things and count them as rubbish in order that I may gain Christ and be found in him, not having a righteousness of my own, based on law, but that which is through faith in Christ, the righteousness from God that depends on faith, that I may know him and the power of his resurrection, and may share his sufferings, becoming like him in his death, that if possible I may attain the resurrection from the dead.'

This was different. Paul's preaching was different. It caused in me strange feelings of intimacy and distance at once. No, it wasn't the substance that had changed. Not his teachings, exactly. But the way he gave them. Softly. No longer charging headlong into argument, or so fiercely *willing* the people to believe as he did. And, most importantly, this: Paul had never been so *personal* before.

'Not that I have already obtained these things,' he said, 'or am already perfect. But I press on. I press on to make them my own, because Christ Jesus has made me his own.

'O my dear ones! I do not consider that I have made it my own; but one thing I do, forgetting what lies behind and straining forward to what lies ahead, I press on toward the goal for the prize of the upward call of God in Christ Jesus!'

In the early mornings, Luke, with strong hands, worked the muscle, the dry ruined flesh, the bunching spine of Paul's back.

'You've lost three fingers,' Luke said.

He was using the Jewish measure. He meant that Paul was shorter by the breadth of three fingers than when they first had met. I thought about that. Almost dwarfish was my teacher. I had begun to feel awkward, lumbering camel-like beside him.

Paul, face-down on a pallet and blankets, spoke in a nearly inaudible voice. I could hear him only by holding my breath.

'Priscilla used to do this,' he murmured. He was talking to himself. 'She leaned her weight against my bruisings. Not well, but charmingly.'

Suddenly he wailed: 'Merciful Jesus, save Priscilla! Save my sister alive.'

A season passed. The hot midsummer came. And Paul could no longer wait in Troas for Titus. Suddenly he announced our passage to Macedonia, and we, three of us, left. Demas and Justus remained in Troas to oversee the churches there. Luke and I sailed with Paul to Neapolis.

We walked to Philippi. We were wonderfully received by the redoubtable Lydia, that powerful woman who kept running her hands through my hair and cooing, 'Never get it cut. Don't ever lose a lock of this.'

It was Paul who, standing by the river, raised his eyes and first saw Titus approaching.

'Titus,' Paul told us that night, squealing with laughter. 'Young Titus came over the green field wearing the bridle of a horse and jingling as he came. A jubilation of jingling!' Paul giggled in delight. 'Because that bridle was sewn from the bit to the headband with bells! Little silver bells! And over his shoulders he wore a cloth that was cut for a rich man's rear. He walked bow-legged, blistered between his thighs, *mincing* as if he'd been beaten in battle – and in his eye a gallows-glare, the baleful stare of a madman.

'"Titus!" I cried. "Oh, Titus, how good it is to see you!"

'And the lad, he greeted me with these words: "I killed the horse at Thermopylae and sold its hide for a pair of sandals."'

aul

83

Paul, an apostle of Christ Jesus by the will of God,
   And Timothy our brother:
   To the church of God at Corinth, with all the saints who are in
      the whole of Achaia:

Grace to you and peace from God our Father and the Lord
Jesus Christ!
   Oh, blessed be the God and Father of our Lord Jesus Christ!
Blessed be the Father of mercies! Blessed, blessed be the God of
all comfort, who comforts us in our affliction and makes us able
to comfort the afflictions of others by the same sweet comfort we
received! For as much as we share the suffering of Christ, even so
much will we share in his comfort.
   O Corinthians, if we've been afflicted, it's for your comfort and
your salvation. And when we are comforted, that too is for your
comfort, the comfort you can experience even while you suffer
the same as we.
   Our hope for you is unshaken!
   We know that as you share in our suffering, so will you share in
comfort.
   Comfort, comfort –
   Listen: I'm talking about the affliction I experienced in Asia.
I was so utterly, unbearably crushed that I despaired of life itself.
I felt I'd received a sentence of death. But all that was to make
me rely not on myself but on God, the blessed God! – who raises
up the dead! He delivered me from the mortal peril, and he *will*
deliver me. I have set my hope on him to deliver all of us again.
Dear Corinth, pray for me. Pray for us, so that many, many will
give thanks on our behalf for the blessings granted to many
prayers.

In all good conscience I tell you, I've behaved – both in the world and to you – with holiness and godly sincerity, not by earthly wisdom but by the grace of God. Whatever I wrote you, I wrote it as clearly as possible, and I hope you understand it completely now, as once you understood in part. Oh, I hope you can be as proud of me as I will be of you on the day of the Lord Jesus.

In Ephesus I began to plan a final trip through Achaia and Macedonia in order to pick up the Jerusalem collection. I thought I might start with you, travel north, then return to you a second time (a double pleasure!) on my way to Judea. It hasn't happened that way. I'm starting in Macedonia after all. Please don't think me fickle, though. Don't think I make plans according to whim and my *own* advantage, saying Yes and No at once. As surely as God is faithful, my word to you has never been 'Yes and No'. For the Son of God, Jesus Christ, whom we preached among you, Silvanus and Timothy and I, was never Yes and No. In him it's always *Yes*! For all the promises of God find their clarion *Yes* in him. That's why I cry 'Amen!' through Jesus to the glory of God.

At the same time, I'm conscience-bound to tell you that even before events overtook me, I had already decided not to start my trip with you. I wanted to spare you. I didn't want either of us to suffer a visit as painful as the last one was. Instead I wrote you. I wrote so that when I *did* come I wouldn't be wounded again. I wrote you, dear Corinthians, out of a bottomless sorrow and anguish of heart. I wrote with tears – but not to cause you pain! Truly, truly, I wanted you to know how great is my love for you.

And if somebody there has wounded me in the past, well, it wasn't just me. In a way it was all of you who were wounded. But that's over now. Titus describes how you've reproved the sinner there. Please: it's time now to turn and forgive and comfort him, or the man could be crippled by his sorrow. I beg you, reaffirm your love for the poor fellow. Those whom you forgive, I forgive. And what I've forgiven, if I have forgiven anything, has been for your sake in the presence of Christ – to keep Satan from gaining advantage over us. (Oh, don't I *know* his wicked ways!)

This summer I was in Troas, preaching – succeeding, in fact. But I tell you, it gave me no relief, absolutely none, because Titus hadn't come with news of you. So I picked up and rushed over to Macedonia, and the God who comforts the troubled comforted me by the coming of Titus! Not by his coming only, but also by the comfort with which he was comforted in you. He told me of your mourning, your yearning, your zeal for me, and I laughed for joy. Oh, I clapped and cried together!

Don't you see? If I made you sorry with my letter, I don't regret it (well, but I did regret it). Instead, I rejoice because it grieved you a while. Oh, I don't mean I rejoice in your grief, but in the repentance grief causes. You felt a *godly* grief, so you suffered no loss, because godly grief produces a repentance that leads to salvation. It's a *worldly* grief that produces regret that leads to death. (I know the difference!) And look what earnestness the godly grief has given you, what eagerness to clear yourselves, what indignation, what alarm, what yearning, what zeal, what speed to reprove!

I rejoice: I have perfect confidence in you.

And besides my own comfort I rejoice even more in the love that Titus feels for you when he speaks of your obedience, and the fear and trembling with which you received him.

Oh, blessed be God who leads us in Christ to triumph! Blessed, blessed be the Father who breathes the sweetness of knowing him through us to people everywhere. We *are* – aren't we? – the very fragrance of Jesus!

On another matter, now: the collection for the poor in Jerusalem.

You should know how liberal the Macedonians have been despite their serious poverty. They've given beyond their means, of their own free will, *begging* us, as a favour to them, to let them take part in the relief of the saints.

You, too, Corinthians: you who excel in everything – in faith, in tongues, in knowledge – should excel in this gracious work as well.

This isn't a command. I'm just using the zeal of others to prove that your love, too, is genuine. For you know the grace of our Lord Jesus Christ, that though he was rich he became poor for your sake, in order through his poverty to make you rich. Not as a command, I say, but as advice: let your present abundance supply the want of others.

I'm sending Titus again to you (well, and he comes of his own accord) to arrange for your gift in advance of my own arrival –

Oh, but this is superfluous, isn't it? – writing you about the offering for the saints in Jerusalem. I already know your readiness. Haven't I been boasting about it here in Macedonia? And hasn't your zeal already stirred them up? Yes, and I'm confident that you would never humiliate me, to say nothing of yourselves.

Here's the point: those who sow thin will reap thin. Those who sow thick will reap a thick, rich profit. Make your donations freely, not reluctantly or under compulsion, for God loves a cheerful giver. And God is able to provide you with every blessing in such thick abundance that you always will have enough. He who supplies seed to the sower and bread for food will himself multiply your planting and increase the harvest of your righteousness.

Under the test of this service, you will glorify God by obedience. And by the generosity of your contribution you will prove the surpassing grace of God in you.

(Are you listening, Erastus? Are you learning how to give a gift in glory?)

Thanks be to God for his inexpressible gift!

Titus, yes. Titus first – then me.

I am coming, my children. I'm coming too. Have patience. Wait a season. Wait till autumn, late in autumn when the rushing wet weather begins, then look to the east and watch for me. I shall be setting forth on the greatest journey of my life: through Corinth I shall go, to Jerusalem, then on to Rome, and after Rome – to Spain.

I am taking the cross of Christ to the very ends of the earth!

But first I'm coming to see you, to embrace you, and to give you kisses too. (Yes, and there's a kiss on my lips for that dear prodigious brother of mine, the Manager of Markets in Corinth.)

Until the blue sky blows to grey, then, wait: and the peace of the Lord be with you all.

Amen.

Luke

84

When he had finished travelling through Macedonia, encouraging the churches, Paul came to Achaia and Corinth. There he spent three months.

Just when he was about to set sail for Judea, a plot was discovered against him, and he determined to return by way of Macedonia.

Sopater of Berea, the son of Pyrrhus, accompanied him. Of the Thessalonians, so did Aristarchus and Secundus, and Gaius of Derbe, and Timothy. Two Asians, too: Tychicus and Trophimus. These all went on and were waiting for us at Troas; but we ourselves, we waited in Philippi until the days of Unleavened Bread were complete.

Timothy

85

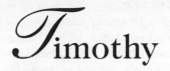

I go to Jerusalem, Paul wrote to Rome.

I was one of the seven men who shipped eastward from Philippi to Troas ahead of Paul. We weren't as interested as he in celebrating the Passover, nor did we feel constrained to sit idle during the festival days. Moreover (as I said to Paul, regarding myself) someone had to act as a temporary leader for the group till he should cross and meet us in Troas.

We had all provided ourselves with new robes and new tunics for the journey to Jerusalem; but Lydia insisted on having Paul's garments sewn at her own expense and under her instructions. She would have used the rich material of her trade, but Paul refused for reasons that had nothing to do with modesty. 'We can't call attention to ourselves,' he said. He asked for the toughest, plainest sort of cloth, because it had a plain, tough job to do. And 'though the raiment be not rich,' he said, 'it will *contain* more riches than anyone must guess.'

Big-boned Lydia gave Paul a poke in his ribs. They made a sly couple, for she knew what he meant. He meant the money on his person. But she meant more: she meant the crumpled person himself, and his parts.

So plain were we all to appear, in fact, that we walked the ditches in the middle of the city streets, did not lift the hems of our robes, wore our clothing night and day, never brushed it, never washed it, never changed it.

We were our own pack animals, you see. We were ourselves the carriers of the heavy coin cargo for Jerusalem.

I go to Jerusalem, Paul wrote to the believers in Rome. Oh, but how he yearned to be in Rome, and then to travel farther. Friends were there. The wife and son of Simeon Niger had moved to Rome when Simeon died: Rufus, whom Paul called *eminent in the Lord*, and his mother, whom Paul declared was *my mother, too*.

To me he said, 'Timothy, what of Prisca? What of Aquila? Do you think they're in Rome? Did they make it safely to Rome, do you think?'

But to the Romans, in fierce hope and with a fainting boldness, Paul wrote. *Greet Prisca and Aquila, my fellow workers in Christ Jesus! They risked their necks for my life, and everyone owes them thanks. Not just I, but all the churches of the Gentiles owe them a holy thanksgiving!*

Paul hungered to rush west to Rome immediately. First, however, as he wrote it to them, *I must go to Jerusalem.*

I must go to Jerusalem with a contribution for the poor among the saints in that city. But when I have fulfilled my obligation, when I've delivered what has been raised, I shall go on by way of you to Spain; and I know that when I come to you I shall come in the fullness of the blessing of Christ.

Oh, my friends, I beg you by our Lord Jesus Christ and by the love of the Spirit: strive together with me in your prayers to God on my behalf, that I may be delivered from the unbelievers in Judea! – and that my service for Jerusalem may be acceptable to the saints, so that by God's will I may come to you with joy and be refreshed in your company.

The God of Peace be with you all, Paul wrote.

Amen, he wrote.

And again he wrote, *Amen*.

Luke

86

We sailed for five days from Philippi to join the rest of our group in Troas. There we stayed seven days.

On the first day of the week, when we were gathered together to break bread, Paul began to talk with friends and believers in Troas. Because he knew his departure would take place on the morrow, he talked long, much longer than usual.

There were many lamps in the upper chamber where we had gathered. As Paul kept talking a young man named Eutychus, who had settled himself on the ledge of a window, sank deeper and deeper asleep. Suddenly, just about at midnight, completely overcome by his slumber, young Eutychus tipped and fell out the window – three floors down to the ground.

We ran downstairs. I took up the poor lad's body and pronounced him dead.

But then Paul came down and bent over him. He embraced Eutychus and said, 'Don't be alarmed. His life is in him.'

Paul went upstairs again, broke the bread and ate, and continued to talk with the people all night long, even to daybreak. Then, finally, he departed.

But he had been right. They took young Eutychus away alive, and they were greatly comforted.

Going ahead to the ship, now, we set sail for Assos, intending to take Paul aboard there, since he had chosen to walk the shorter way by land.

And so it was: he was waiting for us at Assos where he boarded, and we sailed to Mitylene and anchored for the night. The next day we went as far as Chios, the next to Samos, and on the third day we arrived at Miletus. Paul had decided not to land at Ephesus, so that he might not have to spend time in Asia. He was hastening to be at Jerusalem, if possible, by the day of Pentecost.

At Miletus he sent to Ephesus for the elders of the church, and when they came, he asked them privately about Priscilla and Aquila.

'They vanished,' the elders said, 'suddenly after your escape.'

'Dead?' Paul asked.

And the elders answered that they did not know.

Publicly, then, Paul addressed them all, saying:

'You yourselves know how I lived among you all the time from the first day I ever set foot in Asia until now, serving the Lord with all humility, with tears, through trials and the plots of my enemies. You know I did not shrink from declaring to you anything profitable, teaching you in public and in your houses, testifying both to Jews and to Greeks regarding repentance to God and faith in our Lord Jesus Christ.

'And now, bound in my spirit I'm going to Jerusalem, not knowing what shall befall me there, except that the Holy Spirit testifies to me in every city that imprisonment awaits me, and afflictions. But I don't count my life as something valuable or precious to myself. This is my treasure: to accomplish my course; to finish the ministry which I received from the Lord Jesus; to preach the gospel of the grace of God!

'Listen,' Paul said, 'I know you will see my face no more. Therefore I testify to you this day that I am innocent of the blood of every one of you – for I did not shrink from declaring to you the whole counsel of God. Watch out for yourselves and for the whole flock over which the Holy Spirit has set you as overseers. Care for the church of God which he obtained with the blood of his own Son.

'I know that after my departure fierce wolves will attack you, not sparing the flock. And even some of your own people will rise up to utter perversities and try to draw the disciples after them. Be careful! Remember that for three years in Ephesus and Asia I never ceased, night or day, to admonish every one of you with tears.

'And now I commend you to God. I give you over to the word of his grace, which can build you up and give you an inheritance among all who are sanctified. I coveted no one's silver, no one's gold, no one's raiment! You saw me. You know that I laboured

with my own hands to meet my needs and the needs of the
people with me. In all things I've shown you how by toiling to
help the weak, ever to remember the words of the Lord Jesus:
It is more blessed to give than to receive.'

When Paul had said these things, he knelt down and prayed
with them all. And they all wept and embraced him and kissed
him, sorrowing most of all because of the word he had spoken,
that they should see his face no more.

And they brought him to the ship.

When he had parted from Miletus, we sailed by a straight course
to Cos, and the next day to Rhodes, and from there to Patara.
Finally, having found a ship that was crossing all the way to
Phoenicia, we went aboard and set sail.

We passed Cyprus on the left and sailed straight through to
Syria, landing at Tyre where the ship was scheduled to unload its
cargo.

For the seven days while the ship lay in port, we sought out
and stayed with the disciples in Tyre.

They told Paul not to go on to Jerusalem. They spoke through
the Spirit. But when the days were ended, we prepared to
continue on our journey after all; so with their wives and their
children, they brought us out of the city, down to the beach.
There we knelt and prayed and bade each other, 'Farewell.
Farewell.'

Then we boarded the ship, and they turned back to their
homes.

At the conclusion of the voyage from Tyre, we arrived at
Ptolemais, where again we were greeted by the believers, with
whom we stayed one day.

On the morrow we departed and came to Caesarea. There we
stayed in the house of Philip the evangelist – he who had been
one of the seven men of Stephen's circle years ago. Philip had
four unmarried daughters, each capable of prophecy.

At the same time another prophet came down from Judea,
Agabus. As soon as he entered the room where we were sitting,

he took Paul's belt and bound himself hand and foot with it. Then he said, 'Thus says the Holy Spirit: *So shall men in Jerusalem bind the man who owns this belt and deliver him into the hands of the Gentiles*.'

Now we, too, joined those who had been begging Paul not to go up to Jerusalem.

But he said to us, 'What are you doing? Why are you weeping and breaking my heart? Listen to me: I'm ready not only to be enchained but even to die for the name of the Lord Jesus.'

He would not be persuaded. In the face of his convictions, we ceased the struggle, and we all said, 'The will of the Lord be done.'

After these days we made final preparations and went up to Jerusalem. Some of the disciples from Caesarea went with us, bringing us to the house of Mnason of Cyprus, an early disciple, with whom we should lodge.

Timothy

87

'Paul.'

I thought I heard moaning.

'Paul, are you awake?'

It seemed he was moaning in his sleep.

'Wake up. Wake up. You're dreaming.'

There was a breathing pause. Then the moaning continued.

'Paul? Is everything all right?'

Well, it wasn't so much a moaning as a series of deep, heaving sighs. I could hear his lips puff, like a dog blowing through its flews.

'Are you sick?'

We had come to Mnason's house under cover of darkness. In the morning we would walk through Jerusalem in sunlight, open and exposed. I – this my second time in the ancient irascible city – I was scared. For me and for my teacher, my father. I couldn't sleep. And the sighing beside me was making me shiver.

'Paul!'

'Shut up,' he said. 'I'm praying.'

'Sorry,' I said.

But there were no words to the prayer.

And once I knew he was awake, I couldn't control my own need for companionship. I waited as long as I could, then blurted: 'But how can you be praying? – without words, I mean?'

He broke off the groaning.

We lay in silence.

I stared through blackness to the ceiling.

Perhaps Paul was doing the same.

Unless I'd made him mad at me. For interrupting his strange praying.

'I'm sorry,' I said.

'The Holy Spirit,' he said.

Ah, he relented. He was speaking to me.

'What?' I said.

'Sometimes, Timothy, I just don't know how to pray – '

'*You*?' I said.

He made a sort of honk, an exasperated snort: a Paul-sound.

'Sorry,' I said.

'When events outrun me,' he said into the darkness, carefully choosing his words. 'When the fight is a war as vast as the world, too vast for my understanding. When the end of this race and the crown for the victor are too far in the future for me – I don't know the words to pray. I... utter... nothing. I groan – '

'Oh, Paul!'

' – I make it a cry of the heart, and the Holy Spirit intercedes for me,' he said. 'And God, who searches the heart, knows the mind of the Spirit.'

'Oh, Paul! Oh, my father!'

Father, I said. The word erupted on its own and slew me with knowledge: I loved the man so much – that it consoled me, and then, immediately, it terrified me too.

'What if,' I whispered. 'What if they kill you in Jerusalem?'

Again, he made that honking sound, and I discovered a swift, surprising giggle in me.

'Then you will carry on,' he said. He wasn't joking.

The giggle died. I suffered an internal convulsion at his cold word, the terrible word so easily spoken. I drew breath through my nose and said: 'When that time comes, if Jesus wills it, I will surely carry on for you. But that time hasn't come! It can't be now. I cannot, Paul... I don't have the strength to mourn the loss of another father. Not yet. Not yet.'

Silence. Darkness. We lay side by side on our separate pallets. My eyes saw nothing. My sight found nothing to see. But my looking went on and on eternally, and that's what eternity seemed that night to be: endless nothingness.

What would happen when morning came?

What, when we walked forth into the city of angers? Invisible daggers?

'Timothy?'

'What?'

'Yes, you do.'

I knew what he meant, that I had the strength. But I didn't want to hear the possibility he implied.

'You don't know me,' I said.

Honk!

'Laugh, Paul! Laugh! What *do* you know about me?'

'Exactly what you said,' Paul was whispering softly. He had turned his mouth to my ear. I could hear the click of saliva and feel small puffs of his breath. 'I know as much as a father knows his son, which is always less than the father wants to know – but more than any son *thinks* his father knows.'

My father! My father! – the chariots of Israel and the horsemen!

Paul continued speaking softly, in something of a lover's tenderness. 'The sufferings of this present time,' he said, 'are not worth comparing to the glory that waits for us. Timothy, son of my soul, if God is with you, nothing can prevail against you. Do you understand this? He didn't spare *his* own son. He gave him up for us all. Don't you think he'll give us all things else with this his greatest thing, his son? Jesus Christ died,' Paul said slowly, carefully, rehearsing for me the story told ten thousand times. 'Jesus was raised from the dead. Jesus sits at the right hand of God, interceding for us. Who, then, can separate us from the love of Christ? Timothy, Timothy, tribulation? Or distress? Or any kind of persecution? Timothy? Nakedness or peril or the sword?'

He took my hand. His long fingers wound through mine, then clutched them tightly.

'No,' Paul said. 'No, in all these things we are more than conquerors through him who loved us. Timothy, listen to me. I know this well; I know it true; I know it for the both of us: nothing, neither death, nor life, nor angels, nor principalities, nor things present, nor things to come, nor powers, nor height, nor depth, nor anything else in all creation will be able to separate us from the love of God in Christ Jesus our Lord!'

And so it was that the morning came.

And when my father Paul stood up and shrugged himself into his robe, preparing to go out into the streets of Jerusalem, I was astonished to see how short he was. And how bent. For he had seemed in the darkness as big as the beam that bears the weight of a temple.

James

88

As I began, so now I conclude with an admission: the peace
I most have striven for, the healing of the divisions among us...
I don't know. I don't know. Truly, I do not know if these shall
come to pass. Whether we who call Jesus 'Messiah' shall still be
free to worship with the rest of Israel in the Temple. Whether
believers Greek and believers Hebrew will come to terms both in
the Spirit and in practice – I don't know. I cannot tell.

There was an incandescent moment when I was moved to think
all would be well. There followed a full seven-day week when the
conviction increased: yes, yes, the Greek yet might return to find
the face of God in the Laws of God. For if that greater renegade,
Saul, could sweetly and willingly re-Pharisee himself...

But on the seventh day it all blew up, Temple, city, the
incipient peace, Saul, hope, and my convictions; and the eighth
day was worse than the first.

I will recount these events as precisely as I can, and so be
done, unable to utter another thing.

The first day began while I was at my window praying. It began
with a greeting unanticipated.

Behind me a man said, 'James, the peace of the Lord be with
you.'

I turned to see an old man standing between the doorposts of
my little room. His neck, like a vulture's, was thrust forward from
the shoulders, bearing his great head overly low. His eye sockets
were enshadowed, his hair scarce, his skull a crosshatching of
scars, his robe profoundly filthy, his body roundish, his manner
friendly, his person almost, almost familiar –

'Who? – '

'James,' the old man said, stepping forward, spreading his arms; and in the bow-legged bounce of his tread I recognized him. Saul, come back again. Saul, whom I had not seen in six years.

He put his arms around me, drew me close, and embraced me with such pressure it caused his arms to tremble. Thus he held me, forcing some response, and when I returned the gesture by placing one of my hands on his back, I was surprised to feel pebble-like tumours there, scabrous welts wherever I happened to touch him, spine, ribs, and waist.

'Saul,' I said, releasing myself. 'What happened? What's the matter with you?'

His face split into grinning. 'I'll show you what I have,' he said, winking, then turned and called, 'Come!' and into my room there now trooped a company of men as soiled as Saul.

They filled the tiny space where I lived and prayed and slept not only with their persons, but also with a stinging mansweat and with noise. I was not gladdened by this intrusion.

One man I knew: Timothy from Lystra. The others Saul introduced. And as he did so, each man began to strip himself of his clothing.

'James, meet Sopater,' he said. Sopater laughed and took off his robe.

'Meet Aristarchus, Secundus, Gaius,' Saul said, all of whom greeted me with nods and friendliness, then likewise removed their robes – while Sopater was stripping himself yet further. Off with his tunic. Off with everything else, down to his loincloth!

I said, 'Excuse me – '

Saul said, 'And Tychicus and Trophimus and Luke – ' who straightway followed their fellows toward nakedness.

'Excuse me, this is not a public... I mean, I don't have accommodations...'

'No, no, James! No,' Saul interrupted me. 'We need no better accommodation than this. Look!'

He tore off his own robe.

I mean that literally: Saul *tore* it off, separating the seam, and laying it all out before me.

'Look.'

I did look. I looked by means of the daylight that fell through my little window, and there in the folds and the linings of Saul's garments were coins. Gold coins. Several score of golden Roman coins, all sewn individually in place so that, as I supposed, they would not clink together.

All the men tore open their robes, showing me the faces of Claudius, Agrippina, Nero duplicated hundreds of times, causing something like a dull fire in my room – and a sickness in my heart.

'James,' Saul said, fixing me with a glittering eye, 'I never forgot my promise. I am keeping it now, yes, and before witnesses. This money represents the entire contribution of the churches in Achaia and Macedonia for the poor in Jerusalem.' He grinned, pleased with his accomplishments – though more with the success of his journey, I think, than with the size of the collection. 'As heavy as gold is,' he explained, no one more clever than he, 'it's lighter and smaller than the heap of silver we'd have to transport in carts. And a jingling, jangling cart would never have made it two miles on a narrow road without some thief appearing to give us advice.'

Saul was pleased. His companions were pleased. All Achaia, no doubt, and Macedonia too were pleased. And none was not a drooling fool.

'I wanted to send you a message,' I said – I, in whom there was no pleasure at all. 'But you needed no message from me. You should have known.'

'Known what?'

'Not to come. Not to come to Jerusalem.'

Saul grew sober. 'I received the message, James,' he said. 'By way of Simon Peter.'

'But you came anyway? Why would you tempt disaster?'

'Because I made a promise. I am prepared for disaster.'

'Saul! You tempt it for us *all*! You can do nothing here that does not affect every believer in Jerusalem. We are constantly under suspicion. *We* are! All who call upon the name of Jesus – and zealots don't distinguish, no, not in these times when anything Roman stinks in their nostrils. Nor does the Jewish leadership distinguish when any sect is seen as subversive, a threat to their power.'

I paused. I breathed. I waited.

But Saul did not leap to the defence. He tugged at his ear and ducked his head and, childlike, smiled. He smiled!

'How,' I asked sharply, 'do you expect the church to accept this money?'

'Well,' he said, 'I don't know.'

I saw something like mischief in that smile of his, and I felt heat rising along the back of my neck.

'We are under siege here, Saul,' I said with a growing severity – though it was as much at myself as at him. I was losing control. I never lose control. 'Everyone, everyone in Judea is under a murderous siege: the Jews by Gentile Rome, and the church by Jews who despise our Gentile taint. They expect treachery! Zealots are convinced of collaboration. The *Sicarii* will kill us in secret, while the high priest is planning to make it a public slaughter!

'*No lord but God! No lord but God*, angry men cry in the streets of Jerusalem. *No lord but God!* Yet look at this,' I said, heaving up Saul's robe and ripping out a golden coin. 'Look at the portrait! Look at the image! Look at the false god emblazoned here, this... this *Nero!*' I was yelling, holding the coin directly in front of Saul's smiling face. 'Saul, Saul, you have brought a thousand idols into Jerusalem, ten thousand into my own room. You, Saul!' I said, flinging the coin to the floor. 'You more than any other single man – you are responsible for the Gentile taint of the church! Don't you know they come with every festival? Jews from every nation under heaven, cursing you for plundering the synagogues and turning Jews into Gentiles and blurring the boundaries between us? Go away,' I said, whirling round to face my window. I fought to suppress the emotion in my voice. I spoke as one indifferent, except that the words came hissing through my teeth and cracking as they came: 'All of you, put on your clothing all dripping with riches, and get out of my sight.'

I never lose control. I have schooled myself in a politic restraint. It is the requirement of leadership. I always cloak ungracious passion in sober, gracious words. But on that day I lost more than control. James the Just abandoned himself and his own character.

How could this be?

Well, the Pentecost was almost upon us. The city's population was swelling four and fivefold. Diaspora Jews, pilgrims of a hundred tongues and countries, were throwing things wildly out of balance. Threat, menace, revolutionary zeal all increased with the influx. Felix's troops were anxious. And Jewish *believers* were arriving to celebrate the Pentecost of the Holy Spirit's descent.

These needed me for space and safety in the city. These placed their trust – nay, their lives – in me. For who was left in Jerusalem *but* me? All the apostles had gone away; all whom the Lord had chosen – and those whom the chosen had chosen as well – all were gone. I alone was left. I had, therefore, almost exhausted my personal force through watchfulness and endless negotiations. Then into this dry tinder strolls Saul and his band of happy men all studded with Caesars against their skins!

Under such circumstances, who would *not* have lost control?

James would not have lost control.

But James had lost himself. I had lost the James I knew, and I cannot excuse myself with weariness. No: in these latter days I have come to realize a deeper reason for my failure on that first day of Saul's return.

It was happiness. The giddiness of those men.

More specifically, it was that smile on Saul's face which, the more it lingered, the more I detested; that smile which, the more I fussed, the broader it grew – and the broader it grew, the more I raged! So James lost control because James lost James in contradictions: for the more I believed the sincerity of that smile, the more I took it for impudence!

Therefore I choked off my words, and I turned to the window, and I hissed – furious with myself even for the dribble of spit the hissing produced: 'Get out of my sight.'

There followed the whump and rustle of men heaving themselves into robes as heavy as sepulchres.

Oh, these men set up a fearful stink!

Bare feet departed. Silence entered my room again.

I began to pray out loud. Spontaneously, with tremendous emotion, I prayed a prayer of Jeremiah because I was suffering the sorrow of that prophet.

'O Lord, thou knowest! Remember me and visit me.

'I have not,' I murmured, burning for the thing I was uttering unto God: 'I have not sat in the company of merrymakers, nor have I rejoiced. I sit alone, because thy hand is upon me. Why is my pain unceasing? Why is my wound incurable, refusing to be healed? Wilt thou be to me like a deceitful brook, like waters that fail?'

Then the Lord, there in my small cell, spoke to me.

Jesus said, 'If you return, I will restore you, and you shall stand before me.' In a clear and even voice, the Lord said, 'If you utter what is precious, and not what is worthless, you shall be as my mouth.'

Even when I turned and saw that Saul was still there, in the centre of my little room, watching me; even when I realized that the sound of the voice had been Saul's sound, I did not doubt that it had been the Lord who answered my prayer.

Saul was smiling, gently, completely, full of compassion; and that, too, I supposed to be the Lord's smile. Moreover, when I had turned and was gazing at him, Saul said (not the Lord, but Saul said this), 'James, what must I do to take the Gentile taint away?'

89

'James,' Saul said, 'do you hear me?'

I heard him. But I was speechless.

If you utter what is precious –

Saul said, 'What can I do to cleanse our contribution of its Gentile taint?'

I didn't answer.

He said, 'How can I make the money acceptable in the sight of the saints in Jerusalem, so that the poor receive it freely?'

I kept gazing at him. There was an answer. I wasn't pausing to conjure an answer. What I was doing... why I kept gazing so narrowly at the little man, so silently at him... had rather to do with my fear of the Lord.

If you utter what is precious, and not what is worthless –

In fact, my soul was hollow with disbelief. I felt beleaguered by God and Saul together. Why should it be required of me in a twinkling to cancel suspicions? – suddenly, without a shred of evidence to put faith in the man whose feral passions had sundered the church? My gaze, if the truth be told, was the tool of old, cold pragmatism: I was probing Saul for some sly crack of irony.

But I feared to speak my deeper motive. I feared to utter *anything* at that moment. For the Lord had just intervened between us. Holiness still scorched the air. And what if my words were not precious to him?

Saul cocked his great head to one side, smiling. A genuine smile? A wheedling grin?

He said, 'James, you look flushed. Can I get you a drink of water?'

It triggered language in me. 'In order to remove the Gentile taint,' I said with judicial precision, 'use the money in the service of the Law.' It was a test, of course. I drooped my eyelids to scrutinize Saul's slightest reaction.

But there was nothing slight about the man, not then, not ever.

'Yes,' he said. 'I'll do what you ask,' he said. 'Just tell me how,' he said, and he grinned.

I mean that distinctly, he licked his lip, and lifted it, and showed me his teeth, a fence of ruined teeth – and that was the gesture that undid me:

'Saul,' I said, 'I think you're lying.'

I regretted the accusation the moment I spoke it. It caused my face to tighten with heat.

But Saul, receiving my word as something deserving consideration, said slowly, 'No, James. I'm telling the truth.'

'Then perhaps you don't understand me,' I said. 'Perhaps you haven't taken the full meaning of my words.' Stiffly I collected Saul's robe from the floor. I swung it open to the lining and the coinage. I strove for the tones of an impartial judge, but my voice kept rising. 'I'm telling you to cleanse the money lawfully, Saul, to convert these coins and the evil engraved on them by spending them in the Temple! On matters Levitical!'

'I understand that.'

'Saul! I'm telling you to obey the Law! You! Not someone in your stead!'

'Yes. I know.'

'And you will?'

'I will.'

'Listen to me, Saul!' I insisted, throwing the robe aside. '*Listen* to me! Right now, in this room, I am your Judas Barsabbas! Even *he* would ask no more of you than I am asking now.'

'Yes, James. I agree – and I applaud you for that excellent stroke of rhetoric.'

I gagged.

'What are you doing to me?' I cried. 'What sort of an insult is this?' I shouted. My spirit kept begging the Lord for restraint. I feared that by soft words and smiling Saul was whipping me with my own emotions. Canny, cunning, devious Greek!

But the Lord gave me no restraint.

Saul said, 'This is no insult. I am pure in heart.'

And I exploded: 'But you *hate* the Law!'

'No,' he said. 'No, I don't.'

'Oh, Saul! I know what you write. I know what you say. *The curse of the Law!* you wrote. I saw it: *The curse of the Law!* So what? Are you mocking Torah now? – hating it, loving it? Can you be so cavalier with the Holy Will of God? – using it to drive me mad?'

'No,' said Saul. He wasn't smiling now. If he was pretending sincerity, the pretence was superb, complete, and for this his soul would be cast into the flames of Gehenna – *if*, as I say, it was pretence and not the truth.

'No,' Saul said to me, 'I am not mocking scripture, James – nor you nor the God whom I call Father. I believe that the Law is holy.'

I closed my mouth. I was blinking rapidly, uncontrollably. I went down to my knees, and then to my *hands* and knees, in order to retrieve the golden coin I'd flung to the floor before. I drew Saul's robe as well toward me, replaced the coin in its slip in the lining, folded the cloth with perfect folds, rose up, and laid the garment straight on a stone bench.

Saul watched me. When I was done he said, 'In my inmost self, James, I delight in the Law of God.'

My teeth so tight the jaw-muscles cramped, a red haze suffusing all my seeing, I walked out of my little room and closed the door behind me. I climbed the stairs to a chamber on the roof of the house, and there I knelt down a second time, and there, through my teeth, I began to pray.

'If this is meant as a trial for me,' I said, 'if this is a test I must endure, then grant me, O Lord, sufficient strength. And if I endure to the end, grant me the crown of life.'

I prayed: 'Grant me the meekness of wisdom.'

I prayed: 'Grant me the wisdom from above, to be pure, to be peaceable and gentle, full of mercy and good fruits.'

Holding my body straight up and down, perpendicular from the chin to the knees, my hands extended, empty, I prayed in that place for more than an hour.

I recalled Elijah and the palpable effects of his fervent prayer: for when he prayed for drought there was drought, and when he prayed for rain, there was rain.

Elijah was a righteous man.

I beseeched the Lord to receive my prayer, too, as the prayer of a righteous man.

Because I love Saul.

O Holy God! I detest his ways, I despise his immaturities, I resent his arrogance, I would gladly take Simon's bluster over Saul's *sica*-like, dagger-like, pernicious and stinging tongue. He confuses me. He drives me mad. He has destroyed what little consolation the Lord would afford me in my difficult life.

And on that day I was exhausted almost to death. On that day

Saul had caused me to utter what is worthless in the sight of God. He caused in me an excess of sinning.

But I love him. Ever since that moment twenty-three years ago when we shared the supper of the Lord together in a perfect peace, peace as perfect as a pearl, I have loved Saul.

And now I am laid low by love.

I prayed: 'I am returning, Lord. O Lord, restore me.'

I prayed: 'I beseech your mercy, Lord. O Lord, let me stand before you. Let me be as your mouth again.'

I sagged. My kneeling posture, erect and stiff, now broke all along my spine. I bent and put my forehead against the floor.

And I prayed: 'Saul has spoken. His tongue is the rudder to steer his course hereafter, up or down, in regions of angels or else in the regions of demons. O Lord Jesus Christ,' I prayed, 'let the truth of his word be proved by the works that must follow. Works must surely follow. Without them, his faith is dead.'

When I rose up, having finished my prayer, I knew what I would ask of Saul. I knew precisely the difficult work to be required of him.

What I did not know was whether he would be waiting still in my little room below. But if he was, I was convinced he would be true. I believed he would obey the laws I was about to set down before him.

The door was closed.

I lifted the latch and opened the door, and there stood Saul in the centre of the room, naked save for his loincloth, riven and knobby with scars and beatings, bent at the neck; massive his head, sweet the smile in the middle of his face.

'Ah, my brother,' I said, 'you waited.'

'There is an explanation for my delight in the Law,' Saul said when I returned to him. 'I owe you that. I owe your mind and your spirit that.'

He spoke formally, as if he'd rehearsed the words in my absence. He spoke with humility, calmly. We had not sat down. We stood facing each other.

'I know my weakness,' he said. 'I have learned that nothing good dwells within me, I mean in my flesh. I've learned that though I can *will* the right, I can't of my own accord *do* the right.

It's a wretched, invaluable truth. And how did I learn the thing I would never accept by myself, of myself, in myself? Why, by the Law. Except for the Law, I would never have known of sin. James, what I told you is true: in my mind I delight in the Law. But in my *members* another law battles the Law of God in my mind. Alone I can only fall captive to the laws of sin in my flesh and my members.'

With absolute calm, Saul spoke words that seemed to require anguish – but there was no anguish in him. Contentment only: 'Wretched man that I am,' he said, his moist lips parting. 'Who could deliver me from this body of death? Ah, James, thanks be to God through Jesus Christ our Lord. I am no longer captive and no longer condemned because I am in Christ Jesus. God sent him to fulfill the just requirement of the entire Law. No, the Law is not evil. It is holy and just and good. More than that, it is even fulfilled in me, because I walk according to the Spirit of life in Christ Jesus my Lord.

'James,' Saul said softly, softly, 'look at me. Are you still angry at me?'

And these are the commandments required of Saul, not by me but by the Lawgiver and the Judge.

That Saul should exchange the Roman coin of the Gentile collection for Hebrew coin in the porches of the Temple.

That Saul should spend the money, the greater portion of the money, in the Temple treasury itself on behalf of four Jewish believers who wanted to terminate their Nazirite vows. They had kept their vows a long time, and now the ritual of termination was far too expensive for their purses. It costs each man three sacrifices, a male lamb, a female lamb, and a ram; it costs, too, a cereal offering and a drink. If Saul should take the cost upon himself, he would do more than demonstrate his own good piety; he would also have cleansed the contribution by spending it in service of the Law.

But with regard to Saul himself, in order that he might function righteously on sacred ground – and to silence those who condemn his teachings on the Law – I asked him to do one personal work before he participated in the termination of the Nazirite vows:

To purify *himself.*
To undergo the rite of Levitical Purification;
In the Temple;
Publicly.
Paul should (even in the face of danger) remain in Jerusalem
for seven days, on the first and the third and the seventh of which
presenting himself to the priest in the Temple, twice to be
sprinkled with the waters of atonement.

I said to Saul, 'Will you do this good work? Will you keep these
laws? Will you obey the word of the Lord in me?'
'To those who are under the Law,' he said, 'I become as one
under the Law. James, my brother, look at me.'
I looked: thin body, crooked as a stick, tiny eyes, gleeful eyes,
bird-beak nose – and a smile as ethereal as the morning dreams
of children: what a puzzle, this man of crashing disparities!
While I looked, Saul stepped forward, winked, held out his
arms, and crossed his wrists as if I had cords and might bind
them together. 'For the sake of the gospel,' he said, his voice
bubbling with friendship, 'I have made myself a slave to you.
To everyone. James: I am under the Law of Christ. Of course,
of *course*, I will do this good work.'
And so began my brief moment of incandescent gladness.
I suffered myself to hope for the peace of the church. I allowed
myself, in my inward parts, the dangerous taste of a sweet,
unsullied joy. Lo, I was the mouth of the Lord again. I wept for
the fullness within me.
And I said, 'No, Saul, no. How could I be angry at you?'

90

THE FIRST DAY

On the following day, shortly before the morning sacrifice, I gathered the four men who had taken Nazirite vows and with them descended the long stairs and the pavement from Zion into the lower city. The odours of trade and manufacture met us, even so early in the dawning; they linger in the doorways of the poor. We walked to the house of Mnason the Cypriot, where Saul was staying. As we arrived, he stepped out wearing a tunic newly cleaned. He and Timothy and Luke, all of them freshly bathed, greeted us with kisses. Have I remarked on the hair of this Greek, Timothy? Long, soft, uncommonly fair. And when it is washed, it is in the sunrise a golden epiphany.

The eight of us started to climb the stepped street toward the Temple. This was the first day of the seven of Saul's obedient ritual. After the sacrifice, after the prayers, when priests were free to serve the people, Saul would speak to one of them to arrange for the sequence of his purification. Then, together with the four Nazirites, he would name the day of their vow's termination; and he would, with several immediate presents, two doves and two measures of grain, assure the Temple authorities that he was willing to cover the expense of their offerings.

It was a good morning. Olive trees were in flower. The barley harvest in the hills had been abundant. Sacks of grain leaned against shop walls. Pilgrims would not want for food. And Saul paid double the price for the grain of his offering.

Perhaps my judgment on that particular day was somewhat beclouded. Flushed with the hope that the rifts in the church were truly healing, I had sought out Judas Barsabbas and invited him to attend the Temple with us. He refused. I should have known. He has no trust nor love for Saul. He goes white at the name of the man.

And he disturbed the sea of my own blessed peace. It was as if he planted a brier in my bowels: in the midst of joy a little fear began to grow. *What if – ? What if – ?*

We approached the Temple Mount at the southwest corner. Seventy years ago King Herod filled the valley there and built a wall that extended the Temple's esplanade, raising its edge to a dizzy height. Standing on the ground, looking up to the pinnacle where priests blow the festival trumpet, one seems to be facing the sheer escarpment of a mountain. Stairs ascend from here to there. Level platforms grant rest for the climbers; but the casements require ever greater arches to carry them and us high up to western gates and the pavements of the outer courts of the Temple. The last arch is higher than seven houses of the poor, each placed atop the others.

We climbed in groups, the young men first. Saul would have come last, but that I accompanied him. His spirit was willing. The spirit in his eyes was bright and vigorous. But his body, his back, and his legs were untrustworthy. When he paused he was trembling.

Midway, he craned his neck to look at the pillars above and the leaves of their capitals. I glanced at him and noticed beads of an oily sweat on his brow.

'Is the exertion too much for you?' I asked. 'Should I carry the grain?'

'No,' he said. 'I've climbed rocks higher than this before.'

'But you're sweating.'

'Not from labour. Not from the heat,' he said, grinning and gaunt and gazing upward.

When, I wondered, was the last time he had been to the Temple? Not since he debated Stephen. That was twenty-five years ago, and this – columns and courts, buildings and porticoes and the Temple itself – is the most beautiful edifice in all the world.

'Well, then,' I said, spreading my arms to indicate the entire complex of the Temple Mount, 'it must be the fear of the Lord and his glory that makes a man sweat.' Why, in sunlight the golden sheen on the Temple itself can blind the pilgrim that looks at it.

But Saul turned a tiny, bedevilled eye on me and giggled his ridiculous giggle: *Tee-hee, tee-hee!*

'No, James, not the fear of the Lord,' he said, taking my hand. 'The fear of heights.'

THE THIRD DAY

When we ascended the Temple Mount the second time, for Saul's first washing, none but the two of us went – or so I thought until the very moment he bowed his head before the priest who would pour on him the water of atonement.

Pilgrims crowded every street and region of the city, devout worshippers, Jews from every nation under heaven. Their various tongues created a perpetual murmurous sound, exotic, both oriental and occidental. And the electric press of so many people caused my bowels to tighten around that thorny brier. *Jerusalem, what will you do if someone strikes a spark in you?*

Smiling to mask my concern, I suggested that we climb to the Temple courts by way of the southern interior stairs. And here is evidence of the extent of my affection for Saul: I, James, made a joke.

'The halls, being enclosed,' I said, 'don't offer an aerial view.' And I said, 'One cannot fall off a hallway.'

But Saul must hunger suffering. As we had the first day, so on the third we took the same ten thousand stairsteps up to the blinding Temple of God.

On the way Saul spoke of the smells of sacrifice, animal odour, sheep wool, goat stink, cages tumultuous with birds, the pavement slippery with droppings. He said he had smelled it often abroad.

He spoke of the sweeter scent of thick-running blood, of pagan altars glistening blood and buzzing with flies, of the grooves etched into the Temple pavement by which the blood of continual sacrifice flows eastward and down through pipes to the Kidron Valley below. And this was the dry season, he said. Rains would not come for five months yet to wash the blood and the droppings away – not till after *Yom Kippur*, he said. Not till after *Succoth*.

As we neared the top of our climbing, Saul spoke of the smoke, the cloud of smoke and the hissing meat that broils on the Altar of Burnt Offering. He spoke of the coals and the char and the billowing smoke of the sacrifice ever ascending to the nostrils of God.

'Terrifying,' he said, and he stopped.

I looked at him.

He wasn't smiling.

'Terrifying, Saul?' I returned three steps to stand on his level. 'The height,' I said.

He laid a long forefinger against his chin and shook his head.

'What then?' I said.

'Pagans burn their rams,' he said, 'their lambs, their bullocks, their beasts just as the Jews do theirs. They send the same smoke upward too – and the danger is that they send it to demons. I have climbed the pagan rock. To the very top. In genuine fear to the stormy summit, where nothing was higher than I. And there, in my terror, I met the Lord Jesus Christ.

'But here on Moriah, mountain of Isaac and Abraham,' Saul said, beginning again to ascend the stairs, 'here on the hill of the Jews, there exists a danger more grave. If, James, at the pinnacle of this rock; if, between the fires of sacrifice and the judgment seat, I do not again meet Christ Jesus my Lord as the very savour of the smoke...'

Saul fell silent.

We were at the gate. We faced into the Royal Porches, busy with pilgrims changing their monies, purchasing offerings, praying, talking.

'... If I do not see him here,' Saul finally whispered, 'then I am perishing eternally. Then I am of all men most to be pitied, unworthy the kingdom for which I suffer. This is a danger worse than demons. For the mortal who cannot see in every sacrifice the Christ who loved us and gave himself up for us, a fragrant offering and sacrifice to God – that mortal shall suffer the punishment of eternal destruction, which is exclusion from the presence of the Lord and from the glory of his might. *That*, James: that is terrifying.'

See how swiftly things change in one's association with Saul? I have schooled him. I have restrained, instructed, debated, directed him. Such is my role and my duty in Jerusalem, whether or not he chooses to comply. Yet behold: with no transition I can recall, nor by any permission explicitly given, the man was schooling me. Renegade Saul was my rabbi. My preacher. My elder. And I was not resisting.

All at once he turned toward me grinning like Shobal the thief. 'But thanks,' he cried, slapping my back, 'thanks be to God who gives us the victory through our Lord Jesus Christ! Open your mouth, grim James! Laugh and be glad, my dear brother James. It's a joke for a joke,' he cried, then he scurried ahead of me through the high passageway into the portico, flapping his arms and cackling among the pilgrims with all the discretion of a chicken!

What was that? What sort of theatre was that? For the moment I stood lost in perplexity, wondering whether some insult had just been implied. But there had been love in his eyes – *my dear brother James* – though even his fondness felt avuncular, as if he were not my equal but my uncle.

No, Saul did not ease the tensions in me.

And by the time I found him again – *not* in a private alcove but bold between the Nicanor gate and the altar of burnt offering, standing in the court of Israel where Gentiles would be slaughtered for the trespass – Saul was already bowing his head before the priest we'd met two days ago.

This priest was a ruddy, round little fellow in whom there was no judgment at all. In one hand he held a basin. With the palm of the other he scooped out water, then rained it down on Saul's great head.

But in the midst of these ministrations we heard – we all heard – a strangled cry, as if some beast were drowning in its own blood. The priest raised his eyes. I turned. Only Saul held still, his head obediently bowed.

Only Saul did not see the rage in the face of Judas Barsabbas, his flesh now whiter than polished ivory.

But Saul must have heard his hoarse declaration:

'I would not believe it of you, James. I refused to believe it. I came myself to see what blasphemies this man is willing to perpetrate on holy ground. James, shame on you! But you, Saul! If you sin this sin again, I will not answer for your life.'

'Judas,' I said, 'purification is itself a cleansing, not a sin. You know that better than anyone.'

Judas Barsabbas fairly bleated at me: 'His heart is uncircumcised! How do you wash an uncircumcised heart?'

'Please.' I turned and spoke to the baffled priest in low tones: 'Please, finish. Hurry and finish.'

A crowd was gathering. Curious. Skittish.

Saul remained as unmoving as stone.

And I... my incandescent moment was growing cold.

THE SEVENTH DAY

It had been my plan to gather as many elders of the church as were willing to offer Saul the protection of their persons in exchange for his new Levitical obedience. I wanted to bring ten or twelve men to Mnason's house before the dawn's light, there to take Saul into our midst, to build a wall around him, as it were, that he might go secretly to the Temple once more before he left the city.

I was aware of the time he'd spent in Jerusalem. I had grown ever more fearfully aware that Saul could have come and gone in a bare two days if his only duty had been to deliver the Gentile collection. But seven days had passed. His name was flying from lip to lip among the Jewish believers. Who knew what the Zealots had heard? Or the pilgrims?

In fact, Saul's younger face had not been seen in the city for twenty-five years. Seven years ago certain believers saw him, but these were the leaders only, and then he was a man of health and vigour. At his appearing this time even I did not immediately recognize the older, more haggard visage before me. I counted this a minor advantage: though the name be familiar in Jerusalem's streets, the face and the person to whom it belonged was not.

One day yet. One day more. At the completion of his purification, Saul's Gentile donation would be acceptable to serve in the termination of the Nazirites' vows, paying for their sacrifices and the shaving of their heads. And the rest of the collection, clean completely, could flow to the poor saints of Jerusalem. And done. And Saul, be gone! Be safe, my brother, you and your gospel. Go.

I had planned, I say, to surround him with our sober bodies all the way through the public streets from Mnason's house to the Temple and back again.

But when the elders and the Nazirites and I had all assembled at the house in the lower city, Mnason met us alone, looking perplexed.

'Well, well,' he said, wringing his hands in apology, 'but Saul and Timothy left in darkness. Half an hour ago. Is there a threat? Why didn't you tell me you were coming? They must be near the gates by now.'

We flew. *I* flew. I ran up the paved street with the speed of dread. The young Nazirites ran with me. So there were five of us.

But the flight drew public attention. People stepped out of their shops. People began to pop their lips and round their eyes like fish.

'Slow down! Walk!' I commanded. And, in spite of the tripping haste of my heart, we walked.

Lord Jesus Christ, protect him. Keep him safe.

Where were the elders? What had become of the elders?

'Saul's a small man,' I said aloud to the Nazirites. 'He's a wasted little man. Who fears a little man? Who would see him as a threat? Surely they'll overlook him. He'll be all right, washed and all right and returning when we find him.'

Grey light streaked the highest sky. The days and the nights were nearly equal. Fire ignited morning mists behind the Mount of Olives, a reaching red corona. But the air was cool.

One step at a time, a foot for every step, we climbed, we climbed the stairs that Saul had climbed. Circumspectly we climbed, striving to look as devout as any pilgrim on the Holy Mountain of God.

And the stairways and the tunnels, every approach and all the gates to the courts of the Temple were, indeed, thick with people. And lambs were bleating above us, ready for slaughter by the hundreds and the thousands. And pilgrims were carrying loaves of bread in their hands, wave-offerings which the priests would eat.

High on the southwest pinnacle, suddenly, a priest began to blow the trumpet, causing the hair on my neck to rise.

This was the first day of the week. This was the day of Pentecost. It was Pentecost breaking around us.

'No one will notice him now,' I said. 'He's safe in the cover of crowd,' I said. 'The men will dance around the altar. Priests and Levites will bellow the Hallel.

The trumpet kept blowing and blowing.

I swallowed. I was astonishing myself – a man fragmented by emotion! Doggedly, I tried to retrieve the James I knew. By a dead-eyed act of will, I began to assess my present condition.

Why *should* I be so frightened on Saul's behalf? Once before, the Holy Spirit had chosen to control the Pentecost. There was every reason to expect a glad conclusion for this one too, Saul's final washing, his blessed fulfilment of the Law, his freedom to leave for ever, to travel to Rome...

Except that I hadn't seen the face of Judas Barsabbas since his angry accusations in the Court of Israel four days before.

And it is on her holiest festivals that Jerusalem grows most terribly taut, her passions quick and savage.

And now, in the morning light, it was evident to everyone that the Roman Tribune had already deployed his legions throughout the city, fearful of riot.

As soon as I arrived at the gate, I drove forward past the columns and into the masses of pilgrims, my speed empowered by my purpose. Whether the Nazirites were still pacing me, I didn't know – but with all my heart I hoped they were somewhere close behind.

How would I find Saul? How would I *see* the wasted little preacher?

I struggled through beasts and people, treading manure and straw. I worked my way across the southern expanse of the Court of the Gentiles toward the gate at the Women's Court. Just as I turned to enter the gate, the sun breached the Mount of Olives behind me, shooting its light beams to the Temple, whose eastern face burst into a golden blaze, blinding me.

Shading my eyes, I went through the Women's Court toward the Temple. I had almost reached the Nicanor Gate and the Court of Israel, when a brutal shout was raised to my left. Women began to yip and to cry like birds. As if by an axe, the men were felled; the crowds were cut in two – and through that mess of separation I saw a tall man running. He was the point of a human wedge, twenty men, thirty men roaring behind him, driving pilgrims aside. The tall man wore his hair longer than Samson's, binding its richness in three bright cords. His cheekbones were strong, his face a devastation of beauty –

Mattithias!

It was Mattithias cleaving the Court of the Women, the Zealot, the husband of Saul's own sister, fierce, infuriated, consumed by one thought only.

When he came to the Nicanor Gate he did not go through to the Court of Israel. The gang behind him did. Like battering rams. But Mattithias himself stepped aside to the wall that surrounds the Court. He gathered his force together, and he soared! He took a single astounding leap to the top of the wall.

He scanned the inner court, then stretched forth his arm and pointed down inside. 'Men of Israel!' he bellowed in Goliath's voice: 'Men of Israel, *help*! There's the man who's been teaching everyone everywhere against the Jews, and the Law, and this place, the Temple of the Mighty God!'

Who could *not* have seen their hero standing above the priests and the people? Who was *not* listening to his voluble condemnations? And what mob would not have responded with a horrified outrage, with wrath and a galvanized action?

'Moreover,' Mattithias thundered, 'he brings Greeks into the Temple! He has defiled this holy place!'

Now the whole place began to surge. We were borne along on the violence of disgust. But I saw the bloody eruption in the Court of Israel. I saw a heaving weight of human bodies press toward me through the Nicanor Gate then past me, through the Women's Court to the Gate called Beautiful.

Saul was the goods. Little Saul was the only rider on the back of that swollen man-beast, his tunic torn from his wasted frame, his arms and legs thrown wide apart, his chest made naked to the heavens.

Men cheered at the Nicanor Gate, and I saw that they were swinging it closed.

Of course! They didn't want their prisoner to fly back to the Temple for asylum. Neither did they want him killed in the Court of Israel. Such a defilement could bring down the walls of Jerusalem!

And to me these things were a sign: that's exactly what they meant to do! – to murder Saul in the Court of the Gentiles.

What strength did I have left? I tried to break through the multitude. I tried to follow Saul on the back of that man-beast out of the Women's Court.

Then, suddenly, a way was made for me.

Suddenly it was Mattithias himself striding past me, causing people to part before his dazzling intensity. I ran in his wake.

We entered the outer court together, though he did not know me. We broke for the northern esplanade, and there we came upon Saul, and I discovered in shame how weak I was. I lost composure. I began to wail and to weep for my brother. Because he was kneeling low with his arms above his head. And the people were beating him with cords and belts.

Jesus Christ, where are you now?

But then there came the military might and precision of Rome: centurions, soldiers afoot, and behind them the tribune himself, Claudius Lysias.

I sank to my knees in gratitude unto God and the Lord Jesus Christ who is instant in answering prayer!

On the far side of Saul stood the tribune; on the near side, Mattithias; each man convinced of his own superiority, for the one had power, but the other had passion.

To his soldiers – indicating my brother Saul still kneeling on the pavement – Claudius Lysias said, 'Arrest this man. Bind him in two chains.'

To Mattithias he said, 'Who is this? What has he done to deserve such treatment?'

Mattithias, unblinking, maintaining his metallic gaze, said nothing.

But the crowd, trembling with unsatisfied rage, raised an immediate uproar. Men shouted so many accusations, so loudly, so simultaneously, that the tribune could distinguish nothing. He signalled his men to bring Saul back to the Fortress northwest of the Temple Mount, then turned and stalked away.

Soldiers lifted Saul to his feet. They invited him to walk. And he would have walked, except that the crowd redoubled their roaring. Running forward, swollen-throated, they cried, 'Away with him! Away with him!' The people pressed so close, that by the time the soldiers reached the steps that mounted to the fortress door, they were carrying Saul to save him.

It is at this point that the day changed.

Once before on Pentecost, the Holy Spirit was the utterance of a thousand voices. No one who listened did not understand, since everyone heard a familiar tongue.

But on *this* Pentecost the Holy Spirit was but one voice, a single, whining, high-pitched thrill of a Hebrew voice.

Saul's voice, like a spool unwinding.

At the topmost landing of the fortress the soldiers set Saul on his feet. No one entered at the doorway. Instead the whole company paused while the tribune conferred, as it seemed to me, with *Saul*. Saul gestured. Claudius Lysias gestured. Saul spoke rapidly, nodding, nodding, until the tribune moved backward to the door – and Saul stepped forward to the very lip of the platform, facing us, facing the Court and all the pilgrims therein.

He raised his hands for silence.

Miraculously, the multitude did indeed fall silent. And then a swift drama kept them silent: Mattithias contrived to climb to the portico roof, the hero still ascendant before his people and on a level still with Saul. Saul, having raised his hands, now directed them toward Mattithias in an open-handed, open-hearted sign of greeting, and cried, 'Mattithias!' Mattithias reacted, stumbling somewhat as if the word had been a blow. Amazing! In that moment and on that height the victim was acting like a victor.

A great hush fell upon the precincts of the Temple. The people listened.

And no one old or young, man or woman, could not hear Saul's bright and bugling voice.

'That man!' he called. 'Your man! Mattithias, faithful as Phinehas: he was *my* man, once. And once he loved me very well.

'I am Jewish,' Saul cried. 'I was more Jewish than most, and Mattithias loved me for that. I sat at the feet of Gamaliel. I was educated according to the strict manner of the Law. I became in those days as zealous for God as your man is today. I persecuted the followers of Christ. I bound them, imprisoned them, killed them – and I caused in Mattithias such admiration that he attached himself to me. We travelled together to Damascus to destroy Christ's followers there.'

The bronze Mattithias now seemed moulded indeed, his whole person fastened upon the mouth of Saul.

And what devout attention the pilgrims were paying to him!

Saul said, 'But on the way to Damascus a great light struck down from heaven. I fell to the ground. I heard a voice say, *"Saul! Saul! Why do you persecute me?"*

'I said, *"Who are you, Lord?"*

'And the voice said, *"I am Jesus of Nazareth whom you are persecuting."*

'Now that man Mattithias, who was my man then, saw the light. But he couldn't hear the voice.

'I said, "*Lord, what shall I do?*"

'The Lord said, "*Rise, go into Damascus, and there you will be told all that is appointed for you to do.*" When I rose up, I could not see. I was blinded.

'Joy began for me that day. And the joy has never left me. But sorrow began as well, because my man Mattithias, dear as a son to me, left me. First he took his mind away, declaring my blindness to be a curse of God. Next he took his heart away, for from that day he has hated me with an abiding hatred.

'I received my sight again. But it did not change the mind or the heart of my son.

'In joy I went forth preaching to the Gentiles the love of God in Jesus Christ; but my preaching only increased my son's hatred toward me.

'Ah, Mattithias!' Saul suddenly sang as if he were singing a psalm. 'Oh, Mattithias, my son!'

What happened next I have never seen happen before or since. It was a lightning stroke of holy power, and it seemed nearly to kill the man it struck. But the stroke was love! It was *love* that caused in the poor man such murderous despite.

Saul chanted: 'But I have never ceased to love this man, your man Mattithias. Never. Not once. And in your sight, O people, in the sight of Israel, I declare that I forgive him.

'Mattithias,' Saul sang, turning to face him directly.

As if unstrung, the hero began to tremble.

Saul's face had burst into radiance. It was shining now. 'Mattithias, still a son to me,' he sang, spreading his arms, raising them in benediction: 'I forgive you. In the name of Christ Jesus I forgive you all your hatreds. They are as nothing between us anymore.'

But Mattithias hadn't waited for the final word. He was already running the rooftop, charging the Fortress platform and Saul himself, whose face grew brighter and brighter with smiling.

'Away with this fellow!' Mattithias shrieked, torn and horrid with outrage. 'Away from the *earth*!' He ripped the cords from his long hair, which lashed the air around his face. His lips were twisted, smeared with bile and bitterness. 'Kill him! Kill him! He deserves to die!'

At once the spell was broken. The crowd was roused. Men leaped up and shook their fists, all roaring. They ripped off their garments and waved them, hooting disgust. They pitched handfuls of dust in the air.

Like a mouth, the doors of the fortress opened.

As Mattithias was flinging himself up to the landing, soldiers grabbed Saul and rushed him into an interior dark. The doors swung shut against the angry Zealot, shut and barred against the storm in the courtyard.

I lowered my looking.

Among the churning multitude I recognized two of the Nazirites. One was weeping open-mouthed, like a child who walks forsaken under the heavens. The other was hurling dust and curses toward the fortress, his robes at his waistline, his knees and breechcloth a public shame.

But Saul. Once the doors of the Fortress were closed, I never saw Saul again.

91

That was five years ago. I am myself in prison now. All things are clear for me. Nothing past remains hidden or confused. Only the future. The future of the church, I mean: whether the division between Gentile and Jewish believers will ever be healed.

My own future, on the other hand, is assured. The morrow is my execution day.

As for my past, I know my errors very well, and I have received the atonement of the Lord.

This was my error on Pentecost five years ago: I let passion dominate my piety. If the truth be fully confessed, I even took pleasure in passion, whereas I should have left such destructive storms to men like Saul and Mattithias.

This, I say, was my error: I loved. I delivered my more sober self to the love of another, and *therefore* did I find myself caught in riot and lawless behaviour.

So swiftly and deeply did shame come upon me, in fact, that already that night I fell facedown on the floor of my little room and wept the tears of repentance. Not once in the night did I move or slip into sleep. Rather, I spent my wakeful soul in devotion, recommitting my ways to prayer, to ritual purity, to Torah and solemn reflection. The love of the Lord is no passionate thing! It is the business of obedience.

And here is the proof that the Lord had heard my sorrow and had strengthened me: when it was requested that I go to Saul imprisoned in the Fortress, I overruled passion, and withheld myself from seeing him.

In the earliest hours, dark before the dawning, a timid voice called my name outside. I rose from the floor, straightened my robes, and opened the door.

It was a young man.

He held in his hand a small diptych, two boards hinged together which, when he opened them, contained the record and the witnessed proofs that Saul of Tarsus was a Roman citizen.

I looked more narrowly at the lad. Beautiful, he was. High

cheekbones. The image of his father, Mattithias. This was the son of Saul's sister, Saul's family, Saul's nephew.

But the lad was shivering with fear. His eye rolled with unhappy passion.

He said, 'Can you take this to Saul the apostle? Can you take him a message, too?'

What was the message, I asked.

That the poor boy had that very night witnessed his father swearing some forty men to abstinence: none would eat or drink until they had ambushed Saul and murdered him as he was being led in chains to Herod's palace in daylight. That was the message.

'The tribune himself should hear that message,' I said.

'I don't know the tribune,' he said.

'Neither do I. I don't even know his language,' I said.

But Timothy did.

So I gave Saul's nephew the name of Timothy from Lystra, and told him how to find the house of Mnason the Cypriot in the lower city. I sent him out into the darkness, then knelt down and trembled before the Lord.

Almost my heart had persuaded me to go to the Fortress.

But faith prevailed.

In the end, gracefully, there was no blame for me, since Saul was spirited out of the city before the sunrise. He was placed under the direct authority of Marcus Antonius Felix, Procurator of Judea, whose palace was in Caesarea.

There Saul remained in prison for several years. I prayed for his soul, to be sure; but I grew blessedly cool toward him. When Felix was recalled to Rome and Porcius Festus replaced him, I heard the news that Saul – ever Saul, always Saul, the man of extremes and impetuosities – that Saul had demanded to be tried before Nero in Rome. And I think that such a demand by a Roman citizen cannot be denied.

I assume he went.

And that's where Saul's life ends for me. In an assumption.

Festus, too, has departed his office by now. There's been a vacuum of power in Judea. Annas the High Priest has inserted himself into the vacuum. He wishes to prove himself both strong and popular, a leader of this zealous nation. Therefore, because the taint of faithlessness has clung to my person ever since that Pentecost five years ago, Annas has arrested me.

He has charged me with having 'transgressed the Law'.

I am impervious to the irony.

I am filled with knowledge.

Tomorrow he will, according to the Jewish practice, deliver me over for stoning.

I am not afraid. I know that the Lord will meet me in a rain of blood, even as he met Stephen so long ago. I know he will grant me to abide in his mansion for ever. I do not fear my dying tomorrow.

But I am filled with every kind of knowledge. I know the custom, how it will be done.

They will bind me and throw me over the brow of a hill.

If the fall does not kill me, my foremost accuser will lift a great stone and drop it on my chest. He will try mightily to explode my heart. If even then I do not die, then all the people will begin to cast stones down upon me, pebbles and rocks and boulders – and then I will surely die.

O Lord Jesus, watch over your church. I fear that divisions will only grow wider. I fear the passions among our people. And I have seen with my own eyes the effects of human hatreds.

Therefore, Come, I pray.

On my knees, I beg you, Come!

My dying is nothing next to the torment of believers torn apart from one another. Keep them one. Keep them one. Keep them one until you come – and make your coming soon.

Luke

92

When it was decided that we should sail for Rome, Festus consigned Paul, together with several other prisoners, to a centurion of the Augustan Cohort, a man named Julius.

Then, embarking in a ship of Adramyttium which was about to sail to ports along the coast of Asia, we put to sea, accompanied by Aristarchus, a Macedonian from Thessalonica.

The next day we anchored at Sidon.

Julius treated Paul kindly, giving him leave to go to his friends and receive their care.

Then, putting to sea from there, we sailed under the lee of Cyprus because the winds were against us.

And when we had sailed across the sea which is off Cilicia and Pamphylia, we came to Myra in Lycia. There the centurion found a ship of Alexandria sailing for Italy, and commanded us to board.

We sailed slowly for a number of days until we arrived with difficulty off Cnidus. Then, since the wind refused us a straight route onward, we sailed under the lee of Crete off Salmone. Coasting with difficulty along the shore, we came to a place called Fair Havens, near which lay the city of Lasea.

Since much time had been lost and the voyage was already dangerous (the Day of Atonement was over!), Paul advised them, saying, 'Sirs, I perceive that the voyage will be with injury and much loss, not only of the cargo and the ship, but also of our lives.'

But the centurion paid more attention to the captain and to the owner of the ship than he did to Paul.

And because the harbour was not suitable to winter in, the majority argued that we should put to sea from there, on the chance that somehow the ship could reach Phoenix, a harbour of Crete which faces northeast and southeast, much better for wintering.

So when a light breeze sprang up from the south, causing the captain and the owner to think they had obtained their purpose, they weighed anchor and sailed along Crete, close inshore.

$\mathcal{L}$. Anneaus Seneca

93

Seneca, in Rome,
  To Helvia, his mother, in Cordoba,
  the fifth year of Nero:

Greetings:
A cough can cause a rock slide. Any cough from any man's
throat, if time and the mountain are ready. There need be,
therefore, no guilt in coughing, yea, though a village be buried
and a hundred human bodies crushed. But he who coughs, as
he watches destruction, can't help but be crushed by guilt
nonetheless.

Ah, Mother, by a cough I have undone the world. It isn't yet
apparent, but *I* see the signs and *I* know how vast and sad are
the changes to come. The wheel is turning. Historians, note! In
the fifth year of Nero, several pebbles broke; but they held the
boulder that held the escarpment that held a mountain up. My
political power is all but gone. My influence over the princeps is
gone altogether. Agrippina is gone. (Oh, how spectacularly gone
she is!) Nero has forced his majority. Nero sits alone on Olympus.
He exists in a supernal self-ness, heeding no one. No one
restrains him. No one advises him. No one frightens him. He is
his own man, now. He is completely his own. And when he falls
on Rome to rape her, it will be as if the mountain had.

Mother, stiffen yourself to read the rest of what I write. My
news is dreadful, but my purpose is good. Gallio tells me you lie
on your deathbed. Worse, he says you refuse to sleep, that you
fear the sleep which might keep you for ever. He says you cling
with a grinning, apologetic desperation to the life where your
children and your grandchildren are.

But I say that the times are about to turn mindless and

violent, that there is no good thing worth living for, that soon it shall be better *not* to be.

And I say (with a shame I'll reveal to none but you) that should you look with clear eyes upon me, Mother, you wouldn't find the son you raised. I am compromised. The Neronic atmosphere has spoiled the sweet milk of your virtue in me. Surely, you should not cling to life in order to cling to me. I am hollow.

But I am also right: it is time to let go an existence increasingly evil.

This is my cough: that I sent Acte to Nero with news of a rumour, asking him merely to lay it to rest. The *rumour*, I meant. Lay the *rumour* to rest. But before the day was done he had conceived a plan to drop his mother dead into the sea.

Time and the mountain, of course, were ready even before I coughed.

Gentle Acte has been Nero's mistress for years. Agrippina never felt threat from that quarter, despite the fact that she used Nero's legitimate wife for her own designs and would have suffered divorce as a severe, personal loss. Neither Acte nor Nero ever thought to marry. But early this year a new mistress stole the emperor's heart and brains, and became straightway a threat indeed, for *this* mistress could, in scheming ambition, out-Agrippina Agrippina!

Poppaea Sabina is the most refined, intelligent, luxuriant, handsome woman in Rome. This is not hyperbole. It is fact. She has what we almost never find in Rome, hair naturally blonde (to which our young imperial lion has written perfervid verse: 'Hair of amber', and so forth). She has a tender, expressive nose, melancholy eyes, small feet, and milk-white skin. Oh, yes: let me tell you about that skin. In order to preserve its purity, Poppaea bathes daily in the white milk of asses, in the milk of four hundred asses kept at the farther end of the palace grounds for that one purpose only! Her bathtub is porphyry; her walls are polished silver to mirror the languid self that rises from milk; her servants dry her naked body in swans' down, which leaves a fine white dust everywhere on her skin; her hands they soften and whiten with the mucus of crocodiles; her face they protect from the miasmic night air by a cream mixed with powder to form a porcelain mask.

Poppaea is married to Ortho, one of Nero's closest friends. In fact, it was Ortho's boasting of his wife's night favours that first raised the lion's interest; and when the woman herself cast fluttering glances in Nero's direction, he was lost.

And so was Agrippina, mother of the princeps, lost.

For Poppaea wants the throne.

But that requires a marriage to him who sits on it.

And *that* requires a divorce.

And that would never happen as long as Nero's mother was living. Not just because Agrippina would never agree to such an expedient, but also because face-to-face she still held her son in terrible thrall. Under her bright eyebeams he became a boy again; she could reduce him to a maundering inarticulation; he despised her for it; he had banished her to her villa because of it; he even sent bravos there in boats to roar obscenities at the woman; but he would never be Poppaea's tool while his mother could stare him back to babyhood.

Therefore, Poppaea herself began to strategize. In order to arrive at divorce, she whispered of murder. She called the princeps less than his mother. She raised his hatreds to burning embarrassments. I should have recognized the signs, for he would stumble from Poppaea's apartments in a visible anguish, holding his stomach; but next he would grow red with anger and bark rageful orders, hurting servants and people around him.

I should have known what buzzed between Poppaea and Nero. I should have made it my business to know – then I would not have coughed into their tensions. But I did.

I sent Acte to reveal to him the lascivious rumour creeping through Rome – citizens, Senators, the army, and all: that Agrippina was trying to keep power by using her beauty in a manner more depraved than ever, that she was inviting Nero himself to share her bed and her body. This, Mother, is the state of things on the mountain, soon to be the state of things throughout the *orbis terrarum*. Some people – a minority – even believed that the incestuous suggestion came not from Agrippina, but from her son.

I told Acte to indicate that if the rumour wasn't laid to rest, the soldiers themselves might mutiny.

I coughed. As soon as he heard of it, this rumour drove our sullen emperor to the extremist of action, suddenly.

He sought a means to kill his mother. How should he do it?
What could he use?

Poison upon the woman of poisons would fail – and then what
would become of him?

A direct attack could not be concealed. It would scream forth
its names: *Assassination* and *matricide.*

By the greatest good fortune, then, a man named Anicetus, the
commander of the fleet at Misenum, came forward with the plot
that Nero applauded. 'I'll rig a ship,' Anicetus said, 'so the roof of
the cabin collapses just as a hole breaks open the hull. The
roof'll stun your mother; the hole will sink the ship; the sea will
swallow and drown her. Invite Agrippina to leave her villa and
visit you, my lord, at Cape Misenum – then I'll be the boat that
takes her home again.'

And who would know? Indeed, who would know.

Nero initiated the plot. He wrote his mother a letter of abject
humility and long apology.

Agrippina was overcome with triumph and (could it be?) with
maternal satisfaction. This was more than she ever thought to
receive from her ungracious son. She robed herself in beauty and
flew to Nero, who met her tenderly, who treated her with rapt and
loving attentions, who begged her advice on matters of state, who
gazed at her till tears glittered in the woman's antimonial eyes.
And when the visit came to an end, the son embraced his mother
as if he might never let her go. He whispered, 'Best of mothers,'
then kissed her breasts – 'the breasts', he said, 'that suckled me.'

Agrippina boarded the ship with a light foot and a soaring
heart. The starry night matched her mood. She and two others
entered her cabin and sat, a maid named Acerronia and her
treasurer, Crepereius Gallus; and so the boat cast off. The oars
pulled toward open water. The sail took wind and opened.

But Agrippina was Agrippina even to the end, and Nero has
suffered horrors for it!

For the roof of the cabin came down as was planned, followed
by plates of lead – and Gallus died immediately in the fall.

But Agrippina was only grazed. Instantly and completely she
knew this was more than mere accident. She and her maid crept
out on deck, just as the crew went rushing in a single body
starboard. The hole in the hull had failed to open. They wanted
to capsize the boat. It tipped terribly, and it pitched Agrippina
and Acerronia into the sea.

Acerronia began to scream. 'I am the emperor's mother!' she screamed. 'Help *me*! Help *me*!'

Sailors leaned over and spotted her form in the dark water. They threw her a line. She grabbed it. They drew her to the boat.

At the same time Agrippina was stripping herself of her robes and treading water among the waves. She would never have shouted. She would never have identified herself to men she did not know. This woman had swum more savage seas than these and had survived.

The sailors pulled the maid out of the water, up to the gunwale, then raised an oar and cracked her across the head. Acerronia the maid sighed and slipped into the darkness.

Silently Agrippina contemplated her own execution, since it was she they thought they were dispatching, then she turned and swam. Swam for shore, that woman did, and saved herself alive.

The first word Nero received that night was from certain sailors bewailing the loss of 'poor Agrippina, drowned at sea'.

The second word was brought by a messenger from Agrippina's villa:

We experienced some trouble at sea, his mother's message said. *But have no fear for me, my son. I escaped grave injury, only bruising my shoulder a bit. As much as you wish to come and comfort me, don't. I am well. I just need rest.*

Nero was horrified.

He sent for me and for Anicetus, the plot maker, and he commanded the messenger to tell the story of Agrippina's salvation over and over, as if whipping himself. His eyeballs gaped. His body shivered. He kept clawing at his beard and moaning, declaring himself a dead man, while I... I was hearing the distant rumble of the mountain coming down.

'What'll we do? What'll we do?' Nero beseeched the windows.

I had nothing to offer, nothing to say.

Anicetus, on the other hand, began to act even before he spoke. He drew a dagger, then bent and slid it swiftly across the floor till it caught between the messenger's feet. Immediately he leaped up, crying, 'Help! Help! Ho! A murderer!' He launched himself at the messenger and knocked him hard in the head.

Then, 'This,' he said serenely, 'is what we do, my lord. We arrest this man, sent by your mother to stab you in your own apartments. And now – right now, with your permission – I rush to her villa and kill her for this treachery.'

Nero, ghastly white and mindless, nodded.

Anicetus set off on a swift horse with several soldiers and one centurion. They stormed the villa. They broke into Agrippina's private rooms, finding her washed and dressed for sleeping.

She, for her part, recognized death in her assassins' eyes.

The centurion drew a dagger. Agrippina stepped backward to the wall. She took the hem of her gauzy gown in two hands and tore it open from throat to waist. Here was the treasure with which she had purchased the kingdom.

'*Ventrem feri!*' she said. Strike for the stomach.

The centurion obeyed. He plunged the dagger down to its hilt, and Agrippina sank to the floor without a cry.

Nero, as I say, has forced his majority. He who has no mother cannot be a son. He is no longer a boy; and perhaps this was the only way the princeps could have accomplished it.

But he was not free at first. He was morbid. He lingered away from Rome, fearful that matricide was the single crime the people would not accept, even in a monarch.

And now, O virtuous Mother, I must confess one of the more grievous signs that the world is changing. This one, in me, I have been milled in the wheels of these present events. And if I, in my supreme contempt for fortune, can't remain unpulverized, who can?

In order to prepare for Nero's return to Rome, I wrote the Senate a letter under his name. I am a letter-writer. It's what I do, and I do it well. I've written many a letter and many a speech on Nero's behalf, most of them justifiable. Even this one I justified while writing it, for I sought to preserve some influence over the imperial lion for use in the future. If I did not help him here, I reasoned, I'd never help hereafter. See what a merchant Fortune is? Selling the greater good for a lesser evil.

And I paid with an egregious letter.

I recounted not the story Agrippina's messenger had told to us, but rather the one we told on him, about his dagger, about her plot to murder her son. I wrote that she, afraid of the judgment about to befall her, had committed suicide. And then I described in detail all the atrocities she committed during her life, particularly by means of the enfeebled Claudius. These were, of course, not false. (These constituted a realistic justification for her ending, it seemed to me: as she lived so had she died.) Nero's refusal to let her share his rule, I wrote, had so embittered her that she opposed every gift he made to the soldiers and the people. I characterized him as grieved by the absence of his mother but magnanimous enough to recognize that all the world would benefit thereby.

My lies persuaded no one. And Nero's name meant nothing. Everyone knew I had written the letter. And now I'm accused of killing Agrippina too.

My dear mother, my good mother, I think I am not your son any more.

Forgive me, then go peacefully away.

For neither am I Nero's advisor. No greater good was gained by the sale of my soul. At the end of events Nero has emerged so vastly popular, he sees no need for teachers, guides, counsellors of any sort – and I have lost all influence.

When finally the lion returned to Rome, it was astonishing how gladly the people received him. They ran out to the country to meet him. They applauded all along the way, playing music on a thousand instruments, dancing, throwing blossoms at the emperor's cortege, and crying *Nero divinus! Nero divinus!*

'Astonishing,' I say, to everyone including Nero. He truly had not anticipated such a reception. But his astonishment lasted only half the way home; for then I saw his expression change. The sun rose in his face. He beamed. He accepted this dazzling apotheosis as something due to him. And by the time he entered his palace, he and I had arrived at the same conclusion, though his merriment was my misery: if (we realized) to commit this most wicked of sins, if to murder his mother had only increased the people's devotion, what could Nero *not* do and get away with it? Why, he could do anything. Anything.

The world has a new god, Mother. That is the point of this my painful letter to you. *Incurvat in se!* Our deity is self-absorbed, worshipping himself alone, attentive to none but his whim and his will only. He fed on his mother. He'll feed on the people. A shadow is falling upon us wider than Rome and darker than death itself.

It is time. It is altogether time for your departure. The world is not worth your habitation here. And I shan't linger long behind you.

O Mother, do not fear the going! I don't.

See what a muddy burden our bodies are to us, something like ropes and fetters to keep us here. How sweet to snap them loose! 'I shall die,' you may surely say with ease, because you *mean* thereby: 'I shall cease to risk sickness and pain; I shall cease to risk prisons and hatreds and disappointments and guilts and death.'

I'm not so silly as to sing the old soothing lullabies of Epicurus, who used to say that the fears of hell are idle fears, that there is no Ixion bound to his wheel, no Sisyphus rolling his boulder uphill. You left those tales behind you, my darling, more than seventy years ago. Three-headed Cerberus doesn't scare you any more, nor do the shadows, nor do the white sprites that cling to their bones like a mist. (I'm joking. These are the tales you told me when I was a child, remember? And do you remember how we laughed, then? Do you recall the blessed medicine of your laughter?)

But this is not a joke; it's the most sacred argument I have to offer: either death obliterates, or else it sets us free. If we are released, Mother; if we can drop this muddy burden of body, better things await us at the end of the lightsome flight. And if we are obliterated, well, then nothing remains: good and bad alike are gone, and there is no knowing hereafter.

And we have died every day, you and I.

I mean, with every day a tiny portion of our lives is snatched away. Even when we were growing, our lives were waning. We lost childhood. We lost youth. You have lost your seventy-six – and I my sixty – years. All our past time is lost time, and even this day today we share with death. It never was the last drop that emptied the water clock, but all the drops that had flowed out ere the last drop fell. So it is with us: The final hour, the very moment when we cease to exist, doesn't itself bring death! O my dear, we've been a long time dying. This moment merely completes the process.

I know a philosopher who says, 'How long must I endure the same things over and over? Shall I for ever wake to sleep, hunger to eat to hunger again? Nothing ends! Everything is connected in a circle, fleeing and chasing at once. Night follows day, and day follows night; summer is killed by autumn, autumn is buried in winter, winter is broken by spring, and spring's aborn as summer again. All nature passes only to return. I do nothing new. I see nothing new. Sooner or later one grows sick of this.'

Even if the world were not now beshrouded by Nero's dark will; even if it merely stretched its days out to an endless dullness, there are those who consider living not so much painful, as superfluous.

Vale, Helvia, Mater. Do not grieve for us. Death makes all things well, for it takes all bad away.

Farewell, my dear. Remember our laughter. Remember the green days and all our baby tales. Recall my childhood hopes for a moment, for only a moment – and then, farewell. We end the world by ending ourselves. In a stroke we vanquish suffering and war and every calamity. Nothing need remain.

Farewell.

uke

94

Now then, when a light breeze sprang up from the south, opening a possible passage from Fair Havens to Phoenix some eighty miles farther up the coast, the captain and the owner of the ship believed that they had obtained their purpose. Therefore they weighed anchor and sailed along Crete, close inshore.

But suddenly a tempestuous wind, the violent nor'easter, struck down from the land, catching the ship and turning it out to sea. We gave way. We furled the sails and were driven twenty miles south until we came under the lee of a small island called Clauda. There we managed – but with all hands and all our strength – to haul in the ship's shoreboat and to secure it on deck. We ran cables under the ship to keep the timbers from splitting apart. And because we feared to run on the Syrtis, the sandbanks of North Africa, the sailors lowered the mainsail and threw out sheet anchors to slow us, and still we were driven.

The next day brought no relief. So violently did the storm batter us that the sailors began to heave the cargo overboard.

On the third day they cast out the ship's rigging, baring all its poles to the wind.

And when neither the sun nor the stars appeared for many a day, when we could no longer sight a position, when no small winter tempest lay unabating upon us, we finally abandoned any hope that we would be saved.

It was then that Paul came forward and said, 'Men, you should have listened to me. You should never have set sail from Crete into this injury and loss. But I beg you now, take heart! And I promise you, none of our lives will be lost; only the ship will be lost. For this very night the God I worship, the God to whom I belong, sent an angel to me, saying, *Paul, don't be afraid! You must stand before Caesar. And lo, God has granted you all those who sail with you.* So take heart, men, for I have faith in God that it will be exactly as he said it to me. But,' said Paul, 'we must run upon some island.'

During the fourteenth night, as we were drifting across the sea of Adria, about midnight, the sailors sensed that they were approaching land. So they sounded and found twenty fathoms. A little farther on they sounded again and found fifteen fathoms. And fearing that we might strike the rocks, they let out four anchors astern and prayed for daylight.

Now the sailors, saying they wanted to lay anchors out from the bow as well, lowered the shoreboat into the sea.

But Paul said to the centurion and the soldiers, 'Unless these men stay here, you can't be saved!'

The sailors were planning their private escape.

Immediately the soldiers cut loose the shoreboat and let it go.

Near dawn Paul spoke to everyone, urging them to eat something. 'This is the fourteenth day of our anxiety,' he said, 'and the fourteenth day of a seasick fast. I beg you all to eat. It'll give you the strength you'll need for the morning, since not a hair of your heads shall perish!'

And when he had said this, he took bread and, in the presence of everyone, gave thanks to God and broke it and began to eat.

Watching him, the others were encouraged and began to eat some food themselves. (Altogether, we were two hundred and seventy-six souls onboard.) And when they had eaten their fill, they lightened the ship by throwing all the rest of the wheat in the sea.

When daylight came, no one recognized the land that lay before them, but they saw a bay with a beach, and they planned, if possible, to drive the ship aground in that place. So they cast off the four anchors astern, leaving them in the sea. They loosened the ropes that had lashed the rudders. They raised the foresail into the wind, and the wind blew the ship suddenly, sharply, toward the beach.

But it struck a shoal. The vessel ran hard on a sandbank, where the bow stuck fast while the great sea breakers banged behind us, smashing the back of the ship.

'Kill the prisoners!' the soldiers cried. 'Don't let them escape!'

But the centurion wished to save Paul and forbade them.

'Let those who can swim,' he shouted, 'jump first and make for shore! Those who can't, grab planks and boards! Grab pieces of ship and save yourselves – '

And so it was that all escaped to land.

95

After we had escaped we learned that the island was called Malta. The natives who found us on shore showed an unusual kindness, for they kindled a fire in the rain and the cold, and they welcomed us all.

Paul gathered a bundle of sticks, then reached to put them on the fire; but the heat drove a viper out, and it fastened on Paul's hand.

When the natives saw the creature hanging from his hand, they said, 'The man's a murderer. He escaped the sea, but he won't escape justice! The killer is going to be killed.'

Paul reached over the flames and shook the creature off.

The natives waited, expecting him to swell up or to fall down dead. But when they had waited a long time and saw that he suffered no harm at all, they changed their minds and declared that the man was a god.

Now in the neighbourhood of the beach were lands belonging to the chief of the island, a man named Publius who received us and hosted us for three days. His father, as it happened, was lying sick with fever and dysentery; so Paul visited him and prayed and placed his hands on him and healed him.

As word of this healing spread, the rest of those who were sick on the island came and were cured as well. They brought us many gifts, and when we were able to sail again, they carried on board everything we needed.

And so it was that after three months we put to sea in a ship which had wintered in the island, another ship of Alexandria which bore for its figurehead the Twin Brothers.

We anchored again at Syracuse, where we stayed for three days. From there we made a circuit, arrived at Rhegium, and after a day's wait caught a south wind that carried us by the second day to Puteoli.

In Puteoli we found believers who invited us to stay with them for seven days.

We walked the final miles of our journey. Hearing of our approach, some believers rushed west from the city and met us at the end of the day, just as we came to the corner of the Three Taverns, near the Forum of Appius. Two groups stood in the dusk a while, hushed, gazing at one another. Among the Romans a woman burst into tears. And then I saw that the face of Paul had begun to shine white-silver, like a round and ravaged moon.

'Priscilla, Priscilla,' he was whispering.

The sobbing woman broke from the Romans and ran to him and threw her arms around his chest and spilled her tears on his shoulder. Paul encircled her with his own arms.

'You, my little Priscilla,' he whispered, and then he too gave himself over to a noisy rain of tears.

And so we came to Rome.

Epilogue

*R*ome

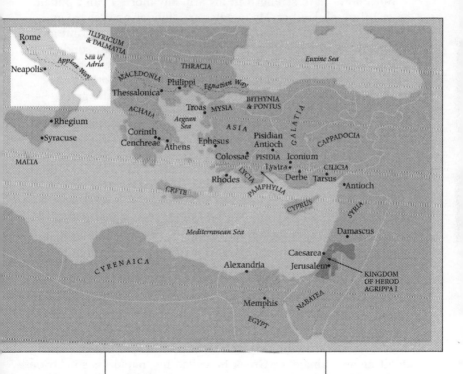

*P*risca

96

I have my eyesight. For that I am endlessly grateful. When I bend at the small bench, even in lamplight and suffering that perpetual pain in my back, yet, I can knot the thin thread; I can stitch a rolled hem finely, tightly, prettily.

But I don't have strength in my arm any more. I can't punch an awl through leather. My needles are slender now, sharp as an eyelash. And my leather is linen these days. I haven't cut an awning in years. I'm sewing soudarions now, too many soudarions, more than is pleasant for me, and I'm using a costly cloth, supple, white, well-knit. The soudarions cover their heads; othonions wind their bodies; my handiwork clothes them for the grave where they will sleep and wait the resurrection.

And the linen shall be left, but they shall fly to the clouds, shall surely meet Christ in the air. Comfort yourself and comfort the people with these words.

On the night before he was crucified, when all that there was to say had been said and all our hymns had ended and we had slipped into a common silence (even the guards to whom he was chained had both of them fallen asleep) Simon Peter suddenly had a notion.

'I want a napkin,' he said. He raised his face and looked around the room. His eye lighted on me.

'Prisca,' he said, 'can you sew me a napkin for my poor bald head?' He was speaking a rough Greek for people like me who don't know Aramaic. In Greek he called his 'napkin' a soudarion.

'Why?' I said.

There was a canny gladness in the old man's eye.

'I'll tell you what it should look like. I'll describe it exactly,' he said. 'Oh! And a winding cloth, too, dear Prisca, good Prisca!' He called the cloth an othonion. 'These are the linens they wrapped the body of Jesus in,' he said. 'Wrap me exactly as Joseph wrapped my Lord.' Peter's nostrils flared for the sheer delight of his idea, and I know he would've jumped up and rubbed his hands together and started to pace the room, except that he was chained between two legionnaires, Africans of massive stature. 'Don't put me in robes like the Romans,' Peter said, 'but shroud me as Joseph of Arimathea did Jesus, then go and tell Nero to look for me. Tell him to seek Peter in the tombs whereto he, the King of Slaughters, sends me – then watch the dog choke on futility. Ha, ha! Nero will find the grave clouts flat and empty, for Peter is taking flight! Ha, ha!'

My arm is weak. My body is bony. My breasts hang like empty purses in my tunic. I stoop. I would scarcely be able to care for myself, but I am not on my own. The church looks out for widows. And Apelles the shoemaker, that vulgar old crank, has attached himself to me in our mutual old age.

Well, he had been grateful to both of us, to Aquila and me together, when we enlisted his vigour to whisk us away from Ephesus the instant Aquila had sprung me from my prison cell.

Mute Aquila, my fumble-tongued husband! At the gravest crisis of our lives, he found his mouth and acquitted himself like a lawyer. While I lay like Paul in prison, Aquila pretended outrage; he scolded the city magistrates; he accused them of arresting the wrong 'man'; he shamed the great Ephesian powers for holding a helpless woman as if she were a danger to the Artemisian peace!

And he prevailed. They released me.

Straight from the cell, in the alley behind the praetorium, Aquila and I tucked ourselves into Timothy's old cart, saved for just this purpose. Then it was Apelles who covered us with rags. It was Apelles who sat on us and drove the donkey south to Miletus, roaring obscenities all the way as if he were a drunkard.

Next, during the voyage to Rome I saw an odd tenderness appear in Apelles the shoemaker, a fondness beneath the bluster. Then, in the city itself, I watched as his love for Aquila grew stronger and stronger. Well, of course! They made a perfect pair, these two, the one as vigorous and verbal as a boiling pot of lye, the other nearsighted and silent, nodding, never interrupting.

At first we lived in the district between the fortress of the Janiculum and the deserted hill which is called 'Vatican' after the pagan chants that once were sung there. Romans fear the place. Jews don't. Neither do believers, and a small church grew up around us, gathering in our house for worship. But several years later poverty drove us to cheaper buildings. Our abilities to work were diminishing. And Rome is crowded. Rome is corrupt and very expensive – unless you praise the rich to receive their favours. But Aquila, Apelles, and I could praise none but one. We praised our Lord Jesus Christ, and we were impoverished by the choice.

In the end we found two rooms in a tenement in the Suburra on the right bank of the Tiber, and there we stayed. This was a flimsy building altogether, constructed of wood and tufa and no true stone. Apelles took a room on the sixth floor, directly over ours on the fifth.

It was in a narrow stairwell of this grim tenement, during the hell of the fires of Rome, that Aquila, my husband of twenty-four years, perished.

For when the air began that midsummer night to roar; when violent winds got up and blew, and when the roof above him burst into flames, blind Aquila lost his way. He stumbled and fell headfirst down the narrow stairs.

I was not there. The whole city was blazing, insane with fire, and I was escaping the incredible cauldron of the Circus, burning like a monstrous crown.

It was Appeles who found Aquila under the feet of screaming tenants. It was Apelles who, by the plain power of his arms, lifted his friend above the wild-eyed panic of the people. Roaring his grief, Apelles bore him out of the building even as it was collapsing inward.

Grief, because he had been too late. The crowds had trampled my husband. He never regained consciousness. Blind and silent below the lurid traffic and terrors of this Babylon, Aquila left us and went to Jesus.

Yet that night the shoemaker and I put our heads together and wept. I inhaled his scent, his sour sweat – which to me in my misery seemed a yeasty thing – warm, familiar, and consoling.

O Aquila! O my dear husband!

Before we separated, Apelles and I, to find which friends had died and which had survived, he coughed. He frowned blackly and growled, 'Don't worry. Don't worry, don't – ' and stopped. It was enough. The rough Corinthian had pledged himself. He'd made me his task for the rest of our lives, and he has served me faithfully ever since.

Apelles, Paul once called him: *approved in Christ*. A blinding transfiguration, wouldn't you say?

My arm is weak, but Apelles' arm is not. He is my good right arm, the friend of my dotage, memorial to my quiet Aquila. Amen.

It was good to laugh with Simon Peter bare hours before he was crucified. For me particularly, the laughter was like new blood in my cold, responseless body. My husband only five months dead, I was grieving. I wonder if Peter thought about that. Do you think he was aware?

And it is good, still today, to have some little labour to occupy me, hand and mind.

Soudarions.

Othonians.

The clothing of those who must sleep a while before the trumpet wakes them.

I've sewn fifteen each in the last three days. Too many. More than I care to think about.

Nero is killing us. He says that we, the believers in Jesus, lit the flame that burned his city down. So, he says, we deserve to die. Well, a flame has been lit, all right. And the world will burn by it. But this fire and the wind that fans it are the Holy Spirit, and no force on earth can extinguish the Spirit.

Nero *thinks* he's killing us. Poor fool, poor fool. The man is nothing more than a passing shadow, brief night before the morning dawns. Sunlight will extinguish him. Just by waking we'll end his rule and the darkness and death that surround him. When Aquila gets up and looks for me; when Peter and Paul and Rufus and Epaphras and Sosthenes and Lydia and Tertius and Erastus and all the saints are roused by the light of the Lord Jesus Christ, Nero will not be.

97

Here's a story: Seneca is dead.

That great and famous man who scorned us, the Jews, for what he called our 'superstitions'; that writer of a thousand books of philosophy, owner of villas and vineyards and farms and houses both in the country and in the city; L. Annaeus Seneca, whom we used to watch as he moved through the forum on foot, refusing the luxury of a litter – he has opened more than one of his veins. He has closed his eyes, and he is dead.

He died four miles from here. The news is everywhere.

There had been a conspiracy among the rich and noble, the lovers of this life: they planned to assassinate their emperor. But the emperor discovered it. Therefore, noble Romans are dying now the way we died last year. No, not the same *way*, since we were persecuted and they are invited to take their own lives in the comfort of their homes. But they're dying nonetheless.

The poet Lucan, Seneca's nephew, is dead. Nero hated that one. We know, because he silenced him. I mean, he forbade Lucan ever to recite his poetry in Rome, so maybe that's the reason Lucan joined the conspiracy.

And Gallio, who set Paul free in Corinth; Gallio, Seneca's brother, is dead – but I think that was for love of his brother. I often saw them walk together, caven-chested men. They touched. They went with their bald heads down, talking, sometimes hand in hand. I liked that. It's my opinion that he killed himself because he missed his brother.

Some Romans still burn the bodies of their dead. We don't. We will rise on the last day.

Old Seneca was burnt. No speeches, no ceremony. They said that's how he wanted it. Just burnt.

How could I make a soudarion for the face that is no more?

They say he was on his way back to Rome from Campania, that he had stopped at a suburban villa to rest for the night. But Nero's command of suicide reached him there, and he obeyed before the night was over.

Seneca asked for his will, but the centurion refused.

Seneca the philosopher turned to the company of friends surrounding him and bequeathed them, in the place of lands and wealth, his way of life.

Old Seneca had married a young wife.

In that hour, her tears were troubling him. Her sorrow was causing his courage to falter. So he begged her to comfort herself by thinking of his virtue after he was dead.

She said, 'No.' She said his virtue was no comfort, and that she was coming with him.

He said that if it was her choice to make a noble end with him, he wouldn't try to stop her.

One swift slice of the knife, then, opened his wrist. One slice opened his wife's wrist too.

But Seneca's body was spare and dry. The blood would not come out. So he opened the veins on his knees and his ankles. This caused him a great deal of pain, unabating and continuous. Soon he was begging his wife to go into another room. Maybe he feared for her to see his suffering. Maybe he feared to see hers.

Out of sight of her husband, the soldiers tied up the young woman's wounds, and she survived. Who knows why this was? We've seen her walking Roman roads, pale and private.

But Seneca died slowly.

He asked for a certain vial of poison which he always kept nearby, the same potion as is used for public executions in Athens. They brought it. He drank it. But it did no good. His body was too cold and numb to allow the poison its course.

They picked him up and placed him in a warm bath.

Finally they carried old Seneca into the hot vapour bath, and they filled the room with a choking steam, and he died of suffocation.

98

Timothy, listen to this. I heard the news today, by way of a ship from Corinth. Perhaps in Ephesus you haven't received it yet yourself:

Erastus has been elevated! Our gorgeous friend has been appointed to the aedileship of the city. How grand and florid he must be! I wonder what he wears, now that he is one of the four supreme officials in Corinth. My, my – he who used to manage the markets now administers the public games. Erastus is in charge of the Isthmian Games! Isn't that something? O Timothy, I think you should increase his joy by writing him congratulations.

And as a gift for the glory and honour, Erastus promises to purchase from his own purse a pavement of limestone blocks for the courtyard east of the Corinthian theatre.

Well, *I'm* going to write him. Yes, and I plan to ask him what treasures he has laid up for himself in heaven.

I will sign my letter, 'Paul'.

99

When we heard that Paul was being brought in chains to Rome,
we all rushed out to meet him, Aquila and me, Apelles, Peter,
Rufus, his mother; Phoebe was there at the time; and friends he'd
never met also rushed out with us: Tryphaena and Tryphosa, the
sisters we call 'Dainty' and 'Delicate,' Andronicus and his wife
Junias. We went with high hearts and jubilation. It took us the
day long to get there. And there he was! There was my dear
friend, standing in the centre of the Forum of Appius. There was
Paul, scarred and skinny and trembling and smiling and *blooming*
so beautifully that I burst into tears at the sight of him. There
was my bright apostle, a prisoner still, as a prisoner he'd been
the last time I'd seen him in Ephesus. Yes, but no prisoner was
ever so supernally free as he. That smile on him! It was in his
eyes. It raised that long, sprouting brow like a Roman arch and
made his huge head seem easy, now – a sun come low to earth.

There was a centurion behind him, soldiers around him – but
no one would stop me. I ran to him and put my arms around him
and wept on his shoulder. I heard the chains *chink* as he raised
his arms and encircled me, too.

'You made it,' I whispered. 'You made it to Rome.'

'And you, my little Priscilla – '

He never said *what* he'd meant to say about Priscilla. He
choked. A sob came up in his throat and a shudder in his arms,
and he held me long and close in his chains, as if he were a sea.

You, my little Priscilla.

You.

'Yes, and I shall rejoice.'

The last time ever we talked, Paul beamed and spoke of dying.

He was living in the busy district between the forum and the
Campus Martius. There was always a guard in his room, always a
chain between himself and the guard, and always a fresh guard
when I came to visit. He would wink. 'They fear my skill at

439

making friends,' he'd say. 'Priscilla, don't you think I'm a champion at making friends?'

In those days I still felt a youthful pliancy. Age hadn't struck me as it has since then, suddenly, in all my vitals.

When Paul called me *Priscilla*, then, something fluttered in my breast. Delicious friendship! Moreover, he used the sweet diminutive all the time, even in front of other people, which he had never done before. He spoke as if the sun could shine upon this intimacy and all eyes could delight in it.

Everyone calls me *Priscilla* now. And I am glad of it now. It keeps the breath of the man in my ears, even when he is not here and breathing.

I said, 'My father died during my absence from Rome. No one sent a message. I don't know when he died or how, but I think of him because you are here. You don't know it,' I said, 'but you eased me at my mother's death. I think you could have eased him, too – my father, I mean. He disowned me. He turned and showed me his back, and that is the last I ever saw of him.'

Paul said, 'I would have talked to him. I would have shown him my own condition. I would have let my joy in spite of all persuade him.'

'In spite of all,' I said.

'Chains, old age, a ruined body, untried trials, an uncertain future.'

'In spite of all.'

'Yes, yes, O gentle Priscilla,' Paul said softly, his eyes as bright as polished walnut, 'and I shall rejoice. I know that through your prayers and the help of the Spirit of Jesus Christ, all this will turn out for my deliverance. And I know that I won't be ashamed. Instead, with courage I will honour Christ in this body, whether by life or by death.'

He ran the tips of his slender fingers over his lips.

'For me to live is Christ,' he said, 'and to die is gain. If I'm to continue in this flesh, that means fruitful labour for me. Yet which to choose – I don't know. I'm hard pressed between the two.'

Paul leaned forward. He reached and took my hand, raising the chain that ran from his wrist to the wrist of the guard.

'My desire is to depart and be with Christ,' he said, searching my eyes as if for some deeper, unbidden response. 'That is the better part, Priscilla, by far,' he said, searching, searching.

'But to remain in the flesh is the more necessary on your account.'

He leaned back again. The chain lay down on the ground like a dog. He smiled. His whole face burst like sunshine on me.

'I'm convinced of it,' he said with a sudden certitude. 'I shall remain. Yes, I shall continue with you all, for your progress and for your joy in the faith, so that in me you will have good cause to glory in Christ Jesus. Yes!'

He never ceased speaking. Paul talked that whole day through. As long as I lingered, still sitting before him, Paul talked. And during the night, even when I was not with him, he talked.

And the days and the years thereafter, when he was not with us, he talked.

Paul never ceased speaking. He talked into the skies. And from the skies that Voice descends as from clouds like rain, as from heaven like the daylight, for my beloved has climbed the holy mountain.

O dear ones, you have always obeyed, Paul's Voice falls upon us: *Continue, then, not only in my presence but so much more in my absence, to work out your own salvation with fear and trembling. For God is at work in you, both to will and to work for his good pleasure.*

Timothy, do you hear him? Lydia, do you? Talking, talking, as from down the articulate wind:

Do all things without grumbling or questioning, so that you may be blameless, blemishless, the innocent children of God in the midst of a crooked, perverse generation, among whom you shine like lights in the world, holding fast the word of life, so that in the day of Christ I may be proud that I did not run in vain or labour in vain.

Rejoice in the Lord always.

Listen, I'll say it again: Rejoice!

Let everyone know your forbearance. The Lord is at hand.

Have no anxiety about anything, but in everything by prayer and supplication with thanksgiving let your requests be made known to God.

And the peace of God, which passes all understanding, will keep your hearts and your minds in Christ Jesus. Amen. Amen. Amen.

BIBLIOGRAPHY

A partial bibliography used in research for *Paul: A Novel*

C.K. Barrett, *A Commentary on the First Epistle to the Corinthians*, Harper & Row, 1968.

C.K. Barrett, *A Commentary on the Second Epistle to the Corinthians*, Harper & Row, 1973.

Jurgen Becker, *Paul: Apostle to the Gentiles*, Westminster John Knox Press, 1993.

J. Christiaan Beker, *Paul the Apostle: The Triumph of God in Life and Thought*, Fortress Press, 1980.

Gunther Bornkamm, *Paul, Paulus*, Harper & Row, 1969.

George Arthur Buttrick (ed.), *The Interpreter's Dictionary of the Bible*, Abingdon Press, 1962.

Clement of Rome, *Epistle to the Corinthians*, tr James A. Kleist, S.J., Newman Press, 1946.

C.D.N. Costa (ed.), *Seneca: Essays*, Routledge & Kegan Paul, 1974.

F.R. Cowell, *Everyday Life in Ancient Rome*, G.P. Putnam's Sons, 1961.

William Stearns Davis, *A Day in Old Rome: A Picture of Roman Life*, Allyn and Bacon, 1960.

Terence L. Donaldson, *Paul and the Gentiles: Remapping the Apostle's Convictional World*, Fortress Press, 1997.

Bart D. Ehrman, *The New Testament and Other Early Christian Writings: A Reader*, Oxford University Press, 1998.

Ed Engberg-Pedersen, *Paul in His Hellenistic Context*, Fortress Press, 1995.

Eusebius, *The History of the Church from Christ to Constantine*, tr. G.A. Williamson, Penguin, 1965.

Jack Finegan, *The Archaeology of the New Testament: The Mediterranean World of the Early Christian Apostles*, Westview Press, 1981.

Francis Holland, *Seneca*, Books for Libraries Press, 1920.

Josephus, *The Antiquities of the Jews*, tr. William Whiston, Hendrickson Publishers, 1987.

Josephus, *The Wars of the Jews*, tr. William Whiston, Hendrickson Publishers, 1987.

Carlo Maria Franzero, *The Life and Times of Nero*, Philosophical Library, 1956.

David Noel Freedman (ed.), *The Anchor Bible Dictionary*, 6 vols, Doubleday, 1992.

Pierre Grimal, *The Civilization of Rome*, Simon and Schuster, 1963.

Richard Mott Gummere, *Seneca the Philosopher and His Modern Message*, Marshall Jones Co., 1922.

Martin Hengel and Anna Maria Schwemer, *Paul: Between Damascus and Antioch*, Westminster John Knox Press, 1997.

Ronald F. Hock, *The Social Context of Paul's Ministry: Tentmaking and Apostleship*, Fortress Press, 1980.

Harold Whetstone Johnston, *The Private Lives of the Romans*, Scott, Foresman and Company, 1903.

Peter Jones and Keith Sidwell (eds), *The World of Rome: An Introduction to Roman Culture*, Cambridge University Press, 1997.

Sebastian Junger, *The Perfect Storm*, W.W. Norton, 1997.

Gerhard Kittel, *Theological Dictionary of the New Testament*, Wm B. Eerdman's Publishing Company, 1964.

Helmut Koester and Ann Graham Brock (eds), *Archaeological Resources for New Testament Studies*, Vol. 1: Athens, Corinth, Olympia, Thessalonike, and Vol. 2: Athens, Corinth, Isthmia, Philippi, Ephesus, Trinity Press International, 1994.

Emil G. Kraeling, *I Have Kept the Faith: The Life of the Apostle Paul*, Rand McNally, 1965.

Gerhard A. Krodel, *Acts*, Augsburg, 1986.

Abraham J. Malherbe, *Paul and the Thessalonians: The Philosophic Tradition of Pastoral Care*, Fortress Press, 1987.

Wayne A. Meeks, *The First Urban Christians: The Social World of the Apostle Paul*, Yale University Press, 1983.

Otto F.A. Meinardus, *St Paul in Greece*, Lycabettus Press, 1972.

Jerome Murphy-O'Connor, *Paul: A Critical Life*, Clarendon Press, 1996.

Arthur Darby Nock, *St Paul*, Harper & Row, 1938.

George Ogg, *The Chronology of the Life of Paul*, Epworth Press, 1968.

Ovid, *Metamorphoses*, tr. Mary M. Innes, Penguin, 1955.

Philo Judaeus, His Works, tr. C.D. Yonge, Hendrickson Publishers, 1993.

Kevin Quast, *Reading the Corinthian Correspondence: An Introduction*, Paulist Press, 1994.

Rainer Riesner, *Paul's Early Period: Chronology, Mission Strategy, Theology*, Eerdmans, 1998.

Seneca, *Ad Lucilium Epistulae Morales*, 3 vols, Harvard University Press.

Seneca, *Moral Essays*, 3 vols, Harvard University Press.

Seneca, *Naturales Quaestiones*, 2 vols, Harvard University Press.

Marion L. Soards, *The Apostle Paul: An Introduction to His Writings and Teaching*, Paulist Press, 1987.

Villy Sorensen, *Seneca: The Humanist at the Court of Nero*, University of Chicago Press, 1984.

Krister Stendahl, *Paul Among Jews and Gentiles and Other Essays*, Fortress Press, 1976.

Anthony J. Tambasco, *In the Days of Paul: The Social World and Teaching of the Apostle*, Paulist Press, 1991.

Robert C. Tannehil, *The Narrative Unity of Luke–Acts: A Literary Interpretation*, 'The Acts of the Apostles', Vol. 2, Fortress, 1990.

David Trobisch, *Paul's Letter Collection: Tracing the Origins*, Fortress Press, 1994.

Ben Witheringtom, *The Paul Quest: The Renewed Search for the Jew of Tarsus*, Intervarsity Press, 1998.

Other books published by Lion:

THE BOOK OF GOD
The Bible as a Novel

Walter Wangerin

> '**Powers along with great stamina for hundreds
> of pages... Terse and punchy... it will be read
> and enjoyed.**'
> *Time Out*

Here is the Bible's story as it has never been told before.

The Bible as an epic novel, with all its sweeping action,
its larger-than-life characters, its universal themes of good
and evil, and always, above everything else, its enduring
story of a love that staggers the imagination: the love of
God for his people.

The Book of God unfolds the Bible's story in a clean,
continuous thread, free of repetitions, lists of laws and
genealogies. Award-winning author and storyteller Walter
Wangerin draws on his theological and literary scholarship
to add flesh and bones to biblical characters – exploring
their motives, their feelings, their relationships – and
painting the lavish backdrop against which their story
is told.

Extraordinary stories of love and conflict, of the
human and the supernatural, unfold alongside the
compelling claims that have brought millions to this
book of books.

Wangerin unravels the Bible text to reveal the entire
Bible story in all its drama. He has created a compulsive,
engrossing saga for all who enjoy an epic story. And he
brings a wealth of new insights to those who already
know the story well.

ISBN 0 7459 3983 X (paperback)

DESIRE OF THE EVERLASTING HILLS
The World Before and After Jesus

Thomas Cahill

> 'Cahill's book does a masterful job of depicting
> what the world looked like in ancient times.'
>
> *The Daily Telegraph*

Jesus of Nazareth, the central figure of Western
civilization, is the subject of this invigorating book
by Thomas Cahill – author of the best-selling *How
the Irish Saved Civilization* and *The Gifts of the Jews*.

Introducing us first to 'the people Jesus knew', Cahill
describes the oppressive Roman political presence, the
pervasive Greek cultural influence, and the widely varied
social and religious context of the Judaism in which Jesus
moved and flourished. These backgrounds, essential to
a complete understanding of Jesus, lead to the author's
original interpretation of the New Testament – much of
it based on material from the ancient Greek translated
by the author himself – that will delight readers and
surprise even biblical scholars.

Thomas Cahill's most unusual skill may lie in his
ability to bring to life people of a faraway world whose
concerns seem at first to be utterly removed from the
present day. We see Jesus as a real person, sharp-witted
and sharp-tongued, but kind, humorous and affectionate,
shadowed by the inevitable climax of crucifixion, the cruellest
form of crucifixion ever devised by humankind. The portrait
of Mary is fresh and alive, and shows her as a vivid and
forceful influence on her son. And the apostle Paul, the
carrier of Jesus' message and most important figure in the
early Jesus movement (which became Christianity), finds
rehabilitation in Cahill's revealing, realistic portrait of him.

This unique presentation of Jesus and his times is for
believers and non-believers alike. With the same lively
narration and irresistible perceptions that characterize
How the Irish Saved Civilization and *The Gifts of the Jews*,
Thomas Cahill invites readers into an ancient world to
commune with some of the most influential people who
ever lived.

ISBN 0 7459 5099 X (paperback)

All Lion books are available from your local bookshop,
or can be ordered via our website or from Marston
Book Services. For a free catalogue, showing the
complete list of titles available, please contact:

Customer Services
Marston Book Services
PO Box 269
Abingdon
Oxon
OX14 4YN

Tel: 01235 465500
Fax: 01235 465555

Our website can be found at:
www.lionhudson.com